A
PRIVATE'S
DIARY

A PRIVATE'S DIARY

Donald A. Edwards

ISBN 0-9639706-0-7

Library of Congress Catalog Card Number: 94-094229

To all the Men
of the Second (White) Battalion
335th Infantry Regiment, 84th Division
Especially Those
Who Gave Their Lives

CONTENTS

	Foreword	ix
I	Fall In	1
II	Clairborne to Kilmer	7
III	Camp Kilmer	15
IV	Across the Atlantic	25
V	Arrival in Europe	41
VI	Training in England	53
VII	A Visit to London	77
VIII	Across the Channel	93
IX	France	105
X	To the Front	113
XI	Arrival in Germany	127
XII	The First Offensive	141
XIII	Torpedo Junction	159
XIV	The First Attack	177
XV	The Lull Before the Storm 1. Leiffarth 2. Lindern	199
XVI	To Belgium	247
XVII	The Defense at Marche	255

XVIII	The Offensive in the Ardennes	287
	1. Amonines	287
	2. Dochamps	303
	3. Berismenil	334
	4. Biron	349
XIX	The Long Rest	363
	1. Appointment to West Point	363
	2. Xhoris, Belgium	373
	3. Schaesberg, Holland	382
XX	Roer to the Rhine	413
	1. The River Crossing	413
	2. The Breakout	431
	3. At the Rhine	454
XXI	A Pass to Paris	467
XXII	Chase over the Rhine	489
XXIII	The Weser Crossing	511
XXIV	Hannover	523
XXV	The Elbe River	547
XXVI	The Russians and Victory	565
	Appendix 1	577

FOREWORD

This is a simple book. I have attempted to describe some of the activities in which I was engaged during the period from September, 1944 until V-E Day in May, 1945. During that time, a small diary was kept on my person at all times. The entries in this diary were compiled on a day-to-day basis. At the end of a day or night, the highlights of that particular day were noted. There was not a single day on which an entry was not recorded. When my battalion was in the rest area, I wrote notes on what had occurred during the most recent time period. Combat is described only as it affected my personal status. Although I was privy to some planning, little is presented here. I have tried to give the reactions of the men with whom I had had contact during this nine months period.

In retrospect, my Second Battalion of the 335th Infantry Regiment was "lucky" since our unit did not engage in as much direct conflict, nor suffer as many casualties, as other infantry battalions in the 84th Infantry Division. It has been stated many times that "War is Hell" but one should, also, add extremely boring most of the time. This was the cumulative effect of the events as they affected me. It should be pointed out that the experiences of any infantryman in a lettered company will vary widely depending upon his assigned tasks.

I would like to acknowledge the assistance of several persons who assisted me in this endeavor. My daughter, Janet Edwards Van Duyn, was most helpful in the reading of the entire book in its early stages. She proposed many worthwhile suggestions that were incorporated in the text. Next is John V. Crable—my buddy, companion and friend, during that stressful time. He has read the book. He believes that the events that occurred have been accurately described. My thanks to Bernie Cohn and Ed Nelson who encouraged me to publish this book when I thought it would be of little value to anyone who was present during World War II. A word of thanks to my son, Gregory M. Edwards, who assisted in the reading of the text. I am indebted to my friends and colleagues at Ferris State University who assisted me in various ways. I am indebted to Keith MacDonald, my fellow Rotarian, whose counsel was most valuable. If there are any errors in this book, they are solely my responsibility.

Donald A. Edwards

I

FALL IN

Wednesday, September 6, 1944

"Fall in." yelled First Sergeant Holman E. Goodpasteur of Company E, Second Battalion, 335th Infantry Regiment, 84th Infantry Division.

"Fall in." echoed the GI's under the company's mess hall where they lay with their full packs on their backs.

The moment of the call to start an unknown journey had arrived. E Company along with the entire 84th Division was to leave Camp Claiborne, Louisiana for a far, yet unknown destination in Europe. For many, the command had been eagerly awaited. Those were the veterans who had spent nearly two years of training with the 84th—Railsplitter—Division. They wanted to see real battle action—where the guns blazed in earnest and the earth shook.

Others were fearful of the future. It could bring unforeseen disasters. Certainly death would await some. The men of Company E knew that the Infantry in all wars were the ones who suffered heavy casualties. Each man under the command of Captain Dick Von Schriltz hoped to be among those who would return from any battles that might be fought.

Although some were proud to be in the Infantry, most individuals did not feel this way. The average GI was invariably looked down as one whose only task was to walk and shoot a rifle. Yet, the idea of combat had been drilled into each and every doughboy of the five platoons that comprised Company E. For many the period of training had commenced only five

1

months prior to this day. Most were young men in their early 20's and late teens. They had been members of the ASTP—Army Specialized Training Program.

The ASTP had as its objective the training of skilled personnel for the United States Army. Those in the program at Drexel Institute of Technology in Philadelphia, including myself, believed they were safe from any combat duty for the duration of World War II. The "honeymoon" as it was titled lasted nine months. On March 29, 1944, the detachment at Drexel Tech, had boarded their Pullmans. The train journey took us southward into Louisiana.

"Hey, look out there!" shouted Al David.

"What do ya see?" a voice from the rear asked.

"A dumpy camp of tar-papered shacks and I do mean dumpy."

Camp Claiborne, just south of Alexandria, came into view. The temporary home of the 84th Infantry Division was composed of huts covered with black tar paper. A few white buildings stood out. All knew these to be the mess halls, headquarter buildings and other related structures.

All the windows of the troop-sleeper with its two tiered bunks were wide open and filled with craning necks. On the platform of the Camp Claiborne rail station was the 84th Band playing for the arrival of the new replacements. To a man, the collegiate GI's did not believe this to be a happy occasion.

"Better if they played a funeral march as far as I'm concerned." quipped a voice from an upper berth.

"Hey, look, there's a one-star General."

On the platform was the one-star General who observed the proceedings with little emotion. No one was near him. His rank seemed to have left him without any companions.

The steam locomotive screeched to a halt, followed by the usual jolt. The trip from the city of Brotherly Love had ended in the middle of Louisiana.

"Fall out," ordered Sergeant John Thornhill, "Put your barracks bags on the trucks." Everyone quickly followed the order. Then groups of 25 men were formed and marched to a waiting truck. The band continued to blare its welcome as the

2

trucks pulled away. The journey was a short one. The entire train load of ex-Drexel students soon occupied some of the tar-papered huts. Each hut contained 24 double-decker bunks. Everyone was ordered to relax until orders came from the Divisional Headquarters.

"Fall out," a twisted-face corporal shouted.

The entire 1,000 men contingent lined up on a large open field. Names were called. Assignments to various units were made.

"Edwards."

"Here."

"335th Regiment Headquarters Company."

Eight men were assigned with me to this Regimental Headquarters Company. Most of the ex-collegians were placed among the lettered companies of the three Infantry Regiments. These regiments, each composed of three battalions, and other components like the Field Artillery, Signal Corps, Quartermaster and Military Police, made up the Division. The men in these lettered companies were the real foot-soldiers. Very few were given assignments with the elite elements of the Division like the Medical Battalion, the Ordnance Company and the Division Band.

Sunday, April 2, 1944 saw all the replacements take a physical examination. Then followed four weeks of a special training program in which all the former ASTP men were engaged.

In May, June and July of 1944, furloughs were given to almost every man in the entire 84th Division. Upon returning from my furlough on July 17, I had been transferred to Company E. My new assignment was in Squad One, First Platoon of the Company as a rifleman. It lasted only July 18 and 19.

At assembly on July 19, Sergeant Harland H. Smith of the Headquarters platoon addressed Company E.

"Is there anyone who would like to be a messenger between the company and battalion?" he inquired.

As my hand shot up, I replied, "I'll take it."

A voice from the third line of the platoon said, "Edwards, you're nuts!"

A PRIVATE'S DIARY

My new messenger job involved not only the regular marching performed by all the infantrymen, but extra walking was required for relaying oral and written messages from the battalion staff to the Company E commander, when the battalion was on maneuvers. Strangely, I found the new task pleasant. However, a required second permanent messenger could never be found because of the added walking. The last of these field exercises ended on July 29th.

The entire month of August, 1944 was spent in preparation for the big move overseas. Countless inspections were made on clothing and arms. Each dogface was issued a new rifle—filled full of grease. This required untold hours of rubbing the rifle butt plus boring the barrel to make it serviceable.

On Saturday, August 19, 1944, the Commanding General of the 84th Division visited Company E during one of these routine inspection tours. Headquarters platoon had just finished another inspection at 1020 when Corporal Ernest Duffy shouted, "Hell, it's General Bolling! He's coming in here!"

The door had opened and Captain Von Schriltz commanded, "Attention."

The four men in the hut immediately jumped to their feet. General Bolling ordered, "Rest."

He then proceeded to ask questions of the quartet present.

"Private, how do you like Company E?" was his inquiry to me.

"It's a good outfit, sir, but my preference is for something else," was my reply.

Before the words had reached the General's ears, Captain Von Schriltz added, "He has only been with the Company three weeks, General, but I'm sure he will like it."

General Bolling then addressed me, saying, "Private, an infantry company is the best organization in the whole Army to which you can belong."

"Yes, sir," was my meek reply. I was never convinced of that statement.

After a few more routine questions of the other three enlisted men, who all professed to like their lot with Company E, the Commanding General departed.

4

FALL IN

Starting Monday, August 28, 1944, the 84th Division began to leave Camp Claiborne in small units for their embarkation camp. Rumors flew. Was it the East or West Coast? Would we go to California? Massachusetts? New Jersey? Virginia? or some other coastal state?

Soon the entire company knew it was some camp in the eastern part of the United States, but which one was still hazy. Betting took place on sites from Florida to Maine. Most of the wagers were on three sites, namely, Camp Kilmer or Fort Dix in New Jersey or Indian Town Gap in Pennsylvania. On August 31, the rumor mill confirmed that Camp Kilmer, near New Brunswick, New Jersey was to be the staging area for the Railsplitter Division.

On Friday, September 1, First Sergeant Goodpasteur announced at the first formation at 0600.

"There will be no passes this week-end. Company E is confined to Camp."

To the rear of the first row where I stood, a voice exclaimed, "Hell, I wanted to go to Boomtown to get laid for the last time."

Wednesday, September 6, was the last day spent in Camp Claiborne. The barracks were scrubbed for the last time. The entire area was policed, at least, three times for any elusive cigarette butt. Six formations were held during this day where every GI carried his full field pack and duffel bag. At the 1700 formation, Captain Von Schriltz announced, "I'm going over with you. I expect all of you to return with me." His prophecy, as far as he was concerned, turned out to be true. But not all came back.

After the 1800 hour formation, the company was dismissed. We had to keep within hearing distance of any command. With several others, I crawled under the mess hall where relative peace prevailed, as far as foul language was concerned. The language of the average Infantryman was not too gentile.

At 1935, First Sergeant Goodpasteur shouted, "Fall in."

Two hundred men scampered to their feet and took their positions.

II

CLAIBORNE TO KILMER

Wednesday, September 6, 1944

The First Sergeant yelled, "Report."

The squad leaders reported to their platoon sergeants, "All present or accounted for."

The five platoon sergeants repeated to the First Sergeant, "All present or accounted for."

First Sergeant Goodpasteur faced Captain Von Schriltz.

"All are present, sir."

Von Schriltz barked, "Posts."

The lieutenants who commanded the platoons took their positions at the head of their outfit. Headquarters platoon, of which I was a member, had no officer to lead them. Nominally, this was the duty of the Executive Officer of a line company, but Company E was without one. Thus, Sergeant Smith, the platoon Sergeant Smith, now occupied both positions.

At 1940, E Company was marching, for the last time, down the streets of Camp Claiborne. In eight minutes, we came to the track siding where our train was waiting. While marching, the five company officers kept up the usual chant of "Hup, Two, Three, Four." In the ranks behind me could be heard the remark, "It seems like yesterday that I got here. Boy, now I'm leaving this dump for good."

At the siding, the various platoons were assigned cars. The Headquarters platoon, along with the five Company E officers, occupied a Pullman composed of separate compartments. As we milled around, Sergeant Smith stated, "Edwards, you, Crable and Norris go back and bunk with weapons."

This meant that three of us had to sleep with the fourth platoon of the company. Ten minutes elapsed before we found them. After a few minutes of shouting and ordering, the platoon sergeant found the vacant upper and lower berths that had been allotted to the three of us.

Under standard Army procedure, two men slept in the lower berth while one occupied the upper berth. Norris and I agreed to share the lower while Crable took the upper.

The noise in the Pullman of the weapons platoon was that of an uncontrollable mob. But order was restored shortly when the porter, assigned to this car, began to unlock the upper berths. Although all of the men in the Company knew how to make their own beds, the black porter performed this task. After all the upper berths had been pulled down, the making of the lower berths was completed.

The train did not leave for what seemed forever. After much bitching, the platoon sergeant informed us that two other companies from the Second Battalion had to be loaded before the train could move.

At 2130, the locomotive gave a slight chug. Company E began to leave its home. Everyone rushed to the windows. This would be our last opportunity to see Camp Claiborne since we all knew that the camp was but a temporary home. As the train passed over U.S. Highway 51, which ran outside the front of the camp, someone shouted, "There's Boomtown, that damn collection of shacks. All you ever did was take our dough. Goodby forever, you fuckers!"

The train proceeded northward, at a pace not exceeding ten miles an hour, toward Alexandria. Outside, pitch blackness reigned. The members of the fourth platoon and their three visitors slipped into their sleeping quarters.

Just before 2400, the long line of Pullmans carrying three companies of the Second Battalion passed through Alexandria. Twenty-five miles had passed on the long journey. Little activity could be seen on the deserted streets. They had been the play avenues of the Division on week-ends. After bridging the Red River, the locomotive burst into a faster speed.

Thursday, September 7, 1944

Upon arising, the question on everyone's lips was, "Where are we?"

We soon found out that the train was in Arkansas, headed toward Memphis, Tennessee. While I was looking at one of the maps of the area, one of the Company E cooks tapped my shoulder, "Edwards, you're on KP." My reputation as a malcontent had not stayed at Camp Claiborne.

The kitchen car, a plain boxcar, was located between the second and third Pullmans occupied by the Company. Upon reporting to Pete Stoppin, the mess sergeant, the day's work was outlined. The three of us assigned to KP were consoled by the fact that we did not have to sit all day and look out the windows. The tasks in the kitchen car proved to be much easier than those performed in Camp Claiborne. The only difficult work was that of washing pots and pans. The three of us split this task so that each of us did this after each meal. The company cooks tried to cooperate by using as few pots as possible. Each meal was served to the men in their separate Pullmans. The cooks along with the KPs had little difficulty serving, except for pouring coffee for breakfast. Extreme caution had to be used because of the swinging cars on the rail line.

Just prior to 1200, the long train came to a halt on the Arkansas side of the Mississippi River, across from Memphis. The long line of sleepers stood for over an hour. Then, ever so slowly the locomotive chugged its way up the trestle across the wide river into the city of Memphis.

"Hope they let us out so we can see some dames."

"Forget it sarge, you ain't going nowhere," retorted one of the cooks.

The train remained in the freight yards while the locomotives were changed. Up to this time, we had traveled on the tracks of the Missouri Pacific. The rail journey continued. It seemed to be moving at less than ten miles an hour. After con-

9

sulting a map, Sergeant Stoppin announced, "We're on the Frisco line, heading toward Birmingham. How are we going to Kilmer this way?"

After supper, while I was up to my arms in soap suds with pots and pans, a stop was made in Amoy, Mississippi. A surprise awaited the troop train. At the station was a host of pretty southern belles. Their arms were full of cigarettes, cookies, candy and other snack food. Although the Second Battalion had hardly finished supper, every hand was out.

"How about coming with me, sweetie?"

"We can show you a good time, get on board."

"We're all going on a long trip and can stand some good cooking."

The young girls, who seemed to range in age from 16 to 25, seemed to take the remarks in stride. The three KPers were permitted to interrupt their work long enough to watch the festivities. One of the cooks secured some candy for the kitchen crew. They would be enjoyed after our work had ended. Some five minutes later, the train pulled out. How the people of Amoy knew of our arrival was a complete mystery to most of us since our whereabouts were supposed to be unknown.

KP was completed shortly after 2000. After returning to my assigned berth, I inquired as to the days' happenings. The reply was, "Nothing and Nuthling." The slow train trip continued. Frequent stops were made. By 2230, the weapons platoon and their three visitors were fast asleep.

Friday, September 8, 1944

Looking out the window this morning at 0830, Sergeant Robert Arnold, the weapon's platoon sergeant, proclaimed, "Fellas, we're in my home town, Atlanta, Georgia."

"How do you know sarge?"

"I know cause we're only five blocks from my home."

The Sergeant informed the group that the train was on the eastern side of Atlanta and had just passed through the center of the city.

"Men, we're on the Seaboard line," added Arnold.

His statement was soon confirmed. We learned that locomotives had been switched in Birmingham.

Riding the slow train was boring. A few of us read magazines and books that had been brought onto the train. Some of the weapons platoon engaged in the friendly and favorite game of poker. Someone usually lost all his money after which a long recess would be taken. Most of the men just stared out the windows at the landscape and dreamed.

After entering South Carolina, the train came to a halt. This was normal until the command, "Fall out" was heard.

"Fall out for what?"

"Where in the fuck are we?"

"What are we going to do here?"

"Fall out," was now shouted by Sergeant Goodpasteur.

Moans and wailings were of no avail. A few of the dogfaces had to be almost ejected from their seats.

After the usual reports of "All present or accounted for" was made to Captain Von Schriltz, a spread formation, where the men were spaced about three feet apart, was used.

All knew that this formation meant calisthenics. For the next twenty minutes, all three line companies stretched their train muscles. The usual push-ups, touch the toes, turn your neck, move the arms routines were followed. After the exercises were completed, all were ordered back onto the train. The long slow journey continued. Dusk found Company E in Monroe, North Carolina. After that stop, nothing could be seen from the windows.

Saturday, September 9, 1944

The train was in the freight yards of Richmond, Virginia. Further switching of locomotives was needed. The long line of Pullmans stood still over two hours before the tug of the engine was felt. The train was on the tracks of the Richmond, Fredericksburg and Potomac Railroad. Surprisingly, the steam locomotive streaked through the north Virginia countryside. The city of Alexandria, Virginia was reached.

11

"Hope this Alexandria here in Virginia is better than that dump in Lousy Anna." Jeff Atkins volunteered.

"What's wrong with Alexandria back at Claiborne?" asked someone.

"Those whores and bitches cleaned me out just before I left."

"Jeff, that's what you get leaving your pants in the hall."

In the distance, everyone on the train could see Washington, D.C. After waiting one hour, an electric locomotive of the Pennsylvania Railroad was hitched to the troop train. The coal burners which had spit black ashes in our faces were gone. The traffic signal ahead changed to green. With an even gentle pressure, the train eased forward. Everyone's neck was out the open window. As we passed the octagon, shaped Pentagon building, one GI exclaimed,

"There's the place where those bastards are that brought me from my home in Tennessee!"

Slowly the train inched its way across the Potomac River bridge. The Jefferson Memorial came into view. Then followed the Bureau of Printing and Engraving. Constitutional Avenue with its numerous governmental structures could be dimly observed. The Pennsy electric engine picked up speed. The tracks were above street level. The Capitol of the United States came into view.

"Why, it's just like it is in the movies!"

For about five minutes, the men of Company H could see the Capitol Building. Then, the train plunged into a dark tunnel. No further sightseeing was possible. Upon emergence, Washington, D.C. was gone. The green countryside of Maryland was seen only in glances for the speed of the Pennsy locomotive was like lightning as compared to the past two days in the South.

The journey's next stop was at Baltimore. It was only for a signal change. A rapid speed was maintained as the train whizzed through Wilmington, Delaware. In Philadelphia, the Pullmans came to a halt under the 30th Street Station of the Pennsylvania Railroad. A green light signaled the continuation of the journey. One hour later, the city of New Brunswick, New

Jersey was reached. After racing through the city, the speed of the locomotive became that of a night crawler. The electric engine began to make an enormous wide turn off to the right. Back over the main line of the Pennsy on a trestle, it went. Ahead could be seen Camp Kilmer. We knew it would be our last mainland stop before the ocean voyage.

III

CAMP KILMER

Saturday, September 9, 1944

From the train, Camp Kilmer, New Jersey, appeared vastly different from the military post we had left just three days ago. Kilmer looked impressive. The barracks were the two-story wood type painted white. They were permanent and neater. The entire camp could be seen from the train window. It could apparently house at least an entire division of infantry. As the engine slowly approached the camp's rail siding — containing twelve tracks, music could be heard.

"Hey, it's the Division band and some top brass."

"Who are they playing for? It can't be for this dumb outfit." Other comments of a similar nature were heard throughout the car.

"Wonder when I'll get my pass to New York?"

"Man, they ain't goin to give you nothing in this lousy outfit." came the retort. Although New York City was only forty to fifty miles away, few of the enlisted men expected to be able to go there.

The long line of sleepers came to a halt.

"Hey, there's General Bolling."

"Fall out." was shouted to the men on the train.

The three companies lined up on the cement walk adjoining the tracks. Major Edgar L. Hunter, the Battalion Commander, saluted and reported to General Bolling. The two officers held a brief conversation. Another conversation was held with the three company commanders.

15

"Forward march," came the order from Captain Von Sch-riltz. Company E stepped off to the beat of the band. The music faded as the 200 men marched. About one-quarter of a mile north of the loading trucks, a turn was made to the east. In front of Barracks Number 925, the order came, "Halt."

First Sergeant Goodpasteur announced the assigned barracks for the five platoons. Our platoon was to occupy the second floor of Barracks Number 926.

"Fall out."

With this command, a mad dash was made by every GI to secure a bed for his stay at Kilmer. I occupied a top bunk over Deloss Beesch. Each man was required to make his own bed. This was a change from the Pullmans. A few minutes later came the call,

"Fall out for chow."

Company E marched about a half mile to the white mess hall. The meals at Camp Kilmer were served cafeteria style. There were two lines that moved at a rapid pace. Everyone agreed that the food was superior to that we had had at Claiborne.

"Hey, fellas, notice what happened to our loving officers?"

Everyone listened as it was explained that each of the five officers in the Company had to pay 25¢ for his meal. At Camp Claiborne, only one officer was assigned each day to eat with the enlisted men of the Company, but, generally all five officers ate at the mess hall. If they had eaten at the Officer's Mess Hall, they were required to pay for their meals. However, at the Company mess hall, they received all the food they could eat without any fee. At Kilmer, they could not have any seconds. Many believed this would be particularly hard on our company commander, Captain Von Schriltz. While we were stationed in Louisiana, he would often come to the mess hall long after breakfast had been served. The company cooks always gave him as many eggs and slices of bacon as his six-two, 220 pound frame could handle.

After our first Kilmer meal was finished, all wandered back to the assigned barracks. That night the Company's supply sergeant issued each man a lightweight gas mask. We were informed they were given only to troops going overseas. After arranging our clothes and equipment, we were permitted to retire. For some, however, there would be little rest. Company E was required to furnish KP's for the night shift. The company's quota was ten men on KP per day. From later conversations, I learned that KP on the train had been a good deal. For once, being the malcontent of the company had paid dividends.

Sunday, September 10, 1944

Breakfast was eaten at 0700. After cleaning up the barracks, E Company was assembled. The 200 plus contingent proceed to a lecture and demonstration on the newly-issued gas masks. Our company was slightly late for the lecture. We learned how the masks should be placed on the head. We were taught the method to check if there were any leaks in the tube or face piece. This was done in the open air as well as in a gas chamber filled with some type of real poisonous gas. Every mask passed the tests, for no gas was detected by any member of the company.

Upon our arrival back at our new barracks, a First Lieutenant hailed Captain Von Schriltz.

"Captain, could you bring your men to the stands near the baseball diamond?"

"Certainly, Lieutenant."

After the company was assembled in the stands, a long and very boring lecture was rendered on censorship. The Lieutenant emphasized that secrecy was essential. He stressed that no individual should know where the 84th Division was encamped. He stated that no record or diary should be kept by any enlisted man since in the event of capture, the enemy might know of our past happenings. After the lecture, one dogface remarked, "All we can tell them is that we are alive."

One point made during the censorship lecture was that we could write anything about our officers within reason. The enlisted man could say or write almost anything about his non-commissioned or commissioned officers. In later sessions, each of the Company E officers stated he would do nothing to anyone who wrote derogatory items in his letters. Later, I would learn these assertions would prove to be completely false. After this lecture, the five platoons returned to their barracks. Just prior to dismissal, Company Commander Schriltz stated, "The company will receive passes but this is dependent upon how fast and how well our inspections are passed."

In the afternoon, each enlisted man was required to lay out his clothing on his bunk for inspections. The various company officers checked to see that all clothing was in proper order.

In the evening, all were given another physical inspection of a certain type. Why this occurred was a major mystery. No one had had the opportunity to leave the train or camp without permission. Everyone had undergone an inspection of the short arm variety just two weeks ago in Claiborne.

"That's the Army for you, no sense!" echoed several in the ranks.

After passing the physical, a typhus shot was injected into everyone's arm. As usual, many of the GIs were sick the remainder of the night. The shots were, of course, administered quickly and not-so-efficiently with a jab in your arm as fast as the medic could do it.

Monday, September 11, 1944

Before any unit left Camp Kilmer, they had to be inspected by the Transportation Corps. In the morning, an ordnance inspection was held. Each man had to have his own rifle ready. In addition, some had to help the supply room lay out its equipment. As one of the favored malcontents, my assistance was required to help the supply sergeant.

The afternoon witnessed a clothing check by personnel from the Transportation Corps. Our company easily passed both inspections. Rumors were heard that, if the entire 335th Infantry Regiment of 20 companies was successful in the passing of all the required tests, passes might soon be issued.

After our supper, many of the GIs visited the Post Exchange at Camp Kilmer to sample its wares. Most of us found the items to be much better than those we had purchased while in training at Camp Claiborne. The Kilmer PX was stocked full of all types of goods and snack items. The only item that many discovered was the same was the 3.2 beer which easily filled one's stomach but with its low alcoholic content left no hangovers the following morning. Little food was purchased since it was assumed we would be fed adequate food on any ship crossing the Atlantic. We would be fooled!

Tuesday, September 12, 1944

At assembly after breakfast, Company E marched to a replica of a ship built at Camp Kilmer. A short bald sergeant gave a good lecture on the use of life boats; how life jackets were to be worn; how to climb up and down rope ladders on the side of a ship. Each enlisted man then went to the top of the make-believe ship and climbed down a rope ladder to a waiting life boat. The sergeant followed with a lecture on what was to be done if our company was forced to abandon ship. We were warned that several evacuations had occurred during the transportation of troops. We were not to panic under any circumstances. This was followed by a movie in a large hall on the proper conduct aboard an Army transport. We would put this to use at a time in the not too distant future.

At 1330, each man was issued a wool knit sweater. We were also given protective clothing which was to be worn in gassed areas. At 1700, one-half of Company E was issued passes to visit nearby cities. Most of the GIs naturally went to New York City. The pass was good for only twelve hours.

September 13–17, 1944

A mild training program was followed for the next five days. There were lectures on current affairs. Everyone was hoping that the breakthrough which was occurring in France would continue so that the 84th Division would be nothing more than a peace keeping outfit. Numerous close-order drills were followed each day.

We were given a lecture and shown a movie on what was to be done if you, unfortunately, became a prisoner of war. We were instructed more than ten times that we were permitted to give the enemy just three items, namely, your name, your rank, and your serial number. A great many jokes were made of these three items by many of the enlisted men. No one expected to be a PW.

Talks were made on the straightening of your personal affairs. This did not concern many of us, including myself, that were not of the legal age of 21.

Every member of Company E was given a second pass during this period.

Sunday, September 17, 1944

During the daylight hours, all personnel were restricted to the camp area.

That evening, commencing at 2000 hours, guard duty was bestowed upon some members of the company. A small group of us were assigned the northwest corner of Camp Kilmer. The primary duty of the guard was to prevent men from leaving Camp Kilmer illegally. Eight of us worked out a system whereby two would be on watch for an hour while the remainder took a nap. The system worked without a hitch since no officer came to observe us. Our mission of preventing men from entering or leaving was never accomplished for everyone had been told that if you did not enforce this policy, you could follow the same routine of sneaking out the following night. The next morning at 0600 assembly, we estimated that, at least, 100 men had illegally departed and re-entered the camp in our area.

However, we would not permit anyone to bring back any female for that would have been trouble for all concerned. Just before 2300, I was on guard with Deloss Beesch when this condition had to be enforced. We saw two figures coming toward us.

I ordered, "Halt, who goes there?"

"Just returning to camp."

"That's ok, but whose with you?"

"I have a friend going with me."

"What kind of friend?"

"A girl. Someone to keep me warm!"

I motioned to Deloss to arouse the others since the returning GI was well over six feet and had the build to suit his height.

"Advance and be recognized."

The soldier came forward. Beesch had returned with the other six guards.

"Soldier," I commanded, "you can come in but your girl can't."

He quickly looked to ascertain that there were eight of us present.

"OK, but it's a damn shame you can't have any fun in this here Army."

Monday, September 18, 1944

The entire day was spent in actual preparation for the movement to our overseas transport. Each enlisted man had to roll a full field pack weighing, at least, thirty pounds. In addition, an extra blanket in the form of a horse shoe had to fit around the pack. The complaints were loud and raunchy.

"They must think I'm a mule."

"Shit, I hope they don't expect me to carry this on the battlefield."

"Doesn't this damn Army have any trucks?"

When first placed on one's back, the weight did not seem too much. After thirty minutes, the pack seemed to bend you over.

In the afternoon, the entire battalion practiced the loading of the rail coaches that would take us to New York City, where we would board our ships. We were briefed that, tomorrow, we would leave Camp Kilmer.

Tuesday, September 19, 1944

The sun came up in its full crimson glory. After breakfast, Company E was assembled. Each man had on his full field pack with the horse shoe roll. We were ready to leave. The officers, of course, had only a small musette bag to carry since their equipment was hauled by transport. A ten minute march brought us to the rail siding where we had arrived ten days ago. At 0900, Company E boarded the rail coaches of the Central Railroad of New Jersey. After a half hour wait, the steam engine began to pull the loaded military train through the country side. After twelve minutes, the main line of the Central Railroad was met. The long line of coaches proceeded toward the Hudson River.

At 1030, the train came to a halt in Jersey City. Every GI, with his full pack and his duffel bag containing other garments, was ordered to board a nearby ferry. When the lower car deck of the ferry boat was jammed, the gangplank was ordered up. The boat slipped into the Hudson River. A dense fog hung over the water. We could ascertain that we were passing lower Manhattan but none of the skyscrapers could be observed. When we were near midtown Manhattan, the ferry made its way into Pier 57. In front of the slip containing a large passenger boat was a huge sign proclaiming this dock to be part of the Cunard White Star Line.

Everyone was ordered off the ferry.

"Every man find his Company," came the order.

Within five minutes, Company E was in its regular formation. The usual long, long wait ensued.

"Hurry up and wait," moaned one GI.

During this break, the Red Cross women came with their equipment and served the usual coffee and doughnuts. The red and white clothed ladies were very cheerful in their chatting with the blue-capped soldiers. Many of the GIs needed some cheering for it appeared to them that they were about to leave the good old United States.

"Fall in," came the order from First Sergeant Goodpasteur.

Our First Sergeant explained how Company E would load onto the nearby ship. Each soldier's name would be called. The individual called would respond with his serial number. Each platoon and squad would be called in its regular order. Headquarters platoon would be first.

"Murray." "30 144 588."

"Johns." "04 268 142."

"Edwards." "16 106 000."

After giving the correct reply, each GI stepped on and up the gangplank. At exactly 1310, my left foot hit C deck of

H.M.S. 'Sterling Castle.' Playing follow the leader, the Headquarters platoon was assigned to Section d-1. This was located on the port side of the ship, midway between the bow and stern. All made a run for a bunk which were in layers of three. The aisle between the tiers was just wide enough for a person to stand. Headquarters platoon was fortunately placed on bunks next to the wall on the port side.

The upper bunks were in great demand. The lower ones were taken, if nothing else was available. The air situation in the entire compartment, which all of us thought was the former ballroom of the vessel, was poor for there was little circulation due to only two entrances to the huge area. Our platoon was the only one in this area from Company E. Joining us in the compartment was the entire rosters of Companies C and D of the First Battalion and Companies F and G of the Second Battalion. This meant that there were about 850 men crowded into a space formerly occupied by a ballroom of this passenger ship.

At 1700, the call came for our first meal aboard the Sterling Castle. Every dogface proceeded to secure his mess kit from his belongings. Ships are noted for their good food. The exception was the Sterling Castle. The supper was the worst most of the GIs had ever experienced. The bread was extremely dry! The coffee was very bitter! The peas were like tiny rocks! Even the potatoes had a bad odor. Every enlisted man aboard the Sterling Castle must have felt a let-down after supper that evening. Everyone in Headquarters platoon was hopeful that when some of the U.S. Army cooks were permitted in the kitchen, the food might improve. Our hopes were never realized.

That evening, a number of us in the platoon explored our troop ship as far as we were permitted. In peacetime, she was a passenger boat carrying people between England and South Africa. She was part of the well-known Castle Line fleet. Five of her decks were filled with members of the 84th Division. According to rumor, she was to carry a whole combat team consisting of the 335th Infantry Regiment, plus the 909th Field Artillery Battalion and some other support personnel. The total was close to 5,000 men.

23

A PRIVATE'S DIARY

Lights were out at 2100 for the day's hauling of equipment and the poor meal made everyone ready for a good night's sleep.

Wednesday, September 20, 1944

Two weeks had passed since our departure from Louisiana.

After a breakfast that consisted of just two slices of bread and one cup of coffee, we saw in the next pier another passenger ship, the Empress of Australia. On the previous day, American troops had been boarding her. They were rumored to be another regiment from the 84th Infantry Division.

At 0900, a shout was heard, "The Queen Mary's coming down the Hudson."

A rush was made to the stern to observe the fastest liner on the Atlantic. From our viewpoint, the Queen Mary appeared to be crowded with American soldiers. We later learned that she was carrying Prime Minister Winston Churchill who was returning from the Quebec conference with our President Roosevelt.

At 0930, a swarm of tugs came next to the Empress of Australia. With the aid of the tugs, the huge passenger liner was pushed out into the middle of the Hudson River.

We wondered when the Sterling Castle would leave. However, our ship continued to take on various types of supplies during the entire day. The usual card game appeared. Most of the members of Headquarters platoon took long naps during the entire day. It was unbelievable but the food was worse this day. A number of us boycotted supper. Some wondered aloud if they would survive crossing the Atlantic. As the compartment went to sleep that night, murmurs of

"Coffee like mud."

"Peas like pebbles."

"Potatoes as tough as rocks."

"Meat tougher than boulders."

echoed through the bunkers.

The last shout heard was, "If I can live through eating this damn food, not even a German bullet could kill me!"

IV

ACROSS THE ATLANTIC

Thursday, September 21, 1944

The big moving day for Company E! Actually the departure day for the entire 335th Infantry Regiment. Word had spread the previous evening that the ship was fully loaded and ready to sail. Breakfast on that big transfer day consisted of one large cup of bitter black coffee and a single roll because the rancid taste of all other British food could simply not be tolerated.

At 0830, four tugs appeared around the H.M.S. 'Sterling Castle.' After jockeying around the ship for nearly an hour in the placement of various ropes, at 0915 the tugs began to nudge and pull the huge vessel from its berth. Slowly the middle of the Hudson River was reached. Then, the tugs retrieved their two ropes. The Sterling Castle proceeded under its own steam. Slowly, the ships' engines began to pound. The decks vibrated as the tugs steamed away. The ride down the Hudson River was very slow. Soon, the ship passed the skyscrapers of lower Manhattan. The shores of New Jersey were watched by those on the starboard side. Suddenly, the Statue of Liberty came into view.

"Boy, I wonder when I'll see her again?"

"Might be sooner than you expect with the way this war is a'goin."

"Anyway, I'm going to wave my last goodby for a long time to come."

All on the starboard side kept waving their hands and arms until the huge statue faded from view. As the vessel continued to pick up speed, land in any direction could not be seen. The entire proceedings in the New York Harbor had been observed by every man on that British ship. The jamming along the railings eased. Many went back to their bunks. The bluish-gray water was the only thing that could be seen. A slight fog hung over the vessel. Instead of lifting, as we expected, the mist became heavier as the hours passed.

At lunchtime, most of those aboard tried, once again, to eat, but the British food with its intense putrid odor could not be consumed. To conserve their strength for the long voyage ahead, most of us in Headquarters platoon laid on our bunks about 1330.

The afternoon rest did not last long.

At 1430, a terrific jolt awoke everyone in their bunks.

"Has this tub been hit already?" inquired a now wide-awake GI.

None of us could imagine that the ship being hit was possible for the Sterling Castle had only left New York harbor five hours earlier. If the German U-boats could get this close to our shore, the United States Navy was certainly not on the alert. Someone mentioned Scapa Flow — the British naval base invaded in 1939. Anything seemed possible.

The bell for the alarm sounded. Everyone put on his life-jacket. Company E took its positions at the designated drill station on D deck. We were located on the port side of this deck.

"What happened to the Sterling Castle?"

"She been hit!"

"What by, a torpedo?"

"Are you guys nuts?"

"Well, what happened?"

"I was just leaning on the rail here with the fog horn blasting away in this pea soup fog. All of a sudden, a tanker appears right to the left side of the bow. BAM! The tanker went right into our bow. Luckily she hit our boat instead of us hitting that oil carrier. We might have caught on fire!"

"Go on!" All were awaiting his account.

"Both captains must have seen each other before they hit for bells were ringing all over both ships. The tanker's out there somewhere in the fog but you can't see her now."

All the military personnel kept standing at ease at their stations wondering what would come next. No further order was issued. At 1600, all were permitted to resume their normal activities. The fog had become so thick that one could not see further than 20 feet from the ship.

At 1830, when suppertime arrived, the rumor mill was in full swing.

One story was that we would be transferred to another ship from our present position. By what manner this was to be done was never explained.

Another bit of unverified information stated that the damage to the Sterling Castle was slight. The ship would proceed forward in the morning after the fog lifted.

Another stated that he heard the officers saying that our vessel would return to New York harbor. The troops would simply walk onto the pier, then, aboard another waiting ship.

The last of the rumors said that the Sterling Castle would return to New York harbor to be repaired. All of us on board would be returned to some military station like Camp Kilmer. When the English boat was ready, we would board her again for the overseas journey. This last rumor was, of course, the most popular. None expected this to occur for the United States Army did not work in this manner. It seemed too simple.

After what little supper was eaten, I spent most of the evening with Harry Ackerman. He was a rifleman with Company A. We had been acquainted since our school days in Philadelphia.

"You know, Don, I think the war is going to last a long time."

"Harry, what makes you think so?"

"Oh, I don't know. Those Nazi guys are just tough."

"How long do you think it's going to last?"

"At the least, a year."

"You mean the whole thing or just the war in Europe?"

"No, Don, the whole affair. Once the Germans are done, they're not going to have much trouble with the Japs."

"Ackerman, if the Allies keep going like they have been, the European war will be finished in three months."

"I'll bet you a buck it doesn't."

"That's a deal."

We shook hands on the bet. Our chatter continued to 2300. Throughout the night, the fog horns continued to bellow with their ear piercing sound. Compartment D-1 was extremely quiet when I retired.

Friday, September 22, 1944

"We're a'going back!"

Joy was rampant aboard the Sterling Castle. Our ship was returning to New York City. The last and the best of the rumors had come true. The entire 335th combat team was to return to Camp Kilmer while our vessel was being repaired. The back-slapping was evident among everyone on deck. Even the Limey chow didn't taste too bad this morning.

"How long do you think this tub will be in drydock?"

"No one knows but it could be anywhere from one to four weeks."

Everyone was hoping for the layup of one or more months.

Just before 1200, the Statue of Liberty again came into view. A return visit to her was totally unexpected.

Slowly the Sterling Castle went up the Hudson River. People on the numerous ferry boats must have thought we were returning veterans from overseas duty. All of us returned their greetings although, in all probability, our ship had never gone past the legal three mile limit beyond the shores of the United States.

The Sterling Castle stopped its engines in the middle of the Hudson near Pier 57. The same tugs which had pulled her from the pier yesterday were again at her side. The four midget boats soon pushed the giant passenger liner into the boat slip. At 1430, the docking process was completed.

28

The majority of us skipped lunch in hopes of getting better food in the near future. Instructions were given over the ships' loudspeakers.

"Everyone should be prepared to leave the ship at 1600," came the order.

Since all knew the 335th was returning to Kilmer, the chow lines for supper that evening were very short. Only five men from the 32 in Headquarters platoon took their mess kits to the ship's dining room.

At 1600, the first outfit departed from the Sterling Castle. We were told that Company E would not be among the first to leave. A number of us watched as the long and laborious process began. Each GI had to carry his full pack plus his duffel bag when he departed.

At 2000, Sergeant Smith yelled, "Everyone get ready to move!"

We waited 100 minutes before the first person from our platoon left the ship. Company E was the next to the last company to depart from the Sterling Castle. Company F had the distinction of being the last to depart.

Headquarters platoon came off the ship onto the second floor of the pier. We had to drag our duffel bags down to the stairs to reach the first floor. This is where we would depart on the ferryboat. Standard procedure meant a good wait for further transportation.

During our wait for the ferryboat, the women from the Red Cross served coffee and doughnuts. Most of us who had skipped lunch and supper were happy to have this snack. Since there were no other troops on the ship to be unloaded, the ladies were gracious and let us dogfaces clean them out of all their supplies. The women could not understand our hunger until the food situation aboard the Sterling Castle was explained to them.

The ferryboat arrived for loading at 2200. With our duffel bags dragging behind us, we of Company E marched over the gangplank onto the car deck. A short ride down the Hudson, with Manhattan barely visible, brought us to the Central of

29

New Jersey Terminal. After our Company's coaches were designated, all proceeded inside.

Along with Hal Cope, Ernie Duffy and Wiley Ponder, I occupied the first compartment in the first vacant coach.

"Edwards, what do you think you and the others are doing?" shouted Captain Von Schriltz.

"We're sitting in these seats, sir."

"Well you men should know that this first seat is reserved for me, so you'll just have to leave."

We did as we were ordered, although Ponder muttered something under his breath.

In the next coach, a vacancy was discovered next to Deloss Beesch.

Everyone drifted off to sleep while the train was still motionless.

Saturday, September 23, 1944

Captain Von Schriltz shrieked, "Everybody out!"

Sergeant Smith echoed, "Headquarters platoon line up!"

It was 0130. Company E had arrived back at Camp Kilmer.

The five platoons quickly assembled on the train platform.

"Put your duffel bags on that truck," ordered Sergeant Goodpasteur. All of us were happy to comply with this order.

Slowly shuffling down the streets of the camp, we made our way to area Number 7, which was located in the center of Camp Kilmer.

In front of one of the battacks, orders were issued. Headquarters platoon was to occupy the second floor again. After dismissal, a search for beds began. Within five minutes of the dismissal order, all had located a bed. Blankets were just thrown on each bed. We were fast asleep within seconds.

No reveille sounded this morning.

But most of the men from Company E arose at 0700 for breakfast. The meals experienced aboard ship had made almost everyone yearn for some good American victuals. At least the food at Camp Kilmer could be digested. On our return from our fresh egg breakfast, we learned that Headquarters platoon was located in Barracks 701.

At 1300, the entire company assembled for a lecture from the Company Commander.

"No one, not even your own mother, is to be told about what happened aboard the Sterling Castle. Just continue writing as if nothing has happened. Don't mention that we have returned to Camp Kilmer," admonished Captain Von Schriltz.

Apparently the men did not hear too well. Each of the four lieutenants spoke at least fifteen minutes a piece on the same topic to the enlisted men. After dismissal, it was apparent that very few would heed the warning that had been given. It was too easy to mail a letter outside the confines of Camp Kilmer.

Most of the enlisted men were granted passes to leave Camp Kilmer at 1500. Those of us who left had, again, to return for reveille the next morning. I went to the City of Brotherly Love for a date with Bertha Kleinert. I had met her at a roller-skating arena while attending Drexel Tech.

Sunday, September 24, 1944

Today was another moving day. The entire 335th Regiment had to be transferred to Area Number 1. Incoming troops that afternoon were scheduled to occupy our present barracks. Everyone was up at 0700. However, Company E was very lax in getting organized and moving to their new location.

Thus, outside Barracks Number 701, Captain Francis Price, the head of the S-3 section of the Second Battalion, gave a bitter tongue lashing to our Company Commander. Captain Von Schriltz accepted it without a single murmur. Most of us smiled inwardly.

September 25, 26, and 27, 1944

Company E settled into a daily routine. The morning hours were spent on drills and calisthenics. The hours after lunch were spent in the playing of all types of sports. The

31

favorites seemed to be volleyball and baseball. Outside passes were granted only on Monday, September 25.

The usual inspections were not lacking for both equipment and personal items such as clothing, shoes, haircuts and so forth.

Thursday, September 28, 1944

At 0600 reveille, the First Sergeant announced, "Everybody be ready to leave sometime today. You'll be given the orders later."

After lunch, Company E had the usual 1300 formation. At that time, it was announced that the final meal at Camp Kilmer would be at 1600. This would be followed by formation at 1700 for departure to New York.

Since all the dogfaces knew we would be returning to the Sterling Castle, every Post Exchange in Camp Kilmer was jam packed during the day. No one in Company E had to be told to be prepared. Although I knew that I would probably lose some weight on the overseas journey, I, too, wanted to be prepared. My purchases consisted of numerous cookies and no less than 84 candy bars. I would carry the extra weight. The clerk of the Kilmer PX inquired of me,

"Hey, private, what's all this buying that's going on?"

"Well, we are supposed to go back on board the British ship, the Sterling Castle to go overseas," was my reply.

"So what, don't they feed you on that ship?"

A further explanation of what some of us had consumed in the single full day we had been on board ship convinced the clerk of the seriousness of the situation. Any and all food items that the GIs could carry were purchased. The food shelves at the Kilmer PXs were absolutely bare at 1645.

At our final meal at Kilmer, the rule of thumb for any enlisted man in Company E was to have a minimum of three servings. Some of them had no less than four helpings. A number of us had a difficult time explaining to the cooks at the mess hall why their chow tasted so delicious. Most of the time the cooks usually faced verbal abuse over the food they had prepared.

Formation with full field pack plus the blanket roll was at 1700. At 1701, the heavens opened up in full force. Down came a heavy rain. Every man was pelted in the face. Orders were given to march to the rail siding of the Pennsylvania Railroad. Coaches were there for the entire battalion. Little time was wasted in boarding, although, being in the Infantry, we had been outside in all types of weather in drilling and marches.

At 1730, the electric engine gave a short tug. Company E was on its way again. The trip to Jersey City seemed much faster this time than on the previous Thursday. At the rail terminal, we were ordered to take ourselves and the usual duffel bag down the stairs to the first floor where the ferryboat was waiting. Darkness was descending. The ferry ride was short and swift. Soon Company E was at Pier 57 where the Sterling Castle was berthed. There were numerous murmurs about the boarding of this ship but all knew it had to be done. As soon as the ferryboat emptied its human cargo, the loading of the Sterling Castle commenced. There was little delay in moving up the gangplank as the names were called for all of us had had some experience in boarding a passenger liner.

"Boy, are we lucky," said Sergeant Smith, "We've got staterooms on C deck for this crossing."

The luck of Headquarters platoon lasted just fifty minutes.

"The Captain decided the company cooks needed their sleep more than us," announced our platoon sergeant. "They have to work every day in the ship's kitchen so it's back to D-1."

The 32 men moaned and groaned but did as ordered. The various groups in the platoon were again assigned the first two rows of the three-tier bunks next to the wall on the port side. We, at least, had a small opening of air near us which made breathing easier than was possible in the center of this huge sleeping dorm.

A PRIVATE'S DIARY

Friday, September 29, 1944

About 0330, when looking at my watch, a cool breeze was felt in the lowest part of the three tier bunks. My only reaction was to reach for another blanket which was at the foot of the cot.

Upon hitting the deck at 0830, a search was made for Manhattan but no land was to be found in any direction. The cool breeze I felt the previous night had meant that the ship had cleared New York harbor and was out on the sea lanes.

In the middle of the afternoon, a convoy started to form around the Sterling Castle. Various types of ships began to form rings around our troop carriers. On the outer ring, we could observe the U.S. Navy's D-E's. These were the Destroyer Escorts which were to be on the lookout for German submarines on our journey across the Atlantic. Most of Company E were disappointed that we were denied the opportunity to see again the skyline of New York City and the Statue of Liberty. Nevertheless, it was quickly forgotten since this was our second departure from the United States. We assumed that the remainder of the 84th Division had probably reached Europe.

September 30–October 9, 1944

The trip across the Atlantic took over eleven days. Convoys traveling together were extremely slow since the slowest vessel governed the pace of every ship. After a few days of looking at the beautiful blue sea, there was little to do.

The quarters on this passenger liner were very poor. Although everyone had complained about the conditions of the barracks at Camp Claiborne, the comparison was made between a deluxe suite at the Waldorf and a flop house on the Bowery. We were at the Bowery on a boat. In reality, Headquarters platoon was in good shape as compared to most of the GIs aboard ship. The majority of the infantry companies were quartered in huge compartments on Decks A,B and C. In peacetime, we believed these areas were used to store cargo. On those three decks, the biggest complaint was the lack of fresh air. One particularly large area on Deck A had only two tiny doors at either

34

end to admit air to a minimum of 800 men. To alleviate their situation, many of those in these cargo holds came to Deck D or E for sleep. They simply laid down one blanket and with another covered themselves against the chill of the night. On several occasions, my bunk was occupied during the day by someone who was trying to get some sleep after being awake all night.

Sleeping quarters were poor, but the meals aboard the Sterling Castle were abominable. In the twelve days spent on the ship, I ate only five meals. Each day as the convey progressed eastward, the mess line became smaller and smaller. During the last few days of the sea journey, a soldier could walk straight into the dining area without any wait. Although most of us lost a minimum of ten pounds aboard ship, we managed to stay alive. The reasons were simple. First, a number of us had purchased vast quantities of snack food at Camp Kilmer. Second, a Post Exchange did open on the Sterling Castle. The biggest item in demand was canned fish. Those of us who still had money after leaving the States could make a small purchase every day. Sardines were not one of my favorite foods but these small fishes, along with tuna and salmon, were the principle staples of the majority of the men in my platoon. My usual daily ration, food for a full day —, consisted of one-half can of fish, one small box of cookies and two candy bars. We bartered food we had purchased at Kilmer for other items that could be eaten. The big joke among the enlisted personnel was that if the 335th had to invade Europe from the Sterling Castle, the Germans would win since all of us would surrender for a good meal from the Wehrmacht.

The cooks of our company reported that the basic material received by the kitchens of the Sterling Castle was good. However, they reported to us that the cooking utensils and other kitchen equipment was alive with bugs and vermin of all types. If our cooks could have had the opportunity to scrub down and thoroughly clean the kitchen, they believed the food would be better. Near the end of the sea crossing, it took less than forty minutes to feed the supposedly 5,000 men aboard. To serve the first meal on September 21 had taken over four hours.

This housing and food situation was valid only for the enlisted men. All the officers of the 335th Regiment were in the regular staterooms of the ship. Each stateroom had forced air piped into it and was either on D or E Deck. The dining room for them was the envy of every enlisted man. White table cloths were on each table. Waiter service was available to them. From our chats with the officers of Company E, we learned that a different set of meals was served to them. After being told that steak was served to them one evening, Rodriquez of our platoon exclaimed, "No wonder the civilians never have any meat back home."

Most of the enlisted men would have not been envious if our superiors had tried to do something about the food situation. It appeared to us lowly privates that Colonel Hugh Parker, the chief officer of the 335th Infantry Regiment, never seemed to care how the men felt as long as we still managed to survive in some fashion. Brigadier General Charles Barrett, the chief officer of the Division Artillery was also on board, but he, too, seemed indifferent to the food conditions.

A few days out of New York harbor, our small convoy of about fifteen ships was joined by another and larger convoy. Rumor spread that the joining convoy was carrying the 99th Infantry Division. As the total convoy spread out over the blue sea, we could count almost fifty ships. Included was a baby air craft carrier. Surrounding the convoy and on the horizon at all times were the D-Es. They kept bounding up and down out of sight during the entire voyage. To the left of the Sterling Castle was a lane of six tankers. During the Atlantic storms, the waves seemed to come over the top of these oil-carriers. On the starboard side and to the rear of our ship was a mass of various types and sizes of boats. We were told by some of the crew that our speed across the Atlantic was just ten knots.

We discovered on the sea journey what a real blackout was like. At night every ship on that convoy was pitch black. The Sterling Castle was no exception. Smoking was prohibited on all decks at night. This rule was strictly enforced. In our training sessions at Camp Kilmer, many warnings had been issued on this subject because the glow from a cigarette could be seen many miles across the sea. Smokers in the companies had problems. At night they were not permitted to smoke on deck and vile threats were made if they smoked in their crowded sleeping quarters. Becoming accustomed to darkness took a few days. Even the transition of going from the sleeping quarters, which had a few dim lights, to the total darkness was found to be difficult. However, by the time of the landing, everyone believed the normal thing was to have total darkness.

I spent many of the evenings with Harry Ackerman. We discussed every item from world affairs to women. Harry's outlook for the future was very pessimistic. He was deathly afraid of going into combat.

"Ed, if I only knew what was going to happen."

"Harry, just hope for the best."

"But in this damn outfit, you can't look at battle in that light. Some infantry units are wiped out just like that, if they get into a bad place. Sometimes, Don, I wish the end would come. I don't want to come out with only part of me alive."

"You're a good guy, you'll survive."

"There isn't much future no matter who you look at it as a member of Company A."

"Maybe, the war will end. We're already in Germany."

"Ed, you're right. But the situation looks as if the Americans are being stalled."

"Ackerman, they may have another breakout like Patton had in France."

"Not this time. Then, the 84th will be in it."

My efforts to cheer up Harry never succeeded. And Harry's outlook turned out to be correct.

One evening in our discussions, Harry noted, "You ever notice, Don, how blue the ocean is out here in the middle of the Atlantic."

"Yes, I have."

"I've often wondered why some sailors like to be on the water all the time. Now I've seen it. The Atlantic seems to have a color that I've never seen in any stream, lake or river. I don't think I'd like to be out here all the time but it sure is beautiful."

37

A PRIVATE'S DIARY

The passengers aboard the Sterling Castle were in the U.S. Army. They were not allowed to forget it. A training program was instituted. To insure everyone's physical well-being, the men were engaged in calisthenics. At exactly noon each day, the moaning and groaning would commence. For a few days, some of us, including myself, managed to escape the physical drills. Sergeant Smith soon caught those who couldn't seem to find the area on Deck E that was used for pulling and pushing.

After drill and physical exercises, a lesson for learning the French language was conducted. Since I had had one year of French in high school and was a college student, I was designated to be one of the teachers. Everyone's attention and motivation to learn was next to nil. The general attitude was expressed by Corporal Joe Deak who said, "If they need us, let them speak English."

Every morning between 0900 and 1000, a boat drill was conducted as a precautionary measure. Participation was usually 100% because all remembered what had happened on the first drill on September 21.

News from the British Broadcasting Corporation in London was played over the ship's public address system each afternoon. After 1600, there was a record program. The latest record hits were played for everyone's enjoyment. During this music program, the announcer from the Sterling Castle would instruct us to set our watches one hour ahead. This occurred every two or three days.

On the evening of October 8, Harry and I became engaged in conversation with a member of the Sterling Castle's crew.

"Where does this ship regularly sail?" inquired Harry.

"Between Southhampton and Capetown, South Africa."

"How do you like sailing the North Atlantic?" was my inquiry.

"Not too much difference, only it's not as hot as going around Africa."

"Do you have any idea where we are now?" continued Ackerman.

"Oh sure. Just a minute and I'll show you two just about where you're headed."

38

Less than five minutes later, he pointed off the port side.

"See that light. The one going on and off. It's not very bright, but it's there."

"Yes, I see it," we both replied.

"Well, that's on the southern tip of Ireland."

"If we're in total darkness, why do they have that light?" I asked.

"You'd better remember that the Irish aren't in the war. They still have the lights on in their cities."

"That means, I guess, that we're getting near the end of the trip."

"It sure does. I think we're supposed to dock at Liverpool on the morning of the 10th. The ship will have to wait outside the Mersey River for the tide tomorrow night. It's not like New York you know where you don't have to wait."

At 1215 the next day, while doing pushups for 25 times, a shout was heard,

"Hey, there's land on the starboard side!"

Everyone broke formation to dash and see land once again.

We guessed that the Sterling Castle was passing one of the islands off the coast of Wales. This Atlantic crossing was coming to an end. As we in Headquarters platoon retired that evening, we were instructed that tomorrow, we would be in the Kingdom of England.

V

ARRIVAL IN EUROPE

Tuesday, October 10, 1944

At 0700, everyone from Section D-1 was up on deck to see our arrival in England. H.M.S. 'Sterling Castle' was slowing making its way up the Mersey River. The banks could be seen from both sides of the ship. Visibility was very poor. A light fog hung down on the buildings that were on both sides of the river. From the liner we could not observe any evidence of German bombings on land. But the situation in the Mercey River was vastly different. In two separate locations were signs entitled "Wreck." We were informed that these were sites where ships had been sunk as the result of the German air attacks. And no attempt had been made to remove them from the shipping channel. Since the river was quite wide here, it was easy for any incoming ship to avoid the sunken vessels.

At 1000, our transport ship was docked with the aid of a few tugs. The Sterling Castle slipped sideways into the dock. This was not like the New York harbor where the piers extended outward from the land.

No one was permitted to leave ship except the crew of the Sterling Castle and a few of the regimental officers. Guards were posted at the gangplank to enforce this regulation.

After docking, everyone was trying to see as much of Liverpool as possible under the circumstances. The fog had disappeared. This large English city appeared to be built low in comparison to large American cities which usually had some tall buildings. Most of the structures looked quite old and in need of repair.

While roaming the decks, we noticed a ferry boat that shuttled back and forth across the river. The passengers on the ferry waved continuously to the men of the 335th.

"Wonder why there's no bridge for all that traffic?" inquire Hal Cope.

"Maybe, the English don't need one since they can't drive any cars now." replied Deloss Beesch.

"Still seems like a slow way to me."

During our stay in England, we learned that there was a large tunnel connecting Liverpool and Birkenhead, the city on the south bank of the Mersey.

Just after 1200, John Crable noted, "Ed, there's one of those English policemen."

"I think, John, they are called 'Bobbies.' You've seen them in the movies."

The solitary English Bobby was about six feet in height and very slender in build. We could not see if he carried any gun but we all noticed his helmet and his night stick which appeared to be about a foot long.

At 1300, the unloading of the ship's cargo began. Most of the freight seemed to consist of items like records and files. We believed they belonged to the units aboard the Sterling Castle. The English longshoremen that were conducting these operations seemed to be much shorter and slimmer than the ones in New York. They were the first English civilians that we saw.

At 1500, a meeting was held of the Headquarters platoon. Sergeant Smith said, "Company E is going to leave ship tomorrow, just after 0600."

"Do we get breakfast on this damn ship?" inquired someone.

"If you want it, get it at 0530. Anyone going to eat?"

No one answered in the affirmative.

"Every guy is to get his duffel bag from the back storage room. Make sure everything is packed tonight, not tomorrow morning when it's time to leave. Everyone got that? Now listen closely. After we leave the ship, we'll march through Liverpool to the railroad station. Then we'll get on a train. We're going to a camp in southern England. I don't know where the place is exactly but it's somewhere around Winchester. Any questions?"

"When do we eat some food?"

"I don't know but all of you have survived so far. Everything is settled. Pack your bags tonight. Be ready to leave at six."

On E Deck that evening, many of us in Headquarters platoon expected to see what a blackout in a city was like. All were disappointed. A dim-out was in effect in Liverpool. The lights on the docks on the Mersey River burned all night. We felt that the English believed the war had finally gone away.

Wednesday, October 11, 1944

"Everybody up," yelled Sergeant Smith at 0515.

Since our duffel bags had been packed, the only item necessary was to roll the back pack. Breakfast was then available to those that wanted some food. Only three men from Headquarters platoon ate. They said nothing about the meal. Every officer and enlisted man in Company E knew that the whole ship would be served in less than thirty minutes. We continued to wait.

At 0645, a semblance of a Company formation was made on E deck.

Captain Von Schriltz ordered, "Everyone down to D deck to depart."

Some of the company lost their way to the deck below but soon we lined up on D deck. Each platoon was checked to insure that each man had the proper duffel bag.

"The Company is to proceed single file down to C deck and off the ship. I'll lead the way. Headquarters platoon will come first. Everyone ready?"

My left foot hit English soil at exactly 0737. It was not ground but the second floor of the dock along side the Sterling Castle. Every enlisted man of Company E just dragged his duffel bag down the stairs to the first floor. Here was an Army

2½ ton truck. Two husky GIs took our bags and heaved them onto the vehicle.

"Everyone fall in their position after they leave the truck," was the command from the officers and our platoon sergeant.

After the regular formation was secured, Captain Von Schriltz went on, "You men are going to march through the city before we get on the train. I want all of you to be in the best military conduct. That means no talking in ranks. No remarks to any of the civilians in the streets. Is everything clear to every man?"

A march was begun through the streets of Liverpool. The first thing to be noted was the elevated railroad which was about one block from the pier where the Sterling Castle was berthed. From the ranks was heard,

"Just like my old town, Chicago."

The other means of transportation seemed to be like that of our own country. One remarkable difference was noted. In the United States, few cities had double-decker buses. Here in Liverpool, every bus was of the double-decker variety. The trolley or street cars were also of the double-decker type. These were the first I had seen. Comments were made about the personnel manning the buses and trolley cars. Most of the conductors collecting the fares were women. Yet all the drivers were male.

The effects of any German air raids could be seen in only a few isolated spots. The few buildings that had been hit were cleared of debris. Usually a few walls were still standing.

The item that drew our immediate attention was the rule of the left. Although there were very few autos on the streets, every bus and trolley car had its driver on the right side of the vehicle. Since we of the 84th Infantry Division were strangers in this country, this new rule was followed. We marched on the left side of the road.

Our route of march seemed to take us through part of the downtown section of Liverpool. The only familiar store to most of the GIs was Woolworth's. In England, the "5 and 10¢" store was appropriately titled the "3 and 6d" store. We would learn that the symbol 'd' meant cents in the British currency.

Most of the English spectators that were on the streets of Liverpool stopped to stare at us. Their faces seemed to say, "Still more Americans coming."

The march through Liverpool lasted less than half an hour. We came to a halt in the Mercey Railway Station. Various coaches for the five platoons were assigned by the First Sergeant. Within five minutes of our entry into the railway station, we were ordered to our coaches.

The American Red Cross was present with its coffee and doughnuts. For most of us in the Headquarters platoon, this meant breakfast. A very rush job of dispensing was done by the red and white ladies.

Headquarters platoon was assigned to a coach similar to those on American railroads. However, most of Company E were in coaches of the small European compartment type. Most of us had known about them from motion pictures. Eight men were assigned to a single compartment. It was crowded.

At 0837, the steam engine gave a gentle pull. It entered a long dark tunnel. The train apparently went underneath much of Liverpool for on our emergence we observed the flat green countryside of England.

"Gee, these Limey locomotives are small, compared to our back home."

"Yea, take a look at the size of those English box cars. One American box car could take about three times as much stuff in its hold."

"And take a look at those coal cars. I'll bet they don't hold ten tons of coal."

"The size of the engine, the small box cars and coal cars. It makes the English railroads seem like a toy along side our railroads."

The gauge of the rail line was the real answer. The smaller equipment was made for the small and narrower gauge. For its size, the railway locomotive for our train seemed to have a much faster pick-up than its American counterpart.

All of us noted that, in one aspect, of rail travel, the English railway seemed to be far ahead of those we had traveled in the United States. Our train did not seem to cross a street or road on the flat countryside to the accompaniment of flashing lights and warning bells. Every road, regardless of size, ran over or under the rail bed.

The English countryside seemed well supplied with railways. Around Liverpool, rails seemed to run in every possible direction. Shortly after leaving the darkened tunnel, I noted that our train was on the tracks of the London and Northeastern Railway.

Green was the color of the English countryside. To the water-sored eyes of the men of Headquarters platoon, it was a welcomed sight.

"See how well those fields are kept."

"Everything looks so green and neat."

"And all the hedges are trimmed to perfection."

"Boy, it's just like a scene from some travel movie."

"I'll tell you fellows, it's just like my home state of Pennsylvania."

Denials came from everyone in the coach. Everyone started to compare the English landscape to his own native state.

One item which everyone seemed to agree upon was the large number of small towns that passed by our windows.

"Hey, we're in another town."

That phrase seemed to be heard every three minutes.

Many of us now realized how forty million persons could live in an area comparable to the state of Michigan. In almost every town there were civilians waiting for a train. They waved at us and shouted some type of encouragement like "Glad to see you Yank" or "Take care of those Jerries for us."

"Don't they have any wooden houses in this damn place?"

"These Englishmen don't have to be like Vermont." was the reply.

From our coach we could see no wooden structures. Almost every house seemed to be made of brick. At each end of the dwelling was a chimney stack. In the rear areas of the homes in the large cities, there was an air-raid shelter which probably had been in use a few years ago.

After leaving Liverpool, the first large city that our train entered was Stockport. Here our train made a fifteen minute stop. Nobody was permitted to leave their coach. We guessed that our journey had taken us due east.

"How are we going to get to south England if we don't change direction?" piped up Wallace.

"Don't worry Bill, we'll make it." stated Sergeant Smith.

The next large city we entered was Sheffield. The city appeared to be a heavy manufacturing town like Pittsburgh or Detroit.

Leicester was next. Our train, which had slowed to a bare crawl, did not arrive there until 1330. Sergeant Smith stated that we were permitted to leave our coach. On the train platform at Leicester was a contingency of ATS girls. Each man on the train, which contained both Company E and F, was allowed to have one and one-half cups of tea. This was lunch. The tea was poured from huge pots which must have contained a minimum of ten gallons. After downing my last ounce of tea, I walked over to a sign on the platform which gave mileage to different points in England.

"Edwards, get back in that car and stay there." shouted Captain Von Schriltz.

"Captain, I just wanted to see where we are and how far it is to southern England."

"That's no excuse. Other people have decided where you're going. That's not your job."

"Yes, sir."

I followed his order after glancing once more at the large directional board.

Our next stop was the college town of Oxford. The famous university could be observed from the railway tracks.

Just after 1700, the coaches came into the town of Newbury. After leaving that city, we were instructed to pull down all shades and curtains. A blackout was in effect on the train. All of us had learned in training that a lighted train made a perfect target for a raiding enemy plane.

Everyone then fell fast asleep.

At 2050, a voice suddenly announced, "Hey, fellows, we're in Southampton."

"Are you sure?" asked Sergeant Smith.

"I'm positive."

Some lips muttered, "Maybe they gave out the wrong dope yesterday. They meant Southampton, not southern England."

In back of me, a GI yelled, "Don't tell me we're going to get on another English tub. I've got to have one square meal before I go back to sea."

"Please God," echoed another. "Just one meal."

"Shut up you numb skulls," stated the platoon sergeant. "How can anyone tell if we're really in Southampton?"

"Lift up the shades and see."

A few curtains were raised.

"Look at the lights. They're everywhere."

Everyone then raised their curtains. The harbor lights of Southampton were ablaze. It was as if there was no war going on. Since the railway station sign read 'Southampton,' everyone knew where we were.

For the next thirty minutes, rumors of all types were prevalent.

Would we leave the train here? Would we board the ship resting at anchor in the Southampton harbor? Would we stay in the station overnight, and board the next morning?

At 2100, all the questions were answered when the train left the Southampton rail station. A sigh of relief fell over the entire coach.

At 2140, the voice of Sergeant Smith announced, "Headquarters platoon, fall outside on the platform."

After shaking ourselves from a sound sleep, we complied and left the rail coach.

When both rifle companies were on the platform, the empty coaches pulled away.

"Hey, Ed, you were looking at the directory in Nottingham, where are we?"

I replied, "How do I know, that board didn't tell me where we were going."

"Hey, Sergeant Smith, where are we?"

48

"Stockbridge, England."

On the pitch black platform, Captain Von Schriltz tried to find some of the officers of Company E. As he walked up and down the platform full of whispering GIs, who had been ordered to keep absolutely quiet, his voice rang out, "Lusby, Gavin, Burke."

He sounded as if he were calling, "Popcorn, Peanuts, and Cracker Jack" at an American baseball game.

Everyone in the Headquarters platoon started laughing at his hawking. Sergeant Smith bellowed, "Keep quiet. He's serious."

The unique calling method of our Captain did succeed. The three officers were found. Five minutes later, our platoon sergeant barked out the order, "Everyone's to go up the hill behind this station. Then right on the road. Trucks will be waiting for us."

In the very still darkness, the order was quickly followed. Minutes later, our truck journey commenced.

A somewhat bumpy ride of twenty minutes ensued.

"Everyone out," was the order after the trucks stopped.

As the company lined up on a one track country lane, I noted that on one side was a large open field. On the other side, where the trucks were parked, was a large grove of trees. The moon, which had appeared, gave some light to the Company which was in its regular formation. A conference was had between all the officers and Sergeant Smith.

The Company Commander gave orders to the five platoon leaders.

Sergeant Smith led our Headquarters platoon to a Quonset hut which was about 70 yards from the gravel road. The trees with their leaves made the area pitch black. The hut was entered in total darkness. Since we possessed no electric lights or flashlights, this hut remained in total darkness. The entire platoon went on the floor to discover what was there.

"I've found a sort of cot." remarked a darkened figure.

"What is it?"

"It's a wood frame with some strands of wire hooked between some two by fours."

49

In the next five or seven minutes, each member of the platoon had found his own bed frame. Each man laid a tent shelter half on top of the wires. Our beds were ready for occupancy. Within the next fifteen minutes, still in the dark, all the men of Headquarters platoon were on top the shelter half with his blanket over him ready for sleep.

At 2245, one of the Company E's cooks stuck his head in the door.

"Hey, you slumbering duckheads, chow is being served at the mess hall."

"Where is that?" grumbled a half-asleep soldier.

"Find it down the road, you numb skull."

Since almost the entire platoon had existed on just one cup of coffee, two doughnuts and some English tea for the full day, all threw off their blankets. Because of our limited meal taking on board the Sterling Castle, all of us in the platoon were ready to eat.

We filed out of the hut and went down the travel lane about three hundred yards to another Quonset hut. This was Company E's mess hall. Two candles flickered. As we walked down the line where the food was in large kettles, the various items of food were simply dropped into our mess kits. Because of the lack of light, few knew what it was supposed to be. No one complained. A square meal after 12 days was heavenly.

At 2345, Headquarters platoon, now back in its darkened hut, retired for the second time.

Thursday, October 12, 1944

At 0015, a voice shouted into our Headquarters platoon hut, "Everyone fall out on the road. The duffel bags you left in Liverpool are on the road."

"Who said we have to do it now?" asked a darkened sleeper.

"The Captain, that's who, you bastard."

The sleepy voice answered, "Why can't we let it go till morning. We'll have plenty of time."

"The Captain said it's got to be done. Before you go sacking, get your gear. Do it if it takes all night. Is that plain enough for all you wise guys? Now everyone out and down on the road. On the double!"

With loud protests, all in the Headquarters platoon struggled down to the road. Every man from Company E was there. The struggle over 200 duffel bags commenced. Although each man's name was stenciled on the bag, everyone seemed peeved. There were just three flashlights to aid in the search for the bag for each enlisted man.

A half hour after searching in semi-blackness, John Crable shouted, "Hey, Ed, I've found your bag."

"Thanks, John, now I'll do the same for you."

One hour later after finding bags for all the members of Headquarters platoon, we returned to the still dark hut. For the third time, we laid down on the new cots. By 0200, everyone was asleep. About 0400, some of us heard planes buzzing overhead. Since no warning of an air attack was given, no one stirred out of his blanket.

VI

TRAINING IN ENGLAND

Thursday, October 12, 1944

Reveille came at 0730. At Company E's formation that morning, we could observe the English countryside in the daylight. My supposed dream about airplanes buzzing in the early hours turned out to be true. About a half mile away from the huts of Company E, across a green field of grass, was an English or RAF airfield. I could see that some Mosquitos bombers used by the Royal Air Force were sitting outside some hangers. Some of us guessed that the Mosquitos had been returning from a bombing mission early that morning. After roll had been taken at the morning formation, our First Sergeant announced, "After you eat, we'll have a company formation at 1030 hours. Dismissed."

At the mid-morning formation, the five company officers lectured us about our general welfare. We learned that Company E was stationed on an estate owned by a certain Mr. Donald Young of London. He was leasing it to the British government for military purposes during the war. As the United States was an ally of Britain, our Army was entitled to use these grounds near Andover on which the circular shaped huts had been erected. The last talk came from Captain Von Schriltz who reminded us, "Men, we're over here to fight, not to go sightseeing and pleasure hunting. I'm going into battle with you and I want all of you to come out with me."

From the rank in back of me, a GI muttered, "How can you do that if you're in the Infantry. No way you dumb bastard."

After the noon meal, Sergeant Smith was given permission to let the men of Headquarters platoon proceed across the open field near the English airfield to some vacant military huts where some straw was available. We were issued some ticks — a sheet with two sides and an opening at one end — which were to be filled with straw in order to sleep more comfortably. Everyone in the platoon was complaining about sore backs from the previous night's rest on the wire covered by the shelter half.

The remainder of the afternoon was spent in cleaning our Quonset hut. It took little time since the previous occupants had left the barracks in good condition. The real problem of the day was trying to light a fire in the huge black pot belly stove which stood in the middle of the huge room. The entire platoon, singlely and in unison, had no good suggestions in getting a fire to burn. We must have wasted over 100 matches in our efforts. Since we never changed clothes to retire at night, the loss of a fire to warm us was taken in stride.

Our big success story was that our Sergeant Harland Smith had found a single electric light bulb to use in the hut. Although we could not read by its glow, we could see the locations of our beds and our duffel bags.

At dusk, three of us were ordered to install blackout boards on the two windows at each end of the hut. In putting them into place, Wiley remarked,

"Boy, what a lousy waste of time. If the Germans are going to bomb something, they'll be able to see Southampton miles away. What do you think, Ed?"

I replied, "Don't think it's important here but on the continent, if we're some place with light, we'll have to rig up something like this."

During the afternoon, our platoon leaders announced, "You can write letters back home telling folks that we are in England. You can't mention what ship we were on or when we got here, but you can say you're some place in England. The rest of what you were instructed in Kilmer still applies."

TRAINING IN ENGLAND

Friday, October 13, 1944

As usual, this was my unlucky day.

At 0600, Sergeant Smith shook me and stated, "Edwards, you're on KP for today. Report to the mess hall by 0630."

"Sarge, what day is it?"

"Your lucky day, Friday the 13th."

Kitchen Police duty turned out to be easy for the entire day. There were no dishes to be washed since each soldier had to use and clean his own mess kit including his own silverware. The jobs this day consisted of dishing out the food and washing the pots and pans.

After lunch, Company E received its first pay on foreign soil. This was our first pay day since leaving Camp Claiborne. Since we were in England, the United States Army paid us in British currency. Very few of the company members knew what coins and bills constituted the Limey currency. My pay amounted to 10 pounds 15 shillings and 8 pence. This totaled $43.50. A deduction of $6.50 was made for my $10,000 GI insurance.

The poker games that were played that afternoon and evening were of a most unusual variety. Most of the British coins that were bet were given the same value, whether they were 1d, about 2¢ in American currency, or 2s, about 50¢ in United States value. There was a great deal of haggling but no real arguments arose. At the end of the game about 2300, most of the card players in Company E had learned the true value of each British coin and bill.

Saturday, October 14, 1944

At 0430, Sergeant Smith yelled, "Everybody get up."

"Hey, Sarge, it's only four-thirty, are you serious?"

"I mean it, our Headquarters platoon has a special detail for today."

Our platoon sergeant shook the bed of each man in the platoon. By 0500, we were in marching order. We proceeded to a spot near the Officers' Quarters which were located about a half mile north of our hut.

An unknown Technical Sergeant approach Sergeant Smith and announced, "Sorry you came Sergeant, but we don't need you. Thanks for coming. Sorry you and your men had to come for nothing."

Headquarters platoon proceeded back to our hut. We crawled back under our blankets.

At 0700, the call for reveille came. Most of us arose to report for the first day's formation. Sergeant Smith said, "Forget about getting up. We've missed enough sleep going to that detail. I'll explain to the Captain what happened."

We returned to our beds again. At 0745, First Sergeant Goodpasteur stuck his head inside our hut.

"Where was Headquarters platoon this morning?"

"We went on a detail and told we were not needed." replied our Sergeant.

"Don't matter, Captain wants you in line in fifteen minutes!"

At 0800, we were in formation before Captain Von Schriltz.

"Where was Headquarters platoon this morning, Sergeant?"

"We went to a detail this morning, sir, at 0500. Later we were told to return to our hut since we weren't needed."

"I don't care what happened before reveille, Sergeant. If your platoon is present in the area, I expect it to be present at reveille. This morning you were here. There is no excuse why the men were not here. Headquarters platoon will have an extra half hour of drill this morning."

The order was carried out with loud mumblings later in the morning after the usual Saturday inspection of rifles and barracks.

Except for the extra drilling, the afternoon was left free.

John Crable, Deloss Beesch and I decided to walk around the surrounding countryside. We noted that Company E was stationed on the bend of a small country road running through the Young estate. On the inside of this bend were the woods where the Quonset huts housing our company were constructed. On the outside of the road lay open spaces which ran as far as the eye could see. The open fields were cut up into small farming patches. On one of these patches was the British airfield housing the Mosquitos bombers.

While walking across the large open field where our drills and calisthenics were held, we ran into a British Sergeant whose last name was Caldwell. He was well over six feet tall with a thin drawn face. We fell into a conversation with him.

"Sergeant, what part of the British Army are you from?" inquired Beesch.

"Oh, I'm a member of a glider team living just beyond your boys. My platoon is near that target range which you can see from here."

Beesch continued, "How long have you been here?"

"We've been here for quite a spell. It doesn't look like we'll leave very soon. How long do you boys expect to be here?"

"Oh, about a month. Then we'll most probably go across the Channel."

"We're sort of anxious to go back into the thick of things. But we just stay here. We're to guard against any surprises by Jerry."

At that moment, a British Lieutenant shouted, "Sergeant get over here!"

"Well cheerio lads. I have to do and drill the platoon. Best of luck to you three. Hope we meet again."

Our walk took us to the nearby airfield. Here we noticed that both the Mosquitos bombers and Spitfire fighter planes were lined up outside the two large hangers.

"Look Don and Deloss, there's no concrete runway." stated John.

"How do they take off?" was my question since I had expected concrete was a necessary item at any airport.

"Let's wait around and see if anything happens." answered Crable.

During the next ninety minutes, we observed what occurred at this small airfield. The British planes simply started at one end of the field. The plane sped over the grass and simply lifted itself into the air.

"Boy, that must be hard on you, especially your rear end." noted Deloss.

"I agree. That bouncing over the grass must really hit you. I'll bet they're glad to get into the air as soon as they can." was my answer.

Our walk around the airfield brought us to the highway which ran along side the airfield. We noted that we were on Road 3057 between the towns of Andover and Stockbridge.

While walking down the highway, John spied a bread truck delivering to a small English farmhouse.

"Let's buy some baked goods, fellows."

Deloss and I agreed. The three of us came to the truck where the driver was making some notes in a small book.

"Have you any bread or pastries you would like to sell?" asked John.

"I'm sorry lads, but that was my last call for the day. I'm out of everything. Aren't you lads getting enough to eat at your place?"

"Yes, we are," stated John. "But we'd like to have a change. We want something that might be a little more tasty."

"Sorry I can't help you lads. Now I've got to get back home. Cheerio."

The bread truck was on its way to Andover.

Sunday, October 15, 1944

The day was spent as one for resting with one exception.

After lunch, while in our hut, Sergeant Smith gave us instructions regarding Post Exchange items available to United States Army troops in the European Theatre of Operations.

First, each of us was given a small wallet size card giving the soldier's name, his Army serial number, his organization and his APO (Army Post Office) number. The card was signed by both the individual soldier and his unit commander.

Each week, each American soldier in this theatre was allowed a tobacco ration which included cigarettes, matches, candy, gum, cookies and toilet soup.

Every two weeks, each enlisted man was entitled to receive four ounces of peanuts, a bar of laundry soap and five razor blades.

On a monthly basis, fruit juice, tooth paste, shaving cream, writing equipment, pipe cleaners and two women's handkerchiefs were available for purchase at the Post Exchange.

After two months in the European theatre, a GI could purchase articles like combs, shoe polish, towels, ink, books, tooth brushes, et cetera.

After detailing all this information to the men of the Headquarters platoon, our platoon sergeant continued with, "Don't expect these items to be available at all times. This system applies only to the rear areas. When we're on the front, no PX is going to be there. No one knows when and where we can get these things."

No one complained about the cost of any of the articles. It was one of the few times a gripe was not heard.

Monday, October 16, 1944

My lucky day.

After our platoon had returned from our breakfast of dry cereal and powdered milk, Sergeant Smith confronted me.

"Edwards, you're the barracks guard for the day."

"What's involved?"

"Just keep the place clean. Keep the fire going. And make sure there are no visitors looking for something free. Is your rifle available?"

"Yes, it is, sarge. I'll put in a clip just in case."

"OK, but don't have a bullet in the chamber."

After a half hour of sweeping and making a few untidy beds, my sole occupation, outside of the usual reading of books, was keeping the fire going. Because the ashes could not be easily removed from the potbelly stove and no draft was available from the bottom, the fire kept going out. Every fifteen minutes it became necessary to fan the fire to keep it alive. Thus, each night in our hut, the fire would go out and be restarted by the platoon members shortly after breakfast.

59

The rést of the platoon participated in the usual drills and marching.

Tuesday, October 17, 1944

At 0600, the gentle voice of Sergeant Smith came upon me with,

"Edwards, you're on KP again today."

"Hey, what's up? I just had it a few days ago. How come again today?"

"I know, I know. But this time, you're at the Officer's mess. You and Crable are to report up there to the Mess Sergeant."

"OK, Sarge. But I still think it's someone else who should go."

At 0700, we reported for KP. Our assignment was scrubbing the pots and pans. We were permitted to eat breakfast before our task started.

After the pots and pans were finished for the breakfast meal, John and I decided to inspect the housing facilities for the officers.

The dwelling was a large English countryhouse. It housed about 40 officers from the four companies of the Third Battalion plus those from Companies E and F. The main floor consisted of a large dining room where the officers ate their meals; a living room approximately 30 by 40 feet with a small sitting room adjoining it and two bedrooms. The kitchen which consisted of two rooms also occupied the ground floor. One of these rooms was the site where the food was cooked while the other was the place where dishes including pots and pans were washed and stored. Adjoining the washing room was a pantry room for storage.

The second floor had seven bedrooms plus two full bathrooms. Each bedroom was quite large and could accommodate, at least, four beds.

The system of serving meals to the commissioned officers could easily equal that of the finest restaurant in the U.S.A. The service available could be described as super-deluxe. The officer upon entering the dining room for any meal had a choice of eight tables. Each table had eight places. In front of each setting was a cloth napkin and a complete set of tableware. The appropriate tableware was available for each meal.

After an officer had seated himself at a table, an enlisted man — there were always several standing around — went to the table. The GI stated what items were available for that particular meal. At breakfast, fresh eggs were always available. They could be ordered in any number and prepared in any way. After the order was given, the enlisted man repeated it to another who went to the kitchen. Then each item was delivered by a single enlisted man. If six items were ordered at breakfast, each item would be brought by a different dogface. The standing joke among the enlisted men was that no one was available to put sugar or salt or pepper on the food to be eaten.

Since the officer patrons came in to be served only one or two at a time over a two hour period, the elaborate waiter system was not pressed into rapid service. Since I did not have to start my chore of washing the pots until the meals were served in full, I watched the highly organized scheme as it operated that day. At supper, a private from I company, who was one of the waiters, remarked to me,

"Edwards, this reminds me of an old southern plantation before the Civil War. All the slaves standing around to serve their masters with every detail. I sometimes think I'll drop some soup on someone's head."

The only officer who did not follow this procedure was Major Robert Wallace, the commander of the Third Battalion. All his service in the dining room was provided by his own personal orderly.

Although I had complained of being selected for KP this day, I actually enjoyed the tasks performed. The reason was the meals at the Officer's Mess. They were the best I had had since leaving Camp Kilmer. One could taste the difference between powdered eggs and fresh eggs. The same was true for powdered and fresh milk.

The cooks at the Officers' Mess treated us KPs as persons. As long as the work was done in a competent manner, they did

61

not hassle you. No officer came by to inspect your work or ask you why you took so long to complete your tasks.

Since John Crable and I were on the pots and pans detail, we were still working when the other KPs and cooks were finished. The Mess Sergeant told us to finish up and leave by the back door and make sure that it was locked. A half hour later, our jobs were completed.

"Don, since no one is here, let's take a treat back to the hut."

"John, that's a great idea! The fellows would enjoy some of these goodies. What do you suggest we borrow?"

"I think the fellows would like some fruit juice. We never get that at our mess hall."

Thus, upon our departure from the officers' billets which we now tagged the "Castle," we borrowed four small cans of fruit juice.

Upon our arrival back at the hut of Headquarters platoon, I announced, "John and I have brought a treat for all of you!"

"Ed, what have you got?" shouted Corporal Duffy.

"We've borrowed permanently four cans of fruit juice. Get out your cups and everyone can have a little."

Our 'borrowed' treats disappeared is less than three minutes.

A few minutes later a request was made of Sergeant Smith. He was to ask our Company Commander that Headquarters platoon would volunteer someone each and every day to work on KP at the Officers' Mess. Captain Von Schriltz granted this request. Thus, from that day, any member of Headquarters platoon was expected to 'borrow' a few things to bring back to his friends for a snack. This secret was kept from the remainder of the enlisted men in Company E until we had departed for the European continent. No other complaints were ever made.

Wednesday, October 18, 1944

This day I spent at sick call. I was not physically ill.

A regulation of the United States Army stated that every GI who wore glasses should have an extra pair in the event one was broken. Since my extra set had been broken in the trip on the Sterling Castle, Sergeant Smith instructed me to secure another set.

After stating the purpose of my sick call at the regimental medical hut, the medic said, "Report back at 1230. Take the ambulance to the hospital. When you get there, go to the optical section. They'll take care of you, you hope."

At 1230, five of us enlisted men were transported by ambulance to the 34th General Hospital. It was located on Route 272, just east of Stockbridge on the route to Winchester.

The optical department was easily located on the first floor.

"What can I do for you, Private?" inquired a Sergeant from behind a desk at the optical center.

"I'd like to have two new lenses put in these frames. Regulations say I'm supposed to have a spare pair."

"You're right, I'll have it done, but you've got to give me the information on your unit so we can return them to you."

"My name is Donald A. Edwards, Headquarters platoon, Company E, 335th Infantry Regiment, 84th Infantry Division. My Army serial number is 16 106 000."

"Got it. Now, how soon do you need these back, Private Edwards?"

"I don't know sarge. Since we could leave any day, I guess as soon as possible."

"OK. We'll have them to you in three days."

The glasses never came. The remainder of the time spent in Europe was with one pair of glasses.

Since my optical business took less than five minutes, I had to remain in the 34th General Hospital for two more hours before the ambulance would return us to the 335th. During these 120 plus minutes, I toured the hospital.

All types of American wounded soldiers were in the hospital. There were at least five men with only one leg. Another half dozen were without one arm. Several had bandages over one or both their eyes. I had several conversations with the

63

wounded about where they had been hit. For almost 25 minutes, I conversed with Dale Stewart, a Corporal from the 29th Infantry Division.

"Dale, when did you get hit?" was my inquiry.

"Ed, I think it was D plus 5."

"Where?"

"About seven or eight miles from Omaha Beach."

"What happened?"

"Our squad was approaching a frame house, when wham. The Germans hit us with some mortars in the open field. All I saw was blood on my legs and I don't remember a thing after that. When I got here, they had to take part of it off just below the right knee. I could go home any time but I hate to have my folks see me like this."

"Got any suggestions for me, Dale?"

"What's your job?"

"Messenger from the Battalion to the Infantry Company."

"Just be careful. Sometimes, you don't know where the damn front is. In your job, you can easily wander into the Germans without knowing it. Be careful Ed and don't come out of this thing like me."

"Thanks, Dale. Anything else you can tell me."

"Yea, those fucking Germans are the best soldiers in the world. They never seem to give up unless it's hopeless. They're real tough. And that machine gun of their will send chills down your spine. Just be careful like I told you. Those Krauts are real good."

"Have to be going now Corporal. Hope to see you in Chicago some day."

On the return trip in the ambulance to the 335th, the five of us present discussed what we had observed. The results of war had been vividly brought home.

Thursday, October 19, 1944

At 0600, Sergeant Smith again greeted me with the words, "Edwards, you're on KP."

"Where, Sarge?"

"Officer's mess."

"OK, no complaint."

When the three of us assigned from Company E reported to the Officer's Dining Hall, we were politely told,

"Sorry men, but we've got all the KPs we need for today. Company E wasn't supposed to send any today. Report back to your unit."

Upon returning to our hut, reveille formation for Company E had been completed. Since I had been up to the 'Castle' to report for KP, I was duly noted as being absent. At 0900, I was informed that I was to report to Captain Von Schriltz.

"Edwards, you were reported as missing from formation. Why?"

"I was ordered to report to the Officer's mess for KP, Captain. Then we were told we were not needed and to return to our company."

"Why didn't you report to the First Sergeant?"

"Sergeant Smith said it wasn't necessary."

"If you're reported absent, it's your duty to report that you're back. I don't care what Sergeant Smith told you. I'm going to remove your name from the list of those going to London tomorrow. And report to the stock room at 1300 for your extra work detail. Have you anything to say?"

"I don't think it's fair, Sir."

"Private Edwards, you don't do any of the thinking around here. Understand me?"

"Yes, sir."

At 0930, Company E was ready for a five mile hike through the countryside. The march route took us on small village roads near Stockbridge. The village itself was not entered. On the hike, many of us noted that there were two other small airports of the Royal Air Force. We were impressed with the fact that no landing lights were visible and that the meadows were the runways.

At 1300, the three of us who had missed the morning formation were in the stock room for work. Except for a half hour break for supper at 1700, we worked until 2100.

A PRIVATE'S DIARY

About 1600, Corporal James Elmore came to the adjoining orderly room and began discussing his visit to London with five other GIs.

Elmore was describing his journey to the British capital in his slow Georgian drawl, when one of his listeners interrupted him with,

"Yea, Elmore, that's all interesting. What we want to know is the women."

"None of you are goin to have any trouble. There's more than you can shake a stick at. Believe me."

"Come on, give us the details."

"After the blackout starts, go to Picaddilly Circus. Don't worry about finding it. It's easy to reach by subway."

"What's at this Picaddilly Circus?"

"All around the place, you'll see women. Every kind you want. White, Chinese, Black, those Indian ones, you name it. All you do is walk around and pick the one you want."

"Elmore, how much do they charge?"

"The prices are kinda steep. The cheapest is about a pound."

"You mean, five bucks."

"That's what I said. That's not for the whole night either."

"Who do they think they are? Back in Louisiana, two bucks was plenty."

"Maybe so. But you ought to see the guys on pass in London. Most Americans are paying more than that. Most of the prices are three and four pounds. And they're getting it."

"Fifteen or twenty bucks. Are you kidding?"

"Hell, no. When you get there, you'll see how the land lays. Be prepared. Not difficult to get a dame but she'll charge you plenty for it."

"Any ideas what a whole night costs?"

"I heard it's about twelve pounds and up."

"That's unbelieveable!"

Until the call came for supper, Corporal Elmore was besieged with these questions. Since a private was earning fifty dollars a month, the prices that were being charged by the ladies-of-the-evening were not easily comprehended.

After returning from supper to the supply room, I chanced to listen to the conversations of three E company officers who were censoring the letters that had been written by the enlisted men of the company.

"Boy, is this a job for you. Read, read, read these lousy letters." said Lieutenant Charles Gavin, the leader of the second platoon.

"Still, you learn a lot from them you never knew before. Listen to this gem. 'I over you my darling, I lover you. I just can't wait to get home and tell you how much I lover you. I'm your great lover.' This letter continues like that for four solid pages. Here's his P.S. 'Dearest I love you and I hope you lover me." Now that, gentlemen, is a real letter for you." added Lieutenant George Burke, the third platoon leader.

"And listen to this," chimed in Lieutenant James Lusby of the first platoon. "This outfit is getting more chicken all the time. I wish I could kiss a few of the lieutenants with my right fist."

"Who wrote that Lieutenant?"

"Oh, Private Johnson of the second platoon." replied Lusby.

"Be glad to oblige you, Sir."

"You can tell almost who you should trust and who doesn't like you from the way some of these letters are composed." noted Lieutenant Burke.

"But you can't let the men know that we discussed these letters. Just give them something extra to do. They won't know the reason for usually they aren't doing anything right." said Lieutenant Gavin.

Upon my return to the platoon hut at 2115, Bertram Gainer asked, "Well, Don, how did the work go in the stockroom?"

"It wasn't too bad, but I sure learned a lot of interesting things."

"What could you learn in that damn stockroom?"

I then informed Gainer of what he could expect at Picaddilly Circus in London and to keep his letters short and sweet.

A PRIVATE'S DIARY

Friday, October 20, 1944

Besides our usual hiking and drills in the morning and afternoon, Company E was required to listen to various lectures by the commissioned officers and certain non-commissioned officers. These military subjects had been covered at least a dozen times in Camp Claiborne. The most difficult task for the GIs was to keep awake for none of the lecturers were experienced in teaching methods. Although they tried, the vast majority of the enlisted men failed to pay attention. If one fell asleep, the penalty was to stand for the remainder of the lectures during that day. Going asleep standing up was impossible.

Our last lecture for this day came at 1600. Captain Von Schriltz explained that the various squads and platoons would engage in night scouting and patroling exercises starting at 1930. He and the other officers would not be present and his last remarks were,

"The purpose of these exercises is to get you men into shape for future events."

A GI seated next to me muttered under his breath, "You should get in shape yourself. You're the biggest slop in this company in one direction and it isn't up."

Our nighttime exercises started as planned at 2000. We were supposed to find our way in the dark with only a compass to guide us. Since no officers were present, most of the enlisted men fooled around a great deal. Those in the Headquarters did an adequate job since our platoon sergeant was our real leader and was present.

Saturday, October 21, 1944

The morning hours were spent in the usual drilling and hiking plus two boring lectures. One again was on the subject of your conduct if you became a prisoner of war. Everyone had to recite several times to his platoon leader the fact that only your name, rank and serial number needed to be given in the event of capture. it was emphasized that we should remain calm as possible if that unlikely event happened.

The afternoon was spent by those in Headquarters platoon in letter writing. Several were absent visiting London. Although it might have been easy, this usually proved to be a difficult task in writing to one's family and other friends. Very little, if anything, could be written about the real activities in which the company was engaged. We could state we were in England, Period. The letter really said, "I'm living! How are you?"

One solution that Deloss Beesch suggested was to write large; tell the person you loved him or her; and comment on every detail on any letters that you had received from them. On one in our platoon ever criticized the officers. My warning was known by all 32 men. No one mentioned our 'borrowing' activities.

Sunday, October 22, 1944

Being Sunday, no one was expected to arise at any hour. The only exception were those who attended any type of church service. Less than one-half of Headquarters platoon were church goers. Only 14 arose before noon. This was the highest percentage of any platoon in Company E.

Mass for the Catholics was held at 0900 in the mess hall of the Third Battalion. Our regimental Chaplain brought the required equipment. It was set on a table that served as an altar. A few benches served as seats. Kneeling was done on the floor. The simplicity of the service seemed to make some more conscious of religion than if the Mass had been celebrated in an elaborate church.

John Crable and I noted the arrangements that prevailed for the men of the Third Battalion in their eating facility. They had ten benches on which to sit for their meals. Company E had exactly two benches. This meant that most of our company had to stand while eating or one could kneel or stoop over and eat from the table. Our mess hall had only two lights with no windows. This one had six lights and two windows. On our walk back to the hut, John remarked, "Don, let's eat with the Third Battalion."

"Good idea, but you realize it can't be done."

"You're right, but it was a good idea."

After our noon dinner, Sergeant Smith informed six of us that we were on guard duty that evening. I asked, "What are we going to guard, the airfield?"

"No, Edwards, you're just going to patrol some grounds near the 'Castle'.

"You mean, someone's going to steal the officers in their beds?"

"No, damn it! Edwards can't you just do as you're told?"

"Yes, Sarge."

At 1600, thirty men from Company E and other units assembled at the horse stables that were part of the Castle. An inspection of the guards was made by the Officer of the Day who was Second Lieutenant Domenic Bertetti of Company I. In passing me during inspection, he gave me a strange look but said nothing.

But I recognized where I had previously seen him.

After inspection was completed, the Lieutenant motioned for me to come before him.

"What is your full name, Private?"

"Private Donald A. Edwards, Sir."

"Where are you from?"

"Detroit, Michigan, Sir."

"Haven't I seen you before?"

"Yes, Sir."

"Can you tell me where?"

"If I can call you Sergeant Bertetti, it would be at Redford High in Detroit where you were the ROTC (Reserve Officers Training Corps) instructor."

"That's right. How did you remember that?"

"If you remember Sergeant, I mean, Lieutenant, I took ROTC for a year. You were my teacher."

"Edwards, how did you end up here? Also I won't get upset if you call me Sergeant."

For the next fifteen minutes, I told him about my experiences in the Army. Lieutenant Bertetti stated that he had been

70

in the military his entire adult life and was hopeful that any experience gained in combat would further his military career. In parting, I asked him,

"Lieutenant, any guess on when the war might end?"

"No, Edwards, but I think the Germans will still be battling at Christmas."

"Are you worried about combat like some of us Lieutenant?"

"Yes and no. A little luck should see all of us through."

Upon our departure, we shook hands.

Lieutenant Domenic Bertetti never saw another Christmas since he was killed in action on December 23, 1944.

We were divided into groups of ten. One-third of the guards began their tour at 1800. The other two-thirds slept. Since there were no horses in the barns, there was adequate room for those who slept while others guarded. At 2000, another one-third went on duty. Thus, the system operated so that you spent two hours on duty and four hours off. The first complete tour ended at 2400 with the second at 0600 the next day.

My two stints of duty came at 2000 on the 20th and at 0200 the following day. The first stint passed without too much difficulty. The second one in the early hours of the next morning was not too difficult for one reason.

During my first stint, I made the acquaintance of Michael Hatzis, a fellow private from the First platoon of Company E. He was assigned post number nine while I had number eight. Thus, the end of our posts met. We must have spent two-thirds of our guard time at the meeting post. Hatzis, who hailed from Chicago, was worried about one thing, demobilization.

"Mike, we haven't been in the war yet. We don't know when it will end."

"I know Ed, but I'm worried about getting home. The war will end before the 84th gets there. The Army's already fighting in Germany. They can break through any day now."

"I think you're wrong but who knows."

"Anyway Ed, when this thing is finished, I'd like to know just when I'll get out. How will they know who to let out first?"

71

"Oh, I guess they'll work out some system. Length of service and combat could be factors."

"You watch Ed, for I'll bet you any money that the poor guy in this Infantry gets the worst of the deal."

"Well, that might be true. And I think that married men with children will get some consideration."

"I doubt it. This Army doesn't operate in that manner. Those birds that do the least will be the first out. Combat don't mean a thing. Those twerps in the States will be the first out and we'll be stuck here. Watch and see if I'm not right."

We continued to converse in this manner during our shifts. Mike Hatzis could not be convinced that living through combat will be his most difficult task.

Monday, October 23, 1944

At 0600, the thirty guards lined up in formation for reporting. We were dismissed and instructed to return at 1800 for another like tour.

Those on guard duty were excused from any type of training for the entire day.

At 1800, we returned for our second tour of duty. The same format was followed with one-third on duty and two-thirds remaining in the stables. Since some of the enlisted men had smoked on the guard duty posts the previous night, all were warned about hard penalties if anyone was caught with 'a weed in their mouth.' That warning did not apply to me.

My stints of duty were like the previous night. Again I had long talks with Mike Hatzis who was again assigned to post number nine.

Tuesday, October 24, 1944

After breakfast, Sergeant Smith announced to the six members of the communications section of Headquarters platoon that we would attend radio procedure school that day. No one complained although nothing new was taught. The communications section was composed of personnel who had to be acquainted with the tree types of messages available, namely, radio, telephone, and hand carried messages. The latter was the easiest for the only instruction was that it be carried in the left pocket of your skirt. In the event of capture, we were to destroy any messages on our person. By having a standard procedure, there would be no question as to where the message would be, in the event the carrier of the message was injured in some manner.

At the radio school, the British Army procedure was outlined to us. We were required to know their operations in the event our outfit was attached or teamed with the British in combat operations. A review was made of U.S. Army procedure. At the end of the sessions, oral questions were asked of the participants. The question proposed to me was the standard alphabet to be used in spelling out words. This did not pose any problem and the answer of Able for A; Baker for B, Charlie for C, Dog for D, Easy for E and down to Zebra for Z was easily given.

Wednesday, October 25, 1944

After breakfast, Sergeant Smith announced, "Edwards, you're on salvage detail today."

"Sarge, is that good or bad?"

"In your case, it's good. You don't like the drilling and the lectures bore you, so I volunteered you. OK?"

"You're right, Sarge. The amount of drilling we do is ridiculous and, as a future educator, I'd give most of the lecturers about a D grade for their work."

With a jeep and a trailer, the three of us from Company E went to the various companies of the 335th Regiment and collected material that had been discarded.

In the afternoon, we were detailed to assist in the unloading of some heavy covered equipment that had arrived for use by the staff officers of the Second and Third Battalions.

A PRIVATE'S DIARY

Thursday, October 26, 1944

Another day of KP at the Officer's Mess. Dish washing was my assigned task.

Since the food was so superior to that of the Company E mess hall, I enjoyed the task.

At 1810, I had just started the supper dishes when the mess sergeant tapped me on the shoulder.

"Are you Private Edwards of E Company?"

"Yes, Sergeant."

"Someone just came from your company and said you're on the list to go to London tomorrow. Report to the dispensary right now if you plan to go. I'll get one of the other KPs to take your place here."

"Thank you Sergeant. I didn't expect with my reputation to go to London."

Every GI knew that before a pass could be issued, a "between the legs" physical inspection had to be undergone. If you failed, no pass was issued.

Upon arrival at the Regimental Aid Station, there must have been 100 or more men who had to undergo inspection. Just inside the door, I bumped into Ed Nelson. He had been stationed with me while we both attended Drexel Tech in Philadelphia.

"Come on over here, Don," Ed motioned to me.

"What are you doing here, Ed?"

"Just checking names and seeing that things are in order."

"Ed, where are you stationed now?"

"With the regimental aid station."

"What do you have to do in order to get the London pass?"

"Don, pass through the 'short arm' part first. Then, have your teeth checked. You've got to get a Class four, meaning nothing is really wrong with your teeth. Think you'll pass both?"

"I'll pass, Ed."

"Come on, I'll put you in front of the line."

74

Both sections of the physical test were passed. Although I observed no one who flunked the 'legs' test, ten men were denied a pass until their teeth were fixed that evening. Since the Army dentists had nothing to ease the pain of any dental work, a few screams were heard from the adjacent room.

After passing my tests, I resumed my conversation with Ed Nelson. We compared notes on what happened to each of us during the past two months. At 1945, I left to return to the hut.

While packing my bag for the trip to London, I inquired of Sergeant Smith as to my good fortune in getting a pass.

"Edwards, this is the last group from Company E that goes to London. Everyone that requested to go has been granted a pass. I guess the Captain felt you shouldn't be deprived of the right to go."

VII

A VISIT TO LONDON

Friday, October 27, 1944

At 0615, I was up without any prodding from anyone in the platoon.

At 0700, all who were selected to go from Company E were at the Castle. The four trucks departed on schedule. Since it was still dark, none of the green English countryside could be seen from the vehicles.

At 0730, our group arrived at the railway station at Andover Junction. The entire pass group of over 800 men from the Regiment awaited their rail coaches.

Three trains stopped at Andover Junction to pick up and leave passengers. As each of these trains arrived, a voice came over the loud speaker saying,

"All American soldiers, please do not board this train. There will be a special coach train to take care of all Americans going to London."

At 0805, the special train composed of fifteen European style coaches came into view. Over the loud speaker came the announcement,

"This is the train going to London for all American soldiers."

Within two or three minutes after the train stopped, every compartment was occupied. A short gentle tug by the locomotive at 0815 indicated that the rail journey had started.

The fields and meadows on the train trip were like those we had seen on the Liverpool to Stockbridge run. All seemed green

77

and in perfect shape. Our special train passed through only two towns of any size, namely, Basingstoke and Woking. As our cars whizzed by other small hamlets, a GI in the rear of the car noted, "Hey, I'm on the same railroad I ride back in Virginia, the Southern."

At exactly 1000, the special pass train came to a halt in Waterloo Station in London. The coaches were emptied in two minutes flat as everyone streamed toward the exits. Five of us from Headquarters platoon quickly secured a taxi for a trip to the Hans Crescent Club of the American Red Cross. This was the place where we had to register in order to secure our lodging for Friday night. Buses and taxis seemed to out number private vehicles by a considerable number. It appeared as if all taxicabs in London were of the same type and variety. The cab driver had only a small seat to himself on the right hand side of the taxi. Due to the limited traffic, all of them seemed to be speeding. They had the shortest and quickest turns I had ever seen a vehicle make.

The taxi arrived at the Hans Crescent Club at 1030. On our speedy trip, the only famous buildings that were recognized were the Houses of Parliament with Big Ben and the Westminister Abbey. We saw both as our cab came across the Thames River inasmuch as the Waterloo Railway Station was located in the southern section of the huge city.

After arrival at this Red Cross Club, we had to line up Army style in order to register. Fifteen minutes later, I had Guest Receipt No. GI 03693 in my hand. It had cost two shillings, about 40¢, and entitled me to a lodging for one night. Due to the large number of American soldiers in London on passes, the Hans Crescent Club had an annex for sleeping only. These were to be our sleeping quarters. After a walk of a short single block, the building was located. My assigned sleeping quarters were on the first floor in Room 2, Bed M. All the beds were in tiers of three, thus, accommodating many sleeping GIs. I was in the lower bunk. After checking our equipment, we decided that breakfast was in order.

We now started the process of learning London. First, we proceeded up Sloane Street to Knightsbridge where some eating places were located. Just as our group of five started up Sloane Street, we met Bertram Gainer and William Wallace. They had arrived in London just twenty-four hours ago and would return that evening.

"Hi, men, what are you guys doing in London? What have you two been doing with yourselves?"

Gainer stated, "Give you exactly one guess."

"OK, tell us all about it," said Sergeant Smith.

"Last night, about eight o'clock, we picked up these two tarts from Piccadilly. We looked around and these two only wanted four pounds each, for the night. That was the best we could do."

"You mean twenty bucks each!"

"Yea, and that's cheap. Well, we went to a few dives. I think they're called pubs. All of us drank that warm English beer. It's not bad after a few. Then, we went to their hotel room. Wow, what a time we had!"

"What did these two tarts do for you?"

"Everything. They fucked us, sucked us and blew us. I must have come four times. Wallace did the same. We didn't get done until four this morning. I tried for a fifth but couldn't get up. Are we tired."

"Where did you pick them up?"

"Down at Piccadilly. You almost have to beat them off. London is the greatest town for women. You can get any type you want. But it's going to cost you plenty."

"Did you see any of the sights?" inquired our Sergeant.

"Haven't had time. Wallace and I are going back this afternoon to Rainbow Corner. They have taxis that take you around London. Right now we're going to get some sleep. Boy, what a time!"

"See you back in camp Sunday." stated Sergeant Smith.

The five of us left Wallace and Gainer who looked as if they had been in a night long fight.

We entered a small cafe on Knightsbridge. Tea and cakes were the only items available at this time. Each of the five ordered one cup of tea. Several cakes were placed before us. After biting into one, Hal Cope exclaimed,

"Why, these cakes are just plain cookies."

After paying our bill, we had a conference on what was to be done. Three of us decided to go to the Rainbow Corner Club of the American Red Cross. It was located just off Piccadilly Circus.

In order to get to the Rainbow Club, it was necessary to ride the Underground or Tube. In my previous experiences with subways in New York City and Philadelphia, a person needed to descend only one normal flight of stairs in order to reach the train level. London was quite different.

After a descent of one short flight at the Knightsbridge Station on the Piccadilly Line, we reached the ticket booth. Here a ticket was purchased for Piccadilly Circus. The fare was based on the distance traveled. After procuring the ticket, we boarded an escalator. This took the Underground passengers about two or more floors into the earth. At this level, the trains ran. At the end of the escalator ride, a right or left turn was made depending upon which direction one wished to travel.

Around the train platform were advertisements of various English products. And, in addition, we discovered beds that looked as if they were still in service.

"Ed, what are these beds doing here?" inquire Cope.

"Hal, I think they came down here to escape the air raids that London had a few years ago."

Within five minutes, the Underground train came into view. The train consisted of ten long curved-shaped subway cars. In the front was a motorman. Half way down the ten cars was a conductor who controlled the doors to the cars. The doors rolled slowly back. Everyone walked quietly into the cars. This seemed like a distinct change from my experiences in the United States. Rarely did I ever see a Londoner run for or shove his way into an Underground car, regardless of how crowded the platforms might be.

The ten cars started off in an easy fashion and gradually increased in speed. Hal Cope noted that one could not see the trains coming from the opposite direction on this Underground line. Three stops and five minutes later, the station of Piccadilly Circus was reached. A trip was made up the escalator. At the end, the ticket purchased at the Knightsbridge station was turned into a ticket-taker, all of whom seemed to be women.

Upon emergence from the Underground station, a whirlpool of humanity was met. It seemed as if every GI on leave was there. The motor traffic consisted mostly of buses which entered the circle from other streets. This was Piccadilly Circus. Since Hal and I could not find the Rainbow Corner, we hailed an English 'bobby'.

"Where is the Rainbow Corner Club, officer." I asked.

"See Shaftsbury Lane, there, it's just up the street. You can't miss it."

"Thank you, officer. Anything happening now."

"No, it's only at night that we have all the activity."

We quickly found the Red Cross club. At the front desk, Hal Cope asked where he might exchange his French francs for English currency. Hal had been with an advanced group from the 84th Division that had been to France in order to secure camping sites for the whole Division in Normandy. A pert English lady gave us directions to the American military station near Oxford Circus.

Hal and I then walked up Regent Street through Oxford Circus to the American military station where the finance section was located.

Upon entering from Regent Street, we inquired from an MP where the money could be exchanged.

"Men, it's on the third floor. You can't miss it."

"Thank you, Corporal."

"Say I've never seen that patch before. What is that?"

"It's supposed to be an axe splitting a log," was my reply.

"What outfit is that?"

"84th Infantry Division."

"You haven't been here long, have you?"

"No, about two weeks in England."

"I expect you'll be going across in a short while. Most of the fellows in Infantry Divisions aren't here long. The only ones that stay are the 8th Air Force guys. They're always in London. Here's the elevator for you."

"Thanks for your help, again, Corporal."

"Best of luck to you in the 84th. Hope it's over before you get there."

On the third floor, a delay was experienced while the Finance personnel checked Hal's story about being in France. He satisfied them that he had been there a week with the 84th advanced party.

On our way back to the Rainbow Corner Club, we stopped at a small eating place called 'The Regent Restaurant' located at 8 Princess Street. Our lunch consisted of baked fish, a vegetable, dessert and tea. The cost was two shillings, six pence. We both agreed that for 50¢, we had an excellent meal.

At the Red Cross club, we attempted to book a taxi tour of London. Our efforts were unsuccessful. Arrangements were made to take a taxi tour the next day.

After consultation with one of the Red Cross ladies, we agreed upon a short walking tour of London. Since we had been issued maps of London upon our registration, we anticipated no difficulty.

Upon leaving the Red Cross club, Hal and I were immediately stopped by two Air Force Lieutenants who were acting MPs.

"Just a moment there, soldiers," cried one of the officers.

"Yes, Sir," replied Cope as he saw their silver bar.

"Don't either of you know anything about military regulations?"

"Yes, Sir," was my reply.

"Why didn't you salute us, then?"

"We didn't expect to see any officers as MPs, Sir."

"I know it's strange but you should be on the lookout for such things. The Lieutenant and I have just completed our thirty missions. We're waiting to go back home. I haven't seen that emblem before, what outfit are you men from?"

"84th Division, Sir."

"New outfit then, just got here, I suppose."

"Yes, Sir, we arrived about the first of the month."

"Good. I suspect you leave soon. Another thing, soldier." The shorter Lieutenant pointed to Cope, "Always keep every button buttoned. There's one open down there on your pants."

"Yes, Sir."

"You two can go now. But don't let us catch you again."

As we started our walking tour, Cope and I soon learned of the complexity of London. Very few streets had names that lasted more than five blocks. Then the name of the street changed. We found out that it was possible to walk three blocks in a straight direction and have been on three different streets. Our map of London was absolutely required by a visiting American soldier. In our walk, Cope remarked,

"How does the average Londoner get around? It sure is a mystery to me."

I answered, "I guess they become accustomed to the layout and really don't have too much difficulty."

Our first planned stop was the famous British Museum. We found it closed because of the war since many of the articles had been removed from London for safekeeping.

Oxford Street was walked its entire length. This was about six or eight blocks. The street had all types of shops. We thought they were well stocked considering that Britain was still engaged in the war. On the sidewalks were service men from all over the world. We saw soldiers and sailors from France, South Africa, India, Australia, Canada and New Zealand. Just after we passed Selfridges, the large department store, we came to Hyde Park.

Hal and I had arrived at the famous 'Speaker's Corner.' Just after entering the park, we noticed a man on a small box talking or speaking to a small group that surrounded him. He kept saying things like,

"We don't need rent control. We don't need petrol control. All we have from this bloody war is control. When can we get back to running our own lives. Churchill got no sense. He don't know what to live with these controls. Let's get him out of office. I say No Controls!"

The crowd that was listening to him seemed very patient. About every five minutes, someone in the small audience would make some remark to the orator who would answer him back.

We moved to listen to two other speakers. One was denouncing the idea of having a Russian ally while the other was upholding the virtues of a socialist state where everything was owned by the government.

Nearby all three speakers was a solitary English 'bobby.' He would walk from one speaker to the other. He appeared very disinterested in the speeches and speakers. Heckling came at infrequent times to all the speakers.

Although we were fascinated by the remarkable display of free speech in the middle of a war, Hal and I decided to push on into the park itself.

"Hey, Ed, look at all those ack-ack batteries over there."

"Hal, there must be, at least, twenty-five of the anti-aircraft guns, all pointed skyward. Wonder if they still fire at night?"

Around the guns were packed sandbags. Next to the guns were barracks where the army personnel must have resided. In addition to the guns, there were numerous air-raid shelters throughout the entire Hyde Park acreage.

In the huge park itself, many of the English folk were walking their dogs or just sitting on the numerous benches that lined the park. It was peaceful.

At the extreme west end of Hyde Park were the grounds of Kensington Palace. The Palace looked to be very old but the grounds were in excellent condition. Since the clock was approaching 1700, we decided to return to the Hans Crescent Club for supper. With our maps still in our hands, we walked back across the south end of Hyde Park. On our journey, we went past Albert Memorial and Hall, the home of the London Symphony. We tried to enter the building but the doors were locked.

Our supper at the Hans Crescent Club cost exactly one shilling, four pence, or about 25¢. For this price, a GI had meat, potato, vegetable, dessert, and a beverage. No one complained about the price. For the evening, it was decided to attend the nightly dance at the Rainbow Corner Club.

Since large scale bombing of London had almost ceased, a dim-out was now in effect. This meant that a few of the street lights emitted a small slit of light. Actually, most of us would have preferred total darkness for the dim-out was a very difficult adjustment for one's eyes.

The route taken to the Red Cross Club repeated the route used in the morning. But Piccadilly Circus at night was a spectacle to behold. No American GI who has been there during the war would ever forget the open flesh market.

Around the huge circle were females of every kind, description and color. The only one that was not observed was an American Indian or red female. As the American soldiers slowly walked around Piccadilly Circus, comments of all types came from the girls.

"Hey, soldier, I'm available."

"Good looking, you'll never find anything better."

"Come on up here and find out what I can do for you, baby."

"I've got what you need Sarge, let me show you."

"I do it all Corporal, I'm ready."

"I'm ready for the Infantry to lay me down."

As the American service men walked very slowly looking over the flesh merchandise, one or two or a group would stop and chat with the available ladies. After a bargain was made, you would see the soldier or sailor walk arm in arm with his chosen female up one of the streets that led away from Piccadilly.

In the street were peddlers of all types. They would shout in loud voices,

"Get your torches here, get your torches here."

Then, in a low tone, they added,

"Kundrums, Rubbers, Kundrums, Rubbers!"

It was obvious that very few flashlights were being sold.

After taking the full circle tour, I managed to get out of the heavy foot traffic and made my way up Shaftsbury Lane to the club.

The dance held at the Rainbow Corner Club was very crowded. A number of us from the Railsplitter Division noted that there were a large number of GIs from the 99th or 'Checkerboard' Infantry Division. Upon inquiry, we found that they were encamped about 25 miles west of our 84th Division in southern England. They, too, had no idea when they would depart for the continent and combat.

The English girls were no different from their American counterparts except for one item. They seemed too enthusiastic about jitterbugging. Many of them wanted to dance in that style no matter what tempo was played by the dance band. My last few dances were with one Nancy Walls who hailed from Lancaster. She worked as a typist in a government department near Parliament. At 2300, when the dance ended, she said, "Thanks, Don, I had a nice time. And you were a gentleman."

"Can you explain that?" I inquired.

"Nine of the last Americans I met here want to go home with me after the dance. Although I like dancing, that's the end of the evening for me. I know they know the Tube stops running and they can't get back anywhere if they take me home. And it's obvious my folks live up in Lancaster."

Nancy's last statement was the reason the dancing ended at 2300. The Underground ceased complete operations at 2330. If one wanted to rest at the Hans Crescent Club, he had to be there by 2330.

Upon emergence from the Rainbow Red Cross Club, it was distinctly noted that Piccadilly Circus was deserted. All the ladies-of-the-night had departed from their business stations. Everyone was scurrying to make those last subway trains.

When those of us returning to our sleeping places emerged at the Knightsbridge station, the beds that had been unoccupied in the morning were full of people who were about to go to sleep. However, until the Underground stopped running, these people would secure little rest of any type.

Just as I was about to open the door to the dorm where my bed was located, a voice shouted,

"Hey, Don Edwards, is that you?"

"It sure, is, Al Barkey."

Al and I had been good friends in the ASTP at Drexel Institute. One of our favorite activities was roller skating at the Chez Vous in Western Philadelphia. Al always seemed to be in a dilemma about his numerous girl friends. We agreed to go over to the Hans Crescent and have some hot tea and talk over old times in Philly.

It was a mistake that would cost me over two hours of sleep, however. I inquired of Al:

"What happened to you today in London?"

"Same old trouble, Don, women. No matter where I go, I always have trouble with them."

"OK, Al, give me the details."

"After I got here, this friend of mine, John Johnson, asked me if I'd like to meet an English girl. I said 'sure', I've nothing to lose. Seems like my pal has relatives over here and they got him a date for his visit here."

"What did he need you for, Al?"

"Well, his date had a friend. So I thought, I'd help him out. We went over to Paddington, that's another railroad station here in London. We met these two females. No trouble. Both were pretty good looking. I felt kinda funny for both of these girls were officers in the ATS, just like the WACs back home. My girl's name was Pam Hansen. This lieutenant I got fell for me immediately."

"You meet her and two minutes later she fell for you. How did you know that?"

"All you got to do, Ed, is look at their eyes. I looked at her a couple of times. Her eyes looked so dreamy. You know what I mean."

"After what you told me about that cute little dame you met at the Chez Vous in West Philly, I know what you mean, Al. Now, what did you two do all day long in Londontown?"

"Had a swell time, Don. These lieutenants took us privates all over London. Showed us all the important sights. We took them to two nice places for lunch and dinner. After supper, we went to a live show and a bar. Then, we had to get them back to Paddington."

"Why, couldn't they stay in London?"

"No, they had to be back at their base, wherever, it was by 2330."

"I understand, just like you and I. Tell me about the sweet parting."

"Boy, Don, it was really tough. Pam just kept looking at me with those eyes. I just kept talking about something. She asked

me to come up and see her at the camp on my next leave. Finally
we kissed goodby. Boy, Ed, what a kiss that girl had. I can still
feel it, two hours after."

"Al, what town was she from in England?"

"Reading."

"Did you tell her about the girl back in Reading, Pennsylvania to whom you are supposedly engaged?"

"Don, I should have done that first, but after an hour, I
couldn't. Those eyes got me."

"Seems like you're always getting yourself in this type of
jam. Al, what do you tell them?"

"Honest, Ed, I don't tell them no line. They just fall for
me. Can I help it?"

"Maybe not, but now you've got girls in Reading, your
home town in Pennsylvania, Philly and Reading, England and
some other places in between."

This line of conversation continued until 0200 the next
morning. We mutually agreed that each of us should retire. We
could stay up the whole night discussing Al's women troubles in
many places throughout the entire U.S.A. and now in England.

For the first time since early in September, I slept between
real white sheets. It seemed like a dream. I wondered when the
next time would come when this would occur. I knew it would be
far in the future.

Saturday, October 28, 1944

After finishing breakfast at the Hans Crescent Club at 0830,
I took a bus to Oxford Street. The purpose was to purchase
some English goods for shipment back to my parents and other
relatives, plus a few girls I knew, back in the United States. Since
my next opportunity to shop was strictly unknown at this time, I
had to take advantage of my present situation. All the polite
English clerks assured me that my purchases would arrive in time
for the Christmas holidays.

After lunch at the Rainbow Corner Club, I was ready for a
taxi tour of London. Hal Cope and I were coupled with two
American sailors, as the foursome to take one cab. We learned

that the sailors were stationed on a Destroyer-Escort which had just escorted a large convoy across the Atlantic. They were stationed in Plymouth until the return journey back to the States. Hal mentioned to them, "Sailors are sure outnumbered here in London."

"Yes, but we expect it. If you men are in places like Philadelphia or Norfolk, all you'll see is sailors. We've been treated very well in London. No one bothers us." replied the younger sailor who hailed from Scranton, Pennsylvania.

The four of us were assigned to a young cabby in his early 20's. Apparently he had some type of physical ailment which prevented him from serving in the British armed forces. He kept up a constant barrage of chatter throughout our whole tour of London.

Our trip started right through Piccadilly Circus. Our driver termed it "Commando Corner."

"Gents, if you can fight your way through Piccadilly, the Jerries won't give you any trouble."

We drove first to Trafalger Square where the monument to Admiral Nelson is located. Then we turned left onto Strand and Fleet streets, where the headquarters of most London newspapers are located. We were told that London papers are more national in scope than our newspapers were in the United States, since the London papers were distributed throughout the entire United Kingdom every day. Most of them were limited to four or eight pages because of the shortage of paper. Next came our first stop, St. Paul's Cathedral.

We were conducted through this massive church by another guide. The Cathedral had suffered two large bomb hits. One was behind the main altar and the other to the left of the apse. All around the cathedral was destruction. There were tremendous open spaces where homes or dwellings of some type had been located. Although I had heard from the broadcasts of Edward Murrow how St. Paul's had been spared, it was until this moment that I saw how it stood alone among leveled ground. A small miracle had taken place here.

Our taxi tour continued. We went past the Bank of England and the Royal Exchange. Then, we crossed the Thames River and recrossed it on the old Tower bridge. The Tower of London with its peaked towers was the next attraction. Our driver then came along the Victoria Embankment next to the river. The cab then veered onto Whitehall. This avenue was an extremely wide one. On each side of the street were various buildings of the British government. We briefly noted the residence of the Prime Minister at No. 10 Downing Street. At the end of Whitehall were the Houses of Parliament and Westminister Abbey.

Our next stop was this famous church of the English monarchs. Our cabbie walked us through the different parts of the Abbey showing us the burial places of famous English personages. In one special corner were the burial sites of great English poets. The tomb of the British Unknown Warrior's Grave was observed. On the grave was a large bronze slab with the appropriate inscription.

The taxi tour proceeded to Buckingham Palace. Our driver said, "In peacetime lads, you can tell if the King is in by the flying of the Royal Standard. During the war, it's been discontinued."

After passing St. James Palace and viewing the Pall Mall, our cab returned to Rainbow Corner. The total time consumed was less than two hours. Each of us gave our talkative cabbie a good tip for his viable comments.

A walk was then taken around the area of Piccadilly Circus. The four of us noted that London had no skyscrapers comparable to New York City. The tallest structure was St. Paul's Cathedral.

Hal and I returned to the Hans Crescent for our supper at 1730.

As I just entered the snack bar at the Hans Crescent, I ran into my friend, Harry Ackerman. After exchanging greetings, I inquired of him, "What happened to you in London?"

"Nothing much Don, but I thought the end had come."

"What do you mean the end had come?"

"Last night, Randy Fellows and I went to a restaurant downtown somewhere. We picked up two nice girls there. We went to a movie. We took them home on the Underground, way out in west London. After taking them home, it was past 11:30, and we discovered that we couldn't get a subway back here."

"Then, what happened, Harry?"

"Gwens' parents, that's the girl I was with, invited us to stay overnight upstairs in their house. We went to bed. The girls went into another bedroom. About two o'clock, I felt a tap on my shoulder. Gwen said, 'Tell Randy to go next door with Polly.' I'm coming with you."

"She took off her gown and we went at it. About an hour later, I finally got into her. Just as I was about to come, there was a terrific explosion. I stopped. I collapsed. I thought I had been hit. Gwen explained to me that it was one of those rockets the Germans were hitting London with. It had been so loud that I couldn't get back to my task. I kept waiting for the next one to hit this house. Finally she calmed me down. We went back to screwing around until Randy came in about six o'clock."

"What time did you get up then?" was my next inquiry.

"Oh, about seven, her folks came to wake us. All of us had herring for breakfast. Randy and I went to the Underground and came back here. I took a nap to take care of my nerves."

After another delicious supper for 50¢, Harry and I took the Underground to Waterloo Station. We were scheduled to board a special train at 2030.

After finding the correct gate for our train, Harry and I engaged in some talk with the two Military Policemen who were guarding the entrance.

"Where are you fellows stationed?" asked Harry.

"Here in London."

"What a deal that must be." I added.

"It isn't as great as it looks." was the reply of the taller MP.

"Why not?" I asked.

"For one thing, our duty comes about eighty per cent of the time at night. Next, when we do get a day off, you always have to be ready to deal with any emergency."

"What kind of emergency?" Harry inquired.

"You always have guys getting into fights with either the English civilians or the home military. Usually, it's in some pub over some dame who they've picked up. We have to go in and drag them out and put them away for a few days. It's a lot of dirty work cause you're always getting hit by some drunk GI."

"Had anything serious?"

"We haven't but two weeks ago some Air Force Sergeant tried to shoot two of our buddies."

"How long have you been stationed in London?" Harry questioned.

"About six weeks before the invasion."

"Seen any difference since June?" I questioned.

"Oh, yea. All the infantrymen have gone. They used to raise lots of cain whenever they were in London. Aren't you two from the Infantry? You have blue on your caps."

"Yes." was our joint reply.

"What outfit?"

"84th Division."

"Expect to be here much longer?"

"No." was our joint answer.

"From what we've heard, you'll have it tougher than we do. A lot more danger. The guys that come here on pass from the hospitals really have some stories to tell. You can hardly believe them."

"We hope for the best." Harry answered.

"I think you two can get to your train now. Goodby and Good Luck!"

The special train pulled out of Waterloo Station at 2155. A peaceful sleep was gained as we rolled through the darkened countryside. We arrived at Andover Junction exactly two hours later.

At 2400, Harry and I bid each other goodby.

At 0030, the trucks came for the enlisted men from Company E. In less than twenty minutes, we were back in our hut ready to retire.

VIII

ACROSS THE CHANNEL

Sunday, October 29, 1944

At 0700, I felt the usual tap on my shoulder from Sergeant Smith who said, "Edwards, guess what? You're on KP at the Castle. Report immediately."

"Oh, Sarge, I am the lucky fellow in this platoon."

At 0730, I reported to the Mess Sergeant at the Officers' Quarters.

"Sorry, Edwards, but I already have enough men from the other companies for today. Tell the Sergeant not to send any more men unless I notify him. Also want to tell you that you and that other fellow, I think his name is Gabel, do a good job whenever you come here. Both of you should make good husbands for some lucky girls."

"Thanks, Sarge. My friend's name is John Crable from Pennsylvania."

"Another thing Edwards. I notice that when you two are doing the pots or pans, you discuss other things rather than the usual conversation of Women, Women and Women. How come?"

"John is quite intelligent. Sarge. I don't think either of us is sterile but there are some other interesting things in this world besides females, but I do think they're important. Don't get me wrong."

"Hope to see you again Edwards. Don't forget the message."

"I won't Sarge."

A PRIVATE'S DIARY

I was permitted to eat a fine breakfast at the Castle. Upon my return to the Headquarters platoon hut, Sergeant Smith was happy to learn that he did not need to awaken any more of his men for KP duty at the Officer's Mess.

After attending church with John, the remainder of the morning was spent in cleaning our hut along with the others in the platoon.

During any of the chores that were performed in our Quonset hut, Headquarters platoon always had some entertainment. Our Sergeant Harlan Smith had carried with him overseas a radio. He was the only leader of all five platoons in Company E who had thought of his men in this regard. Thus, our small platoon often had visitors from the other four platoons who came to enjoy the music and news that we heard daily.

Only one station was used. This was the AEF—BBC (Allied Expeditionary Forces of the British Broadcasting Corporation). Each hour news was broadcasted. Thus, Headquarters platoon was up-to-date on the happenings on the front line. The other programs were both live and recorded. Those that were on record were American shows that had been heard about four to six weeks earlier in the States. Everyone noticed that all commercials or ads had been deleted from the shows. This was especially noticeable when the commercials were worked right into the regular show.

The news was prepared by the BBC. Corporal Duffy would often remark, "You would think listening to the Limey news that the British were doing all the fighting. Five minutes about the First British Army and thirty seconds about the two American Armies.

But most of us seemed to agree with Lou Novak who usually answered, "Be happy we can listen to anything. What do you expect from the BBC? News like NBC would give you? We're in England, period."

In addition to our radio for the current news, Company E had been receiving the Army newspaper, 'Stars and Stripes' since early October. This gave us the American side of the news and rarely mentioned anything about the British military forces. It usually consisted of four pages. Most of us believed it was well edited. The paper tried to give news that would be of interest to the average GI. One of its daily features was the B-bag. At the top of the column were the words, "Blow it out Here." The column contained the gripes of the American soldier on every conceivable subject.

In the afternoon, every enlisted man in Company E had to draw some additional equipment. Each man was given a new pair of shoes, an extra pair of woolen underwear and a sleeping bag. Most of the personnel in our platoon did not like the new shoes which had a six or seven inch leather top in addition to the regular shoe. I took the usual kidding about my large size, namely, an 11D. The sleeping bag proved to be the new big novelty. A soldier just slipped into the bag to sleep. The only item removed by a GI was his shoes. Only his face was exposed. The new 'sack' was warmer than our blankets and one's head was covered while sleeping. While all of us were commenting on the new item, Sergeant Smith announced, "Most of you have been having a grand time in England."

"Who are you talking about, not me!" cried Gainer.

"I mean everybody. No exceptions. Especially you Gainer, while in London. Listen and keep quiet. We're going to leave here within the next few days. From now on, I want everyone to be on his toes. No more horsing around. We've got a job to do. It's going to take a lot of hard work. If you need any help, be sure to see me first about it. Everyone's to be ready to leave at a moment's notice. Does everyone understand?"

No one answered.

After dismissal, our platoon Sergeant came to have a chat with me. "Don, I think you know you're the only permanent messenger in Company E at the present time."

"I know Sarge."

"As soon as we cross the Channel, the Company's got to have another. Any suggestions?"

"I'd like to have Crable first, next Beesch and, then, Norris."

"I talked to the Captain last week and I think he selected Norris. Crable and Beesch are to get other assignments. Do you think you and Ed can work things out as a team in delivering messages?"

"Sarge, I get along with Ed. I prefer the other two first but I've got no complaint if Norris comes with me to the battalion message center. Should I tell him now?"

"No, we'll wait until you're assigned to battalion. Norris should have no objections since he gets along with you. I know you don't like some of the women-chasers in the platoon."

"I'm not against girls Sarge, but some of these guys think a female has no brains and exists only for them."

"Did you ever have a date with a real smart girl?"

"Well, I once asked the top student in my high school class for a date but she turned me down cold."

"Remember her name?"

"Yes, it was Cornelia Groefsema."

"Give you any reason?"

"No, but I believe it might have been I wasn't her equal for brains. Anyway she already had a boyfriend whose name was Herb Marshall."

"Just take it in stride, Edwards. It's agreed then that Ed Norris will be your partner as the other company messenger."

"Agreed."

After supper, most of the platoon went to another mess hall to see some unknown movie. After waiting over 75 minutes in discontent, a Corporal announced, "Sorry men, but the movie never arrived from Division."

There was very little commotion since the average GI in the 84th Infantry Division had come to expect this as normal.

Monday, October 30, 1944

After breakfast, Sergeant Smith asked, "Any volunteers for salvage detail?"

Although only three were needed, at least, ten volunteered since the details were preferred to the drilling and marching that the Company usually had. I was picked to be on the salvage detail. I believe it was due to the fact that I had been the first to bring the 'goodies' from the 'Castle.' The task took us the entire morning.

After lunch, the three of us were permitted to remain in Stockbridge. Hal Cope wanted to purchase a battery for his flashlight which had ceased operating. Cope, Crable and I entered a small hardware store to buy the needed battery.

"Afternoon lads, I'm happy to see you. Tell me about yourselves."

For the next twenty minutes, the three of us engaged in a long conversation with the short stocky storekeeper. We learned what experienced he and other Englishmen had endured in 1940 when it appeared as if their island kingdom would be invaded. At the end, he said, "I think we're going to whip those bloody Jerries."

Hal inquired if the size of his battery was available. It was not. Then, I asked, "Can we buy any food here in Stock-bridge?"

"You can try lads, but I don't think you'll have much luck. Things are still kind of tight, you know. Most things are still rationed. But you might be able to buy a few things. Don't they feed you?"

Crable answered, "They do, but we'd like to try some English food."

We visited several food shops. Because of rationing, we were successful in buying only one small loaf of bread and a dozen cookies.

That evening after Wallace and Gainer returned from the 'Castle', Headquarters platoon had a feast. Those two, who had been on KP, took a duffel bag with them. At the end of their day, they loaded the entire duffel bag with food of all kinds. They brought twenty cans of juice, three dozen cookies, a whole cake and other assorted items. Everyone slept on a full stomach that night.

A PRIVATE'S DIARY

Tuesday, October 31, 1944

After breakfast, Sergeant Smith announced, "Men, this is our last day here. We're going across the Channel to France."

"When are we leaving Sarge?"

"Can't answer that. We're to turn in our things today. The call can come anytime after noon. I'll let you know when you should pack your duffel bags. You'll have to take them with you and carry them on the boat. Any questions?"

"Sarge, why can't they pick them up like they did when we came down here from Liverpool?"

"I don't know. I just receive the orders and pass them on."

In the morning, we turned in our blankets since our platoon had been previously supplied with sleeping bags.

In the afternoon, every item of clothing that each man possessed was checked. After this, each man had to roll a full field pack.

At 1700, an announcement came from Sergeant Smith,

"Supper will not come tonight until we are just about ready to leave. We don't know exactly when your next meal will be. After last night's feast, no one in the platoon should be hungry."

There were a few murmurs, but no loud complaints.

At 1900, an order was given to pack our duffel bags. Because of our new and old issued equipment, every enlisted man had a difficult time in closing his bag. A system was instituted whereby two or three men would pack a single duffel bag. In order to close the bag, one or two men would jump on the bag while the other held and tied it. By 2030, everyone in the platoon had his bag packed. At that moment, Sergeant Smith returned with new orders. He said,

"Men your mess kit cannot be carried in your duffel bag. It's got to be available to eat on board our ship. I realize everyone has it packed away but no one told me until five minutes ago.

The loud complaints spewed forth in a torrent.

"Just like the Army."

"Why can't they make up their fuckin minds once and for all."

"They do it every time, it never fails."

"My mess kit is on the bottom of my duffel bag."

Nevertheless, everyone in the platoon complied with the order. By 2103, the duffel bags were all repacked.

At 2230, Company E had completed its last meal on British soil. Within the next hour, everyone in Company E was on the truck and ready to depart. At 2345, we departed in pitch blackness.

Wednesday, November 1, 1944

At 0020, Company E arrived at the railway station in Stockbridge. We dragged our duffel bags to the railway platform which was only 250 yards from where we detrucked. Most of the enlisted men sat on their duffel bags and began to doze off. Captain Von Schriltz was constantly about and saying in a loud voice, "I want all of you to keep wide awake until the train comes."

In the semi-darkness on the platform, his words had little effect.

At 0230, the special train arrived. Dragging their duffel bags and loaded with full field packs, Company E still filled its assigned compartments within five minutes after the train arrived. I settled down in a corner of our compartment and went off to sleep.

At 0500, the compartment door was opened. A voice shouted, "All out, we're in Southampton!"

"Fall in," came the commands from platoon leaders. Within five minutes, the company was formed.

At 0515, a march to the dock at Southampton was started. Since the entire Second Battalion was at the Southern Railway Station, a guide came to lead the 800 plus contingent. Whoever the guide was, he made himself very unpopular. The marching pace that he used was near that of double time where the average GI runs at about 180 steps per minute. Since every GI in this large group was loaded with a pack and a duffel bag, the men began to drop along the wayside after less than two minutes of this torrid pace. After one and a half miles, I, too, joined the sitters along with Deloss Beesch. After a few minutes of rest, we proceeded to walk at a normal pace. Thirty minutes later, we completed the two plus mile hike. However, the column of straggling soldiers stretched as far as the eye could see. Less than ten men from Company E managed to complete the journey with that double-paced guide. Ever so slowly, Company E and the other four companies of the Battalion assembled. This took nearly sixty minutes. When all the Company had arrived, the Company Commander sounded off,

"Men, I was very disappointed that the majority, and a big one at that, had to drop out and rest. The pace was a little fast. But not too fast for any man in E Company. I want this company to be the best in the whole regiment. You certainly didn't live up to my hopes and expectations this morning on that march. We're going to have some harder and tougher marches coming up. I want every man to keep up. If you're not in condition, get in condition. No excuses in the future."

While Captain Von Schriltz was giving his little speech, most men just sat and looked glum. The company was then dismissed and permitted to sit down.

From behind me, a voice sounded off.

"Why that son-of-a-bitch. What was he carrying? Just a little musette bag, weighing less than one-fourth of the pack I'm carrying. And where's his duffel bag? Don't tell me. It's with the company jeep. He couldn't be bothered to carry one like us jerks had to do. If he thought it was so easy, why didn't he carry someone's bag. He just plain he went bouncing along with himself to carry, then he's mad. Fuck him."

Another member of the platoon added, "I have to agree with you but you can't do a damn thing about it. It's tough buster."

True to Army fashion, Company E proceeded to wait the remainder of the morning. We did nothing except talk, sleep, and visit the nearest lavatory. I couldn't read since my books were packed away. To open the duffel bag was to invite a minor disaster. The total waiting time was five and one-half hours. The hurried journey through the streets and yards of Southampton had been totally unnecessary.

Our place of waiting was a large warehouse near the dock area. On one side of the warehouse was a railway siding. On the other was the water where two ships were berthed. Just prior to 1200, the Red Cross appeared. We were served the usual coffee and doughnuts. Breakfast this morning was a little late.

At 1230 came the order, "Fall In."

"Follow your platoon leader in single file to the ship," was the order.

At 1137, my left foot hit the deck of H.M.S. "Leopoldville." She was a Belgian ship. Sergeant Smith led Headquarters platoon to Compartment E-1. This was one deck below the open deck of the vessel. We were lucky again not to be assigned Decks A through D which were below us. Our assigned compartment was filled with tables and benches.

"What are these for?" inquired Cope.

"This is where you are going to eat our meals until we leave ship." answered our platoon Sergeant.

Above the tables were hammocks stored in neat rows.

"Sergeant Smith, don't tell me we're going to use those for us?"

"Private Cope, you have two choices. The floor or the hammock. Take your pick!"

After depositing our packs and duffel bags in the compartment, all of us visited the open deck. We could see very little of the City of Southampton from this open deck. As Crable, Beesch and I stood at the rail, Sergeant Smith appeared.

"You three have volunteered to secure the food for Company E."

"We didn't say anything Sarge." answered Deloss.

"I know you didn't, but I think I can trust you three to find the kitchen and bring back everything in order. That's a compliment if you didn't know it."

"We didn't know that Sergeant Smith, but we'll be happy to do it." chimed in John.

"Pick up container from me about 1730."

Just after 1530, the Leopoldville left the pier. She proceeded slowly southward through the wide Southampton port facilities which were enormous.

When darkness descended at 1730, we three, who had supposedly volunteered for the type of KP, went forward on the ship to its kitchen to secure food for the entire Company.

Upon entering the kitchen, one of the ship's officers asked us, "Your unit, please."

"Company E." was my reply.

The officer checked the roster for the number of men in that outfit. Orders were issued to some Negroes standing nearby. The language was something other than English or French. Next to each of the four black men were huge containers of food. An item was placed in each of the four containers we had brought. The officer said to us, "You can pick up your food now."

We returned to Compartment E-1. Here the food was distributed by each of the platoon Sergeants. The meal consisted of hash, canned corn, bread and coffee. Compared to the fare served on the Sterling Castle, it tasted excellent. Another factor was that this was our first full meal since leaving the Quonset huts near Stockbridge. Since every enlisted man ate from his own mess kit, everyone had to clean his own dishes in a large tub located in the compartment. The three KPs had to clean the pans in which the food had been carried. By a flip of a coin, my task was to take the containers back to the kitchen. Crable and Beesch had to do the actual cleaning.

On my return to Compartment E-1, I went past the Officer's Mess. In peacetime it apparently was the vessel's main dining room. Like the crossing of the Atlantic, the same type of de luxe waiter service was available. White tablecloths were present. A brief glance told me that the menu was different from the one I had just consumed.

At 2100, the platoon was required to bring down our assigned hammock. Afterward, little difficulty was experienced in getting into it although everyone was fully clothed, with and including shoes.

No hardship was experienced in sleeping in the "sailor's bed."

Thursday, November 2, 1944

By 0800, Company E had finished breakfast. A few minutes later, most of us were on the open deck of the Leopoldville. We were in the English Channel. The water was very calm and few waves were seen. Our ship was in a large convoy. Only a short distance from the Leopoldville were British Corvettes guarding the precious human cargo.

At 1000, someone on deck yelled, "There's France, boys!"

A set of gray cliffs seem to rise out of the water ahead. We were told that this was Omaha Beach where the Americans had landed on D-day with so much difficulty. Our liner soon dropped anchor. The rumors began to fly.

"When do we go ashore?"

"I heard it would be sometime tomorrow."

"Naw, right after supper tonight. Jerry won't see us in the dark."

"Just heard from one of the Officers that it would be right after lunch."

At 1115, an announcement came over the loud speaker.

"Disembarking from the ship will begin immediately after noon."

IX

FRANCE

At 1430, Company E was along the railing of H.M.S. 'Leopoldville.' We were ready to begin our transfer to a waiting landing craft. At 1500, I was given permission to descend the ship's ladder to the waiting LCP. After taking two steps downward on the ladder, my arm was jarred. Away flew my duffel bag. I had vision of fishing it from the English Channel.

"There she goes," yelled Sergeant Dempsey of the first platoon.

"Catch it!" I hollered.

By some quirk, my duffel bag landed directly in the LCP. Only a few added steps were necessary to recover it.

The line of Company E personnel inched forward. Since the Landing Craft was never stationary, bouncing up and down with the waves, it took ordinarily two passes before a GI got into the LCP. The first time the boat went up, the individual soldier would toss his duffel bag into the bouncing craft. When the LCP bobbed up the second time, the dogface would jump onto a small platform. Because of my accident, I was aboard in one sweep.

Since there was no manner in which this procedure could go any faster, over one hour was consumed doing this. During the loading time, many of the dogfaces began to have trouble with their stomachs—although they had had no lunch. Heads became dizzy. At noon aboard the Leopoldville all personnel had been advised to take seasick tablets. Many did not since the water looked so calm. Since we were tightly packed aboard the LCP, no one wanted to lose their food via their mouth. However, a few men heaved the contents of their stomachs upon their fellow soldiers. Complaints were heard in the usual Army language but nothing could be done to erase or vanish the foul odors.

At 1610, the LCP had reached its capacity. The motor was started. Our craft raced toward the French shore. As the cliffs came closer, we could see the small sandy beach was full of activity. We wondered what was going on at this time since the actual war was far away in Germany or eastern France.

Numerous ships of all types and sizes could be seen as we zig-zagged toward Omaha Beach. We could also observe the famous sunken ships that were used for the floating dock to land supplies after D-day. It was no longer in use.

A final roar of the LCP's motor brought us onto the beach. The ramp was lowered. After one small step in the waters of the English Channel, my foot touched French soil at 1646. Company E was formed on the narrow sandy beach.

Sergeant Goodpasteur announced, "Men, leave your duffel bag right where you are. A truck will pick them up and get them to us later. In about fifteen minutes, we are going to march. Take it easy for a few minutes. Dismissed."

The break lasted over twenty minutes. Many of the men needed this time to adjust their stomachs and dizzy heads. A few needed to brush off and clean their clothes although they could not destroy the odors.

During this long rest, we noted groups of German prisoners of war loading and unloading supplies. A group of about 20 men marched by our company. They seemed to stare in bewilderment as if their eyes could not believe more American troops were still coming. And we were obviously infantrymen.

The order to fall in came at 1710.

A march up an inclined road to the top of the cliff commenced. Mud seemed to be everywhere. Our new shoes seemed to stick to it in clumps and clumps.

At the top of the hill, we could observe the German bunkers and blockhouses that had overlooked Omaha Beach. Most of the concrete structures had been blown up. Hal Cope said,

"I'll bet we blew them so if the Germans had pushed us back, they couldn't use them again."

Dusk began to fall. Company E continued to plod through the thick mud. No one could guess what direction we were taking but the best guess was south and east.

About 1815, Company E passed a large airstrip. It was abandoned. We guessed that it had been a beehive of activity just a few months ago. Overhead we could see some C-47 airplanes. We hoped they were flying needed supplies to the front.

After another thirty minutes of marching, E company arrived at an apple orchard. A tent was pitched in the orchard. From it emerged Lieutenant Gavin who saluted our Company Commander. They went into the tent together. The five platoons were given a break. Many of the men picked some of the apples and ate them immediately. Others stuffed some fruit into their pockets for later use. No announcement on the next meal was available.

Captain Von Schriltz appeared.

"Men, we will continue this march until we reach our camping site. We should be there in another hour. I expect every man to stay with his platoon. No one should drop out. We might not be able to find you."

Complete darkness prevailed. The rumor mill had us at a camping site about eight miles inland from the Normandy beaches. After fifteen minutes of walking, some of the enlisted men began to drop out. To keep his outfit together, Captain Von Schriltz was forced to take a break after marching just twenty minutes. Thus, he allowed the stragglers time to catch the main body of the company.

Our Company Commander kept saying, "I can't understand it men. You should all be in condition. If I can do it, you can too."

Under their breath, several of the enlisted men muttered, "Just take my pack and see what you can do. You'll be sitting down every ten minutes, you fat ass."

Twenty minutes later, Company E had to take another long break. The stragglers numbered about one-third of the entire unit.

107

The march or walk was not too arduous. It was the mud. The wet soil seemed to stick to one's shoes. The longer one walked, the heavier it seemed that your boots became. There was no easy solution.

Thirty minutes after the second break, Company E entered a large field. The stragglers constituted about one-half of the total of 200 men. Our company's kitchen was already encamped. It was 1950.

"Pitch your tents." Sergeant Smith ordered. "Find the best spot you can. Be careful of the wet ground. No one eats until the entire company is ready and I mean everybody."

"Hey, John, where are you?" I shouted at John Crable.

"Over here, Don, get out your shelter half."

Out of necessity, John Crable and I had to camp together. Both of us had the old style shelter half which had an open front end. Everyone had to have a buddy to tent with since each man carried only one-half of the complete shelter. The newer type of tents was closed at both ends. In rainy or windy or snowy weather, this newer type was a distinct advantage.

At 2030, Company E was fed its evening meal.

Friday, November 3, 1944

When daylight broke, all could see that the entire Second Battalion was camped in a huge cow pasture. Company E was placed by the muddy road. While serving breakfast to us, the cooks warned us.

"Do not enter any ditches. All German mines have not been cleared. Stay on the site or on the road."

At 0845, Headquarters platoon was lined up in front of Sergeant Smith.

"Men, we have to put our tents in line. The whole platoon is to be near the stone wall."

The men moved to take down and re-assemble their tents.

"Hey, Crable, you're to pitch tents with Beesch and Ed, you go with Norris."

"But we can't Sergeant," was our joint reply.

"No ifs and buts. That's the way I want you to be and no remarks."

"But," we tried to talk.

"Both of you heard me the first time, didn't you?"

"Yes, Sergeant."

"Well, tear down your tent, and move on the double."

"That's the trouble, Sarge." John repeated.

"Why?"

"It seems Sergeant," I went on, "That John and I are the only two men in this platoon that have the old style shelter. It's better if we stay together."

"Why didn't you say something at the start?"

"We tried to," echoed John.

"All right. You two stay together until you're issued new shelter halves. That'll be pretty soon. You'll get them when the company gets settled."

The new shelter halves never came.

After the platoon's realignment was completed, we had to clean our weapons the remainder of the morning.

At 1330, while I was sitting in front of my joint tent, Sergeant Smith approached me.

"Edwards, you're on guard duty tonight with Duffy."

"What do we do, Sarge?"

"See those men down at the entrance. Just make sure that no unauthorized persons get into the camping area."

"Sarge, who would want to come here."

"I think, Edwards, they're worried about some civilians who might steal something like food if the battalion had no guard around the camp site. And remember about those supposedly hot French women. Report at 1600 to the gate."

"Will do, Sergeant."

At 1600, four men reported. Two from Company E and two from Company F. The tour of duty was to consist of four hours on, then, four hours off. Along with Tom Chesman from Company F, I started guard duty with the first shift. We were allowed to sit down while we were on guard. Thus, two small canvas type chairs were provided. During my first four hour stint, I read the book, "A Tree Grows in Brooklyn." The rest of

109

the time was spent in conversation with Tom. We reasoned that the reason two men from different companies were on the same shift was to lessen the danger that both would go off to sleep. At 2000, Duffy appeared for the next shift. I returned to my tent.

At 2400, Duffy awoke me and said to get ready for the next shift.

Saturday, November 4, 1944

My second shift of four hours on guard duty began at 0002. Tom and I alternated sitting and standing. To keep ourselves warm, we maintained the small fire that had been started by the previous two guards.

"Ed, when you think this war is going to end?"

"Tom, if I could tell you that, I'd be a genius."

"You must have some idea. You went to college, and learned something, didn't you?"

"They don't teach you that type of thing in college, Tom."

"Anyway, what do you think is going to happen to us?"

"My guess is that in about two weeks this outfit is going to be on the front line!"

"What makes you think so, Ed?"

"Well, the Allies are in Aachen, Germany. They are going to make another push against the Germans shortly. My guess is that the 84th is going to be one of the new Divisions that starts the new push."

"Your ideas sound pretty good to me. What do you think the front is really like?"

"I don't know. Why do you ask, Tom?"

"Oh in Company F, they keep telling us that we've got nothing to worry about. But I'm still worried those Germans know what they are doing and we don't."

"Tom, I think they're just as nervous as we are."

We talked through the entire 240 minutes on every topic we could think to discuss. He did allow me a few minutes to read by flashlight. Tom's biggest worry was that he would not get back to Nevada in one piece.

At 0400, I awoke Duffy in order to relieve me.

At 0800, Sergeant Smith shook my sleeping bag.

"Edwards, sleep as long as you want. You don't have to go on guard duty any more."

"Thanks, Sarge. I'll skip breakfast. John can wake me for lunch."

After lunch, my time was spent in sewing an extra blanket around the inner section of my sleeping bag. I hoped to make it a little more comfortable when sleeping on the ground. Both John and I tried to have something under our sleeping bag to insulate ourselves from the cold of the ground. Since we had slept outside on maneuvers in Louisiana, the adjustment to sleeping back on 'Mother Earth' was not too difficult. I learned that one could sleep anywhere if you are tired and need the rest.

In the tent that evening, I almost finished my book that I had started the previous day on guard duty. In the process, I burned out the batteries in my flashlight. Finding a replacement later almost cost me my life.

Sunday, November 5, 1944

After breakfast, John came back to our tent and stated, "Don, Mass is being said in that small town of Mosles at 0900. Put on your coat and let's go with the others from the company."

Mosles was about a mile away from our camp site.

After we had just entered the village, an unknown GI stopped the fifteen of us and said, "Sorry fellas, but Mass will not be held until 1030. Go back to camp and return then."

We walked the mile back to our tent.

At 1030, the fifteen of us from Company E heard Mass in the small French church. The priest, who appeared to be about 70 years of age, was very slow in completing the service. All announcements and the sermon were, of course, given in the native language. From my limited high school French, I recognized a few of the words that were spoken. The congregation of 100 was composed of one-half civilians and one-half American soldiers. It appeared that the French attendants were either elderly persons over 60 years of age or youngsters under 14. On

111

our way back, John speculated, "I'll bet anything the Germans transported all the young workers to Germany to work."

I added, "I think some of the others may have been used to build those concrete boxes we saw back on Omaha Beach."

After lunch, Headquarters platoon was called for formation by our Sergeant.

"Men, this is our last day here. Everyone's to pack their bags tonight. And everybody's to take a shower. It may be your last for a while."

"Have they got a shower in Mosles for us?" asked Wallace.

"The answer is Yes and No!"

"How can that be?"

"The shower is on that stream just before you get to Mosles. Did you see those tents this morning? Well, in those tents are some shower heads for your shower!"

"Sarge you don't mean that we're going to take a shower outside. Those tents don't have or provide any heat. We'll freeze."

"Freeze or not, every man in this platoon is going to take a shower. Any questions?"

Silence prevailed.

At 1430, John and I walked the near mile to the showers. In one tent, we disrobed. A run was then made over cold boards to an adjoining tent where the shower heads were located. I quickly got wet, soaped myself in rapid order and rinsed. The shower took less than three minutes. A run was made back to the dressing room. A quick dry was made. The same clothes were worn. The amount of spray could not be controlled. The temperature of the water did not vary. It was one shade above cold. Everyone was yelling about showering in the open in November. Nevertheless, the shower was refreshing.

As we prepared to retire that evening, Crable noted, "You know Don, it will be two months since we left Camp Claiborne. I wonder if the next sixty days are going to see as many changes as we had in the last sixty?"

"Let's hope and pray, John, that you and I are around to discuss it with each other."

X

TO THE FRONT

Monday, November 6, 1944

At 0400, Sergeant Smith called, "Everybody up."

John poked me in the ribs saying, "Don, we've got to get up."

"John, what time is it?"

"Let's see, exactly four a.m. "Let's go."

Although I wanted to sleep a little longer, I knew I had to arise.

Since we slept fully dressed except for our shoes, little needed to be done before our tent was dismantled and rolled up. Our heavy packs were ready within fifteen minutes. Coffee was available to the enlisted men. Most partook in order to be awake for our long journey. By 0500, the entire company was ready to go. The next hour was just sat talking with each other.

At 0600, regular company formation was ordered. Since each GI had to carry his own pack and duffel bag, Company E proceeded slowly down the muddy road back toward Omaha Beach. After 40 minutes of slow marching, we came to a long line of 2½ ton trucks. Each platoon leader gave the order.

"They're to be 20 men in the back of each truck."

"Twenty guys!" screamed a half-dozen dogfaces in disbelief.

Sergeant Smith repeated himself, "I said twenty men and the baggage. Now let's load up."

This meant conditions were going to be crowded. In normal transit, eight men sat on each of the two benches without luggage. this meant that four GIs had to lay on top of the packs and duffel bags which took up all of the available space between the two benches that were in the rear of the truck. Headquarters platoon was fortunate in that Sergeant Smith rode in the front with the driver. Thus, we had only 19 men riding in the rear. The other four platoons had a full complement of 20 riding in the back of their truck since their officer usually rode with the driver. The usual confusion of who was to sit where ensued. Although tight, we managed to fit in the truck. Since a few of my fellow soldiers knew that I was taking some kind of notes — probably they thought for letter writing —, I was given the last available seat on the right hand side.

At 0700, the truck motors roared. Within five minutes, their wheels turned forward. The journey to the front had begun.

Twenty-five minutes later, at 0730, the motor convoy entered the town of St. Lo. While in England, I had believed that London had been badly damaged. Here a full-fledged battle had taken place. This village had changed hands several times between the advancing Americans and the defending Germans. Where formerly homes and buildings stood, only rubble remained. It seemed as if no one single place had escaped destruction.

"Remember seeing this place on the newsreels in Claiborne?" asked Norris.

"Yes, I do." replied Beesch. "But you've got to see this to believe it. Look at those burned out tanks over there. Theirs and ours. What a battle they had here!"

No one in the entire platoon had been prepared for this total destruction. The famous church which the Germans had used for an observation post hardly stood. The magnitude of the terrible damage inflicted by war was vividly brought home. We could note that to the south of the village was a high ridge from which the enemy would have been able to observe the movements of our forces as they advanced. Although St. Lo had been leveled, there were still a few French civilians walking its streets. As we passed in our trucks, every single one of them

114

waved to us. At the main intersection of this battered town, a left turn was made. We were driving eastward.

From the rear of our $2^1/_2$ ton vehicle, I could see the fields and plains of Normandy. Although the pastures and houses appeared to be well kept, the land did not look as picturesque as England. The main reason might have been the objectives in the meadows. Strung about were numerous battered and burned tanks, half-tracks and other armoured vehicles. Most of them were German. The preponderance of enemy conveyances to American was especially noticeable. At this time, we thought that the American tanks were superior to the German. Later, we would learn that if the American vehicles were not too badly damaged, they could be easily hauled back to the repair depots and reconditioned. Since the Germans were largely retreating in France, they could not do the same. In addition, the air belonged to the Allies.

Along the side of the highway was a pipe line. We learned later in the day that this brought fuel to the Allied armies at the front. At certain designated intervals, there were small pumping stations.

At 0900, the trucks stopped.

"Everybody out for a break. Everybody out. Everyone break," came the call from the company commander and the five platoon leaders.

All complied for the 'necessity' break. All took advantage of the ten minute respite to relieve themselves. No command was needed in this situation.

At 0910, every dogface was back on his designated truck. Prior to reembarking, each man had been issued C and K rations. Our forthcoming lunch was to consist of one box of noon K-rations.

During the day, our truck convoy passed through the cities of Vire, Fliers, Laigle and several other small towns. All seemed to be on the pattern of St. Lo. However, the destruction did not seem as great. The ruin that was imposed on a nation was vividly before everyone's eyes. Newspaper photos and movie newsreels could never portray the ruins we witnessed we we rode through this section of France. We noted that any area around the railway yards and stations would be heavily damaged. Many burned-out coaches and rail cars were visible in the switching yards. From all appearances, the Allied Air Forces had done an excellent job of bombing the railway transportation system in that part of France.

At 1120, the trucks stopped for our lunch break.

Everyone brought out their noon K-ration box in blue and white colors. Inside the small cardboard box was some cheese, crackers, caramels, orange powder and three cigarettes. At 1230, we again re-embarked on the trucks for the continuation of our journey.

At 1430, the truck convoy stopped for another 'necessity' break.

At 1740, the truck turned into a large pasture. The field was large enough to hold the entire 335th Infantry Regiment which meant that over 3,000 men were camped in the huge area. John and I soon had our old-style tent pitched.

At 2030, our supper was served. Since the kitchen personnel and their equipment traveled in the same convoy, we were fed a hot meal that evening. As soon as supper was finished, Crable and I retired into our sleeping bags on good French soil.

Tuesday, November 7, 1944

Election day back in the United States. Most of us believed that President Roosevelt would be re-elected. I was not eligible to vote.

At 0430, the entire 335th arose from its camp. I asked John, "Should we try to eat right away or wait and roll our packs?"

"Don, I think we've got time enough to roll the packs. Breakfast should be served until six."

"OK, let's take the chance."

We arrived for our hot breakfast at 0517. Serving had stopped at 0515. We were not served despite all pleadings. John, who was a substitute cook, could prevail on no one to relax this stiff order. No breakfast for us. I said to John, "Only one good thing. It's a good way to lose weight."

At 0545, Company E was in its regular formation. However, no trucks could be located.

"Does anyone know where we're to get the trucks?" inquired our Captain Von Schriltz.

No one answered.

"Sergeant Goodpasteur, take a couple of men and scout the area."

Within five minutes, the scouting party returning.

"Captain, the trucks are on the main road, waiting for us." reported the First Sergeant.

"Everyone find his truck and take his place," came the order.

The wheels of the 335th Infantry rolled again at 0630.

The first city that we entered was Dreux.

After passing through this town, someone in the back of the truck stated, "Hey, men, notice that Paris is getting closer and closer."

Guesses were made if our convoy would go through the capital city of France. The inquiries were soon answered. Shortly after 1000, the trucks came into Versailles. The famous palace grounds were to the left of the highway. Then, for about three minutes, we observed the massive palace.

Within the next twenty minutes, the convoy was in Paris. After crossing the Seine River, the convoy made a left turn and continued through a large park. Although many bikes were being used, we witnessed only a total of twelve autos. Most of the time we could observe the Eiffel Tower which dominated the skyline of Paris.

Near the eastern edge of this city, a huge airport was noted. A great deal of activity seemed to be taking place. We noticed that large sections of the airdromes had been clearly hit by bombs. However, the buildings and dwellings in Paris itself had no war damage.

At 1200, the convoy stopped for a lunch break.

During the eating of my K-rations, I asked the driver of our truck, "How do you like these K-rations?"

"Oh, they're OK for a fill-in."

"Most of the fellows in Company E seemed to like them."

"That's for now. Wait a little while when they've had them for a steady diet."

"How often as a driver do you get hot food?"

"Whenever we get back to the base."

"When's that?"

"Never can tell."

"Do you ever get good food to eat on these truck runs?"

"Sure. See this box here. Contains Ten-In-One rations. They've got a little variety in them. One thing they've got is butter. Have some on your K-crackers."

"Thanks."

"After a while, you'll find out what's good to eat and what you want to get rid of. But those K-rations will give you food if you need it."

At 1300, the convoy was again on its way.

The truck carrying most of the Headquarters platoon developed engine trouble shortly after the restart. The driver and our Sergeant Smith got out to inspect the vehicle's engine. The rest of us were ordered not to leave our seats. Within the next five minutes the trouble was found and remedied. But the entire Second Battalion had continued on without us. By going at top speed, our truck was able to assume its rightful place in the convoy.

Rain began to fall about 1430. Thus, the tarpaulin was rolled back to prevent the water from soaking us. Comments started to come from the occupants of the truck.

"Are we going to sleep in this shitty rain tonight?"

"Let's check in at a nice hotel."

"Let's face it, fellows, we're going to sleep outside in the rain."

Just prior to 1615, the trucks turned off onto a side road beside a huge open field. Orders were given to get out and pitch tents.

Before detrucking, Norris, Crable, Beesch and I had decided to pitch four shelter halves together in order to have an extra long tent, thus, more space. This was especially valuable to Crable and myself inasmuch as we had the open end type which would have permitted the rain to enter. The pitching of

118

this long tent was done in record breaking time. Although we had ample protection with our helmets and raincoats, the water seemed to penetrate our pant legs and shoes. Since the ground inside was wet, we placed our raincoats next to the ground. Our sleeping bags were laid on top of the coats. After supper at 1900, the four of us had a long talk on what the future held for each of us. We had no crystal ball to assist us.

Wednesday, November 8, 1944

A full day of rest. We would not discover the reason until that afternoon. The grape vine informed us that Roosevelt had been re-elected as president.

We were allowed to sleep until 0715. None of us could guess the reason for this sudden generosity. Later, Sergeant Smith informed me that the 99th Infantry Division was also moving toward the front line. To enable them to do this, the 335th Regiment remained in camp the entire day while the convoy carrying the Checkboard Division passed us by.

Upon arising, one could see that the entire Regiment occupied a huge pasture. The various companies were lined up in alphabetical order facing a small road near the city of Laon. We were thankful the rain had ceased.

After breakfast, foot inspections were held. From the bad riding conditions, and sleeping on cold ground, some enlisted men had developed trench foot. As the Medical Doctor examined my feet, he said, "They're ok now Private, but I'd watch myself. You're likely to have trouble."

"Thank you, Doctor." was my reply.

John Crable was behind me in the inspection line. When the physician examined him, he stated, "Private, you've got bad feet there. You should be evacuated."

"No, Sir, I'm all right. I don't want to go."

"Private, I can order you to be evacuated, but I won't do it unless you want to go."

"Sir, I prefer to stay here. Thank you."

Back at the tent, I inquired, "John, if your feet are in that bad shape, I'd go to the hospital."

119

"No, Don. If I left the company here, then came back, no telling what I would wind up doing. At the present, I'm unassigned although I am supposed to go back to the fourth platoon soon."

Fear was what held John Crable back.

When foot inspections were completed, Sergeant Smith visited us. He notified me, "Edwards, you're on a detail to dig a sump hole for the kitchen. When you finish, you can clean your rifle."

"Thanks Sarge, you're so good to me!"

Upon completion of that task, I returned to our tent. My M-1 Gerand was apart when Sergeant Smith stuck his head in the tent again.

"Don't tell me you have another detail for me already Sarge. I've just finished the digging. I know I'm the favorite in the platoon but let me rest until after lunch."

"Sorry to disappoint you Edwards, but I didn't come for that."

"Not for a social call."

"No, you're to go over to Battalion Message Center to take up your job. Norris, you know, is to go with you. Report to Sergeant Butler as you did in Louisiana."

No one else was in the long tent with me. Norris was nearby visiting a buddy. He returned in about ten minutes.

"Ed, you and I are to go to the Battalion and be the company messengers."

"Don, I don't want any part of it."

"Norris, it's not a bad job. You just have to deliver messages."

"That is right! But it can be any time of the day and night. And you can be exposed to being shot at all that time. NO THANK YOU!"

"You're sure you don't want to give it a try?"

"Don, get someone else to go. I want to stay with the company."

I reported to Sergeant Smith about Norris' refusal. His reaction was, "I don't care who goes with you Edwards. You

120

know there's got to be two of you to protect each other. It's your problem! Get somebody!"

"Could Crable come with me?"

"You can have anybody in the whole company if the Captain agrees to it."

Captain Von Schriltz was at the medical tent where some of the men were still being checked regarding their feet. I explained the situation to him.

"Edwards, I don't want to let Crable go. He should be in the fourth platoon. When there is a vacancy, I'm going to take him out of Headquarters. However, if he wants to go, he can."

Up to this point, John had not been consulted.

Upon my arrival at our tent, I asked him, "John, how would you like to come with me as company messenger to Battalion?"

"Don, I don't like the idea," was his cool reply.

"Are you willing to give it a try?"

"I don't know."

For the next fifteen minutes, I touted the advantages of being a company messenger. To climax my argument, which was not impressing John in the slightest, I added, "If you don't like the work after a few days, you can go back to the company. I'll get another man to come up to battalion with me."

"In other words, Don, if I don't like it after a trial, you won't be angry if I leave."

"No."

"I can return to E company anytime I want to?"

"Yes."

"All right. I'll go over with you. But I think I'll be back with the company in a few days. Is that satisfactory?"

"Yes."

A few minutes more of conversation, John agreed to come. I agreed to several conditions. The most important was that he could leave within one hour if he so desired.

John Crable never returned to Company E. Ed Norris later expressed regret that he had turned down my offer.

John V. Crable—Ellwood City, PA

After lunch, John and I moved our two shelter halves to our new location. This was near the Second Battalion's Message Center tent. John distinctly did not like the idea of moving to a new wet spot on the grounds.

Our new site turned into a quagmire that evening. Just after 1900, the heavens opened up. Down came a rain which beat on our tent. Then water began to flow through the middle

122

of our tent. Although the usual ditch had been dug around our tent site, it was inadequate. Both of us had to go out into the driving rain and dig a deeper ditch. Finally the flooding stopped.

During the rain, two messages had to be delivered to Company E. Although I delivered both of them, this type of work did not impress Private John Crable. After the delivery of the second message and being soaked thoroughly, John began to inquire as to what duties were to be performed. He asked, "What part do we play as messengers in the scheme of things?"

"John, I'll try to explain it this way. In the communications platoon of this battalion or any like battalion in any infantry regiment, are three sections, namely, radio, wire and message center. Each has some type of communication. The radio section sets up a radio network between all the companies so they can have fast communications, if needed. The wire section lays wire to all the various companies. It has switchboard to keep in touch with them. Wire is the best for you can talk as long as you like. It's much better than radio because they're no interference from anyone. Finally, there's the message center. Sergeant Charles Butler is the chief. Then there's Corporal Kern. He's the assistant who has charge of the code machine in case any coded messages have to be sent. There's a jeep driver and two battalion messengers who take messages from regiment to battalion. Last there's the eight company messengers who take messages from the battalion to the four different companies."

"That's all clear but what kind of messages do we carry?"

"All types; one thing we usually have to take down each night is the pass word."

"That I can understand. But what happens if both the other sections don't function as might happen?"

"That's where it won't be so good. We're the last and only thing left in the way of communications."

"Oh."

I attempted to point out that we should know more of what's going on at the battalion level than at the company level. After two more hours of discussion, John was still not convinced of the advantages of being a company messenger. His last words as we went to sleep were, "We shall see."

Thursday, November 9, 1944

The entire regiment arose at 0400. We were expected to reach the front today.

John and I had breakfast with the Headquarters Company of the Second Battalion. We rolled our equipment and returned to Company E. We were assigned to the same truck until the journey ended.

At 0605, Headquarters platoon boarded its truck. Within five minutes, our convoy passed through Laon which could be seen from our previous encampment.

Just after 1000, the trucks passed the border into Belgium. As American soldiers we did not need to make any stops for border inspection.

The first large city that was entered in this new country was Mons. During the next two hours of riding, the convoy seemed to be in one solid urban area. One moment after a city or town was left, our trucks entered into another town or city. From study, I knew that Belgium had one of the greatest densities of population in the world. The proof was before us.

Along certain sections of the highway, someone pointed out, "Hey, aren't those German trenches?"

"They sure look like it."

"Wonder if they fought a battle here in Belgium?"

"Don't think so cause there's no ammo or anything laying around."

Belgium was a lively place. The factories appeared to be in operation. The shops were all open. Children seemed to be attending school. We were surprised. Just two months ago, the Allied Armies had been through this area.

At 1200, the convoy stopped for the K-ration lunch break. Many in the platoon now had an opportunity to inspect the vacated trenches.

"Don, let's look at these three trenches." John said.

"I wonder when and where they were occupied?"

"I don't think very long."

"How did you guess that, John?"

"There's only two small tins in the bottom of only one of these three trenches. And they're not too deep."

As our company was eating its lunch, the Mons-Charloe electric trolley passed. It was jammed right out to its doors. Yet everyone on the trolley seemed to wave at us as they passed.

At 1245, the trip was resumed.

During the afternoon, the convoy passed through the cities of Charleroi, Namur, Huy and Liege. We were riding along side of the Meuse River.

When we passed through Charleroi, one of the men in our platoon threw some cigarettes at a Belgian man. He scooped them up faster than lightning strikes. The practice spread to the rest of the trucks carrying Company E. That afternoon, the three cigarettes that everyone had received in his K-ration box were distributed to the Belgian civilians. We noted how anxious these people were to have our smokes. Everybody from small tots to older grandparents ran after them as the cigarettes were thrown from our trucks.

After leaving Liege around 1700, the sky became black. The trucks threw on their dim or black-out lights. The vehicles seemed to be climbing steep hills. The weather became cold. The tarpolin was rolled back over the rear of our truck to keep warm. Soon snow was seen on the ground.

"Anyone know where we are?" asked a voice in the dark.

"Yea, somewhere south, east, or north of Liege. Is that good enough?" wisecracked another voice.

"That's not what I mean, wise guy!"

"Norris, Edwards, you two are at the end. Can you see any signs?"

"Haven't seen one since we left Liege," was our joint reply.

At 1800, the convoy stopped. We ate our evening K-ration. While we were eating and pounding our feet on the pavement a youth passed the convoy. In his best German, Sergeant Smith inquired, "Herr, wo sind wir?"

"Nederlands."

A PRIVATE'S DIARY

"The Netherlands, Holland? Where are we going?" shouted Wallace.

"They didn't tell me." Sergeant Smith answered.

After a half hour break, we reboarded the trucks. It was pitch black. Most of Headquarters platoon began to take a nap. Norris and I kept looking for signs. The short sleep soon ended.

XI

ARRIVAL IN GERMANY

Thursday, November 9, 1944

A voice in the back of the Headquarters platoon truck at 2030 asked, "Is that thunder I hear?"

"Sounds like it." replied another in the darkened vehicle.

"There it is again."

"Sounds like as if it's further ahead."

"Hey, that's not any rain, that's artillery!"

"By God, I think you're right."

Everyone in the truck was wide awake. Yet the silence under that canvas top was absolute. All of us had heard artillery in Louisiana but this was for real. One could feel the expressions of anxiety on the faces of the nineteen GIs. The truck convoy began to slow down until the vehicles barely crawled. The volume and noise of the artillery fire kept on increasing.

At 2130, our truck stopped. Sergeant Smith came to the tail gate and ordered, "Everybody out and be quiet."

The unloading was done without a single word being spoken. The trucks then pulled away. E company was by the side of a small dirt road in darkness. Up and down the ranks whispers were heard.

"Everyone keep silent, no fooling around," came the order.

None of us wanted the Germans to know we were here. We were frightened that an artillery barrage would start. Company E now walked about 250 yards to a junction of two small

127

dirt roads. We proceeded to wait. It seemed like hours. Muted conversations were heard among the dogfaces.

"Hey, Sarge, what's that down the road there?"

"That's some American artillery." replied our platoon leader.

"Were they the ones who were firing?"

"Yes."

"Have the Germans been firing?"

"I don't think so."

This news gave some relief to those who heard it. Until that moment, no one had any idea of who was firing at whom. None of us knew then how the front operated and sounded. We would learn fast.

About 2230, our Company Commander returned with an unknown Sergeant. He knew where we were to stay for the night.

"All the platoons get in a column of two." was the order.

We then marched, passing over a small bridge.

"Put your duffel bags in the barn." All complied with the order.

A hike was started down the small road where the American artillery guns were observed. At Headquarters platoon approached and was in front of a 105 howitzer, we heard,

"20, 42, 7, Right."

"Fire."

For a moment, Headquarters platoon froze. The ground shook. The noise was deafening. Fear struck all of us. I was scared beyond words. What was happening? Where were we going? Would the Germans start to reply with artillery? There was, however, not too much time to think. About 1,000 yards down the road, we came to a halt. There were woods to our right. Sergeant Smith ordered, "Get in a single file and follow into the woods."

Captain Von Schriltz, who was nearby, said to John Crable and myself, "You two are to be at the end of the line. When the company has found its place, you are to return here to this entrance. This is where battalion is to be located."

"Yes, Captain," was our joint reply.

Each man grabbed a piece of the person's clothing in front of him. The trees made the area one of absolutely pitch blackness. After going about 150 yards, the Captain said, "This is where we'll be tonight. You two can go back to battalion."

We turned around and made our way back to the entrance to the woods. We somehow located the message center which was about 25 yards from the entrance. John and I laid out our shelter halves. On top of the half, each of us laid out his sleeping bag. It was almost 2340. The sky was our cover for the night. Periodically the artillery guns seem to go off. But we were asleep before the end of the day. The excitement had made us exhausted.

Friday, November 10, 1944

At 0230, Sergeant Charles Butler, head of the Message Center, shook me.

"Edwards, you're to take the password to your company."

"Now?"

"Right now!"

After repeating the password, I laced my boots half asleep. My footsteps stumbled down the tree-lined lane. I carefully paced the distance from the entrance to the supposed location of Company E. No one could be found. I became full awake. I tried to search for some member of Headquarters platoon. My boot finally kicked someone.

"OW!" moaned a voice.

"Who is it?"

"This is Lieutenant Gavin."

"I'm from Battalion, Sir. I've come with the password."

After relating the message, Lieutenant Gavin continued, "Edwards, I don't think anyone is interested in it tonight. However, you did your duty. Now you can get back to sleep like what I'm going to do. You better get some rest."

"Yes, Sir. See you tomorrow."

Although the area was still black, I managed to find my way back to where Crable was sleeping.

"Don where have you been?"

129

"Had a hard time finding someone. Kicked Gavin in the back but he excused me."

"Do you know what time it is?"

"My watch says 0330. Think I'll go back to sleep."

At 0800, daylight broke through the trees. We arose. Starting today John and I were assigned to eat, when possible, from the kitchen of the Second Battalion Headquarters Company. Breakfast today consisted of canned juice, oatmeal, toast and the usual coffee with powdered milk.

After eating, John and I pitched our tent. In front of our canvas shelter, we dug our first real foxhole. We discussed how deep to make it.

"John, I think that two feet should be OK. The trees should protect us."

"Don, let's dig to five feet. Then we're safe."

We dug to a compromise depth of three feet.

As we dug, we could see the area in which the entire Second Battalion was encamped. All five companies were in a large pine grove. This small patch of woods was on the upward slope of a small hill. We found out that we were located about a kilometer east of the town of Herzongenrath, just inside the German border. Below the woods, in a hollow, was a Battery of the 30th Infantry Field Artillery.

After lunch, I asked John to take any messages that had to be taken to Company E and strolled down to the artillerymen.

After introductions, I asked, "Why were you firing last night?"

"Oh, for a number of reasons," a Staff Sergeant answered. "One was to protect your movement into the area. Another was for just good target practice on Jerry. Just to keep him upset. If we fired, chances of Jerry shooting back were no too great."

"But you guys scared the daylights out of us, when you blasted when we walked in front of the guns."

The entire crew laughed. The Sergeant continued, "You'll get used to everything pretty fast. You'll soon tell when a Jerry shell is coming in. Everybody's like you were, when they first get up here. Don't worry about it."

"I hope you're right about that. By the way, how far is the actual front from here?"

"We don't know exactly. I'd say about a couple of miles. Might be as close as one mile in some spots, but I doubt it. You're in no danger. The German patrols don't usually get back this far. If they did, they would have a hard time getting back. Anything else you want to know, just go ahead and ask it."

"How have the casualties been?"

"Whose, the Artillery or Infantry?"

"Both."

"So far, I don't think this Battery has had a man killed. That means those back here, not the observators who direct our fire up front. The Infantry is a little different story. I don't know exactly how many they've lost. It's hard to find out. Sometimes they've lost a whole company at one swope, especially back in Normandy."

"How could that happen?"

"At Mortain, Jerry tried to cut us off but he didn't succeed."

"How long has your outfit been on line?"

"Ever since we got off the boat which was six days after the invasion started. That's D plus six. I think today is D plus 157."

After some more assurances that I'd get used to everything, I left. Upon my return, Crable had completed our foxhole. It was time for supper which was served at 1615. One hour later it was dark in the woods.

Just after 1930, while lying in our tent, a strange sound was heard.

"Hey, John, did you hear that?"

"Yes."

"There it is again. It doesn't sound like an American shell like we heard last night."

"I know."

"John, do you think it's the Germans firing tonight?"

"No, it's probably just some other type of American artillery firing."

With that assurance, I drifted off to sleep. I firmly believed the Americans had everything in the way of artillery fire power. I would learn differently.

Saturday, November 11, 1944

Armistice Day.

The war for us was about to begin.

After breakfast, Corporal John Kern came over to our tent.

"Edwards and Crable, did you hear what happened last night?"

"No, but we heard some guns going off," answered John.

"Five German shells came into our area last night. Nobody was hurt."

"Do the Germans know we're here?" was my inquiry.

"Don't believe they do since we haven't been on the front yet."

Upon arising this morning, John and I noticed a heavy covering of dew on our tent shelter. But it was better than the previous night in the open. Besides delivering messages of all types, we tried to light a fire to keep warm. We guessed that the temperature was around 40.

After lunch, we found out that President Roosevelt had been reelected as President for his fourth term. Who was Vice-President was unknown. This was written in the one page mimeographed sheet that was delivered to the company. It was to be the only source of news that the front line companies would get each and every day. Only one copy went to a company. As messengers, we were fortunate to learn what was happening in the world around us. This first bulletin stated that the front was generally quiet. The American Armies had been stopped in their attempts to rush through the Seigfried Line. However, the big city of Aachen had been captured.

About 1400, the U.S. Army newspaper, 'Stars and Stripes', was delivered to the Second Battalion Message Center. The company messengers then delivered them to the respective companies in the battalion. But this newspaper was not received each day.

Commencing today, and every day thereafter, one of our assigned tasks was to secure the morning report. This was made up each morning by the First Sergeant of every company. In this manner, each battalion, regiment, and division in the entire army knew its correct strength. Thus, any day we messengers at the Message Center of the Second Battalion knew the true strength of our battalion that day.

At 1930 while in our tent, a shrill whistle was heard. Then, the ground literally shook. I thought a shell had landed right next to our tent. John calmly said, "You know what that was!"

"Yes, and it wasn't an American shell either."

"I wonder where it hit?"

"Pretty close by but no one is yelling for help."

"Do you think we should go into the foxhole?"

"No, my guess is that's all the Germans will fire tonight. We're pretty safe under the trees."

My future experience would lead to the discovery that being under the trees was the worst possible place to be because of flying fragments from the shells. But my prophecy about no more German shells turned out to be correct.

Sunday, November 12, 1944

At the crack of dawn, every man was up and digging. The reason was that one German shell of the previous evening.

At the nearby battalion aid station, I inquired of Lewis Taman,

"Did that shell last night land near us?"

"Ed, right out there in that open field just where the woods end. It's not too far away to take a look at it."

Less than 200 yards from our tent, in that open field, was a small hole that looked freshly dug. The dirt was splattered about in a haphazard fashion. One could plainly tell from the sod that no spade had dug the hole which was about a foot deep. From further inquiry, I learned that the shell was one of the famous German 88s. We would become very familiar with it.

Almost the whole day was spent with one activity. Our foxhole was deepened and widened. Crable and I differed on the exact depth it should be.

"Don, I think it should be, at least, six feet deep."

"But John, we'll never get out of it, if we have to."

"But think of the safety in it."

"Let's make it about four and one-half feet. Then have a good covering over it. That should do it."

"Let's just dig and make a good one."

When we stopped at 1600, the final depth was about five feet. Over our foxhole, which could easily accommodate both of us, we laid logs or strong branches. Next came pine twigs and needles covered by good solid earth. For added decoration, pine twigs were strewn over the top. To get to the bottom of that foxhole, it was necessary to climb down two small steps. The only way in which either of us would have been killed or injured would have been by a direct hit. This was doubtful considering the trees above us. Although other foxholes would be dug, this proved to be the most elaborate one ever dug or made by either of us. The length of time available to us on that day would be the most we would ever have to dig a foxhole.

At 2000 while lying in our tent, we heard the German shells again.

"John, did you hear what I heard?"

"I did. Let's get to that foxhole!"

Without bothering to put our boots on, we jumped into our foxhole. A few more shells were heard. Then, the American battery in the hollow started to fire. We tried to count. Our score was 25 to 10 in favor of the Americans. We agreed that if this continued, the Allies would win the war without too much trouble.

After a half hour, we returned to our tent. I mentioned to John, "I do believe that if we ever have to get into any foxhole in the future, let's wear our boots or take them with us. I've got cold feet from that ground."

"Don, that's sensible."

Monday, November 13, 1944

At 0430, a noise was heard outside our tent. We both grabbed our rifles.

"Who's there?"

"Corporal Kern."

"OK Corporal, what can we do for you?"

"Edwards, go over to the battalion headquarters tent. Guard there from five to daybreak."

"Will do, Corporal."

After putting on my boots, I wandered for fifteen minutes before I found the tent of the battalion headquarters. I found another messenger that was to guard with me. He was a messenger from Company F. In the pitch darkness of the forest, it was impossible to see his face. As usual we engaged in conversation.

I asked, "How long have you been in the Army?"

"A little over six months."

"Did you come over with the Regiment?"

"Oh, yes."

"They didn't waste any time on you then."

"No, I got drafted right after I registered. Within a year, I'm over here in Europe. As soon as I got in service, they sent me down to Claiborne as a replacement in Company F."

"How do you like this job as messenger?"

"Not too well. You've got to run those nutty messages when everybody else is doing nothing but taking it easy. Then, this guard duty isn't too good either."

Strangely, I never asked his name. He never inquired that of me. When we parted just before daylight, neither of us knew each other except by voice and background. Both of us wondered the reason for the messengers being the guards for the headquarters of the battalion when there was an entire company of men that belonged to Second Battalion, Headquarters Company.

After breakfast, Crable and I learned by the grapevine that a big attack was planned. It would take place sometime this

135

week. Our big question was what part our Second Battalion would play in the attack.

About 1400, I visited the Message Center to confer with Corporal Kern. As we were conversing, I heard Lieutenant Bernice Morgan, the Communications Officer of the Second Battalion, conferring with Sergeant Butler.

"I wish I knew where to get ahold of some experience wiremen."

"Lieutenant, I think one of the messengers was one for Regimental Headquarters Company. I'll call him over. Edwards, could you come here?"

Lieutenant Morgan then inquired of me.

"Have you had any experience in laying wire?"

"Yes, Sir."

"Where?"

"I was with Headquarters Company of the Regiment. I was trained as a wireman."

"Can you climb trees and posts?"

"Yes, I was trained to do that."

"Well, Edwards, I'll try to get a transfer through for you. But I don't know if it can be arranged."

"Thank you, Lieutenant."

"By the way, how did you get in Company E?"

"I guess, Sir, I'm too smart for my own good."

"Explain that to me."

"We had two tests while I was with Headquarters Company. I was just a private but scored higher than anyone in the wire section including the non-coms."

"Did you come from ASTP?"

"Yes, Lieutenant."

"I understand what happened now. You should have cheated and scored lower. You would still be with Headquarters Company. Anyway, I'll try to get the transfer."

Upon my return, I told John of my interview with the Lieutenant.

"Don, you might as well face facts. Captain Dick Von Schriltz won't OK a transfer for you. He's got some peculiar idea about having high-class men up front with the infantry. He thinks that having the fellas from the ASTP joining the 84th was a great thing."

"John, I'm still hopeful."

"Back in England, I heard you talk with Sergeant Smith. Von Schriltz will never get over your statement to the General. You're supposed to be overjoyed that you're up front. Nobody else likes it, but you're supposed to."

John was correct, for the transfer never came.

About 1500, the battalion headquarters or command post tent moved into a small house just in back of the Artillery battery. The Message Center remained in the woods.

That night, we heard both the German and American artillery firing at each other. We were becoming accustomed to the shelling. Unless an incoming shell came close, we did not bother to use our deluxe foxhole.

Tuesday, November 14, 1944

After breakfast, John and I spent most of the morning trying to light a fire. Our main trouble was in the fire supply situation. Any twig or stick that we gathered would be wet. We had no adequate way of drying any of them. A fire was needed by us in order to heat and secure hot water. Neither of us minded shaving in cold water but we both preferred hot water in which to shave and clean ourselves a little. Our last bath had been in Normandy. When the next one would come was unknown.

Our daily routine still consisted of running messages to Company E. Each of us kept in good shape by delivering, at least, ten messages daily. Many were oral like the password that was given each evening. Some consisted of written memos that we could not read.

After our fifth fire went out in the morning, I inquired of John, "After a week, what do you think of being a messenger?"

"The day after you asked me Don, I would have said 'Forget it' since you had to go outside there in France when the rest of us could stay in our tents. And when we got here and you had to deliver that first password. But I decided to really give it a try. The longer I do it, the better I like it. It still will be dangerous at times, but I think it's better than throwing out those mortars. And still better than being a rifleman."

"Then, you're going to stay?"

"Probably yes, for the next week I still reserve the right to go back to the Company. If I don't go and am hit or hurt, I wouldn't blame you Don. It's the chance we all take being up in the front. Someone is going to get hit by those German 88s. Let's hope we aren't the ones."

About 1400 that afternoon, an aerial show was put on for us by two English Spitfire aircraft. The two planes were strafing the German front lines or some object just behind them. The performance consisted of four parts which were repeated over and over.

First, the two planes seemed to be drifting over the Allied or American front lines. Probably some objective must have been spotted.

Next, the planes would climb high into the sky. Then, they would begin their dives toward their objective. Their guns would be blazing.

The third phase would be the German response. Their anti-aircraft fire would commence. It seemed to be largely of some kind of machine gun fire. As the Allied planes came down, the enemy ack-ack would be firing.

Finally, the two planes would pull out of their descent. They would climb back over the Allied lines again.

As we watched, we could imagine the havoc that this raised with the German enemy. They could do nothing but wait.

This aerial action kept up for a minimum of ninety minutes. Apparently low on fuel, the Spitfires must have scampered back to some British air base.

As we observed the planes, all the Message Center understood more clearly what command of the sky meant in this war.

At our retirement this evening, John and I had finally devised a plan between us to take night messages to Company E. It was decided that only one person would be responsible for the entire evening. In that manner, one person would have the benefit of a full evening's sleep. Thus, when Sergeant Butler or Corporal Kern came to our tent, only one of us would take the oral or written messages in the darkness.

Instead of going directly to our company, we found a longer but much safer route. Upon receipt of the message, the lane or open space leading to Company E was found. This path was followed until it was necessary to leave it to find the required person to whom the message had to be delivered. The return journey was the same. Whenever we left the path, we counted the steps to the desired person. This system was required because of the incidents that befell us the second night we had camped in the woods. In my attempt to return to our tent from Company E, I stepped into three foxholes. The shock of falling three or so feet without warning did nothing for my back and legs. I was also somewhat worried that my rifle might accidentally fire which could cause injury to myself or others, although no bullet was carried in the chamber. John had had a somewhat similar experience that same evening. Our solution worked for neither of us had any more sudden drops of from two to four feet into the ground without warning. We were lucky that no one was in the foxholes.

After these nights in our encampment in the woods, our eyes were becoming accustomed to the darkness. Within another week, both of us had little or no difficulty in seeing at night as well as in the daylight.

Wednesday, November 15, 1944

Today was to be our last day in the 'Woods of the Pines' as we nicknamed our encampment. Word had spread throughout the entire battalion that the big offensive to the Roer River was to start in the morning.

About 1400, Mass for the men of the Catholic faith was heard in the woods. A Catholic Chaplain from the 30th Infantry Division conducted the service. Prior to the start of the Mass, the priest turned and quietly said, "Up here, you do not need to fast before you take Communion. If you ate just before

139

you came here, it's permissible to go to Communion. No fasting is ever required at the front or near to it."

This announcement seemed strange to most of us. Later experience showed it was a wise move since no one knew when Mass would be said and where the front would be at any time.

Our meals that day consisted of K rations plus hot coffee. This pleased no one. The kitchens of the various companies of the Second Battalion were still with their units. We could understand why the evening meal might be omitted but no one understood why we had to have a cold breakfast and lunch.

During the evening, John and I visited our foxhole twice when we thought we heard some German shelling in our vicinity. Our visits to the five foot trench lasted less than 20 minutes in total.

We had retired early since each of us had run more than 20 messages and we did not know what tomorrow would bring.

XII

THE FIRST OFFENSIVE

Thursday, November 16, 1944

D-day.

This was the first day in which elements of the 84th Infantry Division would go into actual combat. We had heard that some companies of the 333rd Regiment had engaged the enemy in small patrol action prior to this day. From maps that John and I had seen, the American forces were just barely inside the German border. The artillery men of the 30th Division had warned us that the Germans would fight hard to defend their own soil.

After eating our K-rations for breakfast, Sergeant Butler came to us.

"Crable and Edwards, pack up anything you don't need with you in our duffel bag and take it down to Company E. Return here to await further orders."

"When will we leave Sarge?"

"I don't know exactly when but I think it won't be until sometime after noon. But be ready to leave at any time. You'll be taking some messages down this morning."

John and I packed our duffel bags as instructed. We took them to the Supply Sergeant of our company. We were ready at 0900.

We wanted to discard our gas masks that we still possessed. But Corporal Kern had warned us, "You've got to keep them in case of a gas attack."

By the end of this day we would not have them in our possession. Every GI had confidence that the Germans would not use gas since the Allies could retaliate with air strikes using gas. The equipment that we might need with us was rolled in a large roll and given to the kitchen crew of the Battalion Headquarters Company.

About 1000, the 30th Division artillery started firing. Their guns barked away. The shells seemed to be going out continuously. We could hear the barking of American artillery on the entire sector.

At 1230, the artillery was silent. From our training exercises in Louisiana, we knew the infantry would be advancing. We were told that we would be in back of the advancing infantry from the 30th Division.

At 1300, the entire Second Battalion formed and marched out of the woods. The route took us back past the now silent artillery. At the junction of the two small roads, the battalion took the right fork.

"Hey, look at the Kraut kids." shouted a GI.

"Wonder if they believe we're as good as their own Army," stated another.

The small group of about eight German youths, none of them over twelve, just stared at the marching Americans. The march continued with the column swinging into an open field. Some German farmers were at work pulling up some potatoes. They did not bother to look at our battalion.

The first bunkers of the Seigfried Line were now observed. There were about seven concrete pillboxes scattered throughout the field. Each had been blown up so that it was rendered useless. The concrete walls looked massive. It appeared as if this fortification could withstand a heavy bombardment.

"Wonder how many of these pillboxes there are?" inquired some dogface.

"No idea but Hitler was said to have built quite a few of them to protect his Germany from invasion." was my reply.

Just after 1330, the battalion entered the small village of Wilhelmschacht. The eight messengers were placed in a house already occupied by some GIs from the 119th Infantry Regiment of the 30th Division. We were to stay here when they went forward to their new command post. Since we were 'green' messengers, we asked numerous questions.

A private by the name of Lenham summarized it when he said, "You fellows will catch on pretty soon. The front is not what you think it is. It's not like any movie you ever seen. Your outfit might have a better time of it than ours. We've had a pretty bad time of it. The 30th has always been where the fighting been the roughest. And them Krauts aren't about to give up yet. Some of them still think they can't be beaten!"

By these discussions, the messengers were told how the Germans actually fought; which was that they would hold a position as long as possible and move only when they needed to.

Most of these 30th Division GIs were not very complimentary about our Air Force. One soldier was especially derogatory abou the Normandy disaster and fiasco.

"One bombing by your own planes is enough. When it happens a couple of times, it ain't so pretty. You see guys gettin killed by their own buddies. Someone really gummed up the works. In one place in Normandy, our bombers came over one day and really knocked hell out of the place. We kept radioing back that we held the town. Next day, they were back again. This time, they got my buddy. He didn't stand a chance. We couldn't even fire at those air bastards. They wouldn't let us shoot."

One of the messengers asked, "Is this when the Air Force killed General McNair?"

"Yea, about the same time. He was up front when the bombs came down. The only good thing is that the Krauts must really suffer when our planes hit 'em."

While we were conversing with our like numbers from the 119th, a German lady came to the door. Apparently she was the owner of this dwelling. One of the messengers from the 119th went to the door.

He shoved her back and yelled, "I told you again that you can't come in this place until you're told to. Now get out of here."

143

He proceeded to slap her across the face so that she staggered back.

Upon returning to his chair, he added, "You've got to treat them like that. It's the only language they understand. You may be surprised at that but when you see what they did to the French . . . well, you haven't any sympathy for 'em."

The eight of us were shocked. None of us had ever seen a woman treated in this manner. War had made these men hard and bitter. The 84th would become the same way.

At 1630, the messengers from the 119th left for their new quarters closer to the new front.

Just after 1700, Corporal Kern shouted, "Men, come and see the planes."

Outside we could see the B-17 bombers as they were returning from an air raid on some German city. Although the planes were thousands of feet above us, the drone of their motors could be heard on the street. We thought it was one of the noted 1,000 plane raids that our Air Force used against the enemy countryside.

Upon returning to the bricked dwelling, Sergeant Butler announced, "The messengers are to sleep on the third floor for tonight."

"But isn't that dangerous?" asked the messenger from G company.

"Might be men but that's what orders were given to me. You should get a good night's sleep."

He was wrong.

John Crable discovered an old mattress on the second floor. We dragged it to the third floor for a comfortable night's rest.

We did not begin to use it until 2300. From 1900 to 2300, John and I made continuous trips to the headquarters of Company E which was located only four city blocks away. Before we started our first trip that evening, John noted, "Don, I think we both should take the messages together at night."

"Why?"

"If we run into a German patrol, I think having two of us to cover each other would be much better than just one guy alone."

"John, good thinking."

This suggestion was given to Sergeant Butler who ordered all the eight messengers to follow this procedure during darkness.

At 2300, we delivered our last message to Company E which concerned the radio channel that was to be used during the following day.

Friday, November 17, 1944

My birthday.

At 0100, the German artillery started firing. Several shells fell in the area, literally shaking the house apart. I quipped to the other seven,

"I knew my birthday was important but the Germans didn't have to start the celebration so early."

"T'aint funny, Edwards," said one of the awakened messengers.

At exactly 0330, after just falling back to sleep, Corporal Kern yelled, "Everybody up. Message Center is going to move."

"When?" I asked.

"They didn't tell us. They just said to be ready to go."

All eight of us sat up ready to move. We would later learn that we would rest until the last possible moment.

The wait was quite bearable for Wilhelmschacht still had electricity. Thus, we could still read a book while we rested. This luxury would seldom be available near or at the front.

At 0500, Sergeant Butler announced, "Four messengers, one from each company, come with me."

Since I was the senior messenger from Company E, John and I agreed that I should go.

Corporal Kern was waiting outside for us. We piled into the back of a jeep for an unknown destination. In fifteen minutes, we were in Alsdorf.

145

A PRIVATE'S DIARY

Upon our arrival, we were directed to take over some housing that was occupied by some messengers from the 120th Infantry Regiment. Our Message Center group was placed in a cellar that still housed these 30th Division messengers. Also residing there were two married German women and their five children. Only two of their messengers were awake when we arrived.

About 0600, one of the two GIs turned on an electric light down a darkened hallway. A German woman arose. She proceeded to walk down to the far end of the hallway where there was a bed. The other American soldier followed her. The passageway was soon darkened by the first GI.

After breakfast of the usual K-rations, we began the usual conversations with these veterans of the Old Hickory Division. I learned that just one of the original eight messengers was still with their message center. I asked, "What happened to the other seven messengers who started with you?"

John Ford, who was the survivor, answered, "One by one something happened to them. I think five of them are back in hospitals in England. The other two got hit and are gone."

"When did most of the casualties come?"

"During the Mortain counterattack in Normandy. The Germans broke through our lines for a couple of miles. They ran over a few companies in doing it. The battalion threw every man into the line. Even included the orderly for the commanding officer. If the Krauts had gotten through, it would have been the end. They wanted to cut off the breakout we had made on them."

"What finally stopped the Germans?"

"Sheer guts. Why, I remember one of their tanks was knocked out from a bazooka just twelve yards from me. Jerry threw in everything he had. But when we stopped them, they almost ran. The next day we didn't know what happened to them. They just disappeared. I think they suffered a lot of casualties and couldn't go on."

George Teets, the messenger from G company, then inquired, "Ford, when do you think the war is going to end?"

146

"Longer than you think right now. My folks, the way they write, think all you have to do is shoot a gun and the Germans run. Their army is real good. Don't let anyone tell you any different."

"It won't be over by Christmas, then?"

"I'm just guessing but I'd say the Germans will get through the winter. After that, the Air Force will be able to help us a lot more than they can in the winter. Remember, I'm just guessing."

"Do you think the war could have ended by now?"

"Maybe, if they'd have gotten ashore quicker in France, it could have. Not much chance now. Wait till you see how long it takes to batter down just one of their pillboxes. The Heines are tough. They fight if they have half a chance."

"What's so tough about the Germans?"

"It's the way they use their equipment. They don't have as much as we do but they know what to do with what they have. That machine gun of theirs is better than ours. And that 88 of theirs is the best anyone has."

Just after 1030, I needed to refill my canteen which was now empty of water. I asked John Ford where some water could be obtained.

"There's a kitchen just across the street. They have water."

After ascertaining where the kitchen was, I had just entered the door when a loud crack seemed to come over my head. All the kitchen personnel rushed to the doorway.

"Look there!"

"Where?" I asked.

"Right there, just fifty yards up the street. Somebody been hurt."

We all rushed to lend our assistance to the injured. Two American soldiers had been killed. Four others had been badly wounded. One German civilian was wounded. Two nearby jeeps were summoned. The wounded were carried into them and taken to a first-aid station three blocks away. The two deceased Americans were laid on the street and their jackets thrown over their faces. One of the cooks said, "The grave men will be by shortly to pick them up. They both got it in the chest."

It was the first death I had witnessed in the war.

147

A PRIVATE'S DIARY

After assisting with the wounded, I returned to the kitchen and filled my canteen. As I poured the water, I thought, "Just 50 yards made all the difference in my being alive."

After returning to the other three messengers, I told them of what had happened during my trip to secure water.

At 1200, the messengers of the 120th Regiment left for a new position.

During most of the afternoon, the four messengers and Corporal Kern just waited for further orders. During the lull, a conversation was started with one of the two German Fraus. I was surprised to learn that she spoke excellent English.

"Where did you acquire such good English?" asked Kern.

"Why, I was born and raised in England."

"How did you ever get to this town of Alsdorf? You're a German, aren't you?"

"Oh, yes. My man was working in England when I met him. We were married there. Later he was transferred back to Germany so I came to this town to live with him."

"Where is he now? In the German Army?"

"He was in the Wehrmacht. He was captured in Russia last year."

"How often do you hear from him?"

"Very seldom. The Russians, you know, do not recognize the Red Cross. They don't let the German prisoners write home."

None of the five of us felt much sympathy for her. We were becoming hardened to real war.

Later, I inquired, "Why didn't you leave with the rest of the civilians when you knew the Americans were coming?"

"Marie and I almost did. But we decided to stay. The burgermeister told us that the Americans would kill all the Germans they found left behind. They drove all the cattle away. The Wehrmacht tried to do everything to help the people leave."

"Were you scared when the Americans came?"

"Yes, but since I spoke English, I knew I could speak to the Americans. I don't think the people here are afraid of the Americans as they are of the Russians or French."

"How have you been treated?"

"Very well, I expect the war to leave us because I don't think Germany can win the war any more."

"Did you ever think your country would win?"

"Yes, back in 1940 when we beat France and then in 1941 when the Russians were retreating before our armies. But after Stalingrad, I think most Germans knew victory would not come."

"I notice that the children have the U.S. Army K-rations boxes to play with."

"Yes, the soldiers who left always gave them some boxes each day."

"Oh!"

From her look, I believe she knew that the food was given in exchange for the favors that she and her friend had given to the departed soldiers.

At 1700, the rest of the messengers arrived in Alsdorf.

Our sleeping quarters were the vacated kitchen where I had secured the water for my canteen.

At 1800, Crable and I were ordered to take some messages to Company E. Since we were now closer to the actual front and German patrols were known to slip behind the lines, John and I agreed that we would use a buddy system in delivering the messages. One of us would walk on each side of the road or trail. If any intersection was reached, one would proceed to look down the road to see if anyone or anything was present. Then, one would cross and motion the other to follow. We both kept our rifles ready for any action.

Company E was located over two miles from the battalion headquarters. At our arrival about 1830, we learned that Company E had taken its first German prisoner. They had been assigned 'mop up' operations in back of the advancing 120th Infantry Regiment. To celebrate this occasion, the headquarters platoon of Company E had steak and french fried potatoes for their supper. The food supply came from the Germans civilians with whom the platoon was staying. The meal was served waitress style by the two German fraus.

While this scrumptious meal was being devoured, John and I had to wait while First Sergeant Goodpasteur made out some

149

reports for us to return to battalion headquarters. Each of us looked at the other hoping that we might be invited to join the freshly prepared meal. No invitation was forthcoming. When we left, John said, "Don, that supper is the best way I know how to fight a war."

"John, to me it's the only way!"

"Wonder what headquarters battalion will have for dessert?"

"Forget it, we've got our delicious K-rations waiting for us."

After returning, we quietly ate our K-rations. At 2100, we had to deliver another message for the Commander of Company E.

Saturday, November 18, 1944

All the messengers were permitted to sleep until 0800.

At 0900, Corporal Kern stated, "All of you should be ready to leave within fifteen minutes notice. It depends on how the advance goes on the line."

The movement did not come that day. The Germans were resisting.

During this day, I finally became fully acquainted with all the messengers from the four companies of the Second Battalion.

John and I were the foot carriers from Company E.

The representatives from Company F were Martin F. Innes and James A. Rochester. Martin was a husky lad from Torrington, Connecticut. He and I had previously met the early morning of November 14th when we were assigned the task of guarding the battalion headquarters tent. He was the youngest messenger.

His companion was Staff Sergeant Rochester. He hailed from Salem, South Carolina. He was a short, stocky, ruddy complexioned person. Rochester was the only regular army person in the group. Company F had no position for him to fill, thus, he was assigned this messenger task. He was married and had two children, a boy and girl. After living with him only a

150

short time, all of us understood that the Commander of Company F probably did not trust him to lead men into battle. His reactions to our varied situations would be very interesting.

Company G sent two short men to be their runners. George Teets' home was Scottdale, Pennsylvania. George had a fair complexion, was about five feet seven inches with extremely short legs but was well built. He too was married and had one son.

His companion was Mike Smorado who came from Monoquet, Indiana. Mike had a dark complexion beneath dark black hair. He stood at five feet five inches. He was married. Mike was unusually quiet and rarely spoke. He once remarked that he never wanted to be in any way any place.

Charles Simon and Salvador Munoz were the messengers from Company H. Charles came from Crowley, Louisiana. He was very slightly built and about one inch taller than Mike Smorado. While the 84th was stationed at Camp Claiborne, he went home every weekend since his home was only fifty miles from the camp. Simon had a good command of French which would become useful later.

Salvador's home was Los Angeles. He was a Mexican-American. He rarely expressed an opinion about anything. He weighed only 125 pounds and was the same height as his fellow runner.

Martin was the tallest at six feet followed by John at five feet ten inches. I was just one-inch shorter than John.

Geographically, the group resided in various states ranging from the Atlantic to the Pacific. The composition of the eight would change within a period of one week.

Each of the messengers had three runs that day. But it was a quiet day. We heard little gunfire of any type.

At 1830, the German Luftwaffe paid a visit to Alsdorf. Suddenly we heard a loud drone. We all rushed outside. The fireworks then started. The flak guns about a mile away peppered away. The machine guns shot their tracer bullets skyward. A few of the messengers pointed their Gerands upward and squeezed their triggers. All was in vain. The enemy dropped a few bombs which shook the whole area. None came close to us. Within thirty minutes all the excitement had died down.

At 1930, my turn came to perform guard duty. This had been instituted to prevent any unauthorized persons from walking the streets. The most important task was to awaken those sleeping in case of a German counter-attack or patrol which might be in the area.

Sunday, November 19, 1944

At 0445, Sergeant Butler announced, "Everybody up. Messengers be ready to move in fifteen minutes."

At 0515, four messengers, one from each company, were in a battalion jeep ready to move forward. Our vehicle raced through the town of Mariadorf. At the next town, Hongen, we stopped. Just ahead could be heard some firing which indicated that some type of action was taking place.

After moving to four different partially damaged dwellings, the message center finally settled into a small undamaged house having four rooms on the first floor. The messengers heard numerous rumors that our battalion was to engage in the attack on this day. Several messages were taken to Company E, most of which were sealed.

During a message trip in the early afternoon, I inquired of Ernie Duffy, the company bugler, "Duffy, how far is the actual front away?"

"Ed, just go down to the end of the block. Turn onto that road that leads out of town."

"How far away is the shooting?"

"Ed, I don't know. Jerry might have retreated some more. We were ready to join with the 30th in the attack when one of those messages you brought told the Captain to stay at the edge of the village in case our help was needed."

"Duffy, think I'll go see what's going on."

"Just be careful, don't get into the shooting. I don't think the Captain would approve of you being hit at this time."

Duffy's directions were followed.

152

THE FIRST OFFENSIVE

Less than 200 yards from the edge of Hongen, I came upon three dead Wehrmacht soldiers. I went up and looked at them. All three appeared to be about sixteen years of age. Each of them had been hit in the chest by shrapnel, apparently, artillery fire from our side. One had wounds all over his body. They lay gaping at the sky. Their clothes had been ripped. This showed that anything of value had been removed from them. On their lapel were white lines, indicating they were members of the German infantry. While I was staring at the deceased soldiers, a Captain and four infantry soldiers of the 30th Division passed.

"Captain, how far away is the front?"

"Private, see that burst of fire, well, that's it."

"Am I permitted to come any closer?"

"You are, private, but I wouldn't at this time. It's better to be with your own unit. Are you from the 84th?"

"Yes, Sir, I am."

"In time, you'll see enough of it."

With that remark, they departed.

I noted that less than a quarter of a mile away there seemed to be bursts of machine gun and rifle fire. Periodically, American artillery shells would go cracking overhead. In the distance a thud would be heard. I would later learn that no real front could ever be described since it ebbed and flowed depending upon a variety of situations.

After watching the action for over a half hour, I returned to the Message Center where I told my story of seeing the dead Germans and the front.

That evening, all the messengers had beds upon which to sleep. The usual guard duty of four hours was done by at least two messengers during that time. During the early evening hours, some units of the Second Battalion took over portions of the front from the 30th Division.

153

A PRIVATE'S DIARY

Monday, November 20, 1944

At 1000, all of us in the Message Center heard the artillery and mortar shells start to fire. They were German. A counter-attack was being launched against the portion of the line held by the Second Battalion. During the firing, we heard a loud whistle come near our dwelling place. A loud thud hit in the backyard. There was no bursting of the shell. After twenty minutes everything was silent. Then the reply from the Americans was heard. Over came our artillery and mortar shells. This lasted only five minutes. Then silence prevailed. After we got up off the floor, Teets noted, "Hey, fellas, look at the shell in the backyard. I think it's a dud."

All of us looked at the 88 shell but none ventured out for fear it might explode.

At 1100, George Teets made a suggestion to me, "Edwards, let's go out and see if we can find some bikes. I saw some on my way to my company yesterday."

"OK, George, let's tell Corporal Kern where we're going in case something happens."

George and I took about two hours to find two good bikes. While walking through the village of Hongen, we noted signs on almost every doorway in German. They gave instructions to the Wehrmacht that these homes were to be used as if they were their own. These announcements stated that the American Army would soon be driven out of the Fatherland. No one was in these dwelling since the 30th Division had captured the entire town.

At 1500, Sergeant Butler ordered half of the messengers to return to their respective companies. The number of messages being carried required the services of only one man. Crable, Innes, Smorado and Munoz left. The four that were left agreed to accompany each other on the remaining messages that were to be delivered.

At 2000, I experienced a narrow escape from death or a very serious injury. It did not come from any direct enemy action.

THE FIRST OFFENSIVE

At 1930, each messenger was given a message that instructed the companies of our Second Battalion the type of mortar support that was to be given to the 120th Infantry Regiment on their attack the following morning. George Teets and I decided to accompany each other for safety reasons. We decided to use our newly acquired bikes. We delivered the message to Company G first. Next, we made the trip to the headquarters of Company E.

On the return journey, we were riding our bikes on a very dark Hongen street. At one spot in the roadway, it was necessary to make a wide veer to the left lane in order to avoid a shell hole. Just as I was about to veer back to the right hand lane, George yelled, "Don, look out!"

In back and on top of me was a speeding jeep without dim lights on. A quick turn to the left was executed. My bike glanced off the jeep. I hit the left curb full force with my body pinned under the bike. The jeep driver never stopped. My head was spinning. My back ached. My legs were sore. Hitting the pavement non-stop was not fun. Teets rushed over, "Don, how are you?"

"I don't know, I think so. I had a real bad fall."

"Take it easy, Edwards, for a few minutes. We're in no rush to go. If you can't get up, I'll get the medics. Don't move unless you're ready to do so."

"Just give me a little time, George, I think I'll be ok."

We sat on the dark street for the next hour. Then, we slowly walked back to the Message Center which was about a mile and a half away. My bike was ruined.

Upon our arrival back at the center, Corporal Kern routinely asked, "Anything exciting happen to you two?"

"Yea, Don here almost got killed."

"Did you two run into a German patrol?"

"No, I'll explain."

After the explanation, both Corporal Kern and Sergeant Butler wanted me to go to the battalion aid station but I told them, "If I still feel this way in the morning, I'll go."

I was lucky that we had no more messages to deliver that evening.

A PRIVATE'S DIARY

Tuesday, November 21, 1944

At 0500, the four messengers were ordered to be ready to leave at any moment. The entire 30th Division was to start another attack. We remained in Hongen the whole day.

Because I could hardly move that day, Teets and Simon took my messages to Company E. The men at my company wanted to know why I did not come but George just told them that I didn't feel well.

All during the morning hours, the mortars of the Second Battalion barked out in support of the infantry attack. A few German shells came back in reply but the ratio seemed about 5 to 1 in our favor.

About 0900, Major Edgar Kennedy, the battalion commander, and Captain Francis Price left for an inspection of the moving front. They did not return until 1200.

My whole day except for the delivery of one message was spent recovering from my injuries. I took four aspirins every four hours to relieve my pain. I decided that if I felt this way tomorrow, I would have to be evacuated to the rear. By 1900, my body had recovered from the shock of the accident.

A little after 2000, I decided to pay a visit to the room where the battalion radio was. I was interested in learning what part they had been playing in the communications network.

Corporal Robert Bergett was on duty at the time.

"Edwards, had any experience with this radio?"

"Yes, Bob, I learned to operate that back in Headquarters company. Also out on the target range back in Louisiana."

"Can you relieve me for a few minutes?"

"Sure, Bob, I've been here almost all day getting back in shape from that crash."

"Yes, I heard about that. You almost got it. Be back in about fifteen."

During this time, I heard no radio messages. The only thing was the attempts of the enemy to jam our radio channels. The jamming consisted of some sound on the order of Scottish bag pipes. It went up and down in intensity. The sound was a

156

harassing one. It became very tiring after listening to it for only five minutes.

When Bergett returned, I inquired, "What other devices do the Germans try on the channels?"

"Ed, they've got a couple of things going. You can hear those bag pipes now. Sometimes, they try a vacuum sweeper. Other times, it's like a loud truck noise in starting a motor. I haven't heard it yet but some of the communications guys from the 30th tell me they try to cut in on American conversations and join it. Usually doesn't work because they don't know the slang expressions.

"How do you like it as the radio operator?"

"So far Don, it's been boring. One of us four operators has to listen during the whole day and night. Our battalion hasn't had much except for the counterattack yesterday. I expect to be busy in a couple of days."

The remainder of the evening was devoted to discussions on what and where the battalion would do next. All of us realized that we could not be in reserve forever. Our battalion would have to be on the direct front and attacking shortly. All of us had hoped for a break in the German lines. Staff Sergeant Harvey Gooding, the chief communications sergeant, summarized it in saying, "To me it looks like Jerry has no intention of giving any break at any time. You have to make them give every inch of ground. It doesn't look too good to me. I think we're going to get hurt and soon."

XIII

TORPEDO JUNCTION

Wednesday, November 22, 1944

Everyone was up bright and early this morning. Rumors were rampant that the Second Battalion was about to move.

At 0800 exactly, Sergeant Butler stuck his head into the room where the messengers were waiting.

"All the messengers are to return to their companies. You'll be told when to report later on."

"Any ideas where we're going?" inquired Rochester.

"Not yet, but I expect to see you and the other three sometime this afternoon."

Each of us went to our respective company.

At 0900, Sergeant Smith ordered, "Headquarters platoon, board the first truck."

A light raining was falling. While waiting in our covered 2½ ton truck, all could hear the artillery pounding at something occurring at the front.

At 0930, the convoy started on its way. No one in the headquarters truck knew our destination. The route that was followed went back through the towns of Hongen, Mariadorf, and Alsdorf. Passing our convoy and going forward toward the front were artillery vehicles of all types pulling their artillery pieces. The first group was the 105's. Next we sighted the 155's. Finally we saw one large 8 inch gun being towed. The roads in these German towns were jammed with numerous Army vehicles. The cars and trucks seemed to be going in every direction possible.

A PRIVATE'S DIARY

Our route out of Alsdorf was on Route 57. From maps that some of us had, we knew this highway ran from Aachen to Linnich. This was about 20 miles. Yet the two cities at each end were in the hands of different armies. After riding out of Alsdorf about five miles, the trucks halted. Our convoy had just passed a junction with Highway 56. E company sat in the vehicles for over thirty minutes.

"All out of the trucks."

Everyone sat down on the tree lined highway. The trucks were soon gone.

"Hey, fellas, look at these dead Jerries here!"

Less than 100 yards from the road were two young German infantrymen. From their appearances, we guessed that an engagement was recently fought here. Their bodies showed no sign of rot. We noticed some trenches nearby. Scattered in the rain-soaked trenches and in the nearby muddy fields were tin cans and other pieces of German equipment. A few of the GIs from Company E looked over the discards to see if there was anything of value to be found.

Sergeant Smith then approached the platoon and ordered, "Everyone is to dig. Don't move until that's completed."

Although John Crable and I did not know how long we would remain, both of us started to turn the damp earth. As we dug our new foxhole, John noted, "Look up ahead Don, I think the Germans are hitting that town."

"John they sure are. Wonder if they're battling in that place?"

"Maybe, we'll find out soon enough."

While we were still digging, Sergeant Smith approached John and me. It was just before noon.

"Edwards, Crable. You're to go to the Battalion Command Post up ahead. It will be in the third house on the left hand side of the road as you enter the village. If it's not there, ask around and you'll find it. Everything clear?"

"Yes," was our joint reply.

John asked me, "Isn't the battalion CP in the rear of the Company?"

"Usually that's the way it is John, but I don't know what's going on. Get your things together and let's walk up there."

As we started, Captain Von Schriltz approached us.

"Edwards, Crable. The CP will be in the third or fourth house. Across from it will be a large barn. Hurry up, they've got some messages you have to deliver."

We proceeded up the road. Upon entering, we found the name of the village to be Gereonsweiler. The Headquarters of the Second Battalion were found in the third house not far from the crossroads of the village. The road upon which we were situated was the main road or Route 57 going to Linnich. The other went down into a narrow gulley where the main portion of the town lay. As John and I were walking toward Gereonsweiler, we noticed a large number of burned-out tanks scattered throughout the surrounding fields. It appeared as if there were more American ones standing vacant than those of the German enemy.

On each side of the battalion headquarters dwelling was a tank from the famed Second Armored Division. The two crews were in our cellar chatting away on thoughts and ideas far from the battlefield. Part of the second floor was gone, probably as a result of someone's shelling. This was true of most of the structures in the entire town.

Less than fifteen minutes after our arrival, the 88s from the German artillery started arriving. John and I were thankful the enemy had waited to greet us. A group of us at the side door of the dwelling quickly fell flat onto the first floor.

After ten minutes had passed, the shelling ceased. We went to the doorway again to observe what had happened. Sergeant Rochester blurted out, "The barn across the street has been hit. My company is in there."

We could hear the crying of some wounded. I blurted out, "Those men should be gotten out of there as fast as possible."

Captain William P. Thompson, the company commander of Section Battalion Headquarters Company, who was standing in the doorway, replied to my outcry. "I'd help if I could, only my jeep driver was just hit. There's no one to drive it."

"Captain," I answered. "You have one right now." Back at Camp Claiborne, as a member of the Regimental Headquarters Company, I had taken the necessary training and had secured a license for driving Army vehicles.

John volunteered, "I'll take any messages that come."

Captain Thompson and I jumped into the jeep. We drove to the now partially demolished barn. Inside were five wounded GIs. The worst case was a Private whose leg had been broken by a piece of shrapnel. Moving him was done with considerable difficulty since there was no stretcher available. He was clearly in pain and kept pleading, "Please be careful, boys, please be careful, won't you?"

Then he would blurt out, "Those bastards, those dirty bastards, those dirty God Damn German bastards."

During the next hour, I drove the wounded back about ten miles to the aid station in Baeswiler. After this chore was completed, Captain Thompson said, "Edwards, drive me over to Puffendorf. That's where most of my company is located."

Puffendorf turned out to be another battered German village located just west of the junction of Routes 56 and 57. There, Captain Thompson asked, "Can you take the battalion CP guards up to Gereonsweiler?"

"Yes, Captain, I'll do it."

The first trip was made without incident. But on the second trip, the jeep had just turned the corner from Highway 56 onto Highway 57, when I noticed that every Army vehicle was parked solidly on the right side of the road.

"Wonder what everyone's doing on the right hand side of the road?" exclaimed one of the guards.

"Here's your answer." shouted another, for at that moment, three or four 88s hit the dirt on the side of the road. I could find no place to pull the jeep over so all could jump into the nearest ditch. Instead of just stopping, I pressed the accelerator to the floor. The jeep seemed to sail through the flying mud and metal. In nothing flat we were at the Battalion CP in Gereonsweiler. I sustained a cut on my left hand but never bothered to report it to the medical personnel. Upon our arrival, the guard who had wondered about the parked jeeps added, "Boy what a ride, I'll never forget it."

At 1730, all the driving assignments had been completed. I had returned the jeep to Captain Thompson in Puffendorf. He then asked me, "Private Edwards, how would you like to become the regular driver for this jeep?"

"I'd like to Sir, but I don't think a transfer can be made."

"I'll take care of that."

"Captain Von Schriltz won't let me go, I'm sure of that!"

"What makes you so sure?"

"Last week, Lieutenant Morgan needed a wireman. I've had experience in that field. No transfer was made."

"If I request it, I think he will."

"I've already tried twice, Captain, and he refused both times. Because I'm not one of his favorites, he might punish me in some way if I try a third time. I hate to turn it down, but, I'm afraid that you had better get someone else for the job."

"Alright Edwards, if it's ok with you, I'll just make an inquiry, but I'm certain I can get a transfer for this job."

"I'm sorry Captain, but don't mention that I requested the transfer. I can't take the chance of what Captain Von Schriltz will do."

I walked and thumbed my way back to Gereonsweiler.

Upon my arrival, I related to John all my experiences of the afternoon. After finishing, he agreed with me saying, "Don, I think you did the right thing with Captain Thompson. I think if Dick Von Schriltz got another request from you, he would make you point man in the first platoon. You know, the first man that leads the advancing."

"John, I know. That's why I refused it. What happened when I was gone?"

"Don, you can't believe the shelling here. Every fifteen minutes, the Germans give this place a pasting. You've never seen anything like it. Why it's unsafe to step out the doorway for more than two minutes. Use that john in the back in record time. I hope the Companies don't have to attack the Germans here."

163

That night, most of the Army personnel in the dwelling slept in the basement. Six of the messengers including myself slept on the first floor. All through the night, the German artillery continued to shell the small town. But none came too close to the Battalion Headquarters.

Thursday, November 23, 1944

Thanksgiving. Another day of war.

During the morning, John and I went to the next floor of our Battalion CP. We could see the reason for the constant shelling. Throughout the whole town, next to every building of any type, were tanks of the Second Armored Division. There seemed to be hundreds of armored vehicles. But no soldiers on the streets. Like the two tank crews we knew, the armored GIs were in the cellars.

During the morning, three messengers assisted a Grave Registration Unit in picking up corpses. In front of our battalion CP was a dead American who had apparently been hit directly in the head. None of his skull remained. Sergeant Rochester and I looked in on a wrecked tank. Inside the driver sat. He was a charred skeleton. For nearly two hours, we three assisted in removing the dead. It was an experience that one could not forget. Upon our return to our quarters, Rochester lost all his K-ration breakfast and said, "That's the last time I'm going to pick up human flesh. I can't stand it."

I answered, "I don't think it's the last time we're going to see the dead."

In conversing later with one of the Armored tankers, I asked, "Why don't we shell them in Linnich?"

"Jerry occupies the high ground. He can see all the good targets. We can't see anything without our planes. Notice the weather."

"Yes, it's cloudy but you can still see some distance."

"That's right. Jerry got the best for him now. If it clears, then we'll do something. Also, if Jerry starts anything, we'll let him know we're here. No sense in wasting ammo for nothing."

During the morning, a few tanks and armored vehicles began to leave Gereonsweiler. This continued up to 1400, when the Second Armored was now completely out of the town.

Shortly before 1430, I noticed out the side door which we could see from our room in the back that tanks from the 7th Armored Division were rolling into town. The tanks were lined up bumper to bumper. Five of us were looking at the tanks. They would move slowly forward turning left at the road junction. I pointed out to Crable, "John, look at all those tanks. Wonder if Jerry knows about them or are they asleep?"

No sooner had the words left my lips when the Germans told us they knew the Seventh Armored Division was here. The 88's exploded in droves around the junction. We laid flat on the floor. We kept saying, "Another, another, another," for the next twenty minutes. Then, silence, absolute silence.

Upon looking out the doorway, no more tanks could be seen. Two tanks were on fire. We did not know what happened to the men in the tanks.

During the entire course of the day, numerous messages were taken to Company E by Crable and me. Our procedure was to run or trot until the edge of the village was reached. We then walked the remaining distance to our company which was situated in well dug foxholes along the east side of Route 57. When either or both of us went down the highway, we were asked, "Why is there so much firing up there?"

We then would explain that the Germans still held Linnich which the company could see in the distance from their foxholes.

Since our arrival in Gereonsweiler, everyone was eating the usual K-rations. Because of our location, we expected nothing different this day. But at 1730, John and I returned from a message run, when the CP guard announced, "Fellas, you better get downstairs if you want some turkey."

"Are you trying to pull our legs?" I asked.

"I'm not kidding you, go down and see for yourself."

John and I flew to the cellar. Corporal Kern greeted us.

"Edwards, Crable, get your mess kits for we've got a hot meal. Turkey, dressing and cranberries. And real coffee."

165

Each of us was given only a small portion. We were thankful for the effort that had been made on this day for a good hot meal.

That night, the battalion radio operators placed their jeep outside the window where we slept. All the messengers assisted Sergeant Walt Talerek in stringing the power extension into the basement for the radio could use the battery of the jeep for its power source. As soon as the job was finished the usual bull session started.

"Boy, this is some place to remember." stated Martin Innes.

"Yea, the first hot spot as far as I'm concerned." added James Rochester.

"To do this up right, I think we should give a few titles to prominent sites here in Gereonsweiler," suggested George Teets.

Everyone agreed. For the next hour much debating of appropriate names ensued. By unanimous agreement, the phrase 'Torpedo Junction' was applied to the crossroads located less than one hundred yards away from our occupied dwelling. '88 Boulevard' was the title bestowed upon Route 57 which led into Gereonsweiler which the Germans could see at all times from their high ground. While still discussing names for other places in this battered town, Crable noted, "Fellas, we gotta cut this out. We won't get any sleep. Let's hit the sack and hope tomorrow is a better day."

Friday, November 24, 1944

By 0700, all the messengers were awake and ready for their usual duty. The usual German shelling came about fifteen minutes later but soon ceased.

Shortly after 0900, the enemy let forth a thunderous barrage. Then came the message over the radio, "Counterattack."

Within two minutes the American artillery, which had been silent up to this moment, opened up. Then, the tanks in the town itself began to fire. Shells began going in the direction of Linnich in much greater quantities than we had ever experienced from the Germans. The enemy must have pulled back for

166

silence prevailed again within ten minutes. The German attack had failed.

During the German shelling, the upper portion of our dwelling was hit by a shell. No one was hurt by the explosion. After the attack, one of the battalion guards came in from his visit to the out-house and announced, "Those Heines and their 88's must have hit every square foot of ground around that out-house. But they failed to hit the real thing, I know that!"

All of the messengers kept listening to the battalion radio for further events. At 1000, the 335th Regiment informed the Second Battalion that two German Panzer Divisions had moved across the Roer into Linnich. We debated what would occur.

"I bet they try to attack this afternoon," Rochester stated.

"I don't think they will," replied Crable. "We've got too much in the way of tanks and infantry right here. The mud in those fields is heavy. If they try the highway, our artillery will get them."

John's prediction turned out to be true.

Shortly after 1530, John and I had to go to Company E which was still stationed along 88 Boulevard. We had to carry a 300 radio which was a box-like instrument weighing between 35 and 40 pounds. It was a replacement for one which was not in good operating order. An extra battery was also taken.

We proceeded without incident to our company in its fox-holes. Radios were exchanged. I placed the defective radio on my back since it was the only way that it could be carried. As we were returning to Gereonsweiler, John stopped to chat with a member of the fourth platoon.

"I'm going on John, this 300 is heavy. See you back in town."

"Roger, Don."

My footsteps had taken me less than 50 yards when the familiar whistle of an 88 came through the air. Without any hesitation, my body went into the ditch. I was laying next to an elm tree with my face in the ground. Approximately twenty 88s came into the vicinity. Two of them hit directly across the road from me. Dirt and metal came flying. I could hear it hit my helmet and radio. After the shelling ceased, I examined the radio. The German shrapnel had taken two huge chunks out of the radio. The 300 had saved me. I had sustained no injuries although my back felt a little sore from the weight on it when I had hit the ditch. Crable had jumped into a foxhole and had no injuries.

However, Company E had its first man killed as a result of enemy action. Private Anthony Matarrese was dead. One of the 88s had hit a tree by his foxhole. A fragment had gone through his helmet killing him instantly. Two more men were wounded. I yelled at John, "let's get back into town."

"Don, I just got the morning report from Sergeant Goodpasteur. He might as well make the corrections now. Wait for me."

"Roger, John. I'll walk up about 200 yards and wait for you."

In ten minutes, John was back with the corrected morning report showing the first casualties sustained by E Company.

Just before 1700, the cloud formations around Gereonsweiler began to break. Within ten minutes, four Air Force P-47s were overhead. They buzzed like bees. Their targets were, of course, the artillery guns which had been raising so much havoc with us. Although darkness soon fell, the planes strafed the enemy four times before they left.

That evening before retiring, Mike Smardo, who was normally very quiet, said, "Let's everyone pray for good weather tomorrow. Then, the planes can come back and get those 88's."

"Amen," added Munoz.

Saturday, November 25, 1944

The weather was clear and crisp.

At 0900, the four P-47's appeared. Most of the messengers went across the road to watch the tactics of our Air Force. Their movements were like those of the English Spitfires that had been observed back in the woods near Herzogenrath.

First, the planes strafed the town of Linnich. We could not, of course, know what was going on in the German-held town but we were sure no Wehrmacht soldatens would be on the streets.

*Grave of Mike J. Smorado in the American Military Cemetery
near Margarten, Netherlands.*

Next came the attack by air on the artillery or tank guns. The machine guns of our planes blazed away at the distant objectives. Each of the four planes dropped one bomb. The earth vibrated when each bomb hit the enemy-held area. Rochester and Innes kept chanting, "Get those bastards, get those bastards."

The air activity continued until 1300. Then, the planes left. Gereonsweiler did not receive a single shelling that morning. We hoped it would continue.

During the morning, John and I had to deliver many messages to Company E. One of these orders moved our company from the south side of Gereonsweiler to the west side of the battered town.

Just before 1500, Crable and I were ordered to take some miscellaneous equipment to our company. We were also to return with the morning report. Since the easiest route to the new location of Company E went past the location of Company G, Mike Smardo asked, "Would you two like to go with me? I can show you a short cut to E Company. You go right past my company. I've got to deliver some things."

"Sure Mike," was our joint reply.

"Can you wait a few minutes? I've got to go to the basement to see Corporal Kern and pick up my rifle. I left it downstairs."

We had waited a few minutes when I said to John, "Let's not wait for Mike. We can find the company by ourselves."

"I'd wait for Mike, but I'll go if you want to leave."

We left the battalion and had proceeded about 200 yards when the 88 whistle was heard. Both of us flattened ourselves against Mother Earth. The shells appeared to have fallen near a house on the south side of the Second Battalion Command Post. We continued our walk through the shell-ridden village. We easily found Company E.

However, locating First Sergeant Goodpasteur took us another ten minutes. We asked for the morning report which he had yet to fill out. While waiting for him, John and I inspected the new company foxholes. While on our little tour, the Germans let the Americans know that all their artillery guns had

170

not been knocked out by the P-47s. In came the 88's. Everyone but Crable and myself went diving into their new ground homes. Since we had none, we lay prone on the earth. Captain Von Schriltz saw us out in the open and shouted, "Get in here, you damn fools!"

Without a moment's hesitation, we jumped into two foxholes. A few more German shells hit the area but no one was injured. After the bombardment ceased, there was a conversation on the Company E radio.

"Hello, Chapter 6 to Chapter 1, over."

"Chapter 1 to Chapter 6, over."

"Chapter 1, are Edwards and Crable there? over."

"Yes, Edwards is next to me and Crable is here, over."

"Tell them that Mike has gone to the bar, over."

"Wilco, out."

No explanation was needed. If someone had tried to stun me with a blackjack, a more thorough job could not have been done. The term meant Mike Smardo had been killed. If the term 'gone for a beer' had been used, we would know that the man had been wounded. Immediately my mind flashed back to those shells that had landed just after we had passed 'Torpedo Junction.' They had missed John and myself but had probably hit Mike.

We waited another five minutes while the First Sergeant finished the necessary papers including the morning report. On our return, it was necessary to duck into a dwelling housing some members of the Seventh Armored Division while the Germans hurled in some of their 88s. While waiting, a tanker asked me, "Had any close calls lately?"

"I just had one a few minutes ago."

"What happened?"

"I decided to leave early."

"Leave early?"

"I'll explain some other time," I shouted as John and I departed.

When John and I arrived at the Battalion CP, all the messengers, four wiremen, three radio operators, Corporal Kern

171

and Sergeant Butler were all on hand to greet us. They had never expected to see us again.

After a few minutes of back-slapping and hugging, George Teets explained to John and me what had transpired.

"All of us thought that you three had left together. After an hour went by, Mike had not returned. You two hadn't come back. I started to get worried. G Company is only a five minute walk. Finally I decided to call up on the radio to see if Mike was ok. Walt Talarek called for me. G company said no one had seen Mike all afternoon but they would check with all the platoons. They checked. They called back but no Mike was to be found. Then, I went down to the company. I got the morning report. No one in the whole company had seen Mike. Then, I came back here. Just as I got in the door, the Medics radioed they had picked up Mike, just two doors away. We asked them if they had picked up you two. Their answer was no. Everyone was worried so Talarek called Company E. Did you hear it?"

"George, let me tell you I heard it!"

"Don, didn't you go with Mike?"

"No."

"How come?"

"Well, he went to the cellar and I told John we should go. Why I don't know?"

Why John and I did not wait was a mystery. All the messengers at this time were on excellent terms with each other. Frequently the messengers accompanied each other to the respective companies. The next day we learned that Mike had been killed instantly. His helmet was discovered about fifty yards away from the Second Battalion Headquarters.

That evening, as a result of Mike's death, all personnel were ordered to sleep in the cellar. Only one man, the CP guard, was permitted on the first floor. If there was any emergency, we would be alerted. Most of the messengers did not like the dampness of the basement. However, the order was followed.

Tuesday, November 26, 1944

The morning brought the Air Force P-47s back for another duel with the German artillery. We had learned that when the American planes were present, the Germans did not shoot at us. They were occupied elsewhere.

All seven messengers went across the highway to watch the American pilots at work. While we were observing the usual patterns of strafing and ack-ack fire, Innes said aloud, "Boy, I wonder how it would be if that were the Jerries strafing us?"

His companion, Jim Rochester, answered, "It wouldn't be too nice. Look at those planes. They come after the Germans whenever they want to. Those Jerries can't do a damn thing about it except take it."

The number of bombardments received in Gereonsweiler totaled only three that entire day.

Just after 1300, Sergeant Butler announced, "We're going to leave here. A battalion from the 102d is going to take our place. They'll relieve us tonight."

An hour later, a Lieutenant Colonel arrived to confer with Major Kennedy, our battalion commander. While their conference was going on, the messengers were conferring with the driver who had brought his commanding officer. He tried to impress us by saying, "So far we've been in two attacks. The second one was the worst one. Our companies tried to advance. After a whole day, they gained 300 yards. At night, we withdrew to our old positions. Those Germans are tough."

"What did you expect?" quipped Teets.

"I thought the Jerries were ready to quit. Hell, they won't give up for another two years at the rate we're going now. You fellas know what's ahead, don't you?"

"No, what?"

"At Linnich, there's the Roer River. We'll never get across that thing."

Before we could continue, the driver was signaled to drive his commander back.

Another party from the 102d Infantry Division arrived a half hour later. There were four First Lieutenants in the group. Sergeant Butler came with them to our room on the first floor.

"Edwards, Rochester, Teets, Munoz. Each of you are to take the officer to your company's positions. Introduce them to your company commander. Then return here for further orders. Any questions?"

There was silence on our part.

"Edwards, you take Lieutenant Johnson Green to E Company."

Lieutenant Green then accompanied me to Company E. On our journey, I requested him to stay close to all dwellings since the enemy might shell us at any time.

"Private, I'll take care of myself, I don't need any advice from you."

"Yes, Sir."

As we continued, he asked, "Is there any building in this dump that hasn't been hit?"

"I don't think so, Lieutenant."

"What happened here?"

"I believe there was a battle between the Second Armored and some German Panzer Division. The Germans occupy the high ground near Linnich and can see every move we make here."

"Where's your company?"

"Just west of the village. They're dug in there."

Upon our arrival at the Company E foxholes, I introduced the Lieutenant to Captain Von Schriltz who took him on a tour. I waited for the normal reports.

That evening while eating our now not-too-delicious K-rations, I inquired what the reactions were of the other messengers who had accompanied the Lieutenants from the 102d.

Rochester answered, "The guy I got was a louse. Never stopped crabbing."

"The lieutenant I took to G Company was a creep. Thought the 84th had never done anything," Teets added.

Munoz said, "My lieutenant asked if H company could use mortars. He was real strange."

174

Our introduction, we all agreed, to the 102d Infantry Division had not been a good one.

Just after 1830, Sergeant Butler appeared and said, "All messengers are to report back to their companies. When the next place is reached, report as soon as possible to Battalion. Most of you were late in getting here in Gereonsweiler. Teets, don't forget to get a replacement for Mike."

XIV

THE FIRST ATTACK

Sunday, November 26, 1944

When John Crable and I arrived at Company E about 1830, Sergeant Smith ordered us, "Get in a hole, you two, and stay there until you hear from me. We don't want to lose you two."

The order was followed.

At 1930, when darkness had settled over the Gereonsweiler area, the command came, "Fall in. Regular company formation."

The entire company came out of their foxholes. Everyone strapped on his full field pack. We stood and waited and waited. During this time, a few German shells came into Gereonsweiler. Some of the GIs attempted to go back to their safe foxholes.

"No one is to go back unless ordered. Everyone's to stay in line." shrieked the company officers. From somewhere in the ranks in back of me came some comments.

"Order or no orders, I want to stay alive."

"We ain't goin nowhere, let's stay in the holes."

Yet no one disobeyed the order.

At 2015, the march started. As Company E left the Gereonsweiler area, the Germans gave the town another artillery barrage. We believed they knew that troop movements were taking place.

On this west side of the battered village, more tank hulls were in evidence. It seemed that every 200 yards, another

177

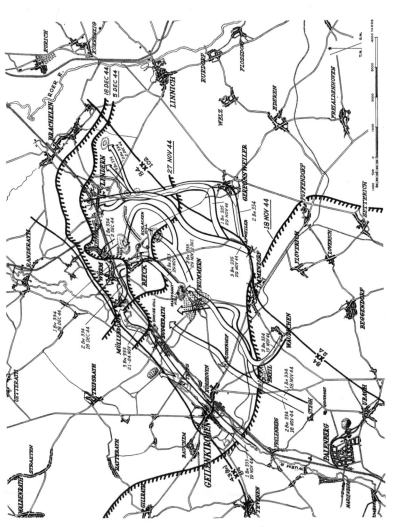

Map of the Siegfried Line

burned out tank would be sitting in the still darkness. On this side of town, the disabled Wehrmacht tanks outnumbered those of the Americans.

The first village that was entered that night was Apweiler. The town appeared to be smaller than Gereonsweiler. It too had been beaten and battered. The march continued without interruption in what seemed a westerly direction. Off to our right as we plodded along, flares that lighted the sky could be seen.

"Gee, I wonder if they're trying to find us?" asked one loaded infantryman.

"No telling. I think Jerry wants some light to see everything he can," answered another.

"Regardless, let's get to our new site. This mud is hindering my walking. Sure wish it wasn't here."

"Yea," agreed his companion. "But just keep going. It's worse than anything we ever had in Lousyana. It's three times heavier than nice firm ground."

The pace at which Company E walked was very slow. The heavy packs only added to the discomfort. Soon, another small village, Immendorf, was entered. After Company E marched through, a break was taken.

Most of the men just flopped down on their packs. Captain Von Schriltz walked back and forth through the five platoons stating, "We've only to go to the next village. That's all for the night."

"How far is the next village, Captain?" came a voice from the dark.

"Not too far away. Perhaps, you can see it from here."

A few of us stood up and looked. All we could see was more rain-soaked earth and the village of Immendorf just behind us.

After fifteen minutes of rest, the company was back on its feet. The shuffling continued through the sticky mud.

Within the next twenty minutes, the village of Prummern was reached. A guide was met at the village limits which guided Company E to its quarters.

As the company made its way to some cellars, Captain Von Schriltz motioned to John and me.

179

"You two are to go with me and Lieutenant Sanborn to headquarters."

After a walk of about two short blocks, we reached another battered dwelling. The two officers left John and me to go to a conference of the battalion staff. The two of us went into a cellar where we met Corporal Kern.

"Edwards, Crable, just lay down in the straw on the floor. There's nothing to do until morning."

John and I took off our packs. Then we found a corner on the straw and went immediately to sleep. The march, although short, had been difficult due to the slow pace and the sticky mud.

Monday, November 27, 1944

At daylight, we were able to see the village of Prummern. As expected, it was in shambles. Every house or building had been hit by some type of shell. None had escaped damage. The Catholic church in the center of town was a sight to behold. Its steeple had been hit several times. It appeared as if a good wind would blow it over. There were some disabled or knocked-out German tanks scattered in the town. These tanks served as guide points for directions of any type. The number of Americans in this petite village was amazing. Every cellar — the only safe place to stay — was filled to capacity. The entire Second Battalion of over 800 men was in the town plus some components of different special forces.

During the morning, all the messengers were placed in a very tiny cellar on one side of the destroyed church. Before the cellar could be occupied, we were given an order by Sergeant Butler.

"Men, this is a potato cellar. It's full of potatoes. They've got to be thrown out before you can use it."

Teets spoke up saying, "Sergeant, is there any chance those potatoes can be saved for someone to eat?"

"Sorry, orders were to just throw them out. I agree it's a waste of food but that's war."

THE FIRST ATTACK

Every potato was thrown on the streets of Prummern to be crushed by our tanks and trucks.

Although every messenger had to deliver numerous messages, the day was relatively quiet. The big treat of the day was that we were permitted to get some cold water in order to shave and wash our faces. This act of cleansing had been denied to us in Gereonsweiler since the only water we could secure was for drinking purposes. Every messenger took advantage of this opportunity. We did not know when the next washing would come.

At noon, we received another treat in the form of a hot meal. The only complaint about the food was that there was not enough of the hot stuff. Everyone, of course, could eat their K-rations, if they desired, as a sort of dessert.

Rumors were rampant. It was certain that the entire Second Battalion would attack during the next few days. The village of Prummern was now less than a half mile from the front. The line was held by the 334th Infantry Regiment. This outfit had captured Prummern.

Since messages were constantly delivered, I fell into a conversation with a rifleman from the First Battalion of the 334th.

"Did you have much trouble driving the Germans out of here?" I asked.

"We got through the town without too much trouble, but then I guess they got organized. The first night, think it was November 18, Jerry was all over this town. It was like a wild animal cage. No one knew where anyone was. As for myself, I just went into some old barn. I'll admit I was too afraid to stick my neck out the door. Thought a couple of times some Heines went past, but didn't try to bother them. Yet, in the morning, they were all gone. I couldn't figure it out. My platoon was all over the place."

"Sounds like the Germans really put up a fight."

"Getting them Jerries to leave was like a slug feast. And our casualties. My company had only 64 good men after we got finished."

"Only sixty-four out of the two hundred when you started!" was my astonished reply.

"That's all we had."

"What about the Germans?"

"My guess is that they suffered about the same rate as we did. They got the advantage of defending. But I think they stayed too long and didn't know we had three battalions around this dump."

After our evening hot meal, Sergeant Butler told the messengers, "Each messenger is to have guard duty for one hour. He's to keep awake. If he sees or hears anything, he's got to alert everyone. They expect Jerry to send out patrols through the night."

Tuesday, November 28, 1944

My shift for guard duty came at 0100. Five minutes before my tour began, Sergeant Rochester shook me, "Don, get up. You're on in five minutes. Don't forget your rifle and a clip."

While on guard duty, the village of Prummern seemed deathly still. Nothing moved. Yet, I knew there were guards of all types like myself watching for a move by the enemy. At 0200, George Teets relieved me.

Another move for the company messengers came just after 0600. This time, our new home was a large cellar with no potatoes. All the message center personnel were in one spot. Just after all seven of the messengers had finished their usual K-ration breakfast, George Teets was told to go to Company G and bring another man to replace the deceased Mike. This would bring complement back to the normal eight.

Hugh Walters from the state of Ohio accompanied Teets on his return. We learned that he had quite a marital history. He had been married and divorced no less than three times. After giving us his entire background, he exclaimed, "I didn't like or love any of those dames. They didn't love me either."

Then Hugh Walters asked, "How come I had to come over here?"

The rest of us explained to him what had happened to his predecessor, Mike Smorado, to which he replied, "You mean you guys deliver messages when the firing goes on?"

"Yes, we do," was our joint answer.

"I don't think I'm going to like this job."

When Walters went to deliver his first message in about fifteen minutes, Teets explained to the rest of us that the G Company Commander, Captain Ted Ketterer, was having trouble with Hugh Walters and wanted him where he would cause no trouble to him. Our group would later experience difficulty with him.

Shortly after 1030, Rochester and I heard a gun shot, and I asked, "Rochester, that sounds close."

"Edwards let's go, it sounds like in the back yard."

We rushed out to the back of the dwelling to find a young GI who had quote 'accidentally' shot himself.

"What happened?" we asked.

"I don't know. I was just cleaning my gun and bang it went off. Bandage me up quick will you?"

"Why did you want to clean your piece out here in the open?" inquired Rochester.

"Just wanted to." he replied in a raspy voice.

Although we had little doubt as to what he really did, we got out our bandages and covered the two holes in his shoulder. I ran to the Medics who came with a stretcher. This type of incident was not the first encountered nor would it be the last. No GI seemed to do this type of thing back in the States. Yet, these type of so-called accidents were prevalent near the front.

Upon our return to the communications cellar, the other messengers told us that the attack tomorrow by the entire Second Battalion was confirmed.

Supposedly the entire sector was to be ablaze since other units of the 84th as well as surrounding outfits were to try to push the enemy back toward the Roer River.

One of my tasks in the early afternoon was to bring Captain Von Schriltz back to battalion headquarters where he and the other company commanders had a conference with Major Hunter and the entire battalion staff. The objectives of the attack were outlined at the meeting.

A PRIVATE'S DIARY

Each time that John or I went to Company E with a message, we were beset with questions as to what was going to occur. Our answers were varied.

"We don't know any more than you do."

"All I can tell you is what I hear."

"They don't tell us messengers what's going on. We just deliver the orders, we don't issue them."

However, later in the afternoon, every soldier in every platoon in every company of the entire battalion was informed of the plan for tomorrow morning. This was the one time everyone knew what the objective of the battalion would be. The objective was a hill between the two small communities called Beeck and Lindern. Later such detailed preparations would not be given since every GI would learn that the situation on the front changes constantly.

That evening, in the battalion headquarters as well as in Company E, everyone was keyed up. Training had been going on for over two years for many of the men. The real test would start tomorrow.

About 1700, Sergeant Butler came with instructions for the messengers for the attack in the morning.

"Men, half of the messengers will go with the Major on the attack. The remainder will be used whenever radio cannot be made with the companies. You must be ready to deliver the message no matter what the conditions are. Does everybody understand his duties?"

We all nodded our heads.

"There must be one messenger from each company. You can decide among yourselves who is to go up front. The other four will remain here in case there must be messages delivered from here to the Major or your own company."

After the Sergeant left, John and I had a discussion as to who would go and who would stay.

"John, I'll go with the Major tomorrow."

"No, Don, I'll go."

"Why, you didn't want to be a messenger. I got you into this mess."

184

"Don, I think I owe you one. If you hadn't made the right decision in Gereonsweiler, I wouldn't be arguing with you now. I owe you."

Our decision-making conference continued for another ten minutes, with Crable winning this one.

The four messengers going on the attack were permitted to retire at 2000. The remaining four ran messages continuously through the night.

Wednesday, November 29, 1944

Throughout the early morning, the messages continued to come. The only individual awake at Company E to receive anything that I brought was First Sergeant Goodpasteur. He checked and re-checked each order or message that I brought to him. My last message was delivered at 0330. At this time, Company E was moving out of Prummern toward their jumping off point.

When I got back to our cellar at 0345, John Crable was awake and ready.

"John, how do you feel?"

"Nervous, Don, just nervous. I think I'll be ok in a while. I think we'll be back early this evening if all goes well."

"Take care of yourself, John."

"I intend to, Don, see you later."

John and the other three messengers, namely, Innes, Walters and Munoz, left at exactly 0400. Corporal Kern then said, "You four go to sleep now. If any message has to be delivered, I'll wake you."

"What time should we get up, Corporal?" I inquired.

"Sleep as long as you can. Just hope you're not needed."

At 0900, I had a nature call and awoke. The other three messengers slept for another hour. During the day, the four of us read or dozed. No messages had to be delivered.

During the afternoon, the Germans periodically shelled Prummern. In the cellar, the four messengers heard all types of rumors. Most of them proved to be untrue.

185

Just after 2200, the four messengers that had gone with Major Kennedy returned. They were completely exhausted. I asked John, "What happened?"

"Don, I'll tell you in the morning. We're due back with the Major at 0700. I've got to get some rest."

With that sentence, he went to sleep.

At 2230, the cellar became a little more crowded. The radio section of the battalion's communication platoon moved in with us. Space was made available to them. During the day, Corporal Kern and I had brought in some straw on which everyone could rest. This was much superior to the boards on which we had been sleeping.

Thursday, November 30, 1944

At 0730, John and the other three messengers left to accompany Major Hunter. Before leaving, Crable explained to me what had happened the previous day.

"One thing for certain Don, was that none of us knew what was happening at any time. The original attack had not gone as planned. Company F led the attack. When they got close to a pill box near a place called Schlacklen Hill, they were pinned down by machine gun fire. That stopped the attack cold. Then, the Germans started to throw some artillery at us. I believe everything the German Army had came through that sky. After the artillery fire stopped, the Major ordered a flanking movement. This apparently was somewhat successful. But the battalion still hadn't reached its objective. I expect they'll try again today."

As we sat in the cellar awaiting further instructions, the battle must have become intensified. The Germans shelled Prummern continuously. During one spell, Bob Bergett of the radio section stated, "I've counted 36 straight shells without stopping. Now Jerry will start again in a few minutes."

For precaution, no one was allowed outside unless it was on official business.

Just after 1330, a voice yelled through the open cellar window, "Anybody know where's there's a jeep driver?"

"Do you need one now?" was my answer.

"Get out here pronto, someone up the street is in bad shape."

Within two minutes, I had driven to the end of a street where a casualty had just occurred.

"Well, if it isn't Don Edwards, himself!"

"Gordon Eaves, what are you doing here?"

"Ed, get that jeep over here will you, this guy's in a bad way."

The wounded soldier must have suffered a near direct hit. His face was bleeding in uncountable places. His neck was ripped wide open. His wind pipe could be observed. One of his legs was shattered. Parts of his body around his stomach had been severed. How he was still living was a minor miracle. The poor GI kept gasping for air. A stretcher was secured by another medical GI. The wounded soldier was placed across the rear seats. I gunned the jeep. With Eaves trying to patch up a few of the oozing wounds, we sped to the battalion aid station.

Upon our arrival, the doctor came out. He tried to patch up the wounded GI in a few spots. The stretcher was lifted from the jeep to the ambulance. In one minute, the ambulance was on its way to the medical clearing station. There more effective treatment could be rendered to this GI. Whether this badly wounded GI survived the war was unknown. We all knew he would never see the front again.

When the ambulance had departed, Eaves asked, "Don, remember that bet you made with me back in Philly?"

"Yes, Gord, I do."

"I think my chances of winning are pretty good, don't you?"

"I think they are. It doesn't look as if the Germans want to end it by the New Year. Nor are the Japs going to give up by June of '45."

"Remember, if you get to New York City, look me up. Then you can buy me and the wife the best full course steak dinner anywhere in town."

"I've got to come to New York or where you live, right?"

187

"Roger, Don, well, I'll see you back in the States next year or later."

With that farewell, Eaves took off for the 309th Medical Battalion of which he was a member.

A half hour after my return to the message center cellar, Sergeant Butler called the four remaining messengers together.

"You four go over to Battalion and relieve the others. Send them back here."

"Yes, Sarge." was our joint reply.

In three minutes we arrived at the Second Battalion Headquarters to be met at the front door by Captain Francis K. Price, the battalion's S-3 officer.

"What are you four doing here?"

"Captain, Sergeant Butler sent us over here to relieve the others," was my reply.

"Each of you go back to the center. If we need you, we'll call you. I don't want you to move unless I give the order. If there's an emergency, you'll be running your butts off. Everyone understand?"

"Yes, Sir."

We returned and gave our report to Sergeant Butler, who said nothing.

Yet, a half hour later, Sergeant Butler told us to come with him to the Second Battalion Command Post. We exchanged places with the other four messengers who had been out toward the front during part of the day. The new cellar where we were located was a huge one which was divided into four different rooms. The messengers occupied a corner of one of the rooms. We were to wait until ordered to go out with Major Hunter. Most of my time was spent in trying to assist George Teets who was ill with some type of stomach trouble. Although Hugh Walters volunteered to stay at Headquarters until Teets was better, George exclaimed, "No, Walters, you went out yesterday. It's my turn. I'll get over this stomach ache right away."

As we sat and did nothing, we discovered that the advanced 335th Regimental Command Post was also in this cellar.

188

THE FIRST ATTACK

A little after 1800, while walking around, I noticed that the regimental commander's orderly, Paul Huppman, came in with some hot food.

"Wonder where he got that?" inquired Rochester.

"I'll find out, for that's Paul Huppman, the Colonel's man. Hey, Paul," I motioned with my arm, "Will you come here?"

"Hi, Don, how are you?"

"As well as can be expected. Can you tell me where you got the hot food?"

"Sure, at the regimental company's kitchen. They're in the cellar next door."

"Think they'll have any extras?"

"You know the cooks, so there shouldn't be much trouble. Go over and see. At least, tell them you used to do KP for them."

The cooks at the regimental headquarters company remembered me. They gave me as much hot food as I wanted. I immediately brought it back to George Teets who had not eaten in over a day. After attempting one spoonful, he refused any more food. I had no trouble finishing the hot meal, complete with hot coffee.

As we sat and waited, we heard rumors of all types. One humorous one was told by Sergeant John Teasdale of the Headquarters Company regarding Colonel Hugh Parker, the regimental commander of the 335th. His tale was as follows:

"Whenever Colonel Parker has to relieve himself, he first sends out his orderly to see if any shells are falling. The orderly comes back and reports. Then, the Colonel goes out to relieve himself."

I asked, "Sergeant have you ever seen this?"

"No, but everybody swears it's true."

"It's a good rumor, but I'll have to see it before I believe it."

The reason for our skepticism was that no one knew when the German artillery would 'open up.' Everyone took the chance when he went outside to perform his natural functions hoping that the enemy would let him do his business in peace.

189

Just after 1900, the cellar was shaken to its foundation. After the shelling ceased, someone reported that the jeep on the side of the dwelling had suffered a direct hit. We went out to inspect the vehicle which was just a mass of twisted parts, with the steering wheel bent up and the seats in shreds. But no one was injured.

At 2030, I asked Sergeant Butler to inquire if we four could return to our usual cellar with the other four messengers. After getting the attention of Captain Price, he came back and announced, "All of you go back to the message center. Stay until you are called."

Upon our return to the message center cellar, we noted that the wire section members of the battalion communications platoon had moved in. Their former cellar did not appear as safe as ours.

I sat next to John Crable. He related his days' adventures.

"We went out with the Major toward the front. We met some officers from the line companies who told of a German counter-attack the previous night which almost succeeded. But the Germans withdrew. Actually the day on our part of the front was very quiet. But off to the right and left of us, we could hear mortars, machine guns and some very heavy artillery. I think our battalion can't move until something happens on each side of us."

"While near the front today, I ran into an Air Force observer. He's the liaison officer for the fighter command that supplies the P-47s. He said that an air group was supposed to come every half-hour and strafe the Germans. Yesterday they did. That's what helped our flanking attack. Today no planes came. He cussed his commander up and down. Said the weather was good enough. Yet no planes showed. I think that's the reason our companies didn't try anything today."

At that moment, Lieutenant Morgan broke in with, "I'd like two volunteers to go with me and the jeep driver back to the rear Regimental CP.

Since he was staring straight at me, I volunteered.

The ride back to the small town of Breil proved to be uneventful. The only reason that we were invited to go, Army

Edwin J. Nelson — Paterson, New Jersey

style, was in the event the enemy was met in some form. Four armed soldiers were better than two.

Friday, December 1, 1944

All the messengers were up and ready for duty by 0600. We were told to sit and wait. However, there were a variety of miscellaneous messages to be delivered during the day.

191

One of these miscellaneous messages came shortly after 0930. I was instructed to deliver a message to the battalion aid station. When I arrived, there were no casualties present. But in a few minutes some arrived. They were three riflemen, all of whom had suffered rifle wounds. They walked in on their own power. One had been hit in the shoulder, another in the foot, and the third in the buttocks. Each had a good size hole with blood smeared around the opening. Their clothes were still intact, which was in contrast to the mortar or artillery wounds which usually ripped clothing to shreds. While talking to the wounded, I overheard a conversation between two of the medical personnel.

"Did you hear about Captain Von Schriltz of Company E?"

"No, what happened to him?"

"Last night, he came back for a conference at battalion. His hand was all bandaged. The CO wanted him to come here but he refused. Said he had to be back to his men for the attack that's going on today."

Upon my return to the message center, I reported the conversation to John who answered, "That's like Dick Von Schriltz. He wants to be in action. He's been preparing for this all his life. Hope he made it safely back to the Company."

Because of my stint with Headquarters Company of the Regiment, I was able to eat hot food whenever it was served. The other messengers did not like my good fortune. I had just finished lunch and had stepped out into the streets of Prummern, when a voice rang out, "Donald Edwards himself, how are you?"

"Why, Ed Nelson, where have you been keeping yourself?"

"Same place you have Don, up here in Germany."

"Where are you now?"

"At Regimental Aid Station. Hey, look there!"

At that moment, seven German civilians were brought into Prummern. Apparently they had been captured in the recent American attack. Two were women. After they finished their walk into the village, they stood along the side of a building across from Ed and myself. In their extremely old ragged

192

clothes, they huddled together. An MP stood with his rifle guarding them. As some of the GIs passed them, they stopped. A few words were mumbled in their direction. The American soldiers were a distinct contrast to them. We wore very good but dirty outfits.

After waiting about fifteen minutes, the two jeeps came. They were placed in the vehicles and departed Prummern.

"Wonder what they'll ask them?" I said aloud.

"I don't think it will be anything like we had this morning at the Aid Station."

"Why, Ed, what happened?"

"About ten this morning some German prisoners were brought in. To be exact, two enlisted men and one officer. They were in bad condition, especially, one of the Wehrmacht soldiers. We just got them laid down when an interrogation officer arrived. He told us to keep right on going. He kept asking questions of those three just as if nothing had happened to them. The two enlisted men were scared. They knew that if we didn't finish bandaging them, they might not live. They really talked. The Jerry officer wouldn't give out much information. He maintained he didn't have to. It was very interesting to see how much information they got from the two of them. I think all of us would change our minds about that name, rank and serial number business if our lives are at stake."

"Ed, have they taken many prisoners?"

"I don't think so Don. I heard the Germans are fighting for every inch of ground here since we've been in the Seigfried Line. They can't afford to have us push them to the Roer River."

"Why?"

"I've heard it's their last defense available to them before the Rhine River."

After a few more minutes of remembering the old days of Philly and Claiborne, we departed. Before leaving, Ed gave me a present.

"Don, here's a capsule of morphine. Keep it on you. If you're hit, jam it into your thigh. Hope you never need to use it."

"I hope so too, Ed!"

About 1730 that afternoon, just as dusk was approaching, someone yelled into our cellar, "Hey, everyone, 'Bedcheck Charlie' is here."

Although we were under orders not to leave the safety of the cellar for anything not in the line of duty, everybody scampered outside to see 'Bedcheck Charlie'.

In about one minute, a lone Lutwaffe plane was seen in the sky. Every multi-purpose gun in Prummern let loose its fire toward the German aircraft. This plane, we had been told, usually came at dusk to observe what was happening on the American side of the front. It rarely dropped any bombs or strafed the American troops. Its sole purpose was reconnaissance. In a few minutes, it was gone.

Before returning to the message center cellar, I obtained permission to visit the basement where two telephone switchboards were housed. One was the board of the Second Battalion. I asked Private Clarence Sharrett, "Clarence, how many lines do you have in?"

"Just two Don, one to the forward Observation Post just behind the front and one to Regiment across the room.

"None to any of the companies?" I questioned.

"None."

"Why not?"

"Understand radio is being used for the communication for the attack. As long as it's ok, I don't think you'll be doing much."

"Clarence, it's boring for me just sitting around and reading. But I guess it's better than the alternative. If we messengers are needed, things aren't too good, I know."

"Don, you're right. Heard something you'd like to know. Captain Von Schriltz didn't get back to Company E. No one knows where he is. The guess is that he might have been killed or wounded. You know he was here last night."

"I know. He supposedly got the information on the attack Company E is going to launch today. Hope nothing happened to him."

"Hope you're right, Don."

194

From the other side of the room, I heard, "Edwards, what are you doing here? Fixing the battalion's wire lines?"

I proceeded to walk over to the switchboard of the 335th Regiment which was being manned by Les Shoemaker.

"No, Les, I'm one of the messengers from Company E."

"Oh, I knew you were a lineman with us. Thought you got transferred to the Second Battalion in that department."

"I tried to, but my Company Commander won't let me go anywhere."

"That's too bad. You know we're short two linemen. I'm sure Captain Read could get you back here if he requested it."

"I doubt it. Anyway, Captain Donovan, I don't think, wants me back in Headquarters Company. He didn't like it back in Claiborne when I couldn't identify some German aircraft after my eye got injured."

"Yea, I remember when somebody sat on you and busted your glasses right in your eyes. Some of us wondered if you'd ever see again. Had any trouble with your eyes since then?"

"My right one bothers me sometimes but I'm happy I can see. When they took that glass out of my right eye, things were blurry. Then, when I couldn't make out those German planes, Captain Donovan got me transferred out. He won't accept my explanation although my right eye was bandaged for five weeks. He sure was mad at me."

"I still think Captain Read likes you, cause he knows you know all about the right way to lay wire. Some of the jerks we've got now don't know what they're doing. Why don't you go over to his cellar and see what he says. Can't hurt to ask."

"I'll try but I don't have much hope. How many lines do you have from Division to here?"

"Two."

"What for?"

"Don, one is for regular calls. The other's for General Bolling."

"You mean they have one just for the General!"

"Correct."

"Can anyone else use it?"

"No."

"Les, is it in use much?"

"No."

"Then, why do you have it then?"

"That's what we'd like to know. It's ok to have two lines from Division. But nobody can see the General having the sole use of one. Either line could be cleared for him in nothing flat, if he needed it. Guess it's just a waste of war."

"Hey, Les, listen to that."

"Well, here go the lines out again, the General's included. Jerry must have thrown in another barrage. You can't do anything here. Might as well go and see Captain Read. I think he'll get you back, Donovan or no Donovan. There's a war going on you know."

"I know Les. Thanks a lot for the transfer suggestion."

In less than five minutes, I had found Captain Read, the Communication Officer for the 335th. I asked, "Do you remember me, Captain Read?"

"I sure do, Private Edwards, what brings you here?"

I explained about my chat with Leslie Shoemaker, who had suggested that I request a transfer back to Regimental Headquarters Company.

"He's right Edwards and I do need a good lineman, but your chances aren't too good you know."

"I think I know why, Sir."

"In the first place, if I know Captain Von Schriltz, he won't let anyone go regardless of what good they can do elsewhere. Then, you know what commander Donovan is unhappy about."

"I know, Sir."

"But I'll try. You know it's easy to get out of Headquarters but to get back in is a little different. I'll do my best for you. But don't expect anything. I've always thought you shouldn't have been transferred out but I don't run the company, you know that."

"Yes, Sir. I'll appreciate your efforts."

Upon my return to the messengers about 2000, John Crable commented, "Don, don't go near Lieutenant Morgan. The line to the OP has been cut by that last barrage of 88's."

196

"Maybe, I can help John."

I immediately went to the Battalion's Communication Officer and offered my services to aid in restoring the severed line.

"Thanks, Edwards, but no thanks. If that line isn't fixed in two hours, you'll be up all night. You'll be needed then. If we need you, I'll remember."

In one hour, the line to the forward Observation Post was back in order.

For this evening, the messengers hoped that the Germans would cease their shelling for the remainder of the night. The enemy did this.

Saturday, December 2, 1944

Rumor reached the message center in the morning that the Second Battalion was going into the final phases of its attack on an object called 'Toad Hill.' For the past two days none of the line companies could move from their positions because of attacks made on nearby objectives by other units of the 84th.

At 1300, Sergeant Butler called all the messengers together. He issued out the following instructions.

"Tonight our battalion is going to be pulled out of the line. Four of you are to meet your companies on the outskirts. Tell your company commander to have his men pick up their equipment they left in Prummern. Then, they are to go to Immendorf. Trucks will be waiting there for the companies."

XV

THE LULL BEFORE THE STORM

1. Leiffarth

Saturday, December 2, 1944

At 2300, four of the messengers walked to the outskirts of
Prummern to await the arrival of the four companies of the
Second Battalion of the 335th Infantry Regiment. We stood and
talked to each other in low tones wondering when the companies would come. The searchlights from the American side of the
line that lighted the sky kept going off and on as if to confuse
the Germans as to what was occurring.

Sunday, December 3, 1944

Just after 0030, Company E came into view. Captain Von
Schriltz was not at its head. Instead, Lieutenant Jame Lusby,
leader of the first platoon of Company E, was in the lead.
Upon meeting the Lieutenant, I repeated the instructions and
orders that had previously been given to me.

"Edwards, are we to leave as soon as the company is
ready?"

"Yes, Lieutenant. As soon as they get their things in Prummern."

I joined the Headquarters platoon which was in the lead. I
inquired of Ernie Duffy, the company's bugler, "What happened
to Captain Von Schriltz?"

Officers of the Second Battalion, 335th Infantry Regiment

"Don, we don't know. He failed to get back to the company after he went into Prummern for a conference. That's all anyone knows. Most of us think he got hit by some shell on the way back to us.

Company E proceeded to pick up any equipment they had left in Prummern. At 0130, we left Prummern. Just outside Immendorf, as outlined, trucks were waiting for the entire Second Battalion. Headquarters platoon was placed in the first truck at the head of the vehicle column. Most of the GIs went to sleep after entering the truck. I asked Sergeant Smith what had occurred during the attack on the German positions yesterday.

"The company finally got to its object late in the morning. Then, we dug in."

"Sergeant, have you heard when we'll go back into the line?"

"No and I don't care. I've spent two years training for this thing. I've had two full days of it. That's enough for me."

Just after 0200, the trucks started their motors. We were going back to the battalion's resting place. Ten minutes later, someone shouted, "Hey, we're back at the junction of 56 and 57."

"Oh no, we're not going back to Gereonsweiler again," wailed another.

The lead truck stopped. Something was said to the MP stationed there. The trucks went back to Immendorf and took another road.

"Wouldn't you know it, just like the Army!" shouted a GI.

200

"They do it every time." added another voice in the darkened truck.

Just after 0300, the convoy stopped. Company E was ordered to detruck. Each platoon was assigned a house in which to sleep. Lieutenant Lusby turned to Crable and myself.

"You two just go to the end of the block. Battalion should be the last house on the right. See you tomorrow."

"Yes, Sir."

Upon arriving at the designated brick duplex, John and I found only Captain Thompson and two other enlisted men from Headquarters Company of the Second Battalion.

"You two can wait in the house here. The rest of Headquarters will be here soon." stated the Company Commander.

We sat in two straight-backed chairs and tried to get some sleep. While waiting for the remainder of the messengers, Captain Thompson began to talk about his experiences during the previous afternoon. His tone of voice was one of extreme anger.

"This afternoon, I went through one of the damnest times I have ever had in trying to arrange to get this space. When I walked into Division Headquarters, you'd think that I had committed some crime. They were all clean back there. They looked as if I should be the same. Some of those Division officers were almost insulting. Couldn't understand that I hadn't shaved this morning. Those nuts back there don't even know there's a war going on. I was ready to hit some of them."

Captain Thompson continued on this track of conversation for the next twenty minutes. He couldn't believe the treatment he had received from fellow officers at the Division Headquarters about his dress and manners. He kept repeating and repeating "none of them have seen any blood yet." The two enlisted men attempted to ask him questions but he monopolized the whole conversation. Finally John and I drifted off to sleep.

At 0430, the Headquarters Company of the Second Battalion arrived. Sergeant Butler quickly pointed out the basement of half a duplex which the messengers were to occupy. No one complained. An unoccupied bed was discovered by John and myself. We simply laid our two sleeping bags on it. Within the next five minutes everybody was fast asleep.

Four hours later, Corporal Kern shouted, "Breakfast is being served. If you want something hot, get there in fifteen minutes. The cooks won't wait any longer."

All eight messengers ate breakfast that day.

During the entire day, numerous messages had to be delivered to the four companies of the battalion. John and I alternated the delivery of reports and messages. The other six messengers did the same.

During our frequent trips to the companies, all of us tried to ascertain how many casualties had been sustained. Later we compared notes of what had happened during this initial attack on the part of the Second Battalion. Innes made the worst report.

"At the end of the attack, F Company didn't have one officer left. Two of them were wounded, one was captured and the rest just somehow left the company. Sergeant 'Buck' Hodges took over. He brought them back in. The second night out, almost one whole platoon was either captured or killed during a German counter-attack. We had about 50 taken from the company in this attack."

George Teets reported on the situation for Company G. "We had some casualties but not too many. I think we had about 45 in all. That's the best of the three rifle companies."

For H Company, Munos stated, "H company got a lot of men hit but no too many killed. The mortar section was ok. But not the machine gun section. They had ten killed and wounded."

Regarding Company E, John gave his report. "At least ten have been killed. They believe over 40 had been wounded. Captain Von Schriltz is missing, and everyone thinks he got killed during the counter-attack on Company F."

"You all know that Major Kennedy was wounded," added Corporal Kern. "Joe Iaconis, his driver, was killed by an 88 just outside the OP pill-box. It happened just before the withdrawal. One guy from the anti-tank platoon was killed. Three others from Headquarters Company were hit."

THE LULL BEFORE THE STORM

All of us wondered if any or all of us would ever live through the war. If the Germans fought like this for every inch of ground, we guessed the war would last another year.

About 1000, I undertook the task of shaving. It turned out to be a minor operation. Six days of growth were tough to remove. The razor blade seemed to take the skin along with the whiskers. The fact that cold water had to be used did not aid the process. However, a clean face was accomplished after six tries. Every man in the battalion had to do the same thing. All the messengers groaned and moaned as they took their beards off.

In the morning, we learned that we were in the German town of Palenberg. The town had not suffered much damage. Most of the brick two-story duplexes were in good condition. The front lines were, however, less than five miles away. Thus, the battalion could be sent, at a moment's notice, to reinforce any weak spots in the front line. We could hear the occasional barks from the heavier American artillery stationed nearby. Nevertheless, Palenberg meant safety. One could walk the streets without fear of a German 88 landing within the next minute or two. The Dutch border was only a quarter of a mile away.

At 1130, all the messengers had to undergo a foot inspection. Many of the men of the Second Battalion had to be evacuated for trench foot. This was a condition that the rifleman incurred when he had to remain outside night and day in the heavy wet clay that existed on the front. Some of the GIs suffered from frost bite. One case, from Company E, was so severe that the entire right foot had to be amputated that afternoon. Orders were issued after the inspection that, in the future, each man had to carry, on his person, an extra pair of socks. Although previous warnings had been issued, few had paid any attention to this order.

About 1330, Corporal Kern came in to make an announcement to the messengers.

"In a half hour, four of you are to get on trucks to go back to take a shower. Then, when the four get back, the other four can go."

203

A PRIVATE'S DIARY

"Why Corporal," joked Teets, it's only been a month since we had our last shower. We thought you'd never ask us."

"Taint funny, McTeets. Anyway, you decide among yourselves who will go first and who will go later. Any questions?"

At 1400, about half of the Second Battalion boarded trucks for the trip to the shower. It had been decided between John and myself that I would take the first shower.

In fifteen minutes, the trucks had arrived at a coal mine in Holland. We went into the building where the Dutch miners changed their clothes upon arrival in the morning and departure in the evening. Upon looking around, Teets asked, "Where are the lockers to hang your clothes?"

"Look up there, those chains will do it." answered Munos.

"Boy, what next?" replied George.

By means of a pulley, the chains lifted the clothes high into the ceiling. The chains were then normally locked so that no one could disturb one's clothes while he worked in the coal mine. The mine house where the Second Battalion took its showers had a large hole in the roof, apparently the result of some war action. Thus, the air was chilly. Yet, the hot water felt great. A month's dirt fell away. The shower coupled with the shave made one almost feel human again.

After the shower was completed, each enlisted man received a complete change of clothing. This meant new underwear, shirt, pants and socks. The same shoes were put back on. The clothing which was shed had been on every man in the battalion for a month.

After supper, conversation dwelt on our new battalion commander, Lieutenant Colonel Charles R. Urban.

I asked, "What does anyone know about Urban?"

"Everyone says he's a prick!" commented Walters.

"Why?"

"Back in Claiborne, he was the strictest officer on every type of inspection. If everything wasn't ok with him, you got no leave to go to Alexandria. I know cause he wouldn't let me go because my shave didn't suit him right down to his ass."

"Anyone else got a comment?" I inquired.

Corporal Kern added, "I hear he was very tough on everyone. He was Assistant Regimental Commander up to now. Supposedly he wasn't doing much back at Regiment. I think they want to see what he can do with a real command."

The general consensus was that if he made a good Battalion Commander, his past history should be forgotten. We would learn his true character too soon.

During the remainder of the evening, numerous messages had to be taken. One was that our short rest would end in about 24 hours. A few new officers were assigned to the various companies. This was particularly true of Company F. The best known of the new lieutenants was 'Buck' Hodges. That afternoon, he went back to the Headquarters of the Ninth Army. He had a Silver Star pinned on him and received his battle commission as a commissioned officer. Later we would learn that most medals pinned upon officers were not truly earned.

By 2100, every messenger was fast asleep.

Monday, December 4, 1944

By the time breakfast was finished, every enlisted man in the entire Second Battalion knew this would be his last day of rest before going up front again. Sergeant Butler informed the messengers that they would be divided in half. Four would be with the forward Observation Post while four would stay with the Battalion Command Post farther back. Each pair had to determine who would go forward.

"John, I'll go forward this time."

"No Don. I don't mind."

"John, you went forward last time. Let's alternate who's to remain with the Battalion Command Post."

"OK, but if either of us gets sick, let's forget the plan. It's fair if we're both healthy."

"I agree."

At 1900, the entire battalion was back on the trucks. After a twenty minute trip, we arrived just outside Prummern. Everyone was ordered off the trucks. I was now with Company E where I was to remain until the company was in place in its new front line positions. Then, my job was to report to the forward Command Post.

While leaning on the truck awaiting the order to move forward, the driver, whose name was John Marsh, asked, "How do you think it is up there?"

"Oh, not too bad or we'd have heard about it. Since I'm in communications we usually hear the news right away."

"Edwards, how far is the front away from here?"

"My guess is about three miles or so. It depends where you go. Is this the closest you usually get, Marsh?"

"Yes. But we've been shelled a couple of times."

"What do you do most of the time with your truck?"

"Jobs like this. Or hauling supplies from the depots back at Corps Headquarters up here. We keep going most of the time. It's not too dangerous but sometimes we don't get much sleep. Still it's better than being in your shoes. How do you think most of the guys like being in the Infantry?"

"Marsh, they'd rather be somewhere else. But you can't do much about it."

"Edwards, how do they like the Air Corps?"

"In my book, they do a lot of work. Especially true when we were over at a town named Gereonsweiler. Have you heard of it?"

"Sure have, Ed. Had a big tank battle there."

"The planes sure took care of the German artillery which kept shelling us. We might think they get too much credit but we can't do without them. Same thing is true of the artillery."

"Edwards, I hate to ask this, but what do you think your chances are of getting through this thing?"

"I really don't know Marsh. It all depends on how the war goes. I wish you could tell me what's going to happen."

At that moment, the order to fall in was given.

"Good luck!" shouted John Marsh as our column moved off.

"Thanks. I think I'll need it. Hope to see you again."

"Same here. Nice talking to you Edwards."

The line of march first taken by Company E was straight through Prummern. It seemed strangely quiet. A short distance out of the village, the marching column veered off the main road onto an open muddy field. A few minutes later Sergeant Smith said, "Four of you come with me to pick up ammo."

The main part of Company E continued on its march while the five of us veered off to the left toward another village. After a ten minute walk, we reached the two jeeps that belonged to Company E. The five of us took the company's bazookas and some extra ammunition from the jeeps. We walked another ten minutes until we reached a haystack in the middle of an open field. We were to rejoin the main body of Company E at this site. Upon reaching the spot, I asked, "Why didn't the company come this way?"

Joseph Deak of the Headquarters platoon answered, "If they had, we would have had a real shelling. Do you know you went right near the lines then?"

"No, Joe."

"You did. That's why we went in such a small group. Jerry won't fire when he only sees a small party like this. But if the whole company had come by, it would have been hell. We still might be getting it now."

"Where did all our platoons go then?"

"They took a long detour around that hill we went by. Jerry can't see them as easily. They'll be here in about fifteen minutes or so."

The five of us proceeded to wait in silence.

Forty-five minutes later, the main body of Company E appeared. Everything was checked. First, it was necessary to distribute the bazookas and the extra ammo. Second, a further check was made to see that all the platoons were present.

It was 2130. Company E proceeded forward on a very deliberate and slow march. Everybody seemed to be edgy. The American searchlights to light up our sector were on. Periodically, they would go off. By conversation, we knew that this was the method to relieve one company in the front line with another. To hopefully confuse the enemy, the lights went on and off in various sectors of the front. However, the Germans apparently wanted to see what was going on. Thus, when the search lights went out, bursting German flares would go up in the sky. The single flare would zoom high into the sky and light the entire countryside for what seemed like miles. At its zenith, the brightness was so great that I believed a book could be read with ease. Every time one of these enemy flares went off, the whole column stopped. We crouched and waited until the flare was gone. The enemy must have realized that something was going on for every ten to fifteen minutes, a few German mortar shells would land in the village ahead of us. Although the ground was wet, the physical strain was not too bad. But the nervous tension of waiting, then, listening to the German shells was on everyone's mind. Very few words were spoken. All seemed to know what was to be done under the circumstances.

We plodded through a huge open field and over a communication's trench. Then we passed through a large tank trap that the enemy had dug to prevent our tanks from coming forward. Company E proceeded into a narrow gulley. Here we met a company from the 334th Infantry Regiment. They were going back for a rest. Nary a word was spoken between those going forward and those going to the rear. We came to the next obstacle. It was a large pile of rocks that had accumulated when the Germans had blown a viaduct in their retreat. Thus, no vehicles could enter the village ahead. After climbing over the rock pile, the village was entered. We broke into a trot on what appeared to be the village green in order to reach some buildings on the other side.

The various platoons of Company E took their places in the front line. The company headquarters were in a farm house just yards behind the front. After the changing or relief was completed about 2300, Lieutenant Lusby turned to three of us in the farm house stating, "Sleep in that barn on the other side of the house. It has some hay in it. If you hear any shell fire, get up ready."

Deak, Norris and I followed his orders. In thirty minutes, we were asleep with our rifles laying next to us.

THE LULL BEFORE THE STORM

Tuesday, December 5, 1944

Daylight came just before 0700. It came with a jolt.

A German mortar shell dropped in the barnyard next to the barn. It must have been a small shell for the wood of the barn easily stopped the fragments.

"I am thinking this place is strictly unhealthy." stated Norris.

"How right you are!" echoed Deak.

"I think we should report to company headquarters. At least, it's in a building that should be safer," I added.

"Lead the way, Edwards, we're coming," replied Norris.

After reporting to company headquarters, I was ordered to go next door to the battalion advanced command post. Only a small pathway separated Company E from the battalion headquarters.

By 0830, the entire personnel of the battalion advanced command post was there. It consisted of the Battalion Commander, Lieutenant Colonel Urban; the S-3 of the Battalion, Captain Price; one radio operator, two wiremen and the four messengers. Three of us had had experience as messengers, namely, Rochester, Teets and myself. The new messenger was Frank Major who was the new runner for H company. During the day, the three of us told Frank what his duties would be. He seemed to think it would be easier than feeding ammo to a machine gun.

The nine of us were housed in the cellar of an old farmhouse. The cellar had an exceedingly low ceiling. My running of messages was very easy because of the near location of my company. During the entire day, very few German shells were heard. The front was very quiet. Actually it seemed too quiet for a normal day. Every two hours, I relieved Corporal Burgett of his task of listening to the radio. During my four hours of being on the radio that day, only one message came to the advanced CP.

Because of the quiet day, the messengers were permitted to remain on the first floor in a room which faced the village green. We learned that the name of the village was Leiffarth. The village was shaped in the form of a triangle. Houses were

209

along the outer edge. In the center was an open space. On this village green, a few goats and cows grazed. Their own concern seemed to be to eat. During the next few days, we noted that these animals would return to their barns for the night. Then, the next morning they would be out grazing. Yet not one single German civilian was there to tend them. In the barn where I had rested the previous night was a trapped cow. During the day, the animal mooed continuously. In front of the cow was a fallen beam. Although several of us could have removed the beam, we did not do so because of a fear of German shelling. After hearing the cow moo for three days, Rochester suggested, "Let's shoot her and put her out of her misery."

Teets replied, "That won't do any good. If the front moves up, then, someone can get that beam removed. If she dies, we can't prevent that, but if she lives, she might do someone some good."

"I agree with George, let her alone." I added.

Major agreed with George and me. The cow was permitted to live. When we left Leiffarth, the cow was still mooing.

After our K-ration supper, the messengers were ordered to sleep in the cellar. We asked to remain on the first floor but our request was denied. No one wanted to sleep in the cellar which not only had a low ceiling but was filled with potatoes. Concrete and ground were difficult to sleep on, but potatoes outranked them in discomfort. The four messengers were also ordered to stand guard duty in single three hour shift. I was to have the last shift the next morning.

Wednesday, December 6, 1944

At 0400, George Teets awoke me. "Don, it's time for your shift."

"Thanks, George, anything to report?"

"Nothing happening. It's just dead silence. Don't forget your hand grenades."

"I won't George. Hope I don't have to use them."

Daylight did not come for another three hours. The main purpose of the guarding was to see that no German patrols were walking in or near Leiffarth.

Just after daylight, I awoke all the personnel of the advanced Battalion Command Post. Upon arising Rochester commented, "I've been in the Army for eight years. I ain't never slept on something so hard. I've been on everything from hard earth to inner spring mattresses. That's the limit."

George Teets added, "Men, we've got to ask to be on the first floor. It may be dangerous but if we do the guard duty, we shouldn't have much to worry about. Edwards, why don't you ask Captain Price?"

"Thanks for the favor men. I'll do it."

Inside of five minutes, I made this request to the Captain. To my plea, he said, "Edwards, I don't want to do it, but I can understand after sleeping on those potatoes. Since you four have to be the guards, I'll let you do it."

"We appreciate it Captain."

An hour later Captain Price was back to ask a favor of me. Although it could have easily been an order, he requested, "Edwards, could you take this fire over-lay back to Major Lamb after you finish eating?"

"Yes, Sir, I will do it for you."

"You must get someone to go with you. The other messengers must stay here. Go over to Company E and ask someone. Let me know immediately when you get back."

In the next few minutes, I had persuaded Ed Norris to accompany me on this journey. Before departing, Ed and I looked at the fire over-lay. We took two deep glups. The positions held by the Second Battalion were extremely exposed. Leiffarth was like a sore thumb in the German lines except where the front ran off the outside joint. We could easily see that if the Germans launched a good counter-attack, they could isolate the battalion from the adjoining American troops.

After folding the over-lay and placing it in the usual upper left shirt pocket, Norris and I left the advanced Command Post. We hurried across the open village green until the gulley was reached. We walked along the edges of the gulley. Lying

still were, at least, twelve dead German and American soldiers.
All had been turned over so that their faces could not be seen.
It was apparent that, because of the tactical situation, the
Graves Registration unit did not have adequate time to pick up
these bodies. Upon passing over the blown overpass and further
up the gulley, we saw a pillbox. We trotted to this pillbox.
Inside was Lieutenant Nablo, the battalion's S-2, and his section
of five enlisted men. This was the battalion's OP or observation
post. It rested on a hill which commanded the surrounding
countryside. With some borrowed field glasses, we could see the
enemy soldiers going in and out of pillboxes on the German
side of the front.

After resting five minutes, Norris and I proceeded on our
journey back to the main battalion Command Post. Although
we must have presented a good target to the enemy, no shots
were fired at us. After a half hour of walking through mud, we
reached headquarters. I turned over the fire over-lay plan to
Major Oakley Lamb, the Second Battalion's Executive Officer.

After my delivery, I turned to face John Crable.

"Don, how are you? What are you doing here?"

"Norris and I came back to give Major Lamb the fire over-
lay that Captain Price made out."

"How are things on the front up in Leiffarth?"

"John, I think it's pretty quiet. But after seeing that over-
lay, I can't understand why the Germans haven't tried to cut us
off from the other parts of the American line."

"Don, they might, but everybody around here thinks the
enemy has lost a lot of men in these battles. Let me show you
around this pillbox. From here you can see why the battalion
had such a hard time getting possession of this place."

Crable proceeded to give Norris and myself a complete
tour of the captured German pillbox. It was composed of four
rooms. The front one had two slits which looked out over a
broad plain. Just a few days ago, the Second Battalion had
attacked across this very field. A machine gun placed in one of
the slits could easily pin down hundreds of men. There was a
small sleeping room with eight bunks. Another was an ammuni-

tion room. In the back was a room which led to the back side of the hill with a single door. Everything was solid concrete.

After chatting with some of the other personnel, we made our way back to Leiffarth. We walked to the OP, rested, then trotted to the gulley and back into the village.

About 1630, the Germans threw about twelve mortar shells into the village green, killing or wounding one goat. No one went to assist the poor creature.

About 2100, the bearers of the K-rations arrived. The party that did this worked anywhere from 1900 one night until 0300 or 0400 the next morning. This hand transportation was night work because of the exposed trail during daylight hours. These supply trains were composed of men from the Ammunition & Pioneer platoon from the Headquarters Company of the Second Battalion. Each night at least two trips had to be made. On the first trip, a minimum of 2,000 K rations had to be transported since there were approximately 600 plus men on the front line. On the second trip, ammunition for the mortars and machine guns were brought. If required, miscellaneous items were brought on a third trip. The rations and other supplies were always brought to our dwelling. Then, each messenger had to notify his company of the arrival of the supplies. Each of us then assisted in the transportation of the supplies to our respective company.

Just after 2230 that evening, I had to deliver a message to my company. As I stepped in the door, a voice greeted me.

"How are you, Don?"

"John Crable, what are you doing here at this ridiculous hour? You're supposed to be back at the CP!"

"Just came to get the morning report."

"But why so late, don't you know it's 10:30 at night?"

"We're lucky that we got here at all. We started from the command pillbox about seven o'clock."

"What happened? It took Norris and me about forty-five minutes to walk from the CP."

"The first part of the trip was ok. We reached the OP pillbox without any trouble. Lieutenant Nablo then told us about the gulley we had to make in order to get into Leiffarth. We

213

left soon after. But we couldn't find the gulley. We kept wandering about those open fields without any sense of direction. We didn't want to wander into the enemy lines and be captured. Finally a voice said, 'Halt!' We gave the right password. The rifleman in that foxhole said that if we had gone about another 300 yards we would have been in German hands. We were just plain lucky. Then he showed us how to get back to the OP. We were there in ten minutes. Lieutenant Nablo had one of his S-2 men take us down to the gulley. He left us and we made it into Leiffarth."

"John, do you think you and the other messengers can find your way back?"

"Don, I don't think we'll have any trouble getting out. How have things been up here today?"

"Nothing to worry about so far. Did you see the fire overlay?"

"Yes."

"Then you know the tactical situation we're in."

"I realize it. No tanks can get in here to support you. It could turn into a mess."

After a few more words, John received the necessary reports from Company E and departed.

Upon my return to the other forward messengers, we decided that two hour shifts on guard would be used during this night. But our sleeping quarters for this night would be on the first floor. Everyone of us was delighted to sleep on a hard flat wood floor instead of bumpy potatoes.

Thursday, December 7, 1944

My tour on guard duty came from 0100 to 0300. The hardest task was to keep alert since silence prevailed. During the two hours I was awake, not a single sound was heard.

At our usual K-ration breakfast around 0800, the four messengers discussed the fact that this was the third anniversary of Pearl Harbor. We were unanimous in our opinions that the war with Germany was far from over. The day was unusual in that not a single shot of any type was heard.

Because we had very little to do except our usual routine of delivering messages, the four of us decided to clean all the rooms on the first floor in order to make it a nicer place to exist. Rochester secured a broom and pan from one of the vacant village stores. He also brought some rags for dusting. We then moved furniture about and tried to rearrange things so that they looked presentable. During our labors, Captain Price came up from the cellar to observe our cleaning job.

"Men, I've got to admire you. You are putting in a lot of effort for the short time you'll be in this place."

"Well, Captain, we might as well do something with our time than lay around." replied Teets.

"I guess you're right. If you want to do the cellar let me know."

"No thank you, Captain, those potatoes can't be cleaned," I answered.

When Captain Price departed, Teets remarked, "You know Edwards, he's just about the perfect officer, if there ever is one."

"George, I agree."

"Captain Price can actually give you an order, and, yet, you think that you're doing it cause it's the right thing. Also, Don, he's one of the smartest guys I've ever seen in this Army. Wonder how he ever got here?"

"I wish I knew, George. All I know is that he's from some place in New York. I think it's from somewhere around New York City."

After lunch, I wandered about the village of Leiffarth in a very careful manner. I went into the vacant shops and houses looking for an item like a rug to furnish our newly cleaned quarters. Just after 1550, I returned to the messenger's quarters when Teets asked me, "Ed, have you heard the latest?"

"No George, what has happened in the hour I've been gone? I didn't hear any shells falling."

"Urban is going to leave!"

"What, you've got to be kidding. Lieutenant Colonel Charles R. Urban is going to leave and go where?"

"He's going back to the regular CP."

215

"When George?"

"Heard it's going to be just before dark. Guess he got cold feet and wants to go back to a safe place."

"Who else is he taking with him?"

"Captain Price and Burgett. Don't worry, we messengers are going to stay right here in Leiffarth."

At exactly 1708, our battalion commander scurried across the village green to the gulley.

"There goes our hope for the Colonel," said Rochester.

"Just look at that walk," added Teets. "I didn't know he could walk so fast. He sure is in a hurry to leave this place. He didn't get out of that cellar during the whole time here unless he had to piss or shit."

Although there was no one to order us to stand guard, the four messengers decided after supper that we would maintain the usual guard procedure of two hours per man. I was selected to maintain the first watch from 2230 to 0100 the next morning.

During my shift, one of the wiremen was sick with diarrhea. But he was afraid to leave since he feared there would be no replacement for him. He realized how vital the wire link to the rear was to the forward Battalion Command Post. Upon his return to the cellar after his third trip in less than ninety minutes, I asked him, "Why don't you go over to the medics and be evacuated?"

"Edwards, there's no one to take my place."

"They'll send someone up if you leave. Don't worry about that."

"Ed, I'll get over it tomorrow."

"By that time, you may not be able to move. Then you'll be more trouble than if you go over there now."

"Are the medics still up?"

"Go over to their bunker. Wake them if they're asleep. I don't think they are since the ration party hasn't come in for their second trip."

"Edwards, I'll do it. Let me get my rifle and see what they say."

As he departed I said, "You'll be back in a few days, fit as a fiddle."

"Ed, I hope so. I've been getting the trots fairly regular. Again thanks for helping me, you've been a real friend."

It was the last time I ever saw him. The next morning, I learned he was evacuated when the ration party came for their second round trip. His name was never known to me but the rumor mill stated he was sent back to the rear for easier and lighter duty because of his run-down condition.

Friday, December 8, 1944

The daylight hours were spent in the usual dull do-nothing routine. While chatting with George Teets, he pointed out something of interest to the other three messengers.

"Fellas, the next time a barrage comes in, look at those animals out there in the center of this place."

About 1000, the Germans threw into the center of the town ten to fifteen mortar shells. Every bull, cow, goat or horse stood absolutely still. They would not eat when the barrage was going on. After the last shell exploded, they would wait approximately ten minutes, then, resume their eating of the village green grass.

The messengers witnessed this three additional times during this day.

Since water was a necessity to us, the messengers went periodically to a well located about 200 yards north of our dwelling. A water can was then filled and returned to the CP to be used by everyone until a re-fill was needed. On my first trip in the morning to fetch water, Jim Rochester decided to come with me. When we arrived at the well, Rochester exclaimed, "Don, look at that dead Corporal there!"

"Rochester, he can't do us any harm now."

"I know, but let's get him out of the way. It's easier to get water for us then."

"Sounds like a good idea to me, Sarge."

"You move him, please."

"OK, I'll do it."

With my left foot, the Lance Corporal was turned over so that his face looked upward at us. This German soldat appeared to be about 17 or 18 years of age, a ruddy complexion with the usual long hair that the enemy seemed to wear. His face had an expression of relief. Apparently the end had finally come. This Wehrmacht corporal had been hit by three bullets right through and around the region of the stomach. It appeared as if he was going onto the village green when he had been hit. After looking at him with Rochester, I took both his limp arms and dragged him about ten yards away. That evening he was evacuated to the rear by the Graves Registration unit which had been gradually clearing Leiffarth of deceased bodies.

Just after darkness fell, the messengers had company in their newly cleaned living room. They were thirty replacements for the three rifle companies. They were made comfortable until someone from their respective units came for them. Inasmuch as the four messengers had secured some candles from the vacated stores, we invited them in until they had to leave. We were talking with these new replacements telling them how quiet things were in Leiffarth, when a shout was heard.

"Grenade!"

Everyone hit the floor. Candles went out. Darkness reigned. Confusion was prevalent. My first thought was that a German patrol had slipped into the village. Probably the patrol had thrown a grenade when ordered to halt by the guard which we always had after dusk. Yet, no rifle shots were heard. Two minutes later, cries and yells were piercing the air.

"Help! Help! Somebody help me!"

That was strange. I thought the shouts came from the backyard.

"Let's get up off the floor and see what's wrong," suggested Rochester.

At that moment, Frank Major, the person on guard, came into the room.

"There's seven men out here who were hit by the mortar."

"We better bring them in here. There's some light and some blankets for them to lay on," I answered.

The replacements were ordered to go into the cellar to wait. The rest of us carried the wounded into our living quarters.

"Don, can you go across and tell the Medics what happened?" shouted Teets.

"I'm on my way, George."

A quick dash was made across the open village green. Upon entering the Aid Station, I was ordered to give the correct password. After doing this, I stated, "Seven men have been hit across the way. Can a couple of you come along with the Doc?"

One of the medics answered, "We'll do what we can but the Doc isn't here."

"Where is he?"

"The Colonel took him back with him last night when he left."

"Well, let's hurry as fast as you can. We'll hope for the best."

Upon returning to the messenger's quarters, all seven wounded men were laid out on our blankets. The worst case was the lieutenant who was in charge of the group. His head was hit in at least five places. Fortunately for the injured, I knew it was, probably, only a 60 mm mortar shell that had hit them. If it had been an 88 from an artillery gun, none would be alive.

Three medics from the Aid Station came in a few minutes. They tried to assist the wounded as much as possible. It seemed that, in most of the cases, fragments were lodged in their bodies. These fragments could not be removed in Leiffarth. We presumed that if the Doctor had been present, something more might have been done for these wounded. Upon hearing where the Doctor was, one of wounded exclaimed, "Boy what nerve! Taking the Doc back for himself. That jerk only thinks of himself."

One-by-one the wounded were taken away on stretchers. Each had to be carried back to the forward OP. At that site was a weasel — an open track vehicle for carrying infantrymen — on which the stretchers could be placed. The wounded were driven back to the village of Beeck. At 2300, the task of transporting the wounded was complete. I turned to Frank Major and asked, "How did this happen?"

219

"Just a few minutes after you took those replacements in, Don, these fellows from the Anti-Tank Company came by wheeling their gun. I asked them where they were going. They said up the hill to put their gun into position. Just as they got their 57 gun into the backyard, WHAM! I think I heard two mortars hit. They were all out on the ground when I got there. They were crying for help. That's when I went to fetch you. All of them got hit you know."

Saturday, December 9, 1944

After my quiet tour of guard duty from 0500 to 0700, I was allowed to sleep another hour before delivering my first message of the day to Company E. During the morning, the Germans lopped a few mortars into Leiffarth, but there were no casualties, either human or animal.

After delivering a can of water about 1500, I said to my fellow messengers, "I'm going down to that little village store just before the well."

"OK Don, just don't walk out into the open." answered Teets.

"I won't. It doesn't look as if the Germans are going to try anything today."

I proceeded to the little store which still had some clothes in it but I could not find any extra blankets that might be needed by us. We were short due to the lending to the wounded the previous night. Just before 1600, a goat appeared at the doorway, as if to enter. I moved to the doorway, intending to hit the goat with the butt of my M-1 rifle. I never made it. Down on my helmet came the ceiling and part of the overhang. I looked down to see that the clothing of my right forearm had been ripped. A cut which was bleeding had been made. My guess was that a mortar shell had just hit above me. I placed my rifle down and secured my whole bandage which was carried by all front line soldiers. I easily wrapped it around the cut.

A quick trip was made to Company E. The Germans had started their attack to push us out of Leiffarth. Mortars and 88s began to rain down all over the village. Since none of the battalion staff was in Leiffarth, the defense was to be conducted by the officers of Company E. Upon reaching the headquarters of Company E, I went to the second story where the front lines could be seen. Lieutenant Charles Gavin, platoon leader of Company E's third platoon, was observing the German attack with his binoculars. Norris, Deak and myself were with him as he watched the Germans mount their attack against the upper joint of the thumb that extended into the German lines. After the preliminary bombardment, the enemy infantry started to come out of their foxholes, crawling very slowly. The three of us in a prone position were ready to fire our rifles from the second story windows, if required. No window had any glass in it. Downstairs, the forward artillery observers were calling their battery.

"Charlie Two, this is Charlie One, over. Charlie Two this is Charlie One, over."

For over a minute, the intermediate radio possessed by the artillery personnel between the front and the artillery positions could not be reached. Norris asked, "Edwards, what's going to happen if the battery can't be reached?"

"Ed, don't worry, they'll reach it, otherwise, we've got trouble spelled with a capital 'T'."

We all knew that we would have one grand retreat for without artillery, the Germans could have blasted their way through our lines. But, after a few more calls from Leiffarth, a voice replied, "Charlie One, this is Charlie Two, over."

"Counter-attack is underway. Ready battery, over."

"Will repeat to Charlie Three, Roger."

We could hear Charlie Two alerting the artillerymen that an attack was underway. Charlie One then gave orders to zero in on a certain designated target. Within two minutes, a few trial shells were fired. Then a salvo was ordered. Now the mortars on the American side began to spit out their shells. The 60 and 80 mm. shells could be heard zinging overhead from all directions. Within five minutes after the American fire power was observed, the German infantry withdrew back into their

221

prepared positions. The men of the Second Battalion did not fire a single shot. But everybody was ready.

"Fellows, they've got back into their lines," commented Joe Deak.

My answer was, "I think they wanted to find out how strong the line was held by us."

"Don, I think you're right," added Ed Norris. "Seems they came out of their line very slowly as if to see if we were ready. We were so that's that."

Dead silence again prevailed at 1620. I returned to the other messengers who had remained at the battalion forward CP.

The enemy did not hurl a single shell during the entire night. After my tour of guard duty from 2200 to 2400, I slept soundly.

Sunday, December 10, 1944

Since the messengers were so confident that the Germans would not attack us this day, we did not arise until almost 0900, at which time a message had to be taken to all the companies.

After returning from my trip to Company E, George Teets remarked, "Don, what happened to your right front sleeve?"

"Not much George, just before the attack yesterday, the roof at that store came down on me."

"Were you hurt?"

"I just got a cut on my right arm."

"Don, didn't you go to the medics with it?"

"No, I just bandaged it and came back to watch the Germans come out of their trenches and then go back in."

"I think you ought to report it to the medics and let them take a look at it."

"George, it's only a cut about three or four inches long."

"Private Donald Edwards, if it becomes infected, you might have real trouble. Get over to the medics."

Jim Rochester added, "Edwards, we'll cover for you if a message needs to be given to E Company."

Two minutes later, I scurried across the open green to the medics.

"Halt, who goes there?"

"Private Edwards from Company E."

"What can we do for you?"

"I got a cut on my right arm just before the Jerry attack yesterday."

"Is it serious?"

"I don't think so. I have a bandage over it and it doesn't hurt."

"I'll get the fellows and we'll take a look at it."

The examination by the medics took only a few minutes. A new thinner bandage was placed over the wound. Instructions were given that if it began to hurt to let them know. Otherwise, they would not expect to see me again.

Just after our K ration lunch, Norris came to visit the messengers.

"Edwards, did you hear the good news?"

"No, Ed, what's going to happen?"

"The battalion's being relieved tonight."

"What time, Ed?"

"Sometime after darkness falls."

At 1830, the four messengers each reported to his respective company. We knew from previous experience that each of us would return to learn the rest location of our company. Then each messenger would report to the battalion headquarters.

Darkness fell. The floodlights came on. At times, one or more of them would go off. With one person always on guard, we continued to wait. Midnight came. Not a single unit had been relieved.

Monday, December 11, 1944

My time for the guard shift came from 0001 to 0100. Silence prevailed the entire time.

At 0200, Sergeant Smith announced to the headquarters platoon, "Ten men from the platoon are to leave now."

"Where do we go Sarge?" asked someone.

223

"We're to go to the anti-tank ditch and wait until the whole company is there. Any questions? The rest of the platoon will follow in about an hour."

The order was followed. Each man trotted across Leiffarth until the blown-up railway debris was reached. He proceeded up the ravine to the battalion OP. In a half hour, the ditch was reached. With one man standing guard, the rest of us curled up and attempted to snooze.

From 0230 to 0330, small groups of men from Company E would reach the anti-tank ditch. Most laid down on the hard cold soil and tried to rest. Those from the rifle platoons seemed particularly tired from their vigils in the foxholes.

"Where's that sack?"

"I thought you guys would have my inter-spring ready."

"Where are those deep cushions?"

Similar remarks continued throughout the hour. A few men from Company E went deep into the trench to puff away on their cigarettes. The tension was present at all times, although there was no immediate danger. Every fifteen minutes, a few shells could be heard falling somewhere along the front. Little attention was paid to them. However, none were falling in Leiffarth.

By 0330, Company E was fully assembled. The trek to the trucks started. A ten minute walk brought us to the jeeps belonging to the company. Here the bazookas and other heavy equipment of the company was deposited. No ammunition of any kind, except that which each GI carried, was brought out of Leiffarth.

After the equipment was loaded, the march continued across a wide open flat pasture. The pace was fast. As we walked, it was noticed that a large number of jeeps seemed to be going and coming. I learned that extra vehicles from other battalions were being used to shuttle some of the men to the trucks. I did not ask for this service since I knew that others were in worse shape than myself.

Just before 0430, Company E entered the town of Prummern. It seemed fast asleep. But everybody knew that guards were posted for any emergency. Next to each structure in Prummern seemed to stand some type of U.S. Army vehicle, largely jeeps.

Outside of Prummern, the 2¹/₂ ton trucks were waiting. Company E was the second outfit of the battalion to arrive. After boarding, everyone went to sleep.

"Hey, soldiers, wake up, we're here." came the command from Sergeant Smith.

All the GIs pulled themselves up and jumped from the truck. Company E was standing in front of a group of terraces. On the other side of the street was a railway track which was in need of repair. Orders were given to the various platoons to move into a designated dwelling. After all had disappeared, I approached Lieutenant Lusby.

"Edwards, battalion is supposed to be in the same place as it was last time."

"OK, Lieutenant, I think I can find it."

My answer was a surprise for it indicated that we were back in Palenberg. A walk was undertaken to find the center of town. Once I located this spot, I knew the message center was easily located. I took only ten minutes to find the message center. My arrival came just before 0800. I found four of the messengers, who had been back at the battalion CP, sound asleep. I turned around to see George Teets.

"George Teets, where have we met before?"

"Knock it off Don, let's get some sleep."

"I'm with you George."

My rest lasted exactly twelve minutes. At 0812, John Crable, poked me in the ribs with the greeting, "Don, breakfast is ready."

"John, I've just got to sleep."

"I don't care. Don you'd better eat the hot meal now. I'll take any messages this morning. Eat, then sleep till noon."

John's idea was followed that day.

During the morning hours, the four messengers who had had adequate sleep went to other vacant Palenberg residences and took some mattresses for use by the eight of us.

At lunch time, the tension I had felt in Leiffarth had left.

225

At 1300, John brought letters from our loved ones that had been received during our stay at the front. My super beard that had grown in Leiffarth was taken off during the afternoon hours. During this time, I went to the battalion switchboard and telephone Al Barkey, who I had not seen since London. I made arrangements to meet him at 1900.

After the hot supper was served at 1800, I walked over the area that was supposed to be occupied by Company A of the 333rd Infantry Regiment. Upon my arrival, I met a GI who was looking at the vacant houses.

"Can you tell me if this is where Company A is located?"

"It was."

"What do you mean it was?"

"Company A left for the front about a half hour ago. I think it was sudden. My own outfit's due back tonight."

"Thanks for the help." I answered.

Although disappointed, I realized that sudden decisions could always be expected in the war zone.

After writing a few letters back home, I retired. Every messenger was in bed by 2100. One had to sleep whenever the occasion presented itself.

Tuesday, December 12, 1945

At 0745, Sergeant Butler yelled, "Men, it's breakfast at 0800. They're going to serve until the line runs out."

Every messenger was in line at 0800.

After breakfast, we were informed that hot showers were available to us either in the morning or afternoon. John Crable and I discussed who would be the first to take a shower.

"I'd appreciate it, John, if I could be the first this time."

"It's agreeable with me Don, and let's keep this arrangement. Whoever is up front gets to go first."

"I agree. From the looks of things, we're going to be here in this general area for a long, long time."

My prediction turned out to be incorrect just a short week later.

226

At 0930, four of the messengers were off to the showers in Holland. We went to the same coal mine where we hung our clothes up in the air.

Upon my arrival back, John had secured my duffel bag. This enabled me to secure clean clothes for another period of time. My cut had healed and only a scar remained from the roof falling in on me.

During my absence, John had heard a rumor which none of us wanted to hear.

"Don, I heard we might to go the front again tonight."

"What happened? Did the Germans try again at Leiffarth?"

"Somebody thinks they did since they knew a new unit was in the line."

"Who replaced us, John?"

"First Battalion of the 334th."

"Are they low in men?"

"About half our size. They lost a lot of men taking Prummern. They've had some replacements, but they're still below strength. One of our companies might have to go to reinforce them. Everyone thinks it will be Company G. Let's hope it's just a rumor. Four messengers will be in Leiffarth if G goes into the line."

"I hope it's just a rumor John. But in my opinion, as long as the artillery is there for use, Leiffarth can't be taken."

By evening, we heard that our artillery had fired numerous rounds at the Germans and this must have deterred the enemy from any attack.

After lunch, John Crable went to the nearby Catholic Church to inquire about the possibility of attending mass in the church. After he returned from his shower at the mine, he told me about the interesting conversations he had had with the German priest.

"Do you remember, Don, that I went over to see the priest at the church?"

"I sure do, John, what did you find out?"

"Well, Mass is said each morning at eight. He invited me to come to church tomorrow if we are here."

227

"Do you want me to come along too?"

"I sure do, the two of us can protect each other if needed."

"How did you talk with the priest?"

"The father understood English quite well. I asked him how everything was. He told me about the treatment he had received at the hands of the Americans. When our Army entered the town, he claimed that the Americans had ruined all his vestments."

"Anything else?"

"The priest claimed the Americans damaged his church."

"Did you ask him if the Germans tried to use it as a defense post?"

"He claimed the Germans would not do such a thing."

"I can say one thing, John, he hasn't been around very much. Those steeples are the best place in the world for artillery spotters. I'll bet he was in the cellar the whole time our Army was driving the Germans out. What else did he say?"

"One interesting thing I found out was when I asked him about the Nazi people and his treatment by them."

"What was his reply to that, John?"

"His English failed him. He didn't seem to understand what I was talking about. Yet, he understood everything else I said to him in English. Personally, I think he didn't want to care to discuss it. You'll see him in church tomorrow morning. Tell me what you think of him."

"After mass, I'll tell you what I think. That is one of my shortcomings."

The evening was devoted to letter writing and chatter among the six remaining messengers. The other two had gone to Holland. In the afternoon, after his return from a shower, Hugh Walters, the new messenger from Company G, asked his fellow runner, George Teets, if he could depart.

"George, would you mind if I took off for a few days?"

"I don't think so, where are you going?"

"That's a lousy question, I think you know where I'm going."

"You mean you're going to shack up somewhere."

"That's right, George, I'm going to get some ass and plenty of it when I've got the chance."

"I think I can handle the messages, but will you be back when the battalion leaves?"

"I'll check every day. I want some pussy, but I don't want to get locked up over some bitch."

"As long as I don't get blamed if you miss our leaving for the front. I'll take care of all the messages."

"Thanks, George, I'll be enjoying myself all night long. And maybe part of the day too. See you in a few days."

After Walters left, Frank Major asked a somewhat like favor of this partner from Company H, Charlie Simon.

"Charlie, I'd like to take off for a few days. Can you handle the messages for Company H?"

"Frank, are you going with Walters?"

"No, he's going to some cat house he heard about in Holland. I think it's in Heerlin."

"You're going to some other cat house?"

"No, I'm just going to stay with some Dutch family where we took our showers. I've just got to get away from this Army stuff. It's driving me nuts."

"Any dame with this family?"

"I don't think so. I'm not going to shack up with some dame. Believe me."

"OK, we believe you, but don't come back here bragging about your conquests later. I'll cover for you while you are gone. But be back here when we leave."

"I'll be back every day about noon to check on the situation."

Wednesday, December 13, 1944

At 0720, John poked me in the ribs, "Don, it's time to get up for Mass."

"Roger, John, just let me wash my face and I'll be ready."

After accomplishing this task, I inquired, "Shall we both take our rifles?"

"No, one should be enough. You take yours, Don. One of us will stay with it at all times, church or no church."

By 0800, we were in the German church. We sat in the next to the last pew. Ten minutes later, the priest appeared. He saw us and came to our pew.

"Are you going to Communion this morning?"

"Yes," replied John for both of us.

Nothing was said about the rifle which was between the two of us.

Close to the front of the church were about ten German civilians. Several glances were made in our direction. My guess was that we were the first Americans to attend this German church.

Mass was said in the usual Latin form. We followed our agreed-upon-procedure in the taking of communion — one man always with the rifle. The German priest was fully robed. There were two candles lighted upon the altar and full wafers were given to the communicants. The interior of the church had suffered no damage. Outside, the structure had only a few bricks that had been hit by some bullets or small mortar fire. In comparison to the churches in towns like Prummern and Gereonsweiler, the church was in excellent shape. Outside after service, I remarked, "John, he doesn't seem to be lacking for anything as far as I can see."

"I think you're right but that's not the way he looks at it."

At 1000 that morning, the Headquarters Company, Second Battalion had a treat in the form of the Red Cross Clubmobile. Every GI was out to see the girls. Because of our location, civilians were a rare sight. Along with the serving of the doughnuts, the Red Cross representative from the 335th Infantry Regiment was on hand to assist with any home problems that a GI might have. After a half hour, the Red Cross personnel left.

When I was returning from lunch, Private George Booth stopped me.

"Don, would you ride with me to Regiment this afternoon?"

"I have nothing to do, if John agrees to take the messages for our company."

"Let me know in ten minutes, will you?"

"Will do George."

Crable had no objections.

At 1315, the ride started. Booth was the messenger from the Second Battalion to the 335th Regimental Headquarters. The ride was pleasant. It afforded an opportunity to see what was behind the front lines. The first surprise was the large number of artillery guns. They came, it seemed, in all sizes. The largest was the huge 155 millimeter howitzers. However, none of the artillery batteries were firing as we passed them.

The second surprise was the vehicle traffic that prevailed. All of it was military. It appeared that trucks of all descriptions, troop carriers and hundreds of jeeps were all going somewhere.

Along portions of the badly torn roads, the U.S. Army engineers were at work with their shovels, picks and other tools trying to put the roads back in shape.

The usual half wrecked houses, burned out tanks, discarded rifles, abandoned gas masks and countless strands of telephone wire were seen everywhere. The entire trip went without incident.

That evening, at 1830, a movie was scheduled to be shown at the local cinema house. All six messengers were in attendance. Permission had been obtained from Sergeant Butler for everyone to attend. We arrived at 1800. We waited for sixty minutes. Every seat in the theatre was taken. At 1900, a Staff Sergeant made an announcement, "I'm sorry to say that there will be no show tonight."

"Boo, Boo!!"

"Just like the Army."

"This chicken-shit Army never does anything right."

However, the dejected soldiers quietly filed back to their German dwellings.

A PRIVATE'S DIARY

Thursday, December 14, 1944

By 0800, all six messengers were up. We were ready to depart for breakfast when George Teets announced, "My company is having pancakes today, why not join Company G?"

Innes inquired, "Will they let us eat there? Besides what's Headquarters having today?"

"I don't think we'll have any trouble if you go in line with me. Headquarters is having the same old powdered eggs. Pancakes are better."

The five of us followed George through the G Company's chow line. Each of us had three servings before going back to our cellar.

At 1000, Protestant services were held for the men of the Second Battalion. Innes, Rochester and Teets attended. Upon their return, Crable asked, "How was attendance today?"

"Best they ever had," replied Innes.

"How many were there?"

"I don't know. But they all couldn't get into that room. It was that full. It's surprising how many are going to church now."

"Guess war does something to men."

"It must by the number we had today."

The most pronounced change among the messengers was noted in Sergeant James Rochester. While we were at Leiffarth, he had begun to read the Bible at least twice a day. During our rest in Palenberg, he continually quoted Bible passages to the other messengers. He prayed that he might be protected during these trying times. When he left later in the morning, Innes commented, "Fellows, you watch Rochie. If things appear safe, he'll forget all about this religion and Bible stuff."

At 1600, Catholic mass was said for the members of the battalion. It was held in the same German church that John and I attended the previous morning. As expected, every Catholic of the Second Battalion was present. Everyone was very serious in their worship. As we returned to our billet, Crable remarked, "Did you notice, Don, the Catholic services have also increased in attendance?"

232

"I noticed John, if this war is ever over, attendance will fall in half."

Just after our return to our cellar, Corporal Kern appeared.

"Men, did you hear the news?"

"John Kern, I'll bet you came to tell us the war is over." I joked.

"No. But Captain Thompson has been put in command of Company E. I don't think it will affect you or Crable."

"Why did they place Captain Thompson in command?" I inquired.

"You weren't there Edwards, but at one time in Camp Claiborne, Captain Thompson had been Company E's commander. Then he went to some infantry training school. During his absence, they put Captain Von Schriltz in command. Then Thompson came back. He wanted his old command back. Instead, they gave him command of Second Battalion Headquarters Company. He didn't like it."

"Kern, you mean he wants to command a line company now?"

"Yes he does, so they gave him his wish. There's also been two other changes."

"What are they, Corporal?"

"First, Lieutenant Nablo is now in charge of Headquarters Company in place of Thompson. He was S-2 you know. For his job, Lieutenant Lusby from Company E has taken over."

"Anything else?"

"Yes, to replace Lusby in Company E, a Lieutenant John Tucker is in command of the first platoon of Company E."

After Corporal Kern departed, Crable and I discussed these changes.

"Don, you know I honestly think that that's the best thing that happened when Captain Dick was taken away. Although he's a likeable guy, he would have gotten our company into a hot spot sooner or later. He always wants to be on the go. What do you think?"

233

"I agree, John. Most likely if the Captain's been captured, which I hope is true, he'll be safe until the war ends. He can't get anyone else into trouble. I think he wanted to make a name for himself in this war."

Just before 1700, Walters and Major rejoined the messenger group. They had heard that the battalion was to go up front that night. They were twenty-four hours early.

That evening, another movie was scheduled for the men of the battalion. The double feature started promptly at 1900. After watching the first movie entitled, "Two Yank Aboard," I decided to return to the cellar to read. The other seven messengers stayed for the second feature which they described as 'horrible' upon their return at 2200. All of us agreed that our rest period would have to end tomorrow. We knew some outfit was waiting for us to relieve them on the front lines.

2. Lindern

Friday, December 15, 1944

We were up at the usual 0800.

At 0900, we learned that we would relieve some battalion tonight. Its location was not disclosed to us. The remainder of the morning was spent packing our duffel bags. My notes were stuffed well toward the bottom of the bag. I had no desire to let anyone know about my notekeeping. John and I left our bags with Company E just before lunch.

Shortly after 1400, two men appeared in our cellar.

"Hi fellas, What outfit are you from?" inquired Frank Major.

"Headquarters, First Battalion, 335th."

"Can we help you?"

"Just came to see your quarters. You men have it fixed real good."

"Where did you come from?"

"Lindern."

"How is everything up there?"

"Very quiet now."

"When is your relief due?"

"Oh, I think you fellows are supposed to come up after dark."

Lindern, we knew, was the village just east of Leiffarth on the front. We had heard that there was a wild fight to drive the Germans out of the place.

At 1700, Sergeant Butler appeared.

"Outside you'll find the trucks which you are to lead to your company. Then tell your company commander to leave when he is ready. Each company commander has all the necessary orders. Any questions?"

Since none was asked, John and I guided the trucks to the quarters of Company E and reported to our new Company Commander, Captain William Thompson.

At 1730, orders were given to board the trucks. Fifteen minutes later, the trucks started their journey. After seemingly endless numbers of stops combined with numerous conferences, the convoy stopped.

As I leaped from the truck, no second glance was needed to realize we were at 'Torpedo Junction' in Gereonsweiler. The usual silence prevailed. After a wait of fifteen minutes, a guide from the First Battalion appeared.

In single file, Company E marched through the battered village. Then, we went through a huge mud field before a hard surface road was reached. Several times contact between members of the different platoons was lost. After a short halt, the single file of men would be in line again. This night, no searchlights lit the front. The night was pitch black.

Soon, the silhouette of a German village appeared. Entrance into the town was easily completed without a sound. At a large house at the south end of the town Company E stopped. This was the headquarters of Company A, 335th Regiment. Waiting outside were their platoon guides. They were to show the various platoons of our company their foxholes and other defensive works. One of the Company A guides exclaimed, "Hey, is that you, Don Edwards?"

"Sure is, Harry Ackerman."

"What are you doing up here?"

"May I ask you the same question?"

"Don, I'm one of the platoon guides. I've got to take your first platoon out to the line. But I'll be back. Can you wait?"

"I'll be here unless I've gone to battalion."

A little over ten minutes later, Harry reappeared.

"Don, how has everything been?"

"Not too bad. Got a little scratch over in Leiffarth. But it's nothing serious. Tell me what happened to you, Harry."

"Believe me I never thought it would be like this! Our battalion took this town on the night of November 29. We were shelled almost the whole time it took us to get here. I didn't know if I'd come out alive. The next day, the Germans launched an attack early in the morning. Some of them got into town through the other end where we had no line then. The whole area was covered with smoke. Then I saw a figure just a few yards beyond my foxhole. I fired my rifle and it fell. Later on I saw it was a German soldier. That's the first person I've ever killed. Since that attack which failed, it's been pretty quiet. My company suffered so many casualties that I've been put in this job. I like it for you aren't in the foxholes all the time."

Our conversation continued for about forty minutes. I related all that had happened to me since our last visit in London.

"Harry, have you had any time for girls?"

"My only concern is to get out of this alive. If this war continues like this, then, the next place I'll see you Don, is in heaven, I hope."

We talked until Harry had to leave with his company which was going back to Palenberg to take over our rest facilities. As we parted, he added, "I don't know the next time I'll be seeing you but let's hope it's not in the hospital. Take care and good luck!"

Company E proceeded to take over the defensive position which always took some time. Everyone from Captain Thompson on down seemed to be straightening out some detail. John Crable and myself sat in a corner waiting for an order. Every ten minutes, one of us would ask Sergeant Smith, "Should we go to battalion now, Sarge?"

"Wait a few minutes until the Captain decides when you should go."

Shortly before 2200, a telephone line was laid from battalion to the dwelling where Company E had its new headquarters. In a few minutes, it rang. Ed Norris answered it.

"Captain Thompson, you're wanted on the phone. Captain Price from battalion is calling."

"This is Captain Thompson. Yes, Captain, Yes, Captain. I'll see that they're sent immediately."

Captain Thompson put the phone down and turned. He spotted Crable and me.

"Edwards, Crable!"

"Yes, Sir."

"Why didn't you two get up to where you belong?"

"Sergeant Smith told us to wait, Sir."

"Why didn't one of you ask me?"

"You were too busy to be disturbed, Sergeant Smith told us."

"After this, I want you two to get up to battalion as soon as you know where we're located. Is that clear? No excuses."

Crable and I departed in record time. A quick dash was made northward on the main street. Second Battalions' Headquarters were about twelve houses away. Upon our arrival, Corporal Kern met us.

"Where have you two been?"

"Edwards and I went through that with Captain Thompson," was Crable's reply. "Our new company commander was too excited to let us go until that call came from Captain Price."

"It's all right as long as you got here. Follow me. I'll show you where you're to sleep for a while."

Our new abode was the cellar in the house next door. This cellar was separated from the main headquarters house by a small vacant lot. A shell of some type had provided the cellar with a wide entrance. Additional ventilation had been provided by other shells. Since the German lines were about 400 to 500 yards away, the three of us set a new cross-the-lot record. A quick jump was made into the cellar. We found the other six messengers had already arrived and were ready to retire. John and I quickly found a dark corner, put down our blanket and went to sleep.

Saturday, December 16, 1944

At 0500, every messenger awoke. The German artillery had fired a tremendous barrage. The messengers had a hurried conference. I volunteered as follows:

"Men, I think there's a counter-attack under way. Four of us should be out there ready to meet it. I suggest that Major, Innes, Teets and myself get over to that railroad embankment I saw last night, about 30 yards away and see if we can help the riflemen."

"What will the others do?" inquired Rochester.

"If a message has to be run, you're available. If the four of us need you, one of us will come back for the other four."

All agreed.

The four of us leaped out of the cellar and raced to the railroad embankment. The shelling by the Germans continued. It seemed to last forever. Just as daylight appeared after 0600, it stopped. I peered over the tracks of the railroad. Off to my left at the southwest corner of the defense perimeter, the German infantry was crawling up a slight slope toward the lines of Company E. None of the Wehrmacht soldatens directly opposite the four of us seemed to be moving. For five minutes, the enemy advanced. Then, the American machine guns chattered. Next, it seemed as if every American artillery and mortar piece in the entire area opened up. This continued for, at least, fifteen minutes. No reply was made by the German mortars or artillery.

In the next half hour, numerous Germans struggled to their feet with their hands in the air surrendering.

The four of us returned to our cellar. I related to the other four what I had observed.

At 0800, Crable and I were ordered to find out from Company E how many prisoners had been taken in the attack. We proceeded to the company. Outside of the Company's Headquarters, we counted twenty-seven prisoners. The Germans were compelled to stand outside the dwelling in full view of their observation posts. Yet no fire of any type was directed toward our area.

We learned that these Germans had been told that both Leiffarth and Lindern were lightly held. Their orders were to go through our positions at Lindern and dig in on the other side of town. Later all of us would realize the real reason for this attack.

Company E, which bore the brunt of the attack, had only four wounded men. One of them was Charles Syrlos, with whom I had been friends in Philadelphia. I was detailed to carry him on a stretcher to the medics' dwelling. He had been hit by a mortar shell just below his stomach and was bleeding profusely. Numerous bandages were strapped over his abdominal area. He attempted to talk to me but I kept saying, "Charlie, save your breath. Don't talk, don't talk."

After reaching the first aid station, I left. In my own mind, I did not believe Charlie could live much longer. He died a week later on December 23.

After the usual lunch, I decided to pay a visit to the battalion's Observation Post which was located on the third floor of the house next door. Upon reaching the top floor, the whole area around Lindern could be observed. I had learned that one did not stand in front of any window since these high spots were excellent targets for snipers. A prone positions was used. Or one could take a quick glance from the corner of the open window since none had any glass in them. From the OP, I could easily see that the Germans held the better defensive positions. The enemy had pillboxes and other fortifications in front of the next town which was Randerath. At various times, a German soldaten would run from a pillbox to some foxhole. But the front lines looked lifeless from this salient view point.

239

Except for the dirt from the foxholes and some wire strung around them, it seemed as if the quiet country fields were ready for plowing.

After our supper, Corporal Kern informed us, "The messengers do not need to post any guard in Lindern."

"What's the reason for this good news?" asked Innes.

"Since the battalion is just across the lot from you, the guard for the battalion CP can watch everything. If anything develops, he'll wake you."

All of us retired when darkness fell.

Sunday, December 17, 1944

A very monotonous day.

The only time any of the messengers would leave the safe cellar was when a message had to be taken to the various companies. This usually occurred, at least, once an hour. During one of my morning runs, I trotted through the whole town of Lindern. The entire village had been freely hit by all types of weapons. Every building showed some effects of the battles that had been fought here. Not a single person was found on the streets. Telephone lines, both German and American, seemed to be strung everywhere.

During one of my visits to Company E in the afternoon, I decided to look around the house. My discovery led to some letters and notes written by an officer in the German Wehrmacht. He was a Lieutenant in the German Infantry. After the fall of France in 1940, he had been married in Lindern during a furlough. His wife was a beautiful German blond—the type that Hitler spoke about but that we had not yet seen in this section of Germany. Letters in 1941 spoke of his experiences in Russia. In one letter, it was stated that the Stalino Line had been broken and the Russians would soon give up. The numerous letters ended in October of 1943. All the letters and photos were well kept. This indicated that they were to be treasured memos.

One of our favorite topics during the dull times was when the war would end or when we would be rotated back to the States.

240

"I think we should have some sort of rotation system like the Air Force," mentioned George Teets.

"What do they have?" inquired Innes.

"Well, after thirty missions, you are sent back to the States."

"What do you think the Infantry should have?"

"Oh, something like thirty days of fighting. Not like today, since no one is firing anything these days. At least, not around here."

"Do we have anything now, George?"

"Yea, if you last six months, then, you get out."

"Six months!" yelled Innes. "Nobody but nobody can last that long. My outfit, Company F, lost twenty percent on the first attack."

"Skinney, you've got it right. There are only two ways to leave here. Either back to the hospital or you're dead."

"That's some choice. Wonder if any guy ever went six months?"

Monday, December 18, 1944

After breakfast at 0800, John Crable and I reported to Corporal John Kern for our first message run of the day. This was our usual time to pick up the rumors which were always rampant.

"Don, John, have you heard about the German advance?"

"What advance?" was our joint reply.

"According to reports over the radio, the Germans broke through the American lines and advanced ten miles."

"Ten miles! Corporal, you've got to be kidding. We've hardly advanced two miles in one week," I exclaimed.

"That's what I heard, Edwards."

"Where did this supposedly happen?"

"Down near Belgium."

"Corporal, how far is that from here?"

"I heard it's about fifty miles from our location."

"When did this supposedly happen?"

"I think it was yesterday."

241

"Have you any way of checking?"

"Ed, I can ask Sergeant Telerak to check on the radio at find out all he can. Sure hope it isn't true. We've got enough to worry about here."

"Do you think it will have any affect on us?"

"I don't think so. Also heard that Division is planning to have our battalion mount an attack on those two towns you can see from the OP, you know, Randerath and Brachelen. We're supposed to go to the Roer River along side of the 102d Division."

"Where's the 102d?"

"I think you know that they drove the Germans out of Linnich and are now sitting on the Roer. But the word is that until the 84th gets there, there'll be no attempt to cross that river."

In the afternoon, I made another visit to the OP to take another quick look at the front lines. I wanted to see how far it was to the two towns of Randerath and Brachelen. Some type of artillery firing exercise was in progress. Sergeant Paul Kottage, one of the radio operators from the Second Battalion, was present.

"What's happening, Sergeant Kottage?"

"Edwards, the Lieutenant from our 327th Battalion is trying to knock out a Jerry machine gun. Here, take these field glasses and see what's happening."

"Thanks Sarge, but don't you need them?"

"No, I borrowed them from downstairs. After you finish, get them back to me."

"Will do, Sarge."

I observed the action with these field glasses. After each salvo was fired by the Field Artillery Battalion, the Lieutenant would radio back instructions giving changes for the next round. I could hear the orders to back. Then the shells could be heard coming over Lindern. Looking through the field glasses, the targets were being missed. Three sets of instructions were ordered. Three rounds were fired. After the third round, the Field Artillery Officer announced, "Mission accomplished. Machine gun nest neutralized."

I looked through the glasses. The machine gun was still there. It was in excellent shape. If an attack was ordered for our battalion, it would give a good account of itself. The Lieutenant had clearly lied. But I said nothing. The enemy, of course, could not engage in such practices. All of us knew we had more shells than the Germans and could engage in this type of target practice.

After all the messengers retired that night, we listened to a "game" that was sometimes played on the front at night. First, an American Browning automatic rifle would burst out with six or so bullets cutting the air. Next, a German machine gun would reply with six or more shots. All of us could easily distinguish the sound of each weapon.

"Don, listen to that Jerry machine gun. What do you think of it?"

"Crable, it's good. It puts out more bullets per minute than ours. What's your opinion?"

"I agree with you. But they have nothing to match that BAR. And, have you looked at their rifles?"

"I sure have. I tried in Leiffarth to shoot that gun that dead Corporal had next to him. But it was too dirty. I saw they had to reload after five shots when our Garand can fire eight."

"I guess we have some things better and they have some."

"John, you're right. What do you think's happening tonight?"

"I think both sides have got out some patrols and those guns are covering them."

"John, I agree."

Tuesday, December 19, 1944

After Crable and I reported in the morning, we asked Corporal Kern for the latest rumor.

"What's the latest, Corporal Kern?"

"The advance in Belgium has everyone worried, Don."

"Whose advancing where?"

243

"You remember, I told you yesterday that the Germans advanced ten miles. Now they've gone another ten miles. Supposedly our side has sent in reinforcements to stop them."

"Think it might affect us?"

"No, Captain Price got some dope on how we're going to attack those two towns in the next few days. It looks as if we're going to stay here a while."

"Anything on relief for us?"

"No, it looks like we're going to take those two towns and then get relief. We should hear something today."

For lunch and dinner this day, all the messengers had a treat. Hot meals, of course, were out of the question. We were given a giant box of 10-in-1 rations. The contents of these boxes were more varied than the usual K rations. Everyone enjoyed eating.

That evening, my digestive system revolted against the good food. About 2100, I developed a mild case of diarrhea. A half hour later, I vomited. The diarrhea continued through the night. To defecate, I went to the farthest corner of the cellar where we sometimes performed our daily functions. To go outside in my condition was out of the question.

Wednesday, December 20, 1944

At 0800, I turned to John Crable.

"John, can you take all the messages, this morning?"

"Sure, Don, what happened to you?"

"I think I was up all night. That food was too rich for me. I've got the runs but if I rest this morning, I should be ok."

"Company F's doing the same thing. Rochester was up too. Innes is taking all the messages for them. I think you better stick to the K's."

"I'll do that up here."

My sleep lasted from 0800 to 1200. The enemy and our artillery did not fire a single shot.

Early in the afternoon, I had another conversation with Corporal John Kern.

"Edwards, I heard we are going to relieve the 99th Infantry Division."

"Corporal, what happened to them?"

"The enemy went through their lines. The 84th is supposed to reinforce them and stop the Germans from advancing."

"Have you heard anything else?"

"Yes, the attack on Randerath has been called off. It was to start tomorrow."

About 1500, the German artillery was heard from. But after five minutes, their batteries were silent again.

Just before 1800, a Lieutenant from the 102d Infantry Division along with two enlisted men appeared in our cellar.

"Lieutenant, what can we do for you?" asked John Crable.

"We're going to take over for you tonight. How do you get out of this cellar?"

"The same way you came in, Sir."

"No other way out?"

"You can use those windows out toward the main street."

"They aren't any good. Don't you men know that you've got to have two good exits?"

"Sir, we'd be able to get out of those windows, if we needed to." added Innes.

"Why you men have never been in any fighting if that's the way you look at it."

Before any of us could reply, Sergeant Butler appeared.

"Each company messenger is to take a man from the Ozark Division down to his company. They are going to relieve us tonight."

John volunteered to do this for Company E.

At 1830, Crable returned to the cellar.

"Don, get our things together. We are to report to the company."

"Heard anything?"

"Everyone thinks the situation in Belgium is bad. The 102d is taking our place because we're being transferred to another part of the line."

245

Upon our arrival at the headquarters of Company E, we heard every rumor possible about what was to happen to our Division.

Just after 1900, Sergeant Smith announced, "Half of headquarters come with me."

About a dozen men followed him out of Lindern. The route back was over the open countryside. On the way, we met some of the 102d who were coming to relieve our battalion on the line. Just as we exited Lindern, a few artillery shells whizzed by. The enemy knew that a change was being made.

Forty minutes later, 'Torpedo Junction' was reached. In the next hour, other units of Company E arrived. Over an hour was spent waiting for the arrival of the 2½ ton trucks. We boarded them on Highway 57. In a few minutes, the motors roared down the highway.

At 2330, Company E detrucked. John and I approached Sergeant Smith.

"Sergeant, shall we wait or go to battalion?" inquired John.

"Do you see where we are?"

"Yes," was our joint reply.

"Then, I think you should go. Captain Thompson doesn't want to get in trouble over you two again."

"Where is battalion?"

"Same place."

"We'll find it. See you in the morning."

Battalion Headquarters was only three blocks away. We reported to Sergeant Butler.

"Crable, Edwards, you two wait until all the messengers get here. It'll be another hour."

XVI

TO BELGIUM

Thursday, December 21, 1944

By 0100, all the eight messengers were assembled. Sergeant Butler ordered us to an adjacent house.

"Go to the cellar, men. But get ready to move at any time. I've heard the situation in Belgium is bad, very bad."

In ten minutes, we had laid our blankets on a beautiful, white, cold cement floor.

At 0230, someone was shaking me. Sergeant Butler was talking to me.

"Edwards, you're to get Captain Thompson. Bring him back to the battalion CP for an important conference. Do it as soon as possible, and don't go back to sleep."

"I'm awake, Sarge. As soon as I get my boots on, I'll get him."

In the rest area, boots were removed for sleeping. This was never true at or near the front line.

Five minutes later, I was at the Company E Headquarters. After awaking four or five persons, I found Captain Thompson.

"Captain Thompson, this is Private Edwards. I've been sent to bring you back to battalion for an important meeting."

"Edwards, I hear you. Just a minute and I'll be with you."

Less than five minutes later, we were walking toward battalion headquarters.

"Do you know what the meeting is about?"

"No, Captain, but I have a pretty good idea."

"So have I. I hate to think about it. It means nothing but trouble."

"It must be important, Sir, or they wouldn't bother to get you up."

"Is this the first time you've done this, Edwards?"

"No, it's not the first time I've been out at this hour, Captain. But it's the first instance where you had to be gotten out of bed."

"I don't blame you, you understand, I just hate to think what this is about."

"Yes, Sir. There's the CP, Captain."

"Thanks for your help, Edwards."

Since I still was having a slight case of diarrhea, I did not retire until 0400. An hour later my digestive system gave me another call.

At 0630, Sergeant Butler was back in the messenger's cellar.

"Everyone up. Eat your breakfast, then everybody report to their company."

"Sarge, where are we going?" one of us asked.

"I don't know yet. But everyone's guessing that it's some place in Belgium. Apparently the American line is broken. The Germans have been advancing like crazy. No one knows where the enemy is now."

Fifteen minutes later, John Crable and I were back with Company E. The whole company was up and waiting.

At 0700, the trucks arrived. Since John and I were still part of Headquarters platoon, we rode in the lead truck. The canvas which normally covered the back portion of these $2^1/_2$ ton trucks was rolled back. We were to be exposed to the elements. All knew the situation must be dangerous since this was the first instance where we had not ridden under canvas. As we were loading, I requested of Sergeant Smith, "Sarge, I've had the GIs the last two nights. Can I ride in the last seat?"

"Yes, you and Crable should ride the end of each side of the seats. If necessary, you two may have to go for help."

After our platoon was full loaded on the truck, Sergeant Smith arose.

248

"Men, I think a little explanation is needed before we start. The Germans have broken through the American lines in Belgium. How serious it is I don't know. The enemy came through in two places. They are called the north and south drives. The south drive has been halted. But the northern one is still going. Our job is going to be to stop this northern drive. When and where we stop is another question mark. You are all to be prepared to jump out at a moment's notice. We don't know where we'll meet the enemy. Any questions?"

The headquarters platoon just sat and listened. All realized the situation was very serious.

"If there are no questions, then, the next thing we have to do is post an air guard. One man is to stand at all times looking up. Change every fifteen minutes. If you see a plane, yell. If the truck stops, hit the ditches. Everyone understand?"

There was complete silence.

After Sergeant Smith left for a conference with Captain Thompson, conversations of all types flowed. Instructions came that we were to ride with loaded rifles. We had never done this before inasmuch as loaded rifles on trucks were dangerous. On our previous rides to and from the front, rifles were always carried unloaded. Tensions began to rise.

For an hour we waited. The air guard was not posted for we had no fear until the ride started.

At 0810, the truck convoy rolled from Palenberg. Soon Alsdorf was entered. In this town, the Military Police were stopping all traffic to let us through. The truck journey was becoming a non-stop flight. The convoy turned onto Highway 57. We were obviously going to the city of Aachen.

A half hour later, Aachen was entered. This was the first German urban center that had received the full brunt of the war. It appeared as if every building in the entire city had received some kind of damage. Rubble of every type and description lay about. A few German civilians were walking through their city. We made three stops in Aachen. Their purposes were never revealed to us when the conferences were held by the various officers of the four companies and the battalion staff.

A PRIVATE'S DIARY

Just outside the city limits of Aachen was the normal boundary line between Germany and Belgium. It was clearly marked by concrete dragon teeth which were designed to stop armoured vehicles. Just behind the dragon teeth and about a thousand yards from the boundary was a German concrete pill-box which commanded the highway approaches from Belgium.

Although the convoy was in Belgium, the signs were still in German. We guessed that this land may have been an area that had been given to Belgium after the First World War. In twenty minutes, the convoy entered the town of Eupen. There was not a single civilian on the streets. Every sign was in German.

The trucks left the main highway and seemed to turn west-ward. In about fifteen minutes, the battalion entered the city of Verviers. Upon our arrival, people started to pour out of their houses. Their faces showed delight at our presence. As the trucks stopped periodically, the townspeople came up to the trucks and gave us apples and other food. We took the apples but tried to make the Belgians understand that we were not hungry. One thing that everyone noted was the lack of war damage.

After leaving Verviers, the same greetings were repeated in two other very small Belgian towns. Those of us in the truck began to wonder just how bad the situation really was. We knew that this area was far behind the front, yet, these Belgian civilians seemed overjoyed to see us. It was almost as though they were being liberated.

The convoy went into an area of wooded hills. The terri-tory seemed devoid of people. A strange silence prevailed. Over the trucks hung a heavy fog. The next day we learned that this fog had aided the Germans in their advance. The trucks were traveling only fifteen or less miles per hour. A necessity break was taken at 1400. Numerous twists and turns were being made in order to follow the road.

The next town we entered was Durbury. It was now 1500. No one was on the streets. We began to wonder if the enemy was near. However, we continued for about another hour of riding. It was a continual stop and go. It was now 1610.

"Time for another break," shouted someone.

"No, it isn't. But it looks as if we're not going any farther. No trucks are moving ahead." stated the air guard.

"Anyone know where we are?"

"Nobody knows."

The trucks remained stationary. Everyone was looking every way possible. Sergeant Smith then reappeared since he had been off to a conference.

"Men, this is where we get off."

"What should we do Sarge?"

"Headquarters platoon, scatter over in that field. Start digging."

The trucks started their motors. They turned around and left.

John Crable and I had selected a spot near the road and had our shovels out. We had turned over only a few spades of dirt, when Sergeant Smith appeared.

"Crable, do you know any French?"

"A little, Sarge, but not too much."

"Captain wants you to come along with him up to the town. He wants you to help him talk with the civilians if he needs to."

John turned to me.

"Keep digging, Don, for I'm certain that I'll be back."

The platoon kept digging for another half hour when Sergeant Smith gave a new order.

"Headquarters platoon, fall in. Space yourselves. We're going to continue marching ahead. Everyone be ready. Keep your rifle loaded."

"Where are we going, Sarge?"

"I don't know, but just be ready."

After a very slow march of over thirty minutes, we entered the city of Marche. As Company E went slowly through the city, we noted that every electric light in the entire area seemed to be lit. This was most unusual. At the front we were accustomed to strict blackout conditions. The brightness of the electric glare almost blinded us.

"This place can't be near the front. Those lights wouldn't be on," came a remark from someone marching in the rear.

251

The next night there would not be a single light burning in the area inside or outside Marche.

Company E marched for over an hour. The pace was very, very slow. Then, the two jeeps that belonged to Company E appeared. We knew that the Captain and others had reached the company's destination. The two jeeps began to shuttle the walking soldiers. I secured a seat on one of the late trips. In two minutes, the jeeps entered the small village of Hollogne. Here we were discharged. A voice ordered, "Everybody find themselves places to sleep for the night."

Several of us saw a large barn nearby. We covered ourselves with hay and drifted off to sleep.

At 2130, Sergeant James Dempsey shouted inside, "Every man from Company E is to fall outside. Get ready to dig."

I quickly followed the order. Since John was not with me, I proceeded to dig alone. Sergeant Dempsey noticed and came over.

"Edwards, why are you alone?"

"Sergeant Smith took Crable to go with the Captain."

"Then, I think you'd better get to that farmhouse over there. Crable is there. He might be waiting for you to go to battalion. No one seems to know where Jerry is."

Upon reaching the farmhouse, there was much shouting and ordering. Captain Thompson was ordering the various platoons to dig in their positions. He shouted, "Every man must be in a foxhole tonight. The Germans are expected any minute."

I soon found John. We then went to Sergeant Smith.

"Sarge, should we go to battalion?"

"I think you should. Don't bother the Captain. Get back here if you get any orders on what the other companies are doing."

"You mean Sarge, if the other companies have met the enemy," I answered.

"Yes, tell us if anything is happening."

John and I with our loaded rifles in our hands trudged on to the battalion CP. John spoke of his adventures in coming into Marche.

252

"When I got to Captain Thompson, he took me to a meeting of the battalion staff. I just sat and listened. Lieutenant-Colonel Urban refused to come into the town. No one could persuade him to do anything. There was violent shouting among the officers. Finally Major Lamb and Captain Price took matters into their own hands. They ordered each company to occupy an area on the map. Then, Captain Thompson and I went back to the company's jeep. Novak pulled the jeep into town. There wasn't a soul on the streets. We went slowly through the town. I expected to bump into a German tank at every turn we took. But somehow we went right through. Next, we came into that village of Hollenge. We went to that farmhouse. Novak then went back and got some men. For ten minutes, the Captain and I were all alone in that place. I wondered if the Germans were going to show up. As soon as the first platoon was there, I knew little could go wrong. The gist is that Company E did reach its objective. From overhearing all those conversations, I don't think the enemy is over a mile from here."

Upon reaching the battalion CP, Sergeant Butler met us at the door.

"Where should we sleep, Sarge?" inquired John.

"Anywhere you can find room."

"Anybody know anything?"

"Nobody does. But no contact has been made with Jerry."

"Do we have guard tonight?"

"No, Corporal Kern and I will take care of that tonight."

Every room seemed full of sleeping soldiers. John and I found a small cove in the hallway. We put our blankets down. Before retiring, I still knew I had a sour stomach.

XVII

THE DEFENSE AT MARCHE

Friday, December 22, 1944

By 0700, everyone in the battalion Command Post was up with one exception, the Battalion's Commanding Officer. The organization of the defense of our sector was undertaken. Sergeant Butler gave the messengers their orders.

"Men, the message center is to move to the small house just down the road. Any message that is taken to any company must be run by both messengers. This applies to both day and night runs. Since we will not be with the headquarters, the message center must post a guard of its own during darkness. After I talk with Sergeant Gooding, I'll give you the arrangements."

By 0800, all the message center personnel were housed with a Belgian family. The family consisted of three persons, Mr. and Mrs. Siberts and their daughter, Bertha, who was about 18 years of age. Their house consisted of three tiny rooms downstairs, and one small bedroom on the second floor. Because of the critical situation, we were ordered to remain downstairs at all times. We slept wherever a spot could be found. Only one room, the kitchen, was heated because of the shortage of fuel, namely, wood. The tiny house was overloaded, yet, no one managed during our stay to get in each other's way. As a rent payment, our messenger group gave the family the extra K rations we managed to secure. The Marche family was extremely happy to get these boxes of food since their normal diet consisted largely of potato soup.

A PRIVATE'S DIARY

The messenger from Company H, Charlie Simon, could speak French fluently. This made our stay in this small house very easy since we experienced no difficulty in learning what each party to this arrangement needed or wanted at any time. In the afternoon, Charlie told us, "The Sieberts said the Germans were here in Marche for four years. But none of the Wehrmacht ever stationed soldiers in their house."

"Have they objections to us being in their house?" inquired Walters.

"All three of them are very, very happy, we are here. They were afraid that the Germans, who they call the Boche, would be here first. They don't like the Boche. They are very afraid of them, especially for their daughter."

In the morning there were thirteen of us in that tiny house consisting of three Belgians, eight messengers, Corporal kern and Sergeant Butler. In the afternoon, Sergeant Gooding, the radio and visual chief, joined us.

At 1100, Sergeant Butler called all of us into the kitchen.

"Each man must now carry a gas mask. I know nobody's going to use it. But some Germans are wearing American uniforms. The Krauts probably don't have gas masks since no American is ever captured with one. This is one way to find out if the guy's an American. Each man take one of these things. Don't go outside without one. You might be shot by your own men if they don't think you're from the 84th." Everyone secured a gas mask.

Varied activity was the order of the day. It seemed that every 45 minutes another message had to be delivered by the runners to each of the companies. Fortunately for Crable and myself, Company E's positions were straight down the main road from the center of Hollenge. Our route was not parallel to the front which was not true of the other routes taken by the messengers of the other companies.

After our K-ration lunch, the messengers discussed what arrangements would be used for sleeping. John and I along with the Company F messengers were relegated to sleeping in the storage room. This small room had a cement floor and was always kept cool for the purpose of preserving any food in it.

256

The cold cement seemed to penetrate right through our blankets and clothing while we slept. In the storage room was a motorcycle. John later learned that it had been stored for four years in a barn covered with hay since the Germans would have taken it had it been observed by them.

During the delivery of the various messages, the messengers learned that the Second Battalion had been assigned a sector of over three miles to defend. Thus, large gaps were left open in the line. Our artillery and mortar fire was to cover these open spots. But during this day we had no artillery support of any type. The battalion was fortunate that no contact was made with the enemy that day.

In the afternoon, Sergeant Butler made the guard assignments.

"I think all of you know that the Germans might be able to infiltrate our lines quite easily. The battalion's going to have an interior line. We're going to be part of that interior line. Two messengers will stand guard from 1900 each night until 0600 the next morning. During daylight, only one man will be on duty. We've been given a daisy chain to use. If it's necessary to leave, we're to place these mines across the road. Anybody coming at night must give the password. If no password is given, shoot and get everybody up fast. The shifts will last one and one-half hours. Then change. Only one messenger from a company is to be on duty at any one time."

"Are you or Corporal Kern or Sergeant Gooding going to take turns?" one of us asked.

"Non-commissioned officers are excused. We do enough work."

After we were dismissed, Walters commented, "What a bunch of shit that is. The three of those bastards don't do as much work as one of us. Yet, they don't pull guard."

"That's life, Walters. We'll do all the work and the guys above us get all the glory." answered his fellow messenger, George Teets.

At 1800, I was called to Battalion Headquarters to escort Lieutenant Elmer L. Edwards of the 909th Field Artillery Battalion to Company E. He and two enlisted men were to be the forward observers of the artillery. This meant that if the Germans tried any attack, they would be met with artillery fire. Upon his arrival at Company E, Lieutenant Edwards was met with joy and thanksgiving. Captain Thompson kidded, "Lieutenant, usually I'm not happy to see an Edwards. It means orders. But are we happy to see you!"

That evening, the big conversation topic among those at the message center was the conduct of our battalion commander, Lieutenant Colonel Charles R. Urban. Since all of us had been in the battalion headquarters several times, Rochester asked, "Did anybody see Urban during the day?"

"No," was the joint reply of everybody.

Corporal Kern then came forth with this rumor.

"I heard that he's in the cellar of headquarters. Remember, he did this at Leiffarth and Lindern. He won't come out to direct anything. He's afraid of what might happen."

"Who's taking charge of things, then?" inquired Simon.

"I'll ask you, Simon, who's been giving you most of the orders to take down?"

"Captain Price."

Three times that evening, I went to battalion headquarters to pick up messages. Each time, they were handed to me by Captain Price. I looked in vain for the Battalion Commander. During one of these trips at 2330, I waited while a message was being readied. Captain Price asked me, "Edwards, how did you ever get in this job?"

"I don't know what you mean, Captain."

"You should know what I mean. You seemed like an intelligent chap to me. You're always reading books. Yet, you're a private here in the Infantry. You and Crable, your buddy, seem a cut above the rest of the messengers. How did you get in the 84th?"

"Well, Captain, you may remember all those college kids that came last April. I was one of those from the ASTP."

"Edwards, I understand now. Seems a shame to me to waste potential brains on the Infantry, but I guess you know how it is."

"I think so, Captain."

"Truthfully, what do you make of Captain Von Schriltz?"

"I didn't think he was too bad, Captain. I didn't like his dogmatic idea of having first-class men in a rifle company. He wouldn't let me go to improve my position even within the Division. But he was doing what he thought was right. Do you have any idea of what happened to him?"

"Most of us guess that he was captured the night he left headquarters, but none of us know what happened yet."

"Here's the message I want you to deliver to Captain Thompson. Are you going to take it yourself?"

"No, Captain. Sergeant Butler has given us orders that all our runs must be made by two men in case of trouble."

"I think that's a good idea. By the way Edwards, how old are you?"

"Twenty, Sir."

"Well, let's hope that both of us get out of this alive and live a long time."

"I agree, Captain."

Saturday, December 23, 1944

At 0800, all the messengers sat around in the kitchen wondering what was going to occur. Each one of us was half asleep and half awake since we had to maintain guard duty as well as take the necessary messages to the four companies of the battalion. As we ate, I was designated to confer with Sergeant Butler concerning the arrangement whereby two messengers were required during the day for a message run.

A few minutes later, I spoke to him.

"Sergeant, is it possible to change this idea of having two messengers on every run?"

"Why do you ask?"

"The messengers think that only one messenger is needed during the day to take the messages. In that way the rest of us can get some sleep if we're up all night."

"Edwards, I think that's a good idea. But I still want two to go at night in case you hit a German patrol."

"Thanks Sarge, we'll be happy with that arrangement."

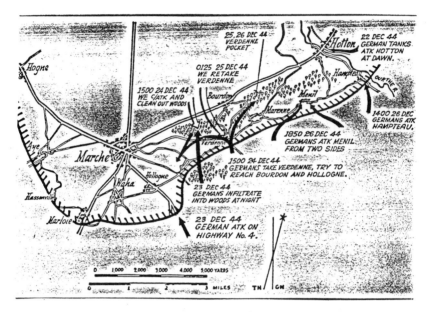

Defensive line of the 84th Division at Marche, Belgium

A strange silence then seemed to fall over the area during the remainder of the morning. As each of the messengers went on guard duty, we were warned to arouse everyone if the need arose. By noon, we heard that every company of the Second Battalion was well dug in and ready for any enemy attack. It would soon come.

At 1530, I took a message to Company E. Upon my arrival, everyone was in a high state of excitement.

"What's up?" was my inquiry to Norris.

"Edwards, Jerry is coming!"

"How do you know, Ed?"

"We just had an attack."

"Where?"

"Down at the nearby junction where this road splits in two. A couple of Jerry tanks followed by some infantry just came wandering up the road. Apparently they weren't aware of us here. Two of the fellows from the first platoon sneaked

260

ahead of our line. They waited until the tank came right along
side of them. then, they let the front tank have a rocket."

"What happened after that?"

"The rest of the Jerry column turned around. They went
back. We're expecting them to attack any minute. The artillery
started to fire after them when they turned. Everybody's just
waiting."

"I think I should get back to battalion and report."

I quickly trotted down the main road. Upon my return to
battalion headquarters, I met Captain Price.

"Edwards, is anything happening down there?"

"I'm afraid so, Captain. Company E just hit a German
tank."

"Thanks, Edwards, for I'll get down there right away."

In a few minutes, the enemy began to throw some artillery
shells into our area. None of us in the center were worried for
we believed we were ready for any attack by the Germans. Our
hosts, the Sieberts, had an entirely different outlook. Anytime a
shell would burst near us, the glass in the little house would
shake. We tried to reassure our hosts that the Boche would not
be coming in the next minute or two. All of us in the center
were worried about the window panes. These panes of glass
added considerable warmth to our temporary dwelling. The
enemy we could handle.

Since the Germans had been contacted, the American artillery continued to fire periodically throughout the afternoon and
well into the night. We learned later that this shelling had
helped to break up planned German attacks in our sector.

On this day, another ten-in-one ration package was issued
to us. Since our hosts still had very poor food, we shared our
entire meals with them. Throughout the day, some of the messengers also brought some coal to our dwelling. Although the
Sieberts told us about the coal located about two city blocks
away, they would not go themselves. They knew that the military could and would take it for their own use. None of us had
any trouble in securing the coal for the heating of the house.
Many of the houses occupied by the Americans nearby had no
civilians in them since they had fled upon learning of the Ger-

man advance in this area. In some of the houses occupied by the rifle companies, the Belgians had been asked to leave. None had refused this request.

That night, no messenger secured more than four hours sleep. Since two of us were on guard at all times, only six could sleep. Four times during the hours of darkness, all eight had to leave to deliver some message. Then, Corporal Kern had to take over as the guard. Nevertheless, we still felt fortunate as compared to others since sleep for some of us was always available during the daylight hours.

Sunday, December 24, 1944

Our sector of the front was quiet during the entire day. There was the usual shelling by both our artillery and the Germans but no direct attacks came. However, to the left of our sector, some type of battle seemed to be raging on and off during the entire day. We wondered what was occurring on other sectors. It was our guess that the Germans were trying to get into Marche and take over the town.

The event of the day was the attempt on the part of my fellow Company E messenger, John Crable, to learn the French language from our hosts. As John explained to me the previous day, "When I came into Marche with Captain Thompson, I would have felt foolish to try to converse in French. If the Siberts are willing to help me, I think I can learn quite a bit."

Thus, during every spare moment, Crable was talking with Mr. and Mrs. Siberts or their daughter, Bertha. The whole family seemed overjoyed that John was attempting to learn their language. The only one who didn't like the idea was Charlie Simon. He didn't want any rival in his contacts with our hosts.

Monday, December 25, 1944

Christmas in Belgium.

My tour of guard duty came from 0130 to 0300. I could feel another case of diarrhea developing. My companion on guard duty, 'Skinney' Innes, tried to comfort me. I left him

262

alone for necessity reason a good part of the 90 minute shift. Upon retiring after guard duty, I could not get any rest on the cold cement floor.

At 0730, John Crable came to awaken me.

"Don, it's time for your shift."

"John, I can't get up."

"You've got the GIs again. I'll see what I can do for you."

Five minutes later he returned.

"Don, Skinney has agreed to take your turn at guard. Do you want me to get you anything?"

"John, I'd appreciate it if you could get some pills from the medics to stop these runs."

"I'll be back in ten minutes. Don't move."

"John, I'm not going anywhere. Even if the Germans come, I can't move."

Fifteen minutes later, Crable was back with the required pills. After taking them, John mentioned, "After you're able, the medics want you to come over to the station. They want to examine you."

"How come, John?"

"Well, if you're too sick, they might keep you at the station or send you back to the hospital to get over the GIs."

"Suppose I don't go?"

"Nothing will happen. It's up to you."

"I'll give myself until noon. If I don't stop, I'll have to go to the station."

My breakfast that morning consisted of just one item, cheese. I traded my K-ration breakfast for another K-ration lunch so that I was nibbling on cheese the entire morning.

Christmas provided us with two big surprises. Both were appreciated.

The first one was the weather. Since our arrival in Belgium, the skies had been overcast. Clouds naturally aided the Germans in their movements. One of our prayers in the morning was for good weather. By 1200, the dark clouds had departed from the Marche area.

Shortly after 1400, someone yelled, "Everybody out here. Our planes are in the air."

Everyone in the message center came out. Other Americans in nearby houses came out to watch our Air Force in action. Sighted above were four P-38s buzzing about Marche like bees. They seemed to be looking for something to sting. After ten minutes, the American P-38s flew away. The disappointment was terrific.

"Maybe they were just observation planes finding out the situation," stated George Teets.

"And maybe they're through for the day," Walters added sarcastically.

An hour later, Rochester yelled from his guard post, "Come out and see the planes."

All thought the P-38s had returned. They had not. Instead, roaring thousands of feet above us were uncountable B-17 bombers. The number was unbelievable. The American Air Force seemed to pass over in formation after formation. After a half hour of watching, those not on duty returned inside.

Just after 1600, Sergeant Rochester again yelled, "Come out and see the planes!"

"What are they? More 17's?" asked Major.

"No, the P-38s are back."

Everyone was back out to watch the aerial display. Along with the four P-38s were four P-47s. After a few minutes of air scouting, the planes began diving at the Germans, spraying them with machine gun bullets. The aerial show was not all one way. The Germans were firing their machine guns and anti-aircraft weapons whenever our planes came over their lines. The targets of our planes appeared to range about a mile away from our location to sights that we could not see or observe. The aerial activity kept up all afternoon until darkness fell about 1800.

The other surprise on this Christmas Day was hot food.

Every company in the entire Second Battalion had a hot dinner. Since there was no ground activity in our sector, a good portion of the rifle platoons came out of the line to eat. This was done in half hour shifts so that the front would be covered in some manner at all times. The bill of fare was turkey with all the trimmings. We later learned that many sectors, that the 84th Division held, did not enjoy this treat since war did not stop for any day.

Two of the messengers griped, wishing that they were back from the front, but the rest of us felt thankful for the small food favor that we had received.

That evening before my tour of guard duty, I went back to the storage room to lay down for some sleep. I had just laid down when Sergeant Butler appeared.

"Edwards, you and the other messengers can't sleep here any more."

"Sergeant, where should we go?"

"There's still some space in the living room. I don't care if the others don't like it, all of us are going to sleep there. If you sleep here again tonight, you'll have the diarrhea again. The next time, cheese won't help you."

Following orders, I moved my blanket to the living room and warmth.

In the evening, I went back on guard duty with Martin 'Skinney' Innes of Torrington, Connecticut. During our duty that evening, he remarked, "Don, I sure wish I knew if I'm going to get through alive. Then, it wouldn't be so bad waiting for the end."

"Skinney, I'll agree to that. All of us would like to know when the end is coming."

"What do you think, Don, about the end of the war."

"My guess is that this is the last big German offensive. If they succeed, the war will last through summer. It will be tough on us."

"What if they don't succeed, Ed?"

"My guess, Skinney, is that the war will end in the spring."

"Why do you say that?"

"Well, if the Americans can ever get across that Roer River back up in Germany and get to the Rhine, the Germans won't have their industry to rely upon."

"Sounds good to me. Are they going to succeed?"

"I don't think so."

"Why not?"

"I think you saw the reason today. We've got control of the air. It means we can move around while they can't."

"Let's hope the weather is good every day."

The eight messengers had worked out a system of who would relieve whom on guard duty. Innes and myself were always relieved by Hugh Walters and Frank Major. They, in turn, were relieved of their guard post by James Rochester and Charles Simon. Then came John Crable and his partner, George Teets. My shift started again after the tour of duty by Teets and Crable.

Our tours of guard duty that evening and night were without incident. While on duty, the guards always kept a clip of ammunition in their rifles. We could take no chances. The good news was that my diarrhea was gone.

Tuesday, December 26, 1944

At 0700, John Crable shook me.

"Don, how are you feeling?"

"OK, John."

"Then, take over the guard post now. We'll leave Skinney sleep this morning."

"I'll be there in a minute."

"Don, don't forget to take some cheese with you to nibble on while on duty."

"John, I won't forget. Not today or any day while we're on the front."

By 0900, the P-47s and the P-38s were back in the air over the enemy lines. None of us bothered to watch their attacks throughout the day but we knew the Germans would not welcome their presence.

Just after 1400, Frank Major yelled in, "Watch out everybody, a P-47 is coming in."

"What do you mean coming in?" answered Innes.

At that moment, a huge bomb from the wandering P-47 hit about 500 yards from our dwelling. The windows in the house shook. The concussion was terrifying. Everyone in the

266

house had hit the floor including our hosts. But no one was hurt.

Just before 1530, I had to deliver a message to Company E. Norris asked, "Did you feel that bomb the P-47 dumped on us?"

"Yes, we did. Did it hit our company lines?"

"No, Company E was lucky. It hit just to the left of our gap in the line. But everybody here is sure ticked off about it."

"What did Captain Thompson do about it?"

"He got on the phone to Captain Price in one minute flat. I think Captain Price phoned somebody in Division because he called back to state it wouldn't happen again."

"Norris, I sure hope it doesn't happen again. I remember that's how General McNair got killed back in Normandy."

There was no activity on our portion of the front that day. But about a mile or two away, we could hear artillery and mortar fire going on in the afternoon and evening. We would learn in a few days that this was the last offensive action taken by the enemy against any part of the 84th Division in the Marche area.

During the afternoon, the message center received a copy of the Army newspaper, the 'Stars and Stripes.' Teets noted, "Hey, fellow messengers, look at this. Stars and Stripes shows Marche in German hands."

"How about this little burg of Hollogne where we are?" inquired Innes.

"From their map, my guess is that this place is in German hands!"

"I think somebody better tell them what's going on," added Major.

I asked, "What's the big story about, George?"

"Don, it's about a place called Bastogne. Apparently the 101st Airborne Division is surrounded by the Germans."

"Are the paratroopers going to surrender?"

"Doesn't say anything here. Looks as if the Germans are far beyond Bastogne. This map has them at the Meuse River."

"Let's hope Stars and Stripes is wrong just like they are about Marche."

Just after 1800 that evening, Rochester, Major and I approached Sergeant Gooding about the guard situation. I politely asked, "Sergeant, do you think it would be possible for you, Sergeant Butler and Corporal Kern to take some guard duty?"

"We have other responsibilities that you don't have, men."

"Sergeant, that might be true but couldn't one of you share some of the guard duty with one of us during the night time. That way, at least, one of the messengers could get more than four hours of sleep at a time."

"No, Sergeant Butler, Corporal Kern and I have to be ready to work at any time."

"But Sergeant, only one of you has to be at the phone to tell any of us to go to battalion to run the messages."

Major, who had been silent to this time sarcastically stated, "Cut out the bull. Tell us you're pulling rank on us."

"I am not. I'm just looking at the situation which might arise. We've got to be ready for it. That's all, men."

We left. Sergeant Harvey Gooding would take his revenge on Private Frank Major.

Wednesday, December 27, 1944

About 0030, I was called to battalion to deliver a message to Company E. While waiting, I chatted with Captain Price which was our usual habit.

"Anything unusual today, Edwards?"

"Nothing, Captain, except some of us tried to get Sergeant Gooding and Sergeant Butler and Corporal Kern to take some guard duty."

"What happened?"

I then recited what had occurred.

"Edwards, do you want me to order them to stand guard duty with you?"

"No, Captain. Gooding and Butler would get back at us without your knowledge. They know they're not pulling their share of the load, but we'll live with it. Thanks for your offer of assistance, Captain."

After breakfast that morning, George Teets and I approached Sergeant Butler with a request.

"Sergeant, can George and I go into town?"

"What for, Edwards?"

"Our hair is getting long. We've heard that there is a barber shop in Marche itself that is still cutting hair every day."

"You two can go as long as you make the necessary guard arrangements."

After accomplishing this task, we managed to secure a ride with Larry Gardiner, the jeep driver for the message center jeep.

This was my first opportunity to see the city of Marche in the daylight. The city seemed to consist of two story apartments along very narrow streets. Numerous U.S. Army jeeps seemed to be traveling about, but the city was very quiet. We saw only four civilians on the streets. After delivering some material to headquarters of the 335th Infantry Regiment, a stop was made at a barber shop. Upon entering I saw Zelson James of Regimental Headquarters Company standing with ten or twelve others apparently waiting for a haircut. I inquired, "Zelson, how long have you been waiting?"

"About an hour Edwards."

"How long do you think the three of us have to wait?"

"I think about that time."

I then turned to Larry Gardiner.

"Can we wait that long?"

"Ed, I don't think I can be away from center that long. You and George can wait but I think I should get back."

George then added, "Don, I don't think we can wait that long. Maybe we can come back tomorrow."

"OK George, let's go back with Gardiner."

For supper that day, we had hot food brought to our area. We guessed that the situation must have settled down somewhat since the kitchens served us in a barn near the battalion headquarters.

While going through the chow line, I noticed an unusually large number of GIs laying on the hay inside the barn. I turned

269

to Corporal Kern, who was seated next to me, and asked, "Corporal, where did everyone come from? Are they from some other outfit?"

"Oh, that's Blue. They're staying here tonight."

"What company are they from?"

"I think they're from Company I."

Corporal Kern did not need to tell me that the GIs were from the Third Battalion of the 335th Regiment. Red denoted the First Battalion. The Second Battalion was termed White.

After finishing my hot meal, I started a conversation with one Stan Evans of Arnold, Pennsylvania. He asked me what experiences the Second Battalion had encountered. After I had finished, he exclaimed, "You boys had it easy."

"What happened to Company I?"

"We came down the same route you did."

"Did you go into Marche?"

"Yes, but that's when we parted company with you. The next day (December 22) the company was out into the countryside to find out where Jerry was. Everything was fine until we got into a town by the name of Rochefort."

"What happened in Rochefort?"

"Jerry found us. He must have got us cut off cause no one stopped their tanks from coming in either direction. About half of Company I got lost or killed. No one knew what to do."

"How did you get out of that town?"

"The next morning our First Sergeant got some of us together and we slipped out of Rochefort and got into some woods. We kept walking back toward Marche. That was December 24. Some trucks picked us up and brought us here after riding around two or three days. It was like leading lambs to a slaughter. I still don't know what the idea was but it was like a nightmare."

"Didn't Company I try to set up any defense?"

"Couldn't do it. There were Germans in every direction. I mean everywhere. On our way back here we met some tanks from the Second Armoured. I heard they're going for that Panzer outfit that hit us."

"Guess the Second Battalion was rather lucky."

"I guess we got it this time. But your turn will come around. You can't be lucky forever."

Thursday, December 28, 1944

About 0230, I was standing my usual guard duty with Skinney Innes, when I felt something wet on my face.

"Skinney, is that rain or snow I feel?"

"Don, I think it's snow."

"I don't think we want this white stuff but we're going to get it anyway."

The snowfall lasted the entire day. By evening, there was three inches on the ground.

After the usual K ration breakfast of six small crackers, a small can of pork and eggs, one fig bar and some powdered coffee, I approached Sergeant Butler with another request.

"Sergeant, is it possible to go back to Marche to get a haircut?"

"Edwards, I can't leave you go. The whole battalion's supposed to shift around today. I don't know when it will be."

"Sarge, do you think there's any chance to get to a barber soon?"

"I don't know. But if you're willing to take a chance, I'll cut your hair if you want me to."

"I'll take the chance, Sarge."

The tonsorial work of the Sergeant turned out to be excellent. After I was finished, everyone in our message center secured a haircut from Sergeant Charles Butler. In the middle of the afternoon, the Communications Officer, Lieutenant Bernice Morgan, came to have his hair trimmed. The Sergeant could have had more customers since his fame had spread but he declined to cut any more heads. After all of us had been groomed, our move was postponed to some later date.

Just after our noon meal, our hosts, the Sieberts, learned that we were planning to move. Both John Crable and Charlie Simon talked to them for over an hour trying to explain that we were not retreating. John commented to me later saying, "I

271

don't think Charlie or I convinced them that we're not leaving. They think the Bosche will be here tomorrow."

"John, didn't you tell them that there are more Americans here than before?"

"Don, you and I know the Germans are not coming. We'd be out there trying to stop them. But the Siberts have much more respect for the military prowess of the Germans than they do for the Americans. They saw the map we received in Stars and Stripes. They believe we're going to give up Marche to the Germans."

"Do you think they're afraid?"

"You bet they are! The only way they are not going to be afraid is when the Germans are miles from here. I couldn't tell them when that will be."

The fears of our hosts seemed to be confirmed that evening about 2000. While chatting, we heard the sound of hobnail boots, signifying German soldatens. Papa Sibert yelled, "Le Bosche, Le Bosche?"

None of us became excited since we knew that there would be some shooting if the Germans had penetrated the line and were approaching our dwelling.

At that minute, Rochester, who was on guard, stuck his head inside the door.

"German prisoners coming up this way."

Crable quickly translated this to our hosts. The front door was opened. A half minute later, seven or eight Germans ran past the door with their hands behind their necks and an American guard urging them on.

This episode helped to quiet the fears of our three hosts. John talked to them. He stated that all of us would be out there with our guns, if needed.

Friday, December 29, 1944

The snow continued to fall throughout the entire day.

Shortly after 0830, it was necessary for me to go to the battalion CP to pick up a message. In front of the battalion headquarters were four German prisoners. They were standing and were guarded by two of the battalion's guards. About three or four Belgian civilians wandered by to look at the prisoners. Suddenly an elderly Belgian male broke and ran at one of the Germans. The civilian raised his right foot and kicked the German solidly in the butt. The Belgian was quickly restrained from further action. The look on the face of the enemy soldat was one of bewilderment but he was not hurt.

Shortly after 1200, the sector which had been occupied by the Second Battalion was reallocated. Blue Battalion took over half of White's front. Where there had been three rifle companies, there were now four. This meant that two companies could be placed in reserve. Company G was selected to rest in the Second Battalion, while Company I was selected from the Third Battalion.

The message center was moved back about 2,000 or more yards to just outside the city limits of Marche. Our new quarters were in a large house. There were four rooms plus a kitchen on the first floor. The second floor contained three huge bedrooms. The Belgian occupants, consisting of two women and three men, had not used the second floor since war activity had begun. Thus, the messengers secured permission to sleep in one of the bedrooms. We were confident that the Germans would not bother to shell us this far back from the front. John and I secured an old rug which we placed in the corner for our mattress. Both of us realized that we must keep away from the windows for fear of concussion from any shells as well as the possibility of glass breakage. The idea of precaution seemed to be discarded by our fellow messengers from G and H companies. Teets, Walters, Major and Simon decided to place their sleeping bags on the two beds in the room. They told John and myself, "After sleeping on the hard floor, we're going to sleep good."

John warned them, "The Germans are still here. They can shell us anytime."

Walters answered, "They won't bother us here."

Supper that day was another hot meal served in the adjoining garage. We brought back some food for our new hosts who

273

tended to stay in the only warm room in the entire house, namely, the kitchen.

All the messengers were happy this evening. Since the area had ample defenses, none of us were required to stand guard. Sergeant Butler had told us that no night messages would be contemplated for a few days. We would be able to sleep the entire night without any interferences.

However, the one party we would not notify would not let us have a peaceful sleep. Just after 2200, the Germans let us have an artillery barrage. All seemed to center around our dwelling. George Teets spoke, "Fellas, I think they're getting close."

"Too close as far as I'm concerned." echoed Walters.

I suggested, "I think everybody better put their boots on in case we need to make a dash for the cellar."

"I agree with Don," stated Major.

Within ten seconds after Major had agreed with me, an artillery shell landed in the backyard. Panes of glass gave way. The room was showered with tiny fragments. Without hesitation, the G company messengers, closely followed by those from Company H, were out of the room and on their way to the cellar. Crable and I waited.

"Don, do you think they'll hit the house next time?"

"My guess John, is that Jerry has quit for the night."

"Do you think we should follow the others? It should be safer."

"I agree. But let's wait. If another comes in, we'll go to the cellar. Besides the roof on this house should stand quite a blow. I think we'll be safe through another hit."

The Germans ceased their firing. John and I unlaced our boots and went quietly back to sleep. A half hour later, the other four messengers came back to the bedroom. We had plenty of fresh air.

Saturday, December 30, 1944

Just before 0200, the enemy fired another round of artillery shells. But none came close enough to warrant any movement by the six sleeping messengers.

Just after 0800, Sergeant Butler called me.

"Edwards, get down to our old battalion CP. Your company is going to move into it for their headquarters."

"How can I help them, Sarge?"

"Show them the whole place. I think some of your company men need a better place to rest than where they are now."

I hurried to the old company headquarters and met Sergeant Luther Sweet. We went to the new company headquarters. After showing him all the rooms and facilities, I inquired, "Why didn't someone else get this job?"

"Edwards, I'm back at our CP for a little rest. My feet are sort of bad."

"Didn't you go to the aid station?"

"No, you couldn't be evacuated unless your feet or hands were frozen. Just couldn't afford to spare the men. Any of us with just cold feet had to stay. It wasn't too bad until it began to snow cause you couldn't get the water out of the holes we were in."

"How are most of the rifle platoons, Sarge?"

"Think most of the boys are in pretty bad shape. But we couldn't do anything about it."

"How many with frozen feet were there?"

"Maybe two or three, Edwards. That's not too many of 'em. Just part of being where we are. Couldn't be helped."

"Wonder Sarge, who gave the orders that men with cold feet were not to be evacuated?"

"Ed, it doesn't matter. All I know is that it's in force. Captain Thompson been trying to help by giving rest to some of us. He's ok by me."

A hot meal was again served that day. It came about 1630. After the first helping was secured by everyone, some of us waited around to see if there would be seconds. To everyone's

275

delight, extras were available. A line of food-hungry GIs quickly formed.

Just as one of the cooks placed a slice of bread on my mess kit, I thought the roof had caved in. I knew from past experience that a mortar shell had hit close by. With the impact of the shell, all just dropped to the ground. No slight hesitation was shown. Food was unimportant. The mess kits overturned on loaves of bread. Coffee was mixed with gravy. Food and men were laying on the ground. Extras had ceased to be served. After laying prone for about five minutes, everyone rose, washed their mess kits in double fast time and left. Upon leaving the garage, I noted that the battalion CP had been smashed. Two sides of the building had been hit by mortars. We heard the cries of some wounded but someone stated that the medics were already there.

Upon arising from the floor, I discovered that the concussion from the mortar shells had knocked the left lens of my glasses loose. The glass itself was still intact. I easily put the lens back into the frame. A loss like this would have affected me immediately.

Just before dusk that evening, I thought I heard a loud noise like that of a low flying plane. The noise was unusually loud. It couldn't be one of ours since daylight had almost disappeared. Someone from the first floor yelled, "Everybody, look what's flying in the sky outside. Come out and see it."

All eight messengers ran down the stairs and outside. In the air was a large oblong object that appeared like a plane and a dirigible. Rochester asked, "What's that thing?"

"It's a V-1 rocket. Those are the things that have been hitting London," answered Teets.

We watched as the V-1 slowly went over the city of Marche. A few minutes later, the motor stopped. The downward flight started. Next came a deafening explosion.

"I think, if that rocket had cut off just five minutes sooner, we might never have seen it." noted Major.

"Yea. And we might never have heard it either." added Innes.

It would be the only rocket we would see during the war.

That night not a single shell of any type was heard. All the messengers slept through the whole night.

Sunday, December 31, 1944

After breakfast, John and I confronted Sergeant Butler with a request.

"Sarge, is it possible for both of us to go to church this morning in Marche?" inquired Crable.

"Will anyone cover for you while you're gone?"

"Yes, any of the F or G company runners will take our messages. They know where E headquarters are located," I answered.

"Permission granted, but come back as soon as you're through church."

The Catholic Church was located in the heart of the city. We proceeded there with both our prayerbooks and rifles. The latter we knew was necessary in case of any emergency.

Upon entering, we found no pews. The entire congregation was kneeling upon the seats of numerous chairs. John and I stood in the rear of the church. Soon we found two vacant chairs near a pillar. Since we were not going to leave our rifles in the rear of the church, we leaned them against the nearby pillar. When several American GIs saw what we had done, they followed our example. There were around 30 M-1 rifles against pillars throughout the church.

Ten minutes after mass had commenced, one of the rifles fell from its position. Immediately several Belgian civilians jumped up. When nothing happened, they resumed kneeling. During the entire service, ten or fifteen rifles hit the church floor. When the last one hit, none of the civilians bothered to turn his or her head.

When the fifth rifle fell, John turned to me saying, "Don, I hope no one left his clip in. If a single bullet is fired, there'll be an empty church."

"John, I'll bet someone forgot. Let's hope his piece doesn't fall."

277

We learned that the chairs upon which everyone knelt served a dual purpose. At the appropriate time, the chairs were turned around. Everyone then had a seat. It was low but comfortable. A little noise occurred when a shift was made. Most of us were fascinated by this arrangement.

Naturally the announcements and sermon were in French.

As we left, I asked John, "What did the priest say in the announcements?"

"The only portion I caught was that prayers should be offered for those working in Germany. As far as I could tell, he didn't say anything about the present situation here in Marche."

On our return to the message center, we walked behind two Belgian women. They were engaged in flowing conversation. They soon departed from our path. John said, "Don, they were talking about us. They were surprised about the large number of Americans in church today. They were quite happy about it. One of them said she had never seen a Bosche soldier in church the whole time they occupied Marche."

During the day, the enemy shelled some parts of Marche but none came in our vicinity. The messengers delivered the usual reports throughout the day. An hour never passed before another message had to be taken to the companies.

Just before 1600, John Crable asked the other seven messengers, "Fellas, do you have any extra K's you can give me?"

"Crable, are you trying to get fat?" inquired Walters.

"No, I've been invited for supper by the Siberts."

"They're not going to feed you this stuff?" Innes asked.

"No, but I think they can use anything we can give them. Remember they stayed up every evening we were on guard to give us hot coffee after we finished duty."

Each of us gave Crable a box of K-rations for our former hosts. John and I had previously agreed that I would take all messages in his absence.

It was New Year's Eve. Everyone in the message center had been given some liquor by our Belgian hosts. Other GI's had managed to secure some alcoholic beverages from various sources. We did not know what the enemy was doing, but everyone knew that this would have been a good time for the Germans to attack. Many were in no condition to fire any type of weapon or gun.

At 2355, our 84th Division artillery thought that a celebration was in order. At midnight, every artillery gun in our sector welcomed the New Year. The Germans must have believed the favor should be returned. A few minutes later, their guns welcomed the New Year. Our area was one of their targets. None of us in the bedroom moved while the remaining glass showered the room. No one was injured. We soon went to sleep.

Monday, January 1, 1945

Although there were a few swelled heads in the morning, the vast majority of the Second Battalion knew where they were. Danger was always present. New Year's Day was just another day at the front.

After the messengers had finished their usual K ration breakfast, Sergeant Butler entered the room.

"Have you heard the news?"

"No, Sarge, don't tell me the Krauts have surrendered cause they know they can't win in the snow." Walters retorted.

"No, Walters, but it's a good thought. Might be true some year."

"Seriously Sarge, what is the latest news?" inquired Crable.

"We're going to leave. Pack your duds and be ready to leave anytime from now on."

"Where are we going? Back to Germany?" Innes asked.

"Don't know. Nobody knows that as yet. Just be ready."

"Whose going to take our place in the line?"

"An English outfit."

"You mean some unit from the British Army?" Major asked.

"Yes, some English outfit. It's supposed to be the 53rd Welsh Division."

"My country cousins." I added.

"What do you mean your country cousins, Edwards. Are you Welsh?" asked Simon.

279

"My father's side of my family came from Wales. I may meet a long lost cousin."

During the morning, we guessed that the Germans might have celebrated the New Year more than us for nary a shell came into our area.

After lunch, Corporal Kern appeared in our room.

"The next time each of you goes to your company, you're to pick up your pay."

Simon, who was usually quiet asked, "What do we need money for Corporal? There's nothing to spend it on around here."

"You're right Simon. But that's the order we received. If you don't pick up your pay, I guess they'll just keep it."

After Corporal Kern left, Major turned and addressed Walters, "I think I know one guy who can use the dough, right Walters?"

"Major, what gives you that idea? I don't need one damn cent!"

"How'd you pay that dame you're visiting down the street in town?"

"Cigarettes, man, that's all you need is cigarettes."

"You mean those whores don't want American money?"

"I don't know whether they want our dough or not. Since we got to France, the only thing I've paid in is cigarettes. For a pack, they'll sleep with you all night. Those twenty weeds must be worth plenty when they sell them. Cigarettes is all I'm going to pay until they want cash."

"You goin to collect your pay today?"

"Sure Major, but on my way back here, I'm still going to pay that slut in cigarettes."

Just after 1500, it was necessary for me to deliver a message to my company. Upon my arrival, there were four or five of the men from the rifle platoons arguing with First Sergeant Goodpasteur.

"Can't they keep my money until I need it Sarge?" asked one of the assembled group.

"Just can't do it men." replied the First Sergeant.

"What am I going to do with it?"

"Keep it until you can spend the stuff."

"When will that be?"

"Can't tell you now."

Observing the disbursement of the payroll was an English officer from the 53rd Welsh Division. After I received my pay in cash, he motioned for me to come over to him.

"Yes, Lieutenant, can I help you?"

"Private what is your name?"

"Edwards, Sir."

"I noticed that you received only a few dollars and some pennies. Have you been fined or disciplined?"

"No, Sir."

"Is there a grade lower than private in the American Army?"

"No, Sir."

"I'd be interested to know why you were paid so little?"

"Well, Sir, I wasn't paid less than the other men. Back in England, I made arrangements to have most of my pay put into like an Army bank. I figured that if my outfit was near the front, there would not be much opportunity to spend it. Most of my buddies thought I was nuts in doing it, but if something happens to me, my folks can use the money back in Michigan better than I can here in England."

"I congratulate you Private Edwards. Jolly good thinking."

"Thank you, Sir."

After leaving the Company E headquarters, I had to make a stop at our former message center to fetch Crable. John had gone to have lunch with our former hosts, the Siberts. Upon my arrival, the threesome of this family was very happy to see me. They thought I had come to have supper with them. John, in his now developed French, told them that this was our last visit with them and that our unit would be leaving that night. The three Siberts began to cry. Crable tried to reassure them that we had to leave in order to drive the Germans back into their homeland and we would win the war. After each of his statements, they would say, "Oui, Oui."

281

A PRIVATE'S DIARY

After a half hour of trying to leave, I finally told John, "Crable, I think they're going to miss us at the center if we don't get back there soon."

John then made one more explanation, picked up his rifle and we departed. The three Siberts waved to us with their handkerchiefs as we marched back up the road and out of their sight.

As we walked back to the message center, John said, "Don, I'm glad you came to get me. I don't think they would have let me go if you hadn't been there."

"You mean, John, I was the bad guy."

"In a way. I told them you came with an order that I had to go back with you or get in trouble."

"That's ok with me John. Did you learn any French from them?"

"I sure did. Speaking with them in their language on a daily basis makes you learn the language in a hurry."

"Let's hope both of us survive this thing and you can see them again."

"I'll double that Don."

We arrived back at the battalion headquarters just before 1700. The English had begun to arrive. It seemed as if they outnumbered us by two to one. All of the messengers were amazed to see the British set up everything they owned right on the front line. The most unusual item was that their kitchen was set up in the very garage where we had been eating our hot meals. This appeared irregular to us for our U.S. Army kitchens were placed many miles behind the front lines. Then, the food was brought up in large cans or jars in which it was kept relatively warm. We wondered aloud what passed if the British ever had to retreat. We knew our kitchens were safe in the rear area.

The other thing we noted about the British Army was their main vehicle. In our army, the jeep was the most familiar in use near the front. Our allies used the Weasel, which was a small tracked vehicle, but must slower than our jeep.

After supper, which was the usual K rations, one messengers from each company went out to assist the trucks in order for the various companies to load. The task took about a half an hour. During the next ten minutes, I had an interesting con-versation with one of the Negro drivers of this Quartermaster unit.

"What's you name, Private?"

"Edwards, what's yours?"

"Fred Jones."

"How have things been for you, Fred?"

"Pretty good, but we don't get to see any of the action."

I shook my head. "You mean you would like to be in the Infantry!"

"I sure would. But you know how the Army treats us Negroes. They think we wouldn't know what to do up there."

"Fred, you may think you want to see the action, but you don't. It's messy and bloody. It isn't like they picture it in the movies."

"You mean, Edwards, you not afiring all the time and the enemy just can't stand up to you white guys."

"Believe it or not, it's one of the most boring jobs there is. You sit and wait most of the time. No one fires unless they need to do so."

"Edwards, you got a whole mess of bullets around your waist. Don't you keep using them and get new ones all the time?"

"No, Fred. I've fired my rifle very few times. In the Infan-try you're always worried that you'll be cut off. Then you'll really have to use those bullets."

"Edwards, you're one of the first white guys that ever told me what it's really like up front. Still I'd like to see for myself. And that goes for most of the guys driving these here trucks."

"Fred, let me tell you that if we could legally trade places now, I'd do it right now. And I don't know what's coming in the next month or two."

"Ed, you might be right. But I'd sure like to try it. Us black boys don't have no choice."

"Fred, I think that might change in the future. I, for one, would welcome the opportunity to choose. But I'd guess that after you find out what it's really like, you would be like me. I can't wait for this war to end. If it goes too long, I'll either be in my grave or in some hospital."

"Don't you white boys get a chance to go back to the States after a while?"

"Yes, after six months."

"Isn't that good, Edwards?"

"Fred, it might sound like it but no one from the battalion forward through the lettered companies will last six months. My guess is that, maybe, one GI out of a hundred will last six months without something happening to him."

"Anything happen to you, Ed?"

"Yes, I got a small scratch on my left hand and cut on my right forearm, but it's not serious like some of the fellas I've seen."

"Still think it's exciting being at the front?"

"Fred, it isn't believe me. I would rather drive a truck any day of the week."

We shook hands a few minutes later. I don't think I had convinced Fred Jones that being up front was not like the movies.

Just after 2000, four British enlisted men and a Captain came into our dwelling. The Captain spoke fluent French. He asked us about sleeping quarters. Then, one of the Belgian ladies came forth and took him to our bedroom on the second floor, minus glass windows. The four enlisted men joined our little circle.

"How long have you lads been here?" asked an English private.

"Since December 21st. Where have you been?" I asked.

"Up in Holland. We were supposed to get a rest. But we came here to help you, I guess."

All eight of us were stunned. We knew quite well that there had been trouble upon our arrival. But we were convinced that the Germans presented no big threat to us under present circumstances. After a few seconds, I spoke, "There's no trouble here any longer. Maybe we're supposed to be back in Germany and our old position at the end of the American line."

I then added, "What part of Wales are you from?"

"I'm from Yorkshire. That's in northern England."

"Aren't all of you in the Division from Wales?"

"Oh no. That's just the name of the Division. We've got people from both England and Wales. None from Scotland or Ireland that I know of."

At that moment, the British Captain reappeared. He commanded the four enlisted men to accompany him. Upon leaving, my new unknown English friend said, "Cheerio, hope this thing is over soon."

"Right on." I answered.

Within the next hour, the order to mount the trucks was given. As we loaded on the 2½ ton vehicles, we noticed the newly arrived British soldiers looking for their new quarters in Marche.

XVIII

THE OFFENSIVE IN
THE ARDENNES

1. Amonines

Monday, January 1, 1945

For this trip, it was ordered by Sergeant Butler that only one messenger from each of the four lettered companies would return to his respective company. It was agreed between John and myself that I would remain with the Battalion Headquarters.

By 2000, all the members of Headquarters Company were loaded on the 2½ ton trucks. By usual Army standards, we knew that some type of wait would be necessary. Many in the truck began to wonder aloud where this next journey would take us. From the darkness under the canvas came different guesses.

"My guess, fellars, is that they're just taking our outfit out of here. They're putting in the Limeys so we can go back up to Germany and get on with the show. So what if the Germans sit here in Belgium. If we can get into their own land, they just have to fall back and defend it. Don't you agree, Harry?"

"It don't make sense, Dick. Why didn't they leave us here and let the Limeys go forward. I'd say we're goin back for a rest. Then we'll come right back and relieve those English. Watch and see if I'm not right!"

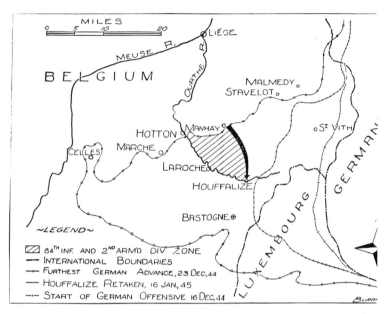

Map of the Ardennes Offensive

Another voice shouted out, "Give us a rest! They don't know what the word means. Did they give us one when we were taken off the line in Lindern? Hell no! And they won't give us one now. We're going right back into the line and push Jerry right out of this area."

Just at that moment, the motors in our truck turned over. The last parting words were, "We'll soon find out who's right."

At 2130, the convoy inched forward. Most of the GIs fell asleep as best they could in the moving vehicle. Others peered out into the darkness to find out where the convoy was going. In a few minutes the Second Battalion was out of the city of Marche. We had passed into the Belgian countryside. After what seemed like constant hours of peering, my eyes went into a state of truck-sleepness. This was a medium between complete rest and actually being awake. This unusual state can only be acquired by those who have ridden U.S. Army vehicles and know the constant stopping and bouncing that occurs. As usual,

288

my seat was at the end of the truck row. I was able to obtain it since it was the coldest spot where one could sit.

Tuesday, January 2, 1945

Where the trucks were going was a complete mystery. Numerous stops were made, but no one was allowed to leave his vehicle. The ride continued for what seemed like endless miles. At 0230, the convoy made another stop. A few minutes later, First Sergeant Salvatore Vignato of the Headquarters Company yelled, "Fall Out."

Every man staggered half asleep out onto the snow. Until we detrucked, no one had realized how cold it was. The chill seemed to go right through out bodies. Soon everyone was looking for some houses. About a half mile away was a small farm village.

We stood around tramping our feet, trying to keep warm. An hour later, one of the men from the Headquarters came with an order.

"We're supposed to stay here. Everybody's to sleep out in the open. Those are the orders from Colonel Parker."

"Why can't we sleep in the town?" a voice asked.

"We're not supposed to disturb the civilians and sleep in their houses."

"Why that God damn no good son of a bitch. I suppose the dear old Colonel is sleeping out in the snow. All he can think of is himself. Not a fucking consideration for us damn souls."

"What about our new commanding officer for the Battalion, whatever his name is, I forget. Did he say anything?"

"Lieutenant Colonel Bond is just following orders."

"What is his name anyway?"

"Lieutenant Colonel Ridgely Bond."

"I'd say he no better than that louse Urban if he won't do something for us."

Before any more muttering could be voiced, Sergeant Vignato interrupted, "Men, I'm going into that village and try to find a place to sleep. If any of you want to do the same, you can."

Everyone followed his unwritten order. Not a person stayed to sleep outside.

Inside the small village, we found numerous vehicles of the Second Armored Division. Their members were sleeping inside somewhere. As I wandered about, I bumped into John Crable.

"John, is Company E here?"

"Yes, Don, where is the Message Center?"

"I don't know. We really do not have one. We were ordered to sleep out in the open fields. But Sarge Vignato told his company to find quarters inside this village. What about Company E?"

"Same thing. They were prepared to sleep out in the snow when somebody told them to move into some farm house and barn. Let's find a place for ourselves if there's no message center."

"Crable, you're a thousand percent right!"

After a search of ten minutes, a barn with an abundant supply of hay was found. We agreed that the loose hay was to be our bed for the remainder of the night.

A little after 0700, I received one of the fastest awakenings I ever experienced. My back received a terrific jolt by two heels that were attached to someone's shoes.

"Ooooooo what hit me?" I mumbled.

A voice replied, "I'm sorry, I didn't realize you were there."

"That's ok. But please watch where you plant those feet. My back isn't up to it."

Crable was easily awakened.

"Hey, Don, look. There's a ladder leading to a loft. Let's move and fast."

Two minutes after our move, more members of the Second Armored Division were ready to jump down to the first floor.

I yelled, "Watch where you jump fellas. Two of us are down here."

After watching five more GIs jump, we decided that our sleep had ended. After strapping our packs, John and I decided that the first order of business was to find Sergeant Butler and

290

the other messengers. Since there were numerous American soldiers wandering about, we had little trouble locating our duty post. Upon our arrival, Innes asked, "Where have you fellas been? We've been waiting hours for you."

"I'll bet you have," was my retort.

After inquiry, it was discovered that all eight messengers had arrived within the space of ten minutes. Only one trip was made with an order that morning. Since John knew where Company E was located, I accompanied him on the run.

We discovered that we were in the small town of Soy. The entire Second Battalion was in the immediate area, plus a unit of the 66th Armored Regiment. Just before 1030, we were ordered to prepare for another move. All five companies of the Second Battalion were shortly out on the road awaiting the next move. During our talks, Teets mentioned, "Was everyone like Company G? We slept out in the snow last night. The guys are sure mad about it."

"George, I think every company was given the order. But nobody obeyed it. Sergeant Vignato told us that he wasn't going to sleep outside. So everybody from Headquarters found some place to sleep," stated his companion Walters.

At 1130, the entire Second Battalion boarded trucks. Within five minutes, we were on our way again. The pace was slow. Along the road, I noted the telephone lines that were being strung by both American and British wiremen. The British line was blue while the American one was the dull black. Later we would see the red lines which were used by the Germans.

Just before 1400, our convoy passed some American artillery pieces which were firing, we guessed, at the enemy lines. We knew the front was less than five miles away. We were not returning to Germany. Just after passing the artillery, the trucks stopped.

"Everybody fall out," barked Sergeant Vignato.

As we detrucked, Rochester piped, "The 84th to the rescue, that's us."

"How do you figure that out?" asked Innes.

"Well, that artillery's firing for one reason only. To keep Jerry from moving forward. He's most probably broken through here and we're here to stop him."

"Doesn't seem right to me. Hey, look at those trucks. They're from the 75th Division. Wonder where they're going?"

A few minutes later, Rochester noted, "Skinney, those trucks are pulling that artillery to the rear. It looks bad to me."

As we stood jawing by the road, a small well-closed-in jeep with two shiny stars on a red license plate drove by.

"Hell, just look at that, the General's here!" shouted Walters.

The jeep carrying Major General Alexander Bolling, the 84th Division's Commander, went slowly past us and continued on ahead.

"Wonder where he's going?" inquired Skinney.

"Guess yourself," answered Teets.

"I wish he'd tell us what's going on," added Simon.

"That will be the day. Nobody knows anything," stated Salvador Munoz, who had returned to the messengers as one of the two representatives from Company H. Frank Major had received orders that he was transferred back to Company H as a carrier of machine gun ammunition. Sergeant Gooding had secured his revenge.

Ten minutes later, the two star jeep returned. It continued toward the rear.

"Things can't be too hot around here or the General wouldn't have shown up," commented Skinney.

During this time, our trucks still remained on the road empty. The order was issued to again board the vehicles.

Shortly thereafter the highway made a hairpin turn. While moving down one side, we could see bursting shells on the next hill. At the base of the hairpin turn was a road which, we assumed, led toward the front. Our trucks turned up the other side of the hairpin. They stopped. Sergeant Vignato came to every truck and ordered, "Everyone stay in the trucks until orders are given."

While John and I were waiting, some members of Company E went walking past our vehicle. My voice rang out, "Hey, fellas, what are you doing here?"

"Hi, Ed," replied Bill Wallace. "We're staying here."

"Where, Bill?"

"See that hotel—about 200 yards yonder up the road. The whole company's staying there. Sergeant Dempsey said that we were going to stay there all night."

Our truck started again. Our convoy made a U-turn and came back past the base of the hairpin turn. We went a short way up the other side and stopped. We detrucked.

We were in the town of Fisenne. Sergeant Butler found a house where the messengers were to be located. Our Belgian hostess, a woman of about 35 years old and her three children, seemed glad to accommodate us. Crable and Simon spoke in French to her about our purpose in coming into her home.

The terrain around us was extremely hilly. Across the road from our new billet was a gully which carried the Aisne River. It seemed to run fifty feet below the roadway.

According to the rumors we heard, the front was less than two miles away. An attack was to be made against the enemy within the next few days. The idea was to close the bulge which existed on the front in the Ardennes. That evening all eight messengers were in bed by 2100. We knew something was up but no one knew what should be expected.

Wednesday, January 3, 1945

All the messengers were ready to operate by 0630. However, almost the entire morning was spent doing nothing. We all tried to guess what the future would bring. None of us ventured outdoors because during the night about three inches of new snow had fallen. Although the flakes looked beautiful, walking conditions were extremely difficult.

Just after 1130, I was directed by Corporal Kern to deliver a message to Company E. As far as I knew, my company was still in the same location. After securing a ride to the small town of Erezee, I learned that there was no Company E in the area. The 335th Regimental Command Post was scheduled to move in that afternoon. Numerous inquiries were made of the GI setting up telephone wires for the new location of the regiment. No one had any information. I found Captain Carl Read and asked, "Captain, do you know where Company E is located?"

"Edwards, I'm sorry I don't. You'll have to wait until S-3 gets here. They'll know for sure."

"When would that be, Captain?"

"Again I have no idea. But it will be, at least, two hours."

"Thank you. I guess I'll have to find them myself."

For the next half hour, I made eight or nine inquiries regarding the whereabouts of Company E. In reply to my question, a corporal from the Second Armored finally answered, "Yea, I noticed a group of marching men walking down that road."

"Corporal, did they turn off, or go up the hairpin?"

"I'm not sure, but it seems they went off down the road."

I hastened to the junction of the hairpin road and the one that led off from it. The road and its surrounding area seemed devoid of human life. I wondered if I had made a mistake. Maybe I would wander behind the German line. After a walk of over a mile, I entered the small village of Blier. Again there were no people around of any type. I continued walking straight ahead. While I trudged along, I noticed the small creek, which was the Aisne River, could be clearly seen immediately to the left of the road. On the other side of Blier, a member of the 75th Infantry Division was met.

"Have you seen anybody from the 84th Division around?" I asked.

"Yes, you bet, I see you're from that Division."

"I am. Are there any more in the immediate vicinity?"

"There sure are. There are some right up that hill and some ahead in the village."

"You don't know the outfits by chance?"

"No, but you might find out from those on that hill."

"Thanks. By the way what's going on here?"

294

"There's some fighting going on ahead in the next village. Seems as though almost all the Germans have left now. But I'm not positive."

"Thanks again. I'll get up that hill."

On the hill, I found Company E. Every man was digging a foxhole in the new snow. First Sergeant Goodpasteur was located. The message was delivered to him. Since a reply was required, I began to help dig the foxholes for some members of the Headquarters platoon. While doing the digging, I heard a message come over the radio. Company E was ordered to move into the village and take defensive positions on the other side.

I inquired from Sergeant Goodpasteur.

"Is the Second Battalion in any fighting yet?"

"No, Edwards. We're not in it yet. The 290th Regiment is cleaning out the town. We're going to relieve them in a few minutes."

"Into what town is the company going?"

"I think it's called Amonines."

As I left, Company E began marching forward to take their new positions.

After a walk of nearly an hour, I arrived back in Fisenne. The Message Center had moved. For the next ten minutes, inquiries were made as to its whereabouts. Its new location was only four hundred yards from the former site.

After delivery of the message, John filled me in on what was to happen.

"Don, the 84th and Second Armored are joined together in Combat Command B. The general in charge is from the Second Armored. The idea is for the tanks to attack and the infantry is to support them."

"John, have you been outside?"

"No. Why?"

"Unless that snow melts, those tanks are going to be worthless. The road is icy and slippery. It took me about an hour to walk about three miles. Usually I can do five. The area from here to the company is full of trees. I can't see any flat land of any type. It might change but the Armored's not going to help the guys in the foxholes. If I know the Germans, they'll have every road mined and blocked. I don't like the looks of it any way, shape or form."

"Don, I think you're wrong."

"What else did you learn?"

"The 84th is one of the main outfits that are supposed to drive the Germans out of Belgium. We're not going back to Germany until the Third Army is met."

"Where is the Third Army coming from?"

"From the south. We're on the north side of the Bulge as part of the First Army. The idea is to trap the Germans in a pocket as they did in France. If it succeeds, it might end the war."

"I sure hope so. But unless the weather gets better, it's going to be tough."

No order was given that all the messengers should retire early. All knew from my report that our Second Battalion would be in real action soon.

Thursday, January 4, 1945

Everyone in the message center was ready by 0630. We knew that a move would be made today. The artillery was firing as soon as dawn had broken. Rumors of all types were prevalent.

At 1100, Sergeant Butler and two others left in a jeep. The jeep was to return as soon as possible for the eight messengers. Just as the jeep left, a unit from the Second Armored Division in two half-track vehicles appeared.

"Are you leaving soon?" asked a Staff Sergeant.

"As soon as we can," answered Simon.

"It's ok then, if we take over."

"Sure thing."

In the next few minutes, several of the Armored GIs came into the house and deposited a few packs to indicate that they had taken possession of this dwelling. Then, they took out their mess kits and left for their kitchen which was located about a

1,000 yards away. Three of them returned with their mess kits containing a hot turkey dinner.

I inquired, "Do you think there'll be any left over?"

"Sure, why don't you get your kits and go. They'll feed you."

All eight of us secured our mess kits. We jointed the chow line. The mess sergeant eyed us as we started down the line. But he said nothing. We secured a good helping of every item and returned to our dwelling to eat. A hot meal was always preferred to a K-ration lunch.

Just before 1330, Private Larry Gardiner returned with the jeep. All eight messengers somehow squeezed into the jeep. The jeep went down the hairpin turn but at the junction, the road toward Bliers was followed. We soon met the 325th Field Artillery. Their trucks were parked along the road. Behind the trucks were the huge 155 millimeter howitzers. Gardiner threaded the jeep past the trucks and weapons with great care since there was little room remaining on the road. The village of Bliers was entered. There were troops and vehicles everywhere. I could not believe the change that had occurred in just twenty-four hours. Our jeep proceeded slowly through the town. Five minutes later, the jeep brought us into Amonines. Gardiner told us that the previous day it had been occupied by the enemy. He sped the jeep right up to the front door of the Second Battalion's Command Post which was housed in a small hotel. At the door to greet us was Corporal John C. Kern of Hinsdale, Illinois.

"Hi, Corporal," we all shouted.

"I've got bad news for you men."

"Who?" piped up Munoz.

"All of you."

"Such as," stated Rochester.

"You're all to return to your companies."

"Why?" was the chorus of eight voices.

"Colonel Bond ordered it."

"Didn't you tell him what our jobs are?" Crable asked.

"No. He gave the order. I'm passing it on to you. that's all there is to it. You're to return to your companies."

"But when are we to come back?" pleaded Innes.

297

"Whenever the Colonel orders it."

"And suppose we're in a nice foxhole and can't get out when that time comes." stated Walters.

"Can't be helped men, you'll have to take that chance."

"Can't you talk to him just once more?" cut in Simon.

"No. He gave the order. When you're wanted, he'll call for you."

For the next fifty minutes, this conversation continued. Corporal Kern had been given an order. He would not plead our case. The torrent of words was to no avail. Corporal Kern pointed out where each company was located. The eight of us set out for our respective companies.

John and I walked slowly.

"What do you think, John?"

"Don, up to now, it's been pretty good. I'm a little worried what Sergeant Smith might do with us when we get back to the company."

"I agree with you. But we'll just have to tell him the truth."

As we dragged slowly along, we tried to convince ourselves of the necessity of our jobs. From experience we knew that if we were given tasks as riflemen, our chances of survival were extremely poor. As messengers, our chances of survival were fair.

We soon found Company E which was situated in a large brick house at the far end of Amonines. The house had two floors and a basement. The second floor was not used except for observation. Upon entering, we reported to Sergeant Smith.

"What are you doing here, Edwards and Crable?"

John then gave the Sergeant the whole story. His reaction was, "I don't understand this new battalion commander, Colonel Bond, but I guess he had his reasons."

Captain Thompson noticed John and me. Sergeant Smith then explained the situation.

"Edwards, Crable, come here. What's the matter with you two?"

"Nothing Captain. We were just told to leave," was my reply.

"I don't believe you two. Can't you two handled the job? Or is battalion unable to handle you two? Tell me what's going on, will you?"

John replied, "Captain, we don't know the reason for this. If we did, Edwards and I would tell you. But we don't, Sir."

"I have enough to worry about besides you two. Keep out of the way now. If you don't get this thing settled by tomorrow, you'll join the first platoon. They're short some men now."

John and I tried to place ourselves in a corner of the cellar. Neither of us said anything to each other. No talking was needed now.

About a half hour of silence was broken by a terrific noise right overhead. All knew that a shell had landed. Within a few seconds, a voice yelled, "Captain, the right side of the house has been hit. Three men have been hit bad. Better call the medics."

The radio operator for Company called the medics. When some calm had been restored, John and I simply, without any words between us, left the cellar for the first floor. We found an old table in the kitchen and laid under it. We proceeded to eat our K rations. Men from the various platoons were constantly coming in and leaving. The company headquarters was the place to gain a few minutes relief from the cold foxholes. It seemed that the temperature was close to zero degrees, Fahrenheit.

Shortly after 1800, Captain Thompson came to the first floor to inspect how the changing of the foxholes was going. He saw Crable and myself under the table.

"What are you two still doing here?"

I answered, "Captain, we were told to stay here until battalion requested us to return."

"I want you two to get back to battalion! Tell the Colonel either he wants you two louses or he doesn't! If he doesn't, tell him he'll get no more men to run!"

"Yes, Sir."

"Now I want you two out of here now! Space is too valuable for you two to stay here. Do you both understand me?"

"We do, Captain."

We hurriedly got our packs and got out the door. As we stepped into the yard, another shell landed on the other side of the house.

As we slowly moved back toward the battalion headquarters, we debated what to do.

"John, we're in trouble. The Colonel says there are to be no messengers at battalion. Is that right?"

"Don it is. But Captain Thompson says we are to be at battalion or else."

"You and I know that what else is. I'm damn mad about it, John, because back in Louisiana, no one wanted this job as messenger. You had a hard time being convinced."

"You're right, but that does not solve our present situation. Any suggestions?"

"Let's try to stay out of the way for a day or two. I think we'll tell Kern we're here, but don't let any of the officers see us. I think Captain Price would want us but I don't know about the rest of them. Getting Bond to replace Colonel Urban back in Marche wasn't too good for us."

"Urban was no good, but Bond, I think, doesn't know what function we play."

"John, my father wants me to be a lawyer some day. Let's see what I can do in talking to Kern."

We arrived at the small hotel which housed the Battalion's Command Post. A request was made of the battalion guard to get Corporal Kern who soon appeared.

"Crable, Edwards, what are you two doing here?"

"Captain Thompson sent us back here."

"But Colonel Bond ordered the messengers back to their companies."

"I know, Corporal Kern, but if John and I reappear at Company E tonight, we will never be messengers again. Captain Thompson is really mad and will put us outside in the line."

"What do you propose to do then?"

"Crable and I will find a room in some vacant house. We'll keep out of sight of anyone from battalion. Only you will know that we are here. Don't tell anyone until we are all recalled. I'm sure we will be, but we'll have to be patient."

"Edwards, I don't like this. But is no one sees you for the night, maybe things will be different in the morning."

"Corporal, think. If there are no messengers, you don't have a job either. The same goes for Sergeant Butler."

"Edwards, you're right! I never thought of it that way. OK then. You and Crable find something. Report to me sometime in the morning and I'll see what can be done."

John and I left.

"Don, I think you hit the nail on the head. Kern never thought that without us, he'd have no job. I'll bet you anything that everything will be all right in the morning."

"John, I hope for both of us, we're back in business."

A suitable place had to be found for our night's lodging. I noticed a large building which seemed like a colonial house. It was located about 200 yards from the CP on the west side of the town square of Amonines.

"John, how does that colonial building look to you?"

"OK. Let's investigate it."

The door made no noise as I pushed it. Inside it was pitch black. This presented no problem since we left the front door open. Upon entering we saw that there were four doors leading from the long first floor hallway.

"John, I'll open each door. But cover me in case someone stayed behind."

"Don, push each one fast. Jump in with your rifle ready."

"Will do."

The first door on the left was locked.

"John, should I break the lock with a shot?"

"No, leave it alone for now. Let's not make any unnecessary noise."

The first door on the right side was open. Inside was a large sitting room complete with furniture still intact. The other two rooms proved to have doors open. They, too, seemed to be sitting rooms.

"John, the last room on the right seems to be in the best shape. Let's sleep there."

"I agree, Don. But let's check the upstairs first. We still don't know if a German or two may have stayed behind."

301

While John remained on the first floor, I ran to the second. After arriving there, John joined me. The same pattern was followed in examining each of the four rooms on the upper floor. All four were bedrooms.

"John, let's each take a mattress down to the first floor."

"Right, we might as well sleep in comfort. You and I could be in a foxhole tomorrow night."

After the mattresses were dragged to our new room, I suggested that we should reinspect the upstairs. John agreed. In my second inspection, I used the small flashlight that I carried.

"Don, keep that flashlight down. We don't know who is out there."

"I'll do it John, but Jerry can't see it from here."

"You don't know that. Watch that light."

After we had settled into our newly converted sitting room, I noticed, "If we could cover those windows John, we could use those three candles that I found upstairs."

"I'll put them up, if you hand me those extra blankets."

The window was covered by two or three blankets. After completion, I inspected the job from the outside. John lit a small candle upon a tap from me upon the window pane. No light could be seen. After getting back into the room, about five or six 88s came sailing into the area.

"Don, I told you the Germans would see that light of yours."

"Maybe they did and maybe they didn't. Let me do my writing now."

Three more candles were now lit. I proceeded to write in my small notebook.

"Don, I sure hope that no one knows you're writing what's happening to us. If any of the officers outside of Captain Price knows what you're doing, you are in big trouble. What are you going to do if we lose this messenger job and you're put on the line?"

"I think I'd give up writing it John. It would be too dangerous to keep it on the line."

"I sure hope you don't wander into the Germans line some day. They'll know everything about this outfit."

302

"I agree they would. But I just want to keep a record of what I've done during this big war."

At 2130, we blew out the candles. The lock on the door was turned. But we still kept our rifles next to us.

2. Dochamps

Friday, January 5, 1945

Considering our previous day of tension, John and I slept well on our Belgian mattresses. Just prior to 0700, I looked out the front door of our dwelling and spotted Corporal John Kern.

"Hey, Corporal!"

"Yes, Edwards."

"Any news?"

"Yes, I just told the Colonel that I would get the messengers back here. He just said, 'Do it, Corporal.' I knew you were here so I went to the other three companies and told them to send back their messengers."

"When will everybody be here?"

"The other six should be here within fifteen minutes."

By 0730, a reunion was in progress between the eight of us. None had experienced any difficulty except John and I. Teets and Walters said they told their First Sergeant they were to remain there just one night until battalion had room for them. All were delighted with the room that John and I had selected. Additional mattresses were brought down from the bedrooms.

At 0800, Corporal Kern appeared at the door.

"Edwards, can you take a message?"

"You bet, Corporal. I think Captain Thompson will be happy to see me at work."

At the headquarters of Company E, Captain Thompson did not say a single word about the previous evening. He wrote his reply on the message form which I had brought. As I was about to leave, Wallace and Gainer asked me, "Edwards, are we going to attack today?"

"Fellas, I haven't heard anything yet. But I don't think we're going to stay put."

"When do you think it will start?"

"I couldn't guess."

But at that moment, the answer had arrived. Captain Price walked into the dwelling with an arm full of maps. As we stood around, he instructed Captain Thompson and the other officers of Company E that the attack would start at 0900 — less than an hour away. Company E was to lead the battalion attack along the road running by the Aisne River. After listening to the full explanation, I returned to battalion headquarters.

At 1100, the two Company E messengers were ordered to take a Number 300 radio and a spare battery to our company. As we walked through Amonines, everything was quiet. The war seemed miles away. Soon we passed the former headquarters of Company E. We could see that a good portion of the house was detached as a result of the shells that had landed on it. Just ahead were ten disabled German vehicles such as Volkswagens and personnel carriers. They appeared to have been hit in an air attack. Less than 500 yards from the knocked-out vehicles was a small house. This was the new CP for Company E. As we entered Sergeant Smith greeted us.

"Crable, Edwards, I see you're back in business."

"Yes, we are, Sergeant," was my reply.

"What have you got for me?"

"We brought the new 300 radio and the spare battery."

"That was fast. Doing a better job after last night's adventure?"

"No, the same usual good job. I think there was a mix-up at battalion. We're back as messengers today."

"If you have to see Goodpasteur, he's out with the Captain. They are just ahead on the road."

"No, but Captain Price asked me to deliver a message to Lieutenant Lusby. Is he with them?"

"Yes, he's conferring with the Captain. You can't miss them, straight ahead."

Just as John and I were about to leave through the front door, a round of six or eight 88s landed around the house. None struck the building. As we left, John noted, "If we had left two minutes earlier, Don, one of those 88s would have gotten us."

"I know, John. Let's hope our luck holds."

We proceeded forward on the road. No more than 150 yards from the house was a tank from the Second Armored. Behind it were Lieutenant Lusby, Captain Thompson and a few others. On either side of the road, lying or kneeling was Company E. I delivered my message to the Lieutenant who had to write a reply. As he pondered what to write, I looked from behind the tank. Ahead about 200 yards was a road block of logs that completely covered the highway from one side to the other.

I inquired, "Can't that road block be reduced?"

"Go right ahead and try, Edwards." replied Sergeant Goodpasteur.

"What's been happening, Sarge?"

"Anytime any of us try to get close, Jerry opens up with a machine gun. We can't move."

As Sergeant Goodpasteur spoke, the German machine gun blazed away. Some rifles also fired. As soon as the bullets stopped, mortars began to fall in the area. All tried to hide under the tank with little success.

When the firing ceased, Lieutenant Lusby wrote his reply. I retraced my steps. Just as John and I reached the area of the small house, another round of 88s landed. Without any hesitation, we were in the ditch. For about five minutes the enemy kept up their barrage. Then quiet reigned. We started a quick trot back toward Amonines. On our way back, Company G, which was approaching, was to try to flank the German roadblock.

During the morning hours, other personnel occupied the vacant rooms. The Belgian family, which owned the house, returned and took possession of the kitchen. This was the room which had been locked the previous evening.

Just after lunch, Sergeant Rochester rushed in. He shouted, "Fellas, they've got two prisoners in the hallway."

We realized that prisoners on this day were very valuable. The stiff resistance that our battalion was meeting might be solved by the use of information gathered from some captured prisoners. What made the two prisoners unusual was that one was a member of the vaunted SS while the other was a plain Wehrmacht soldat. Private Bill Wiles, the battalion's interrogator, was attempting to question the SS soldat. He appeared to be a youth of about 17. A large wallet had been taken from him but it contained no valuable information. Wiles tried and tried to get some answers from the hard-faced young prisoner. He simply would not reply. Although there were ten of us standing around with rifles, the elite German soldat remained firm in his refusal to answer.

The Wehrmacht prisoner, on the other hand, presented a sharp contrast. He was an older man, probably in his late 30's, who was slovenly dressed in his gray uniform. His reaction to all of us standing about seemed to be one of extreme fear. He constantly looked at the SS soldier. Upon questioning, he gave a few answers. On some he refused to reply. Wiles made a request.

"Men, I think the regular soldier is afraid that someone is going to shoot him. I'd appreciate it if most of you would return to your places."

Almost everyone complied with his request. I asked permission to stay which was granted. Wiles separated the two prisoners. I escorted the SS soldat to the end of the hallway. Wiles was about to resume his questioning of the Wehrmacht soldat when a jeep arrived. The prisoners were placed in it with the usual guard. We later learned that the Wehrmacht prisoner was very cooperative back at regimental headquarters when he no longer feared for his life.

Upon my return to the messenger's room, a discussion was in progress on what it would be like to be a POW. Teets expressed it in a few words saying, "They keep telling us that all you have to give is your name, rank and serial number. But I guess if your life is at stake, you'd tell them more. Especially, if a bunch of guys are standing around with guns. One goes off, who cares. This is war!"

A little after 1600, Corporal Kern appeared in our room.

"This time men, I've got good news for you."

"Tell us," stated Simon.

"Lieutenant Colonel Bond has been transferred to be commander of the Third or Blue Battalion."

A cheer went up from all the messengers. Although Colonel Bond had been in command of the Second Battalion just over a week, the messengers did not want a Commanding Officer who would terminate their jobs.

During the remainder of the day, no other messages were taken. From this activity, we knew the forward progress of our battalion was slow.

Early in the evening, I visited the radio room of the battalion. I learned that the road block had finally been taken after a whole day of fighting. Company E had had thirteen men wounded and one killed.

Saturday, January 6, 1944

At 0630, Corporal Kern shook all the eight messengers.

"Which of you is going with the Major today?" he inquired.

"Corporal, what's happening?" asked George Teets.

"As I understand it, Major Lamb, our new commander, is going to lead the attack today. He wants four messengers with him at all times, in order to keep communications with the companies."

"I thought another battalion was going to attack today!" Crable asked.

"No, the orders are for the Second Battalion to take Dochamps today. It should have been done yesterday but it wasn't. Any more questions?"

After a quick conference, it was decided that Rochester, Teets, Munoz and I would accompany the Major. Five minutes later, the four of us were in front of the CP ready to go. As we waited on the steps, we devoured our boxes of K-rations.

Major Lamb appeared just after 0700. The four messengers climbed into a jeep behind his vehicle. Five minutes later, the two jeeps stopped at the exact spot where I had ducked behind a tank the previous day. Scattered around the sides of the road was the entire Second Battalion.

Major Lamb had a conference with the four Company Commanders. This was followed by a conference with Captain Price on some technical details regarding designated places on the maps.

As the four messengers waited in the snow, eight German prisoners with their hands behind their necks came out of the woods accompanied by two men from Company G. These Wehrmacht prisoners looked to be in extremely poor physical condition. We guessed that the snow was affecting the enemy as much as it was the men from the Second Battalion.

"Get those Krauts back to headquarters as quick as you can," ordered Captain Price.

After the Major had finished his conferences, others were held between the four Company Commanders and their respective platoon leaders.

The Second Battalion entered the woods to the right of the road leading from Ammonines to Dochamps. The woods at the left could not be entered since the Aisne River was located there.

"Why are we going into the woods?" questioned Rochester.

"Sergeant Rochester, you amaze me, don't you know why?" replied Teets.

"No, I don't."

"We are going to try to outflank Jerry. He can block the road too easy. Our big problem is going to be that snow. It must be ten inches deep."

The march or plodding through the snow commenced. The three rifle companies—E, F and G—were in two files about 100 yards apart. Behind them came the heavy machine gun section of Company H. The 81 mm mortar section of that company

308

remained behind occupying the former headquarters of Company E.

The battalion team accompanying Major Lamb consisted of six persons. There were the four messengers, one radio operator in the person of Corporal John Mulligan and a single battalion guard. The latter, in our opinion, was not needed except to add more firepower if required.

Attached to this command party were two men from the Second Armored Division. One was a brand new Second Lieutenant. He had never been in combat. With him was a radio operator. Their assigned task was to keep communications going between our battalion and the tanks on the highway.

During the first three hours, there was little activity. The progress of the march through the deep snow was very, very slow. The long column would cautiously move ahead for ten to fifteen minutes. Then a halt of fifteen to twenty minutes would be taken. However, the Major's party did not stop this often. When a break would be taken, we would pass the entire column until the leading elements were reached. The Battalion Commander and one or more officers would hold a conference. The plodding would resume. We would go back past the entire column. Next, Major Lamb would hold a conference with Captain Charles Hilton, the Commander of Company H. During one of these breaks, Sal Munoz inquired, "Fellas, I'm wondering if the Germans know we're here in the woods?"

"Sal, I think they'll have some type of defense prepared for us," was my reply.

"What should we do if they start hitting us with artillery?"

"Sal, just try to get as close to the ground as you can."

"Thanks, Ed. I'll do that."

Just before 1100, Corporal Mulligan had a conference with Major Lamb. I heard him say, "I think I can arrange it, Major."

Mulligan approached me.

"Edwards, you know how to operate this radio, don't you?"

"Yes, Mulligan, I do. But aren't you the radio operator?"

309

"Ed, I am, but I'm sick. The Major says I can go back to battalion if Bergett will relieve me. I've radioed Bob and he's agreed to come. But someone has to take over before he gets here. Can you do it for me?"

"OK, I will. But how long before Bergett will get here?"

"I think he can make it in an hour."

"Mulligan, I think it will be more like two. That snow is heavy. I know he's got a trail to follow but he won't get here in any sixty minutes. I'll do it but I've got to get rid of my pack."

"I've taken care of that. The battalion CP guard didn't come with anything on him. He'll take your pack for protection."

"But I get to eat my own rations. Otherwise no deal."

"He'll agree to that, I'm sure."

In the next few minutes, the 300 radio weighing the usual 35 pounds was placed on my back. My pack was transferred to the CP guard.

Just before 1200, all took a lunch break. As usual we dispersed to protect ourselves against a sudden tree burst. While we ate and rested, Major Lamb radioed back to the Battalion's CP in Ammonines our approximate location. This was done by the use of letters which had been agreed upon prior to launching of the attack.

The battalion's march continued. But we heard overhead shells coming from the Germans. The shells were mortars. We realized that the Germans knew that we were in the woods attempting to outflank their defenses. Longer halts were taken. The usual marches up and down the long column were made.

Just after 1300, the Germans tried another shelling. This time the shells fell just behind the column. The mortars were coming closer.

Just after 1400, Corporal Bergett arrived.

"Edwards, can't thank you enough for taking over."

"Bob, that's all right. What happened to John Mulligan?"

"I think he had the shits. Maybe they hit him again. I was listening at the CP when he called in for a replacement. Said that Major Lamb had ordered me to get up here. So here I am."

"Glad to see you. If that thing gets too heavy, I'll take over for a while."

"I appreciate that, Don. Sure am happy to have someone who knows how to operate this thing along."

Exactly a quarter of an hour after Bergett arrived, the Germans tried another shelling. This time they succeeded. A literal shower of mortars hit the trees. Everyone hit the ground. My body was as close to a tree as permitted. The mortar shells were hitting the trees above us giving rise to a 'tree burst.' This was worse than being in the open. Less than fifty feet from me next to another tree lay Sal Munoz. As I watched him, a piece of shell hit him in the left shoulder, opening a large bleeding gash.

He yelled, "I'm hit! I'm hit!"

I hollered, "Sal lay down, we'll get you when it stops."

"I'm hit! I'm hit!"

Munoz then jumped up and ran toward the rear, the blood streaming from his shoulder. Several others yelled at him to lay down. Apparently Sal was so terrified, he fled. Later, we were told that the doctor said it was a miracle that Munoz had lived. The blood that he lost caused him to collapse at the battalion's aid station. Fortunately, plasma was available when he arrived. Sal Munoz was evacuated to a hospital that day.

After ten minutes, the mortar shelling stopped. We got up to see who had been hit. About 150 yards away lay the radio operator from the Second Armored Division. His left arm and thigh were bleeding. The new second Lieutenant knelt over him. But he did nothing. He acted as if he were in shock. George Teets ran over and pushed the Lieutenant to the ground yelling, "Lieutenant, get out of the way. This man been hit. We've got to do something."

The new shavetail mumbled something incoherent.

"Don, get over here. This guy is in bad shape."

I ran over and literally pushed the Lieutenant further away. He appeared dazed.

Teets and I now applied our two bandages to the wounds. Since another was needed, I simply pushed the officer and took his bandage from him. I believe this third bandage saved the

311

life of the radio operator. We tried to calm the wounded operator, telling him, "Soldier, you're ok. The medics will be here to
get you."

All the time we bandaged, the wounded man kept groaning. After five minutes, we thought we had stopped the flow of
blood. Then Rochester yelled at us, "Teets, Edwards, the
advance is going forward. You've got to come. Major said
you've got to be finished."

"Rochie, we're coming," George replied.

Teets turned to the stunned Second Lieutenant.

"Watch him. If you need to fix him up any more, tear off
your shirt."

"Yes, Sir."

"Then, Lieutenant, call the medics. Get him the hell out of
here. Another shelling and he's gone. Do you understand me?"

It would be the only time in my Army life when I heard a
private give orders to an officer.

The progress of the Second Battalion came to a permanent
halt. The German defenses had been met. The Major's party
went up to the lead elements. While lying flat on his stomach,
Major Lamb conferred with the officer leading the advanced
platoon. Company E had reached the side of a hill. On the
other side was the enemy. Without some type of support, our
battalion was stopped from advancing. The Major came back
from his conference running.

"All right everybody, follow me."

His party proceeded about 200 yards to the left in the
woods. We arrived at the Ammonines-Dochamps road. There
stood a tank from the Second Armored Division. Teets wondered, "Don, wonder why he's just standing there?"

"George, look up there. A German roadblock."

"Where?"

"Look George, about 250 yards ahead on the road. That's
why that tank can't move."

Major Lamb followed by his party slid down a short
embankment to the highway. The Major started toward the
roadblock. He had not taken more than five steps when a German machine gun started to spit out its bullets. They hit just to

312

the left of the five of us. In record time, we were up the embankment and back in the woods. To remain on that road was unhealthy.

Major Lamb found Captain Thompson in order to hold a conference with him. While the party waited, I jumped into a foxhole with First Sergeant Goodpasteur. He said, "Edwards, what a pleasant surprise. I didn't know you were doing this sort of thing."

"Sarge, I'm with the Major today. Also seemed to have the job as a substitute radio operator."

"I thought that was you out there. But I wasn't sure."

From a nearby foxhole, someone shouted, "Hey Edwards, what are you here for, the morning report?"

"I think that Sergeant Goodpasteur is getting it ready now. He's having trouble finding all his things in this foxhole."

Sergeant Goodpasteur then piped up, "Edwards, can you give me a little time in getting it ready?"

"Sarge, under these circumstances, you can have all the time you want!"

The morning report which was not due was not picked up until a day or two later since the First Sergeant had no idea at that moment the true strength of Company E.

While we lay there, a few enemy bullets went zinging over our heads but they caused no alarm.

Major Lamb and Captain Thompson soon finished their conference. Orders were given on the radio that one platoon of Company E would try a flanking movement on the left side of the Ammonines-Dochamps road. Company F was to try a wide flanking movement on the right side of the road. The Major's party withdrew and went back to Company G which was being held in reserve. Teets and I dug a shallow fox hole and lay in it.

During the next hour, we could hear rifle and machine-gun fire on the right and left. The Germans lobbed a few mortars at our advance. But the companies reported that they could not advance. Major Lamb gave an order to withdraw back to the slope of a hill that we had passed during our march. The Major was not going to give the enemy a distinct advantage if he

313

decided to make a counter-attack. The Major turned to Rochester, Teets and myself.

"Would you three get back on the road and go back about 800 yards. There will be an intersection in the road. Get a building for the battalion CP."

"How many buildings will there be, Major?" inquired Rochester.

"I think there're about 10 or 20 of them. It should be like a farm estate. There should be no one in them now."

"Shall we report back to you or wait until you come?"

"Stay there. Corporal Bergett and I will be there shortly. The Battalion should be withdrawing now."

The three of us started back through the woods. We could observe the results of the German shelling. Most of the wounded were from Company G. The medics had not yet been able to evacuate all the wounded. The worst case was a GI who had been hit by a bullet that had gone through his left temple and out his right jaw. His teeth were destroyed. Yet, he was still living. We guessed he would not live through the night. Later, George Teets reported that this GI had recovered. Since all our bandages were gone, we could not be of any assistance.

Since none of us wished to be sprayed again with machine gun bullets or anything else, we carefully kept in the woods until the second American tank was reached. Then the highway was entered.

A third tank from the Second Armored Division was sighted. Behind it was the jeep belonging to Company. Its driver, Lou Novak, recognized me.

"Hi, Edwards, do you know where the company is?"

"Yes, Lou, they're up ahead about 200 yards. What do you want with them?"

"I've brought coffee and doughnuts for them."

"Up here, Lou?"

"What's wrong with up here?"

"Nothing, I'm just surprised. The enemy has got us stopped cold. The company was fighting but I think they're going to pull back soon."

"Give me directions on where they are."

314

"I think you ought to wait here. But if you insist I'll tell you where they are."

Directions were given on the company's location. I added, "But Lou, don't move that jeep. There are three tanks ahead of you. In front of the first tank is a German roadblock. That's the problem today."

"Thanks Edwards, I'll take your advice."

Novak proceeded forward on foot toward Company E while the three of us proceeded back to the intersection. The crossroads were reached in five minutes. But the buildings were not empty. There were personnel from the Second Armored in almost every structure of any type.

Without much hesitation, the three of us found an empty mill and the attached house. It was the only empty structure in the crossroads. Teets and I left Rochester and attempted to search for another empty building. We found none.

In one of the occupied houses, I inquired, "When did you men arrive here?"

"Oh, we came in this afternoon," replied a lanky blond tanker.

"Did your outfit take this place?"

"Yea, the Krauts must have seen us coming and vamoosed."

"Any other outfit help you?"

"Some infantry outfit is assisting us, I think."

My face must have turned beet red when I replied, "Soldier, I know you're from a very famous outfit, but your tanks can't do anything without us doughboys from the Infantry. In these woods and on the highway, all the Germans have to do is erect a roadblock. They had one yesterday and your tanks couldn't move. They have another one about 800 yards up the road. My company and some others are trying to get around them now. If you don't believe me, walk up that road. Get in front of that lead tank. Jerry will let you know he's there with some machine guns. Unless our battalion gets around it, you'll stay here until hell freezes."

"Sorry fella, you must have had a rough day."

315

"It could have been rougher but some guys are out there bleeding so we can get your damn tanks through that road."

Teets and I departed. Outside George remarked, "Don, you really blew your stack."

"Sorry George, but they really got my number. They think they're doing everything and the 84th is just along for the ride."

We returned to join Sergeant Rochester. Ten minutes later, Major Lamb and Corporal Bergett arrived. After the Major inspected the premises, I stated, "Major, we tried to get more quarters, but the Second Armored is occupying all the rest of them."

"Edwards, this will do us. Now I think you three messengers can get back to the CP."

"You won't need us tonight, Sir?"

"No, I don't think so. All the company CPs will be in here. I can talk to the Company Commanders whenever I need to. Corporal Bergett will radio for the jeep to come for you."

After an hour's wait outside in the cold darkness, Larry Gardiner arrived in the jeep.

"I thought, Edwards, there would be four of you."

"Munoz got hit in the shoulder."

"Too bad, get in and we'll get back to town."

In less than ten minutes, the three of us were back with the other four messengers.

After we had taken off our packs, Crable asked, "What happened? We heard Munoz got hit."

I replied, "I think George can tell you what occurred. But Munoz did get hit."

For the next twenty or thirty minutes, Teets described what went on during the attack. Although our battalion was supposed to take Dochamps that day, numerous problems had arisen. The other four messengers were very skeptical of our story regarding the new Lieutenant and his radio operator until we showed them that we had no bandages left in our kits. They found it hard to believe that an officer would 'freeze.'

After we finished our tales of our adventures, Crable introduced me to a visitor who was staying with us that night only. Our guest was Sergeant Michael Citrak from Company I of the

316

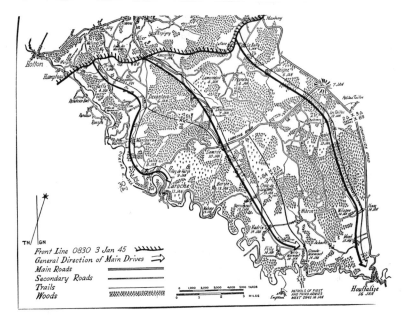

Map of the Main Drives of the 84th Infantry Division

Third Battalion. He seemed very shy and asked a few questions of me about the day's happenings. Just before V-E day, we learned the true purpose of his visit to us. Citrak was a private at the beginning of combat. At this time, his rank was that of a Sergeant. Shortly, he would be a Second Lieutenant. He was later credited with being, probably, the outstanding combat soldier in the entire 84th Infantry Division. I asked him unknowingly why he was here.

"Private Edwards, I've been ordered to report to Regimental Headquarters."

"Sergeant, is it for something good or bad?"

"I think it's good right now."

"Is regiment supposed to be here?"

"They were but I gather from your stories that we've been held up. So regiment probably will not be here until tomorrow."

"We're happy to have you with us."

"Thank you for your hospitality."

317

A PRIVATE'S DIARY

As soon as we had finished our bull sessions, all seven messengers retired. We realized that the attack would continue the next day. Although the front was only a mile or two away, Amonines seemed in another world.

Sunday, January 7, 1945

At 0630, Sergeant Butler poked his head in our room and announced, "Messengers, be ready to leave in five minutes."

Since we used the alternate system, Crable, Innes, Walter and Simon were to go forward with the Major. Three were to be in reserve. The seven of us went to the battalion CP and ate our K-ration breakfast. Although nothing was spoken, all of us realized that another man could easily be lost during this day.

Just before 0700, Private Gardiner with his jeep arrived. The four jumped in. We waved goodby to each other.

During the morning hours, the three of us did little but read and snooze. Three times prior to noon, I visited the battalion's radio room. During one of the visits, I inquired of Sergeant Paul Kottage.

"Sarge, how far it is from Amonines to Dochamps?"

"Ed, it's between three and a half to four miles from here."

"How far did battalion get yesterday?"

"From the maps, my guess is about two and a half or three."

"Do you think they'll get into Dochamps today?"

"I don't know, but you were out yesterday, tell me what you think."

"Sarge, that mile is going to be tough. If Jerry has any more road blocks, I don't know if they'll make it."

Upon one of my trips to the radio center, I met Sergeant Butler who informed me that the 335th Regimental Headquarters were scheduled to move in that afternoon. He told me to be able to move up front any time after noon.

Shortly after 1200, a rap was heard.

"Come in." shouted Rochester.

The door was opened by Major Walter Tice, the Regimental Surgeon.

318

"Men, are you going to leave this room anytime?"

I answered for all three of us. "Major, we're scheduled to go up to battalion this afternoon."

"Can we have the room then?"

"Certainly, Sir."

Looking at me the Major questioned, "Private, didn't I have something to do with you back in Claiborne?"

"Yes, you did, Major."

"What was it?"

"I think you were the one who took those broken pieces of my eyeglass from my right eye. I landed on the bottom of a pile and someone sat on me."

"That's right. Didn't you have a bandage over that eye for quite some time?"

"Yes, Sir. Six weeks."

"How has your eye been since then?"

"I still have some trouble with it Major. I lost some of my vision from it but the new lenses seemed to have helped."

"If you have too much trouble, don't hesitate to come to the station. You may have a real problem there."

"Thank you Major, I'll remember."

"Remember the Aid station will be here before the afternoon is out."

Less than an hour later, there was another rap at the door.

"Come in," I shouted.

For a moment, I saw only a helmet and the insignia of a Captain. The helmet covered the face of the officer. When he lifted it off of his head, I recognized Captain Joseph Donovan, the Company Commander of Headquarters Company, 335th Infantry Regiment. He was my former commander since I had been a member of that company in Camp Claiborn from April to late July of 1944. But he did not recognize me.

"Where are you men from?"

"Captain, we're messengers from the Second Battalion," I answered.

"Are you leaving soon?"

"Yes, Sir, we are."

"This is sure a nice room."

"Yes Sir, it is."

"Has anyone else been here?"

"Yes, Major Tice was here about an hour ago."

"What did he say?"

"He said the Medics would move in here by the end of the afternoon."

"Well, I think I'll reserve this one for Colonel Parker."

"Captain, it's all right by us."

"Let's see. The S-3 can go in right next door. Medics can go to that other building. If the Medics came, tell them this is for the Colonel."

"Yes, Captain, we will."

"Somebody will be here in about an hour. Stay here until then."

"We will, Captain."

The three of us proceeded to gather our equipment together. It was decided that the material left behind by Munoz should be given to Sergeant Butler who could ship it to him in the hospital where he was recovering from his wounds.

Shortly after 1500, another rap was heard. The three of us together shouted, "Come in, the door is open."

"Is this the future residence of Colonel Parker?" asked a squared face Corporal.

"Yes, it is," I replied. "Captain Donovan was here a short time ago."

"We're coming in then."

Behind the Corporal and two privates came two stepladders and numerous pieces of electrical equipment. To assist them, I stated, "Men, there's no electricity in here."

"Thank you, we know that," responded the Corporal.

"Are all these things for the Colonel?"

"Yes, it is."

"Tell us, how is the electricity furnished?"

"Regiment has a special power unit run by gasoline."

"Besides electric lights, what else does the Colonel have?"

"There are two radios. He listens to them every night. And they enjoy liquor when they listen."

"Is there anything lacking?"

"Private whatever your name is, regiment has all the comforts of home."

"Does the Colonel know there's a war going on?"

"Sure he does. He listens to the radio every night and he gets his reports from all the companies on what happened during the last day."

"Sounds good. Can you tell me what job Captain Donovan has?"

"He looks up good future CPs for the Colonel."

"Is that all?"

"As far as most of the guys are concerned, that's what he does, but he does it well."

"What do you guys thinks about this system?"

"We think it stinks. When the British took our places in Marche, their officers all had orderlies. It was out in the open. All they do here is disguise it. But supposedly Division is even worse. They've never eaten K rations back there yet."

For the next half hour we watched the three enlisted men string the wires and prepare the future regimental CP. We decided we would leave. We went to the battalion CP which was still housed in the old hotel. But the radio section had left. First Sergeant Vignato directed us to leave our luggage in the former dining room of the hotel. Due to the German shelling of the village, every pane of glass from this dining room was gone. Air conditioning is nice but not when the temperature is about freezing.

Just before 1730, I noticed that the kitchen from Regimental Headquarters Company was going to set up in the building across the square from the hotel. I suggested, "George, Rochester, let's try Headquarters chow."

"Do you think they'll let us eat there?" inquired Rochester.

"Well, since I was a member of this company back in Claiborne, I think we can try it."

We lined up with the members of this company for the hot food. One of the cooks glanced at me, winked his eye and continued to serve the three of us.

321

After our good hot supper, the three of us began to wonder what had happened to the four messengers that had left us in the morning. Teets remarked, "Don, I wonder if they got held up and are still out in the snow?"

"I just don't know George. If they didn't take the town, Major Lamb should pull them back as he did last night."

"Don't you know some of the men in communications in Regimental Headquarters? Check with them. Since battalion's radio's gone, we can't contact anyone else."

"George, I'll check with them."

The regimental radio section was housed in the same hotel where we were living. Much of the evening was spent listening to the radio reports. Only one thing was for certain. The radio section of the Second Battalion had not entered Dochamps. It was then presumed that the town was still in enemy hands. Nothing else could be given over the radio for fear of interception by the enemy.

At 2300, I returned to George and Rochester with no news. We decided that we should go to bed since we could do nothing to aid our fellow messengers. We laid our blankets on the dining room floor and went fast asleep.

Monday, January 8, 1945

At 0630, Rochester, Teets and I were up. We were ready for any task. I approached First Sergeant Vignato.

"Sarge, have you heard anything about the attack?"

"Ed, I know nothing. No official word has come yet."

"What do you think?"

"My guess is the battalion hasn't taken Dochamps yet."

About 0730, George spotted a field kitchen of the 326th Field Artillery Battalion. We decided to try our luck in getting another hot breakfast.

As we stood in line, one of the mess sergeants growled, "What outfit are you guys from?"

"Second Battalion, 335th," I replied.

"Don't you know my guys come first. After they finish eating there won't be anything left."

"OK, Sergeant," was my answer.

We walked back to the hotel and dined on our usual K-rations.

During the morning, all three of us tried to ascertain what was happening. We could find out nothing.

Just before 1200, Larry Gardiner pulled up in his jeep.

"Edwards, Teets, Rochester, get your gear. I'm to take you to the others."

"Larry, has Dochamps been taken?" asked Teets.

"Yes, it has, but don't waste any time. Climb in and let's get going."

The traffic on the Amonines-Dochamps road was unbelieveable. Tanks of all descriptions were moving forward. The big difficulty seemed to be the speed of the armored vehicles. The highway was covered with ice. Tanks could not get a footing on this ice. At one spot, a tank was causing a traffic jam. The tank tracks had slipped partially off the road. All four of us got out to watch the attempt to get the tank back on the roadway. But no traction was available. Gardiner then slowly pulled his jeep around the sliding tank. His front bumper kissed the front tracks of the tank. Five minutes later, we could see the town of Dochamps. It was nestled in a valley between tree covered hills. After going around another hair pin turn, which seemed to be quite common in this section of the Ardennes, the jeep entered the village. Gardiner pull his jeep before a small house.

"Fellas, the other messengers are on the second floor. Battalion CP is on the first floor. See you later."

On the second floor, we met the four messengers and Corporal Kern. "I blurted out to Crable, "I didn't know John if we were going to see you again. No one back in Amonines knew what was going on. Tell us what happened."

"Don, we left you yesterday at 0700. After some artillery fire, the line companies finally got that roadblock removed. That took about four hours. But the companies still couldn't use that road. The Germans kept that covered at all times. We had to go through the woods. I think you know about the snow. We'd go ahead ten minutes, then, stop twenty minutes. I think that by 1700, we'd covered, maybe, two miles. But the battalion had just gotten to that hair-pin turn that you saw coming in here. We could see the Germans filing up the hill on the other side of the town. Everyone thought Jerry was leaving Dochamps. Boy, we were wrong!"

"Did they leave someone behind?" I inquired.

"They sure did. The Major got the battalion grouped for a final assault. On the road were those three tanks you saw yesterday. We wanted the tanks to go forward first. They wanted the Infantry to go forward and they would support the battalion. After some discussion a Lieutenant in the lead tank agreed to lead the way in. Everything was quiet as that tank warmed up its engine. I could see the attack starting. The lead tank just got into the open space before the town. The Germans let go with artillery, mortars and machine guns. They shelled the entire area including the hill where we were. The lead tank got hit. The tankers were able to escape but they were covered with blood from head to foot. A retreat was made back into the woods. Major Lamb ordered a reformation. I was in a fox hole with the forward observer and radio operator from Cannon Company. They ordered a round fired. The directions were terrible. Their shells landed just in front of our men. New directions were given. The second round hit Dochamps. About ten minutes later, our artillery started to blast the town. H company's mortars started barking away. Finally the three companies slowly advanced into the town. The tanks were no good to them. The lead elements of the battalion just got into town and the Germans started to fire again. We stopped. Darkness was complete."

"What happened next, John?"

"Don, everything was quiet for about four hours. Then the Major got a radio call. He was ordered to take the town that night. He was mad. But Major Lamb got the company commanders together again. Along with us was the Mechanized Reconnaissance Troop from Division. Captain Thompson asked them to aid in the attack. Their commander said he had only 80 men in the group. Captain Thompson replied that that was more than he had but he was going to attack."

"When did the attack finally take place?"

"About 0100 this morning, the attack restarted. Strangely they didn't meet any resistance. By 0400, the whole battalion was in the town. We guessed that the Germans pulled out early in the evening. But none of us saw them go. It was an experience I'll never forget. I think the thing that got everybody was the General's insistence that the town had to be taken. He didn't seem to care if every man in the Second Battalion got killed or wounded."

Although Dochamps had been captured, the Germans let us know they were still defending every inch of ground. At 1300, John and I had to take our first message of the day to Company E. As we stepped out the door of the Battalion's CP, two 88s hit the house directly across the street. John remarked, "At least, they picked the right house for battalion. If we'd have been in there Don, I wouldn't be talking to you now."

"Just luck, John, just luck."

Since John was exhausted from his previous day and night activities, I suggested after the initial run that he sleep the afternoon while I performed all the necessary message taking for the remainder of the day. He did not dissent.

Throughout the rest of the daylight hours, the enemy continued to shell the town of Dochamps with their 88s.

About 1400, Corporal Kern came to Rochester, Teets and me to ask, "Are you interested to see what the Germans did to some civilians?"

"Is it bad?" I asked.

"Edwards, it's not good, that I can tell you."

We walked to a small house at the entrance to the village. A corporal told us to go into the kitchen. On the floor were two dead Belgian females. Both were nude. One was a young girl about 18 years of age. We were told that she had been raped by a member of the SS. Her body bore marks of being kicked in the back by the heavy German boots. Gashes appeared over her entire face. She lay face upward. She looked as if she had been in sheer agony. The older woman, who appeared to be around 40, bore no marks of any type but had been shot three or four times in the chest area. As George and I were leaving, some Army blankets were brought in and the murdered Belgian women were wrapped in them. We had witnessed first hand the evidence of German brutality.

At 1600, the daily edition of the Army newspaper, Stars and Stripes, came. I immediately awoke John to tell him what the paper said. As he read it, John kept shaking his head.

"It's just not true. The Second Armored Division had nothing to do with the capture of this place."

Credit for the capture of Dochamps had been given to the Armored Division. When I delivered the papers to Company E, the officers and enlisted men were about to explode. Someone said to me, "Edwards, you brought the wrong paper today."

Tuesday, January 9, 1945

This was to be a day of full rest for the Second Battalion. Early in the morning, the Third Battalion of the 335th came through Dochamps. They started an attack on the next village, Samree. Several of us watched the start of this attack. We saw the Second Armored Division go into action. The attack went across an open field. Here the Armored vehicles could maneuver. In the morning, the enemy lobbed a few shells into Dochamps. After 1000, none fell. We assumed the Germans were more interested in the attack being launched against them.

About 1030, the messengers had to move into a new house since the CP of the Battalion was at full strength. We were, also, at full strength. To replace Munoz, Company H sent Vernon Dawes. Dawes was a private who hailed from New Goshen, Indiana. He was a big husky fellow, about 6 feet two inches and around 200 plus pounds, with a ruddy complexion in his middle 30's. He was married and had one son back in the States. He was very quiet upon his entrance into the very noisy messenger group, which always seemed to be chatting about some details. Since Crable was still tired, I continued to take all the messages to our company.

Early in the afternoon, the entire battalion received its tobacco and candy ration. Since John and I were non-smokers,

Vernon O. Dawes — New Goshen, Indiana

we easily managed to exchange our tobacco for some extra candy.

About 2000, Sergeant Eric Carlson, the Battalion's Sergeant Major, called three of the messengers outside for a run. He said to each of us, "The battalion has been sent some replacements. You are to take them to your company. Don't

327

scare them. Keep them calm, real calm. They'll learn fast enough what's to be done. Do you understand?"

"We do, Sergeant," I replied for all of us.

Outside our dwelling were 75 scared-looking soldiers. They were huddled together in the cold. Sergeant Carlson began to call their names. They were separated into three groups. I was selected to lead one group to Company E. As we trotted along, I asked, "Where are you fellas from?"

"69th Division."

"Do you know where you are?"

"In Belgium. Can you tell us how far the Germans are from here?"

"My guess is about two or three miles. They haven't bothered us since about 1000 this morning with any shelling."

"Can you tell us what the front is like?"

"No, I'm afraid I can't really describe it. You have to be there to know what it's like."

"What's your job?"

"I'm a messenger from battalion to the company."

"Is it dangerous?"

"It's not safe, that I can tell you."

"What's your company commander's name?"

"Captain William Thompson."

"How do you like him?"

"So far, I think he's pretty good. He tries to look out for the men in the company."

"Do you think he'll treat us all right even if we're new?"

"I'm pretty sure you'll have no trouble with him."

"Has Company E suffered many casualties?"

"Yes, we have. But we're still the lowest in the battalion, and, I think, in the whole regiment."

"How come?"

"I think Captain Thompson's careful in where and when he sends the company."

At that moment, we arrived at the house where the CP of Company E was located. I called First Sergeant Goodpasteur outside and explained who these men were. He was delighted to have some replacements for those who had become casualties. I then left.

Back at the messenger center, Rochester and Teets had had like experiences since the new replacements were truly excited and nervous.

Wednesday, January 10, 1945

In the morning, we could hear the firing ahead in and around the town of Samree. As we heard the American artillery shells going overhead, John remarked, "I sure hope Blue Battalion got more support than we did from the Armored."

Shortly after 1000, four messengers took an urgent message to their respective companies. It was a notice that all companies of the Second Battalion should move up to Samree to reinforce the Third Battalion. However, the movement was not to start until 1200. Company H was to go first. Blue Battalion wanted some assistance from their machine guns and mortars in case of a German counter-attack.

In the afternoon, the messengers learned that the Third Battalion had considerably less trouble than our own White Battalion in driving the enemy back. This was due mainly to the effective fire power delivered by both the artillery and the supporting tanks.

The messengers were ordered to be ready at 1500 to move to the new town of Samree. As we waited, we noticed that the Regimental Headquarters of the 335th were taking our places in Dochamps.

Several times during our waiting, I asked Sergeant Butler, "Sarge let us walk to Samree. It's only about two miles or so."

"Edwards, I know you and the others could go there in about thirty minutes, but my orders are that you are to wait until Gardiner picks you up."

Darkness came a little after 1800. We ate our K-rations. We waited and waited. At 1915, Gardiner showed up with the jeep.

"Sorry, I'm late men, but they wouldn't let me come to get you."

I replied, "That's ok Larry, but what took you so long?"

"I had to go back to Amonines to pick up some material to deliver to some of the companies and headquarters. You can't believe the traffic jams back on that road."

On the road to Samree, we saw some of the effects of the German offensive in the Ardennes back in December. Along the highway were numerous jeeps, half-tracks and tanks of the American Seventh Armored Division. The moonlight did not give us a clear view of the damage inflicted. But it was perfectly clear that the various vehicles had been caught and hit by some type of artillery fire.

In less than ten minutes, the eight messengers were in Samree. The entire village was lit up by fires.

I asked Gardiner, "How did the fires get started?"

"Edwards, I understand that our artillery lit them in the morning when Blue made their attack."

"How long have they been burning?"

"Ever since I got here about noon."

At least, ten or twelve homes were going up in smoke. All of us knew they would burn to the ground inasmuch as no one could take the time, or especially, the risk of putting them out. To do so invited a shelling from the enemy. I turned to Crable and remarked, "John, I sure would hate to be a Belgian and return to find no house."

"But wouldn't fire insurance cover it?"

"Sorry, war is never covered in any first insurance policy."

"Don, what could they do?"

"Nothing, John, simply nothing."

"The expression 'War is Hell' is sure true."

Our new message center was located in a well-built two story house. There was not a single piece of furniture on the floors. We believed the enemy had used it for fire wood. Orders were given that everyone was to sleep on the first floor. At 2100, a non-message trip was made to Company E. The messengers had to know their location for any emergency. None arose that night. The enemy must have been conserving his ammunition since there was just a single shelling during the night. The only detriment was the movement of the CP guards during the entire night. The four of them had taken sleeping positions in the far corner of the room. Since they constantly changed in the night, they had to crawl over other sleeping bodies. Twice during the night, my legs were kicked but I suffered less damage than others whose backs felt the heels of some tough Army boots.

Thursday, January 11, 1945

The message center was full awake at 0630. The first message was delivered at 0700. When I delivered it to Captain Thompson, he immediately ripped it open.

"Edwards, at last, you delivered some good news. Most of the things I get from you I don't want to see."

"Yes, Sir."

"Hey, everybody, hear this. We're going back to Dochamps for a rest. Get the word out to the platoons."

Upon my return to the message center I noted that the fires in the village had practically ceased. But some of the wood was still smoldering. Just after 0800, another battalion started arriving to relieve our White Battalion. Orders were issued to be ready at 0830. It was the usual 'hurry up and wait' routine. While waiting for the march to start, I noticed some wiremen laying some telephone lines. I inquired, "What outfit are you from?"

"Seventh Corps."

"You're kidding. Corps up this far?"

"Well, no. We're from the Corps artillery. Corps Headquarters is somewhat back. Near Liege, I think."

"I thought so. Our regiment is back in the next town. And in back of them is Division. Corps should be even farther back."

"You're right, soldier, but some artillery outfit needs a line up here to support some attack that's going to be made in the next day or two."

A PRIVATE'S DIARY

Just after 1100, Headquarters Company of the Second Battalion assembled. Orders were issued to take a slow leisurely walk back to Dochamps. As Sergeant Vignato stated, "Any time anybody wants to take a break, take one. But men try to get back there by 1230. If anyone can't walk too good, see me."

Clouds had drifted away. The sun shone brightly in the sky. The march was really a stroll. We could notice the beautiful Belgian countryside. About four feet of snow still lay on the ground. The trees were covered with flakes. Skiing conditions looked ideal. Although the temperature must have hovered around zero, no one complained. We were going back, not toward the front. Just before reentering Dochamps, we could see the disaster that had befallen the Seventh Armored Division. It appeared as if fifteen or more vehicles had been hit. We guessed that the Germans had caught the Americans trying to flee. During our walk, Gardiner came by with the jeep and offered to transport some of the messengers. Three took up his offer but the other five including Crable and myself completed the march.

Most of the remainder of the day was spent at leisure. Mail was delivered to all the companies in the Second Battalion. During the afternoon, I attempted to answer some of the numerous questions posed by some of my friends back home. Very few could be answered since censorship of personal mail still prevailed. The only thing that could be related was that we were in Belgium, period.

In the afternoon, I found a well and drew some water for a shave and some general cleaning. I had not shaved since our last day in Marche on New Year's Day. My grooming took over an hour. Although the cold water was satisfactory, I still preferred to have hot clean water to clean myself. After putting back on the same clothes freshened by a little air, I brushed my teeth. I always attempted this on a daily basis. My buddy, John Crable, was the most faithful in his daily brushing. If required, he would use some of his canteen water to brush his teeth. That afternoon, I asked him, "John, why do you take such good care of your teeth?"

332

"Simple Don, if they go, I can't get another set like them. If I take care of them, I'll have them until I'm 92."

"You mean, if you live that long."

"Correct. Under these conditions, my teeth might rot any time. You know from the ads 'brush your teeth twice a day.' Besides, we can't get our teeth taken care of under these circumstances. When was the last time, Don, you had your teeth cleaned?"

"Back in August in Claiborne."

"When's the next time?"

"G.O.K."

"That's right. God only knows. If this thing lasts another six months, no one will get his teeth cleaned by a dentist. I'm going to take care of mine as long as I can."

John's care of his teeth was in strict contrast to that exercised by Sergeant James Rochester from Company F. Every single day, regardless of conditions, Rochester had chewing tobacco in his mouth. His wife constantly sent him more tobacco in the packages that he received from her. Most of us hoped that she would cease this practice but she continued to do this until the end of the war.

Just before 1800, Corporal Kern came in with some unexpected news.

"Men, we have a new battalion commander."

"What's wrong with Major Lamb?" questioned Walters.

"Nothing is wrong. Major Lamb went back to being Exec."

"Who's the new commander?"

"Major Edgar Hunter."

"Where is he coming from?"

"I understand he was attached to either regiment or Division."

"I think Corporal he was attached to the 335th."

"That's the same one."

"Corporal, he's an old man. He can't take walking through that snow. He'll die of a heart attack if he's not careful. It's tough for all of us and none of us is near 60. He might be younger than that but he looks like 60."

333

"Walters, I think you're right. But he's our commander. Division must think he knows what to do."

By 2100, all the messengers were fast asleep. For the first time in several days, not a single shot was heard throughout the night.

3. Berismenil

Friday, January 12, 1945

All the messengers slept until the late hour of 0830. Other than the usual message runs which occurred about every hour, we spent a restful day. In the morning, Sergeant Butler announced, "Men. Regiment will be moving in here today. Be ready to move to another place in town any time after lunch."

"Sarge, you mean they have to get that liquor cabinet for the Regimental Staff," retorted Teets.

"Teets, let's not get too truthful. We're all jealous of them."

During one of my message runs in the middle of the afternoon, I literally bumped into my friend from Company A, Harry Ackerman.

"Harry, where have you been?"

"Don, I've got the same question for you."

"Remember, the last time I saw you was in Linnich. White relieved Red that night."

"I remember Don."

"What's happened to you since then?"

"First you tell me where and when about you."

For the next quarter of an hour, I told him about Marche and the journey to this town of Dochamps. He related his experiences.

"Don, the worst day was January 5. We went off into some woods in front of a town called Beffee. We were supposed to take a town called Cosny. Just behind it was a high ridge. I think the Krauts could see every movement we made. We got about 200 yards into those woods and they let us have it. The guy in front of me got killed. Fellow in back of me was hit in both legs. The shelling by those Germans was unbelievable. We must have had 40 guys hit during the day. Finally, about 1600, they pulled us back into Beffe. God must have looked out for a Jew that day. I kept praying all day long. Some other battalion took over from us and the Germans then retreated."

"Hey, I notice you've got some stripes on your shirt. How come?"

"Believe it or not Don, I was promoted to Sergeant in charge of my squad. Most of the guys who started out aren't with us any more."

"Well, Harry, you can now give me orders."

"Don't worry, I won't."

"What's your company doing here?"

"I think we're going up to some place called Samree to take over part of the line. Have you heard of it?"

"I was there yesterday. The Germans aren't throwing much stuff into the town."

"Glad to hear that. Don, do you think this thing is ever going to end?"

"Harry, it's got to end some day. When, I don't know. My guess right now is Memorial Day."

"That soon?"

"Harry, that's nearly five months away. A lot can happen. But I think the Germans have really tried to break our lines and they couldn't."

Since it was now approaching 1600, I knew that the message center would soon move.

"Harry, I've got to go. We're moving cause regiment's due to take our place."

"My company's scheduled to go up to Samree about 1630. Hope to see you again."

"Maybe, Harry, you might be an officer the next time."

"No chance of that, Don. I'm brave, but not that brave."

I arrived back at message center shortly after 1600. John asked me, "Don, where were you? It didn't take you that long to get to the company."

"No, I met an old friend from Company A on the street and we just talked."

Since we were in a relatively safe area, all five kitchens of the member companies of the Second Battalion served a hot meal that night. The biggest treat seemed to be the fact that hot coffee was available. Mixing our powder in the morning with cold water didn't seem like the real thing.

At 1700 a move was made. The messengers were placed on the second story of a small brown house. Someone had been good enough to leave some straw on the floor which was much superior to sleeping on the bare floor. Just after 1830, Sergeant Butler visited us with an announcement.

"Four messengers be ready to go with Major Hunter."

"You mean, Sergeant, that there's going to be another attack?" I replied.

"It looks like it. All the five Company Commanders are here at the CP for a conference now."

"Do you know the objective?"

"I heard it's the next town."

"What's its name?"

"Berismenil."

"How many miles from Samree?"

"Three."

"What time has been set by Division to take the town?"

"Noon."

"Did you say noon, Sergeant?"

"Yes, why?"

"In my opinion, Sarge, the only way our battalion will take that place by noon is if the Germans desert it. No other way. Are we going through the woods or down the road?"

"That I didn't hear Edwards. You'll see tomorrow."

"That I will Sarge. That I will."

From our rotation system, it was my turn to accompany the Major on this attack.

Just as the messengers were about to retire that evening, we heard something which made us very apprehensive about the attack tomorrow. Below us on the first floor was the battalion's radio room. We could easily hear the usual messages that were being sent. We usually paid little attention to them. However, Sergeant Gooding acting as the radio and visual chief, sent a message.

"Attention all companies. Your attention. For the attack tomorrow, you are instructed to use Channel Three."

The three of us that heard it screamed. If the Germans had been listening to our radio network, they knew an attack was coming. Thus, their troops could be alerted. Teets and I ran downstairs and reported to Sergeant Butler what we had heard. Lieutenant Morgan was called. Sergeant Gooding was summoned. He admitted the mistake he had made. The four messengers that were to remain behind were sent immediately with instructions on the new channel to be used.

As we laid down on the straw, Crable remarked, "Say an extra prayer, Don, that the Germans weren't listening. Otherwise you might be in big trouble tomorrow."

Saturday, January 13, 1945

At exactly 0302 by my watch, Sergeant Butler shook me.

"Edwards, time to get up. Breakfast is being served below."

"OK, Sarge. I'll be there in five. Wake the others."

The four messengers quickly slipped on our boots and took our packs and rifles. The remaining four kept sleeping peacefully.

Breakfast was being served in the next dwelling. But there were no lights. Yet the cooks got the food in the right places. Teets questioned me.

"Don, give you one guess what we're having for breakfast this morning?"

"No guesses George. It's powdered eggs, bread and coffee. Right?"

"Right. And the coffee is good, black and strong."

337

One gulp and I was wide awake.

For the next two hours, the four messengers waited. Then, at 0530, Major Hunter and Corporal Bergett appeared. Gardiner was ready with the jeep. Major Hunter sat in the front while the five of us were jammed in the back. Within ten minutes, the jeep and its occupants had arrived in Samree. On the outskirts of the town, the entire Second Battalion was lined up on both sides of the road.

Numerous conferences were held between the Major and the various officers from the four attacking companies. As we waited Bergett mentioned to me, "Ed, sure am glad you're along on this one."

"Why, Bob?"

"Well, I hope you'll relieve me from this radio job if this thing gets too heavy for me."

"I'll do it Bob, but you've got to take my pack then. Also I get your carbine."

"I agree to that switch."

"Have you heard anything about the attack today?"

"Only that Lieutenant Lusby is coming along to help lead the forward elements. And I think we're going through the woods again. Jerry has another roadblock up ahead. Berismenil, I think you know, is the objective."

Just as daylight appeared, the attack started. Immediately the battalion went into the woods. According to my compass, we were marching in a southeasterly direction. Company G was in the lead this time followed by F and E. Company H again brought up the rear with their heavy machine guns.

The forward elements of Company G plodded ahead. I estimated there was about four feet of snow covering the earth. The progress was slow. First we descended a small hill. Then we started climbing another. What then occurred was the very reason for the existence of the messengers. Corporal Bergett could not get Company G on the radio. The march halted. Teets was sent ahead to contact his company commander, Captain Ted Kettering. His orders from the Major were that Company G should hasten the pace being set.

George left. He came back about thirty minutes later and reported, "Major, the radio in Company G is out of order. Captain Kettering says his men are going as fast as they can travel with the snow conditions."

"Private, the next time you go, tell the Captain that I think they can go faster."

"I'll do that, Sir."

A few minutes after 1000, Major Hunter found out why Company G was not running through the snow. The battalion command party began the descent of an extremely steep hill. To some of us, it seemed like a mountain. At the bottom of the descent was a small creek. There was only one place that it could be crossed by stones. If necessity demanded, the creek could have been waded. At this time, it was not deemed necessary. The Major's party was between Company F and E. It took the six of us ten minutes to get across the water. Then a real hurdle was met. The ascent up the new hill was the most difficult ever encountered in my twenty years of life. The pace was very, very slow. The effect was plainly visible on the Battalion's Commander face. Three times he stopped for a rest. One of them lasted nearly 30 minutes. As we sat in the snow, I turned to George Teets and whispered, "I sure hope the Major doesn't have a heart attack here."

"Don, I'll second that. Do you see the color of his face?"

"George I do. It's beet red. He's straining to keep going."

"What should we do if he collapses?"

"I'll notify Captain Thompson right away. He's just in back of us in the middle of Company E. Then Bergett will have to radio Captain Price for instructions. Let's hope nothing happens."

"Don, I'll second that again."

During the last break, Teets was sent ahead to notify Captain Ketterer that he should halt his advance. At 1230, the Major and his five enlisted companions reached the crest of the hill. Bergett was plainly exhausted. He asked me, "Ed, can you take over for me? Six hours with that thing has got me."

"Bob, you are the messenger for Company E. Here's my pack."

339

"Don't forget to use the alphabet if you need to. Do you still know it?"

"I don't think I'll ever forget it for the rest of my life. Able, baker, charlie, dog, easy, fox, george."

"Don't go on. You know it."

For the next two hours, I was the full-time radio operator for the Second Battalion. I received only one message and sent none during that period.

The trail continued. At times, we seemed to be going in circles.

Just after 1400, some mortar shells came over the heads of the whole battalion. We all hugged the ground but there were no casualties of any type except for wet clothes and snowy faces. A little after 1430, we began the descent of another hill. Berismenil could be seen. It appeared as if nothing was moving on any of its streets. Unless the Germans could see into the woods, the entire Second Battalion was completely hidden from their view. Major Hunter held a hurried conference with the four Company Commanders.

During the conference, we noticed a small cub-type airplane which belonged to some Field Artillery Unit. We knew these planes were the eyes of the artillery. The plane was circling over Berismenil and our positions. I tuned to the channel reserved for the artillery. I heard, "Two columns approaching town. Both columns from west side. Hold fire until further instructions given."

We knew we were one of the columns. Where the other was, was unknown to any of the messengers or Corporal Bergett. We presumed it was the tanks on the highway.

As soon as the conference started, almost everyone in the entire battalion began to dig. Protection was still the first priority. Since I still had the radio on my back, Teets volunteered to start scooping dirt for our foxhole. Rochester and Dawes did nothing except watch everyone dig.

In ten minutes, the conference was finished. We learned that the plan was to have the three rifle companies continue double file through the woods and up into the village itself. If the Germans were met, a general attack would be made by the whole battalion. Company H's machine guns were set up at the edge of the trees so that their bullets could be fired directly into the town. The Preliminaries went as planned. The Battalion Command Party remained on the downward slope where the attack could be easily observed. I was relieved of the 300 radio. The binoculars that I had brought in my pack were put to use.

The village of Berismenil was reached without any reaction on the part of the enemy. Not a shot was fired. Then, the Germans must have discovered our presence. Company G managed to occupy about a half dozen houses before the Germans got organized. The light machine guns from the three rifle companies began to fire into the town. Next, the heavier machine guns of Company H sprayed Berismenil. But the forward elements met one obstacle our infantry could not overcome. My binoculars noted that from behind a house at the far end of the village, a German Tiger tank appeared. It backed into the street. One 88 shell from its turret was fired at an American held building. From the other end of the dwelling, sprang a squad of Company G soldiers. The tank's machine guns began to spit forth its bullets. The enemy at this time reacted with more firepower. Mortars of all types started to hit the hillside. By instinct, George and I jumped into the newly dug foxhole. Sergeant Rochester hit the ground and yelled at us, "George, Edwards, let me come in there with you!"

"Sorry, Rochester, but there's no room," answered Teets.

"But I'm in trouble out here. Jerry's shelling me."

"We know. But there's no room. Get close to that dirt. It might protect you from the tree bursts."

In fifteen minutes, the shelling stopped. Major Hunter contacted all companies. The attack was called off. Yet, we realized that the Germans could not attack us in the woods since their Tiger tank would be of little or no use in the woods. A stalemate had developed. Neither side fired at each other. Both must have figured that it was a waste of good ammunition.

In a few hours, darkness settled over Berismenil and the surrounding woods. Company G still held the six buildings in the town. Major Hunter ordered the Command Party to follow him into the village. We were to go to the first American held house. Before starting, Lieutenant Morgan notified Major Hunter that the telephone crew, which had been stringing a telephone line behind the marching battalion, had run out of wire. By telephone, the Major conferred with Captain Price in Samree. It was agreed that a food and ammunition party would be organized. They would follow the newly strung wire until its end. Someone would be there to meet the carrying party.

It was 2000. Lieutenant Lusby, who had been inside the village, returned to lead the Major's party into Berismenil. The trail went down the remainder of the hill. A small creek was met. Again it was crossed by stones. A small road was met. This brought us within 200 yards of the first house. Upon reaching the first dwelling, we discovered that Company E had already commanded it for their headquarters. Three other American held houses contained the other company headquarters. Captain Thompson agreed to let Major Hunter use the dwelling as his headquarters on a shared basis. After the Major was partially settled, Lieutenant Lusby motioned to Teets and myself.

"Edwards, Teets, you two will come with me."

The three of us retraced our steps down the road, across the creek and up the hill. We met the wire team of three men. The Lieutenant turned to Teets and me.

"Do you two think you can find the way back to the house where the Major is?"

I spoke for us. "Yes, Sir, we can. Is there anything you want us to tell Captain Price upon his arrival?"

"Edwards, just try to explain the situation to him. Point out the houses we occupy and where you think that tank is."

"We'll do that, Lieutenant."

We watched as the Lieutenant proceeded back into Berismenil. I turned to George. "Any bets on how long that carrying party will take to get here?"

"Don, I think they can do it in two hours. That will be about midnight when they get here. What do you guess?"

"George, my guess is six hours. Remember they only have that small wire to guide them. And that snow is still there."

342

During the next hour, the five of us at the end of the telephone line deepened our foxholes. Although we expected no shelling, we always wanted to be prepared. After settling in our foxholes, we talked and talked.

Just after 2200, George said, "Fellas, do you hear that?"

"What's that, George?" I inquired.

"Sounds like an airplane engine. Listen."

Within a few minutes, the plane was heard but not seen. First, the aircraft flew over the area. Next some flares were dropped. As they descended, the entire area lit up. For five minutes a newspaper could have been read. The light from the flares slowly faded away. Two bombs were dropped. Although they were not in our vicinity, we could feel the vibrations. In five minutes, the plane had disappeared. During the dropping of the flares, one of the wiremen wondered aloud, "I sure hope he can't see us down here."

My reply was, "To see five of us down in these trees would take some spotting."

"Edwards, do you think we're safe?"

"Yes, safe from that plane. But not safe from a wandering German patrol. One of us has to be awake until that carrying party comes."

"Sounds like a good idea."

Sunday, January 14, 1945

A new day had arrived. There was no sign of the carrying party. I said to George, "You owe me money Teets, they haven't arrived."

"Only one trouble to that Don, we didn't bet anything on it."

"My tough luck this time."

Yet none of us felt any anxiety that the carrying party had not arrived. We wondered aloud how long it would take them to climb that steep hill. The night was still. Cold had descended upon us. Every twenty minutes, I left the foxhole and tramped my feet and waved my arms. My feet were actually the only part of my body giving me any trouble.

343

Two more hours passed. Each of us urged the other to try some sleep but none of us ever dozed off. The tension kept us awake.

At 0250, footsteps and voices were heard. Teets warned, "Everybody have their rifles ready and handy."

Five minutes later, I shouted, "Halt, who goes there?"

"Edwards, it's Captain Price."

"Advance Captain and be recognized."

The Captain complied with my request. Our rifles were lowered. A conference was held with the battalion's S-3. Captain Price decided aloud, "Teets, you lead me and the carrying party to Battalion Headquarters. Edwards, we've brought some additional line for the wire crew. If you can, stay with them as they lay the phone line to the CP."

The order was complied with. Since the laying of the wire was a slow process, we could easily see Teets and Captain Price enter the CP about 0345. Some forty minutes later the wire party and I arrived there. Captain Price spoke to me, "Edwards, there's some straw in the corner. I think the other messengers are asleep. Why don't you join them?"

"I'll be glad to Captain."

As I drifted off to sleep, I looked at my watch. It was 0435.

At 0630, George Teets shook me.

"Don, time to get up."

"I'm ready George. Do you know anything?"

"No, but I think if we talk to Bergett, he'll know what's what."

Corporal Bergett was soon found. He told the four messengers, "The attack is due to start in about a half hour. The word is that if the tank is still here, artillery fire will be ordered. Battalion will pull back of town so that no one is hit. Supposedly the British are across some nearby river and their artillery will assist us, if necessary."

None of the four messengers had the foresight to bring any food for the new day. We had been confident that Berismenil would be taken in one day. But breakfast was no big worry. The worry was that tank.

At 0730, the attack started. Our machine guns fired. But there was no reply of any type. The firing stopped. The enemy had vanished. We later guessed that the Germans had pulled out during the darkness. However, about thirty members of the Wehrmacht were flushed from the houses. They had chosen to remain behind their retreating army. The new PWs were the best looking members of the German forces that any of us had seen. All of them appeared to be in their 20's. They had full faces indicating they were well fed. Their uniforms, although naturally dirty, seemed well kept. A few of them had some American equipment of which they were relieved. One Wehrmacht soldaten had on a pair of our Army shoes. These too were taken from him. The entire group was calm. All except one or two were privates indicating that their officers and non-coms had retreated without them. Two or three of our officers remarked on the youthful appearance of these prisoners. The new PWs were led away toward a nearby house where they were to be questioned. Whether the German private with the sock feet ever received any shoes was unknown to me.

By 0900, every house in Berismenil had been thoroughly searched. Fifteen minutes later the jeeps belonging to the units of the battalion arrived from Samree. One jeep carried bread and jam. The four messengers and others easily found the food-laden jeep and were gulping down a meager breakfast in record time. While we ate, I noted a dead German soldaten just a few yards from us. He had been shot through the temple from left to right. In his right hand, tightly clutched, was a German potato masher. His left hand still held his bold action rifle. We were looking at him when a rifleman from Company G appeared and said, "It looks like I got him."

Teets, who knew the GI from his company, asked, "What happened?"

"Well, George, we had just taken the fourth house, when I saw this Kraut stick his head out. I took dead aim at the spot. I figured, if he stuck his head out again, I'd fire. I saw his helmet and fired. I can see I got him. Too bad, looks like a nice young kid."

345

Conferences were being held by the battalion staff and the five company commanders inasmuch as Captain Nablo, commander of Headquarters Company, had arrived by jeep. The four messengers found a vacant house and rested. During the lull, I asked Vernon Dawes, our newest arrival, his reactions to our recent adventure.

"Ed, it was both worse and better than I expected. Coming up that hill with Major Hunter, I was sure happy that he rested all that time. My wind was almost gone. But the thing is that you know more what's going on. Back in my company, we knew nothin but nothin. Right now, I'm glad to be with you."

At 1100, I had a chat with Corporal Bergett who said it appeared that another town had to be taken before the battalion would be given any rest.

At exactly 1200, the Second Battalion went out of Berismenil in a southeasterly direction. The pace was very slow although we marched along the road. The battalion command party was to be at the end of this column. While we waited for the column to pass, a large formation of B-17s, the Flying Fortresses, flew overhead. Except for the usual first glance, no one paid any attention to them. Then someone shouted, "Hey, one of the B-17s has been hit."

Just as the bombers flew over German-held territory, a terrific barrage of anti-aircraft fire went up. One plane was on fire. Smoke began to pour from the aircraft. The plane began to lose altitude. All watched in spell-bound fascination. The craft circled and circled as if looking for a landing site. Teets remarked, "I sure hope he makes it. It doesn't look good to me."

The aircraft went down behind a group of hills on the other side of Berismenil. For a moment everything was calm. A few seconds later, a terrific explosion shook the ground. The bomber had met its end. Vernone Dawes noted, "He almost made it. It's sad."

The incident was soon forgotten. The problems of the Second Battalion were more important.

After leaving Berismenil, we walked a short way on the road. Then, a white covered open field was entered. The snow

346

was over my knees. Nothing occurred as the rifle companies trudged across the field. As the lead team approached a Belgian village, a hail of machine gun fire was met. Everyone went to the prone position without any hesitation. It was 1400.

Next to me on the ground was Major Hunter and Corporal Bergett. The Major ordered Bergett, "Call Battalion. Tell them we're pinned down before Madrin."

"Anything else Major?"

"Tell them to get the mortars and artillery ready."

Bergett complied with the order. A few minutes later, the reply came back.

"Nadrin in our hands. You may proceed there."

The Major fumed. He ordered Bergett, "Tell them we're pinned down. Tell them to check the situation. We can't move."

Bergett again complied. Back came the reply.

"Nadrin is taken. Artillery will not fire on our troops."

This meant that our battalion itself had to eliminate the machine gun. Periodically, the Germans would fire a few bursts to keep us in that prone position. Company E was ordered by radio to start a flanking movement. Major Hunter kept ordering.

"Tell Captain Price to find out the situation. Something is wrong."

Ahead I could see the riflemen from Company E bobbing up and down. One would rise from the snow, then land face down in a few seconds. Just after 1500, Captain Price reported, "Nadrin held by 334th. They will come to your assistance."

Bergett tried to contact Company E by radio. There was no reply. Another try was made. No reply. Major Hunter turned to me.

"Private Edwards, get over to your company. Tell them to stop the attack."

"I'll do it, Sir."

For the next sixty minutes, I bobbed up and down in the snow. Only once during my trip through the deep snow did I hear the sound of machine gun bullets. I estimated my speed to be about two miles an hour. After having my face washed, at least twenty times by snow, I reached Captain Thompson.

347

"Edwards, what are you doing here?"

"Order from Major Hunter, Sir, call off the attack."

At that moment, Company F lifted itself out of the snow. They walked around with little concern for that machine gun. Captain Thompson inquired of me, "What has happened?"

"Captain, I think the 334th came and eliminated the machine gun nest."

We later found out that when the German gunners found themselves surrounded on both sides, they meekly surrendered.

Company E lifted themselves out of the snowy field. Company G did the same. The entire Second Battalion went back on the road to Berismenil. The messengers waited. Major Hunter entered a jeep. In five minutes he was in Nadrin.

At 1645, the Major returned from his trip. Orders were issued to return to Berismenil. No one complained. The battalion would spend the night inside.

A half hour later, the four messengers were back in the village. There was no trouble in locating the other four messengers. My buddy, John Crable, had made a quick dash in the new quarters and had secured the only bed in the house for us. Because of his actions, Crable and Walters had a quarrel. The other six messengers were on Crable's side since the various actions of Walters did not suit any of us. I said to John, "Don't let it get you down. That bird is going to get himself in trouble some day. If Captain Kettering couldn't get along with him, he has got problems."

After supper, the usual bull sessions occurred. The four, who had stayed behind, could not understand why an attack was made on Nadrin when our forces already held the town. My reply was, "Simple, the right hand didn't tell the left hand what it was doing."

"Did anyone get hurt?" questioned Crable.

"I think two men from Company F got hit, but it wasn't fatal. Company E didn't suffer anything."

"Did you men hear what happened to Gardiner?" Crable asked.

"Did he get hurt?" I questioned.

"He's all right but not his jeep!"

"How can that be?" was my inquiry.

"Larry first delivered Gooding and the radio crew down to Berismenil about 1130." No trouble. He started back to Dochamps to pick the four of us up. About halfway between Berismenil and Samree, his jeep hit a buried mine. His vehicle went sky high. The four wheels went in all directions. Everything had holes but the driver's seat. Gardiner landed about 100 feet away still in the seat and the wheel in his hand. He only got a few cuts on his hands. How he escaped, nobody knows."

"How did you get here then?"

"Sergeant Butler told us to walk but to stay off the road. That we did."

Since the four of us that had been on duty had had little sleep, we retired at 2100.

4. Biron

Monday, January 15, 1945

At 0430, John Crable shook me.

"Don, it's time to get up."

"What time is it?"

"Four thirty."

"In the afternoon or morning?"

"It's morning."

"John, let me sleep till forty-thirty this afternoon."

"Don, I can't do it. We've got to be on the trucks in half an hour. We're supposed to get to the rest area by eight."

I slowly put on my boots and placed my pack on my back. By 0500, all the messengers were sitting in an open 2½ ton truck. As usual we waited. The air was bitterly cold. All of us in that truck tried to sleep and keep warm by sitting as close together as possible. For some unknown reason, the truck had no canvas top.

349

Just after 0600, the journey started. The convoy carrying the entire Second Battalion went back through Samree, Dochamps, Amonines and Fisnenne. Then into the Belgian countryside to an unknown destination. Very few truck rides were ever enjoyed. In this cold weather, we had no chance to exercise in order to keep warm.

By 0700, my feet had lost all their warmth. By 0800, my toes felt like solid ice. According to all reports, the journey should have ended. The trucks kept stopping and starting frequently. By 0830, the pain in my feet began to increase until it no longer seemed bearable. I tried stamping them on the floor of the truck. With my gloved hands, I kept hitting my toes. Crable hit my feet with his shoes and hands. I asked one of the other passengers to heat my feet with his cigarette lighter. Nothing was working. At 0900, tears began to fall down my cheeks. John kept talking to me.

"Don, hold on. We'll be there any minute. Hold on."

My appearance must have been that of a small baby crying. I simple kept on crying. A few others were doing the same thing. The cold was penetrating.

Just after 1000, the trucks stopped. Orders were given to detruck. I could hardly move. Crable assisted me off the truck. In front of us was a house. I said to John, "Take me in there. I've got to get warm. Another hour on that truck and I've lost my feet."

Inside the dwelling were some members of the 771st Tank Battalion. They had a fire going in a pot belly stove. Crable assisted me to a chair and removed my boots. He warned me.

"Don, don't go near that fire. Just let your feet warm up gradually. You're like a starved person who has got a full meal before him."

"Thanks for everything John. I'll follow your order."

I sat in the chair and went to sleep sitting up.

Just before 1130, I awoke. My feet were warm. John had been kind enough to get my boots near the stove to get them warm. I put them on and left the tankers.

Message center was easily found since it was located directly across the street from the tanker's dwelling. The messengers were on the second floor. We possessed a luxury that he had not seen in over two months. We had an electric light. We all agreed that it seemed strange not to read and/or see by candlelight. The floor was our bed since no straw was available. No one complained since we were many miles from the danger of the front.

At 1145, breakfast was served. We had pancakes which were much superior to the usual powdered eggs. I learned that we were in the small town of Biron. The largest nearby city was Baraux.

After breakfast, I returned to the dwelling of the tankers to listen to their radio. Listening to entertainment on the regular radio was vastly superior to the contacts that I had recently had.

At 1330, I returned to the messenger's room. Crable had been kind enough to secure my mail on a message run to Company E. After writing what I termed 'nothing letters', I decided to visit the medical aid station of our battalion to ascertain what could be done about my feet.

At the aid station, I was given the old instructions about the frequent changing of socks and soaking of your feet in hot water. I sarcastically said to the medic attending me, "Tell me, where do I get the hot water?"

"Wherever you get it when you shave."

"What if you shave in cold water?"

"I've got no answer for that."

"Is there anything you can do permanently for my feet?"

"Nothing, just take care of them the best you can. You probably will have to do that the rest of your life."

"How bad do your feet have to be before you can be evacuated?"

"Your toes must be frostbitten."

"Only then?"

"Yes. If you got trench foot like you did, you stay. Those are our orders."

"You mean they're in writing."

"Edwards, you know better than that. The General can't put himself in that bind. No, they're oral."

"What's the reason?"

"The grapevine says that if we'd evacuate those with trench foot, the casualty rate would be too high. Then, Bolling would get the foot. No General ever wants to lose his command, no matter what Army it is."

"Sure is tough on some men."

"Sure is. But remember, the General's welfare comes before the men's."

"I know that. I saw how our Colonel takes care of himself."

In the evening, the messengers rested. After another hot meal, we seemed content.

About 2000, I was talking with Corporal John Kern and questioned, "Corporal, how far was it from Berismenil to Biron?"

"Less than twenty miles."

"Corporal, you're joking. I could have nearly walked twenty miles in four hours."

"I know Edwards, but the trucks got some bad directions and turned around, at least, twice."

"You're kidding."

"I'm not. Scuttlebutt is that Major Hunter got all mixed up in his directions to get here."

"I'm not surprised. I think this command is too much for him."

"Keep it quiet, but someone told me he's applied for a transfer."

Tuesday, January 16, 1945

A complete day of rest.

No messenger arose before 0900. I was the first to rise at that time. Everyone at both the Headquarters Company and Company appeared in a bright mood. Hot meals were served to us twice that day. There was no limits on seconds. Since our work as messengers never ceased, John and I alternated the runs. Most of the morning was spent reading a book entitled, "They Also Ran." The book had been sent to me by my father as my Christmas gift for 1944 and had just arrived. John Crable had also been sent a book by his parents as his holiday gift. The two of us were commonly referred to by the other six messengers as the 'two students.' Walter, particularly, seemed upset when we referred to our natural duties as 'defecating' instead of 'shitting.' It was the habit of John and myself not to use foul language or swear regardless of the situation. We had agreed that its use would not change what was happening.

Shortly after 1030, Sergeant Butler came in with an announcement.

"Men, showers will be available today."

Innes asked, "Sarge, is that an order that we go?"

"No, but I think everybody would want to go."

The afternoon passed quietly. Supper was served and eaten. The eight of us forgot about the showers. Considering that this was the Army, it was just normal.

At 2130, as the messengers were getting to retire, Corporal Kern appeared.

"Men, time to go take your showers."

Simon, the normal quiet one, exclaimed, "Corporal, do you know what time it is?"

"Sure, nine-thirty British daylight savings time, why?"

"I think it's time for bed not a shower."

"Simon, you're right but the call just came a few minutes ago."

Teets inquired, "Corporal, are the showers out or in?"

"They are outside in a tent in Baraux. Any more questions?"

All eight were silent.

The time and the fact that the showers were outside completely discouraged Rochester and Walters. The rest of us decided to take a chance. Over a month had passed since our last bath. Our body odors could stand some improvement.

The ride to Baraux was a cold one but took less than thirty minutes. The tent showers were set up along the Ourthe River from which the pumps drew the water. The entire group from out truck entered tent number one where we undressed. Some hated to do this, not from modesty, but going nude in the middle of winter did not appeal to anyone. We estimated the temperature about 10°. Next, another tent was entered. Here the showers were located. The system was set up so that two slabs of boards were along each side of the shower tent. The boards were over large troughs for catching the water. Parallel to each slab was a pipe with four or five spigots. Everyone shouted and yelled in all types of languages at those taking showers to hurry up. Standing in the open in the Belgian winter was not fun. After finishing his shower, each man ran back to the dressing tent. Like the shower tent, it was air conditioned, that is, no heat of any type.

Prior to the shower, Corporal Kern stated that each man would receive new underwear and clothes. But only underwear was available. Shirts, pants and socks were gone. Since I was lucky to be one of the first through the shower routine, I went outside to board the truck and get a little exercise to keep warm. I fell into a conversation with one of the Negroes who were in the Quartermaster outfit operating the showers.

"Man, you men sure are noisy in getting them showers," stated a tall very dark-skinned Negro.

"It's cold in there," I answered. "By the way what is your name?"

"I'm Sam Jones from Alabama. What yours?"

"I'm Don Edwards from Michigan."

"You all come back from the front?"

"Yes, my battalion has been in and out of the line since Christmas."

"Sure would like to see what it's like. Ain't never goin to do that given showers all the time."

"Sam, be happy you can't see it. It's no fun, believe me."

"Eddie, you probably right but us black boys ain't never get that chance like you white boys."

"I guess that's true, Sam. But any day you want and can change places, look me up. I'm just hoping to get through this war."

"Rough eh. Maybe you right but I just can't believe you telling me the truth."

"Believe me, Sam, it's the truth. And I'm not a rifleman. If I was, I probably wouldn't be talking to you now."

"Eddie, what do you all do?"

"I'm a messenger. I take messages of any kind from the battalion headquarters to the company headquarters. Sounds easy but still I manage to run into shelling."

"Maybe it's better than toting a rifle. Has you seen the front?"

"I have. Most of the time it's quiet until everything breaks loose. Then you just pray."

"Pray for what?"

"Pray you don't get hit."

"Has you all been hit by a bullet?"

"Not by any bullets, Sam. I been scratched twice by some mortar shells."

At that moment, the call came to board the truck for our return to Biron. I waved to Sam who stood in the spotlights surrounding the shower tents. He waved back until we disappeared from his view. We reached Biron at 2330.

Wednesday, January 17, 1945

At 0700, I looked at my watch. I remembered that Crable and I were to attend mass that morning. John was already awake. We both slipped on our boots and left with everyone still asleep. The small Catholic church was situated only 500 yards from the message center. From the outside the church appeared deserted. Nevertheless, one door was ajar. We entered and found ourselves the sole occupants. The church contained not more than fifteen pews. We sat down in the last pew placing our rifles quietly on the floor. After a quarter of an hour, a small older priest looked out from the sacristy. His eyes seemed to pop as he saw us sitting there. Five minutes later, he came out to say Mass. As he started to say the prayers at the foot of the altar, John went up to assist him. I was the congregation. The aged priest was extremely slow in completing the service. The chill that seemed to prevail in the church must have hampered him. After mass was completed, I joined the priest and

355

Crable in the sacristy. Since John was now somewhat fluent in French, he talked with the cleric for about ten minutes. As we departed the priest said to both of us, "Merci." Then he took both of John's hands and repeated, "Merci, Merci."

As we walked back to our quarters, John mentioned, "I've never seen a person so cold. That priest shook the whole time he said mass. Did you notice?"

"He seemed nervous to me in the back. Maybe that's because of his age. How old was he?"

"He said he was 74. Notice the candle?"

"Yes, there was only one."

"That's right, just one. After mass, he said he hadn't been able to get any since 1942. Remember the German church in Palenberg. It had two candles. And I'll bet that priest was able to get new ones at any time."

After breakfast, Corporal Kern again announced, "Showers are available again."

"Can we take another if we had one last night?" questioned Innes.

"No. Heating the water is tough. But clean clothes are supposed to be available to everyone."

I took the ride to Baraux. A clean shirt, a clean pair of pants and some socks were secured. I felt like a new person.

Upon the return journey to Biron, the usually reliable Army truck broke down. I immediately jumped out and went to the driver.

"How long before you get this fixed?"

"Soldier, I've no idea. Maybe I can fix it. Maybe someone will have to come and tow us back to Baraux."

I then announced to my friends on the truck that I was walking back to Biron.

Someone shouted, "What's the matter Ed, got no patience?"

"I've got patience, but my feet don't have any. If I walk, they'll be warm. If I sit, they'll be cold. I've learned my lesson!"

I started my walking trip to Biron. My march had progressed only a little over a half a mile when a jeep from the

356

Communications platoon of the Second Battalion came by.
They looked at me, then stopped and backed up.

"Hey, Edwards, need a ride?" shouted Sergeant Hal Brazil,
the wire chief.

"Sarge, I sure can use one. Thanks."

I proceeded to jump in the back of the vehicle along with
Privates George Seifert and Hoyt Merritt. In ten minutes, I was
back at the message center. The others who had remained in the
truck did not arrive until four hours later.

Upon my arrival at the messenger's quarters, Teets confronted me.

"Don, have you heard the news?"

"What news, the war's over?"

"No, you smart ass. Battalion has a new CO."

"What's his name?"

"Lieutenant Colonel Birdsey L. Learman. And he's from
your home state."

"What happened to Major Hunter?"

"He's been transferred to some easy post. You remember
how he was at Berismenil."

"I sure do, George. I thought he was going to give way any
minute. Hope the new CO is in better shape. Where did he
come from?"

"A week ago, he was in Washington, D.C. Quite a change
I'd say."

About 1130, I was required to take a message to Company
E. Upon my arrival, the headquarters of my company was in a
state of chaos. It was worst than at any time during the action
at the front. No one noticed me. Usually I was greeted by some
snide remark. I turned to one of the men in Headquarters platoon.

"What's wrong here?"

"Where have you been?"

"Up at battalion where I'm supposed to be."

"Oh, pardon me, Edwards, I forgot."

"What's everybody so excited about?"

"Well here's what happened as near as we can figure out.
J.S. Smith was cleaning his bazooka in the room on the first

floor. For some crazy reason, he had a torpedo in the damn thing. By some accident, he set it off. It burst into the room upstairs. Deak and two others were in the room then. All three were hit. Somebody's leg is in real bad shape. It's a real mess."

"Can I help any?"

"No, Ed, don't go up there. There's enough hands there already."

"Any suggestions?"

"Just drop off what you brought from battalion. Somebody will see it after things calm down. Best if you went back to your center."

An hour and a half later, Sergeant Butler gave a lecture to all the messengers on the cleaning of weapons. Rifles, pistols, carbines and any other guns were to be carried unloaded in the rest areas. Anyone caught with a loaded weapon could be punished.

Part of the afternoon was spent with the 771st tankers. Their radio played the latest new songs and hits as well as giving newscasts. The big event was the capture of a town called Houffalize. It meant that the Americans from the First and Third Armies had met. The Bulge had been closed. The Big American attack had lasted from January 3rd to the 16th. We had won. The significance of our victory would come later.

Thursday, January 18, 1945

After breakfast at 0830, Sergeant Butler gave the expected announcement.

"All the messengers go back to your company at 1100. Stay with your company until you know their CP. Then report to battalion."

"How long will that be, Sarge?" inquired Dawes.

"My guess is that we'll be back up front about 1500."

At 1200, Company E boarded their assigned trucks. The weather was cold. I was apprehensive about my feet. I had put on new socks just before 1100. I had only to hope.

The trucks traveled through Soy, then, around the familiar hair-pin turn through Erzee. Grandmenil, Manhay and Regne were other localities I noted. Although there was snow on the ground, the highways were completely clear. When the convoy arrived at Baclain, the trucks stopped. The order came, "Everybody out. Line up on both sides. Keep ten paces between each man.

The journey continued on foot. Ahead we could hear the sounds of bursting shells. The Second Battalion passed through two tiny Belgian villages. German dead lay along side the road. This meant that fighting had recently taken place here. I also noted that several herds of cattle seemed to have been slaughtered. I remarked to Crable behind me, "What will these people do for food?"

"Good question, Don. Bet there will be some sort of Hoover plan after this war."

Someone asked, "You mean, President Hoover?"

"The same guy," answered John. "He became famous after World War I for sending food to people in Europe."

Along the road we could see the effects of the German break-through. Numerous American jeeps, anti-aircraft mounts and tanks had been rendered useless.

Fifty minutes after the march started, the town of Sterpigny was entered. The village showed the usual effects of war. Just ahead we could hear the sounds of gunfire. Company E marched through the village to its edge. Several vacant houses were entered. Crable and I waited until our company was established in its new quarters. We departed for the message center. We had taken only a few steps when the Germans welcomed us with a mortar barrage. In record time we were flat on the side of the road. The aim of the enemy seemed bad for the shells fell outside the town itself and injured no one. In ten minutes, we arose and walked. We soon passed a section of 4.2 chemical mortars which were firing at the enemy.

We found the CP of our battalion lodged in a farmhouse with a bar nearby. The messengers were initially assigned to sleep in the barn stalls. No one complained. However, a half hour later, we were transferred to the farmhouse itself. We were placed on the second floor which did not meet our approval. To get to our new quarters, it was necessary to climb a flight of stairs on the outside of the building. There was no other entrance or exit. A good shelling might make us uncomfortable. Crable and I quickly grabbed one of the two available beds for our sleep. Four messengers had to use the floor. The room was air-conditioned since all the window panes were gone. We were asleep at 2100.

Friday, January 19, 1945

The messengers were ready for work at 0700. However, the day proved to be one largely of resting. We learned that our Battalion was in reserve in case the enemy would be successful in one of their famous counter-attacks.

After being indoors in our former rest area, all right of us had been cold during the night. Most of the morning hours were spent trying to get some material to cover the broken window panes. Our efforts were successful. We managed to pick up some heavy dark material. Although we would have no natural light at night, we had secured candles to give us the needed glow to see each other.

Just after 1000, a Belgian family of three appeared in our room. Crable spoke to them in French. He stated to the rest of us, "Fellas, they want their mattress back."

"What are they doing here now?" demanded Walters.

"They just came back to their house across the street and their bedding is all gone."

"We didn't take it. The Krauts left it here."

"Walters, I think they know that but they would still like their mattress back."

"What if we don't give it back to them?"

"They'll probably go to one of our officers. Since they don't want to get in trouble with Division, we'll be ordered to give it back."

"Crable, you're probably right. Damn it. Those guys at Division never sleep on a floor."

"If it's ok with Walters, ok with the rest of you?"

"I think it's ok with the rest of us, John," I replied.

Crable then handed their mattress to them.

Upon their departure, Teets noted, "I don't mind them having the mattress. What I don't like is that they came back to their house and the front is only several hundred yards away. If we have to retreat, I'll bet they'll get in our way. I hope it didn't happen to those guys whose trucks we saw coming in here. They should have waited until the front is, at least, five miles away. They wouldn't be any trouble then."

On one of my numerous trips to Company E, I noticed a column of GIs from the 83rd Infantry Division returning through Sterpigny after being relieved in the line. All had scrawny beards, tired eyes and dirty uniforms. They looked tired. Until that moment, it had never occurred to me how different a weary Infantry soldier is from one that has just returned from a rest area. Rests were needed.

In the afternoon, two of the messengers managed to secure a small wood stove from a vacant dwelling for our use. Ventilation was no problem since our windows provided ample air. The number of shellings heard that day was less than five. We guessed the Germans might be switching units in their line at the same time.

Saturday, January 20, 1945

All five battalion companies kitchens served two hot meals that day. Breakfast for the messengers was served in the town's church. The altar was in complete shambles, having sustained a direct hit. The roof of this structure was basically intact but was punctured with about a half dozen holes that appeared to be the result of mortar shelling.

Our evening meal at 1600 was served in the barn where we were first assigned to sleep. The reason for the transfer was that the enemy had stepped up his bombardment of Sterpigny. A few huge shells fell in the village plus the usual reliable 88s. Our guess was that the Germans were using some railway to unload their heavier artillery. In the past, the Second Battalion had not encountered shelling by such large guns. Just after 1200, one large shell exploded next to the battalion's headquarters while three or four more shook the building. That was the worst that

361

day. Whether or not the Germans knew an attack was imminent was unknown to us. But they showed us that their artillery was still functioning.

XIX

THE LONG REST

1. Appointment to West Point

Saturday, January 20, 1945

At 1930, Sergeant Butler came to the messengers' quarters.

"Edwards, we just got a message that you're to report to Regiment."

"Sarge, I haven't done anything wrong that I know of."

"Maybe you're getting a decoration."

"I doubt it. I just hope it's good news."

I quickly adjusted my pack and reported downstairs. Larry Gardiner was detailed to drive me back to Regimental Headquarters. He asked, "Don, what did they call you for?"

"No idea, Larry. No one at battalion seems to know."

"Hope you get some sort of award."

"Doubtful. Do you think you can wait around until I find out?"

"I think so. There's not much going on anyway."

Upon our arrival at Regimental Headquarters ten minutes later, I was taken to the offices of the S-1 and S-4 sections. Captain Roger Taylor, the 335th Regimental S-1, shook my hand.

"Congratulations, Private Edwards, you've been appointed to West Point."

"I'm afraid, I don't understand, Sir."

"I guess you don't. This afternoon, General Bolling received word from Washington that your Congressman had appointed you to the Military Academy at West Point."

"What do I do, Sir?"

"First you're to take a physical examination here. If it's satisfactory, you'll be shipped back home as soon as possible."

"I think I'll have a hard time, Captain, since I do wear glasses. Do you know what the requirement is for West Point?"

"I think you can have 20/40 without glasses and corrected to 20/20. Any chance you can make it?"

"I think my left eye will pass, but not my right. But I'll try my best."

"That's all the general wants you to do. You can sleep with my section tonight. You're to go to the Regimental Medical Station tomorrow."

Larry Gardiner, who had been standing and observing, exclaimed, "Don, you lucky stiff. You're going back home. Wait till all the boys hear about this."

"Larry, don't be too sure. I still think I'm going to have a hard time passing that physical."

"Anything I can do for you?"

"Yes, take my field glasses and give them to John. I've got a few other things some of the messengers might want."

I accompanied Gardiner to his jeep. We shook hands. He believed he would never see me again.

After Gardiner left, I was approached by a reporter from the "Stars and Stripes" Army newspaper. We went into one of the regimental offices. Here an interview was conducted on my appointment to West Point. He asked about my entire background and my job as messenger in the Second Battalion. A few days later, an article appeared in the newspaper entitled "GI Pulled From Foxhole For Appointment to West Point."

A bed was secured for me. At 2300 I drifted off to sleep.

THE LONG REST

Sunday, January 21, 1945

I arose at 0645. Breakfast was eaten with my former outfit, the 335th Infantry Headquarters Company. Several of my friends had heard of my good fortune and wished me the best back in the States.

At 1100, I left in a jeep with Privates Joe Kopesky and Ed Calvert. An hour later we were back in Baraux. We reported to the Personnel Office of the 335th Regiment.

Captain Jack Talbot, the Regimental Personnel Officer, instructed me to report to the 309th Medical Battalion Aid Station in Durbuy. Private Kopesky drove me there. At the Aid Station, the Major in charge stated to me, "I'm sorry Private Edwards, but we don't have the facilities to give a complete physical. You must go to a hospital for that. I'll make the necessary arrangements for you."

A half hour wait ensued.

Private Kopesky and I were given instructions to report to the 102d Evacuation Hospital in the City of Huy. It meant another jeep ride of an hour. On our way to Huy, our jeep was involved in an automobile accident. A run away Belgian sled hit our jeep head on. The vehicle slid into the adjoining ditch but fortunately there was little damage. With Kopesky at the wheel, I pushed the jeep out of the slight trench into which it had slid. We arrived at the hospital at 1600.

The complete physical examination was given. When my blood pressure was taken, the nurse said, "Mm, that's not too good." The last part was the eye examination. Although my left eye tested out at 20/40, I could, with my right eye, barely see the 20/70 figures on the chart. I knew that was not good enough to enter the U.S. Military Academy. The sample of blood that had been taken from me could not be analyzed for some unknown reason. Thus, the Captain who had charge of the physical examination refused to sign until this testing was completed.

Joe Kopesky and I started our return journey in the dark just after 1930. We did not receive any supper but he had some K rations in his jeep which we devoured. At 2130, we arrived

365

back at the Personnel Office in Baraux. Captain Talbot had remained past the normal working hour to wait for us. He examined the papers and asked me, "Edwards, how do you think you did?"

"Captain, I know I didn't pass the eye part. I think everything else was satisfactory."

"You're right there. Also says that you have high blood pressure. Had any trouble in this line before?"

"No, Sir."

"It may be the excitement of today. Or it might be from the tension in your job. We'll see."

My resting place that night was the floor of the Personnel Office. I had no objections since the office was warm and comfortable.

Monday, January 22, 1945

At 0630 the telephone rang. Gulford Hamrick, whose job in personnel seemed to be that of messenger, answered. After he finished, he told me that he was assigned to sleep every night in the Personnel Office as part of his duties. Like myself, his resting place was the floor. Yet, he stated he was thankful for this job where he was relatively safe from any shelling and the front lines.

We ate breakfast at the Division Headquarters kitchen. The meal consisted of canned juice, cereal, pancakes and coffee. It was far superior to any that I had been receiving in the Second Battalion.

During the remainder of the day, I attempted to be helpful in running a few messages as directed by Captain Talbot. Most of my time was spent in reading books that the Personnel Office had available. I renewed my acquaintances with two former schoolmates who had attended Drexel Tech with me in Philadelphia. They were Charles E. Brown and Jack Shepman. The latter kidded me over my political appointment to West Point, to which I retorted, "Jack, you may remember back in Claiborne that you got this job through pull."

"Don, you've got a good memory. That's true. Captain Talbot was sore when they put me in here. But he's used to me now. Hope everything turns out good for you. You're a smart guy and don't deserve to be just a messenger. What platoon were you with back in Drexel?"

"Number one."

"I remember that. I was with three. And didn't they put us into the platoons by academic rank?"

"Yes, Jack, they did. But I guess I'm just a little unlucky now. Most of the men I'm with except for my buddy, John Crable, look down on anybody that's a student. Most of the officers sort of pick on me for the same thing except for one."

"Who is that one?"

"Captain Price, the battalion's S-3."

"We've heard that he's one of the best in the whole division. He looks at every situation carefully."

"I think he's tops."

"What do you think of your chances of leaving here?"

"Jack, I'd say they're extremely poor. My eyes just won't pass the standard for West Point. And I'm not going to cheat to get out of a bad situation. I'll take my chances."

"Your attitude is much better than mine would be, Don. Still hope you pass that exam."

"Thanks, Jack."

At 2200, Hamrick, who liked to be called 'Jack', and I turned out the lights.

Tuesday, January 23, 1945

The telephone rang at 0645 to awaken Hamrick and me. Three hot meals a day were now being eaten at the Division Headquarters. I wondered if I might grow 'soft' if I kept up this routine too long.

Although I again attempted to be helpful, there was little I could do. The Personnel Office's work was cut out for them. Their routine was like that of an office in a large corporation. Their work day started about 0800. A break for lunch was taken around 1200. After lunch they worked until 1730. Except for unusual situations, their day did not vary too much. Their most trying task was probably filing reports of men who had been killed in action as well as those who had suffered wounds or had been injured.

During the day, I spent most of my time reading books and magazines. I wrote several letters. One was to my buddy, John Crable, still expressing my doubt as to my ability to pass the physical. I wrote to him, "I know I'm good enough to do the fighting for my country but, perhaps, not good enough to be admitted to a military academy." Another was written to First Sergeant Goodpasteur asking him to hold my place as a messenger until my return.

At 1400, Captain Talbot addressed me, "Edwards, why don't you go over and take a shower."

My reply was, "Captain, thank you, I just had one last week."

His face showed considerable surprise. He replied, "OK, do as you want."

"Captain, I'm sorry. I guess when you don't bathe for quite a while, you think once a week is frequent. I'll take one just before going back to the company, if that is satisfactory to you."

"That's satisfactory with me. Edwards, I forget the situation with the companies on the line."

That evening I went to a movie entitled "Rhapsody in Blue," with John Edsall, a private from Company I who worked at the Personnel Section.

Wednesday, January 24, 1945

The telephone operator awoke us at the usual time of 0630.

The 335th Personnel Office was scheduled to move to a new location that day. Since I did not know when and where I would have any other opportunity to take a shower, I secured permission from Captain Talbot to go when it opened at 0900. I received clean clothes for everything I had on except my shoes. I felt like a new, new man.

The previous day, I had been told that I would return to the hospital to get the results of my blood test. Since the Personnel Section was about to move, my hospital visit was postponed.

At 1500, their move was canceled.

At 1700, I secured permission to visit the Adjutant General's office to discuss my situation regarding my appointment. I was referred to Warrant Officer Ted Skronski. He was honest and frank.

"Edwards, I don't think they'll send you back to the States unless you pass that physical. Do you think you could do better with another eye exam?"

"Sir, I don't think so. I've worn glasses for about four years. I don't think a doctor would have prescribed them for me unless they were necessary."

"You know the General is very anxious for you to pass. He could then point out that one of his men made the Point."

"I realize that, Sir. But I'm going to pass the correct way. I could easily memorize that Snellen chart and fake it, but I'd be caught sooner or later."

"Let's do this. After the 335th Personnel moves tomorrow, you come back to me. I'll make sure the hospital is expecting you to get those blood tests. Then bring everything back to me. If I don't think you have any chance, you can go back to your company on the 26th. We shouldn't waste everyone's time on this. Besides, maybe your company needs you."

"I hope not, Sir. They were scheduled to make an attack when I left. I hope everything went all right."

"I hear that it did. The whole 84th is scheduled to get out of the line now that the enemy has retreated so much.

"See you tomorrow, Sir."

Thursday, January 25, 1945

We arose at 0600. Personnel was definitely going to move. After the usual good breakfast, I assisted in moving some equipment onto the moving trucks. At 0900, the entire Personnel section was aboard a 2½ ton truck and moving toward their new quarters. We arrived in Aywaille just after 1000. After assisting in the unloading of their equipment, I reported to the Adjutant General's office.

Warrant Office Skronski had already taken care of securing a jeep for my ride to the hospital in Huy. Because of better roads, the journey went through Liege to Huy. The results of the blood tests were available. Three doctors signed my physical examination report. To relieve the monotony of just riding, my jeep driver allowed me to drive the jeep the entire distance back to Aywaille.

I immediately reported to Warrant Office Skronski about 1600. He looked at the report.

"Edwards, I'll forward this to the attention of the General. But, of course, there will be no recommendation that you go back to the States."

"I understand, Sir. I was never under any idea that I wouldn't go back to my outfit. Thank you for your assistance."

"I thank you. Most men would have been very bitter that they couldn't leave. And I venture to say most of them would have cheated to leave."

Friday, January 26, 1945

After breakfast, Captain Talbot informed me, "A mail truck is scheduled to leave at 1000. It's going to Bovigny where the kitchens of the Second Battalion are located. If you find Company E's kitchen, they should be able to get you to your company's headquarters. Good luck, sorry it didn't work out for you."

To prepare for my journey, I went to a small store and purchased a map of the area. It proved to be a fortuitous choice.

As I put on my pack to leave, Jack Shepman came to bid me goodby.

"Don, I'm sorry to hear that you're going back to your company. I thought you would make it."

"Jack, you know the standards to get into the military academy are strict. I just couldn't make it. I'm not bitter about it."

"Well, good luck anyway. How do you think you'll come out of this war?"

"For some reason Jack, I think I'll make it. From what I've heard on the radio here the last few days, our side has the momentum. I don't think the Germans will ever get it back."

At 1005, the mail truck left. Since I was an extra passenger, I rode in the back with the mail. Two hours later after, at least, six stops for various reasons, the driver yelled, "Hey, back there. This is Bovigny."

I searched and searched for any and all types of kitchens. There were none to be found. In my wanderings I asked an MP if he had seen any kitchens that day.

"Yes, I saw some here this morning. I remember that they left about an hour ago. But I don't know where they were going."

"Got any suggestions as to what I can do?"

"Soldier, you're in luck. The Anti-Tank Company from the 335th is still here. I think they're getting ready to move out. Go down that street and see what you can find out."

Directions were given to me as to their exact location. As I approached the Anti-Tank Company, their enlisted men were in the streets ready to board their trucks. Permission was given to ride with them.

After arrival at their new destination, I went to their company headquarters and approached the First Sergeant.

I asked, "Sergeant, can you tell me where Company E and the Second Battalion is located?"

"I can't, but I'll get our radio man to find out for you. Just wait here."

In a few minutes, he returned.

"Private, your company is located in Xhoris."

"Where is that, Sergeant?"

"Oh, about ten miles from here. Do you have a map with you?"

"I just purchased one this morning in Aywaille."

The map was produced. The way was outlined. The First Sergeant said, "Just start going down the road to your outfit. Someone will pick you up."

I walked but not a single vehicle passed me during my travel. Since my feet did not get cold, I completed the journey in just over two hours. The headquarters of Company E was easily located. Upon my entrance, everyone in the company was surprised to see me.

"We thought you were back home after we saw that article in 'Stars and Stripes,'" announced Sergeant Goodpasteur.

"That reporter forgot just one important thing. I had to pass the physical."

"But you passed the physical back in Claiborne, Edwards."

"Right, Sarge. My eyes may be good enough for combat but not good enough for West Point."

"Sorry you didn't get it."

At that moment, Captain Thompson entered the room and exclaimed, "I thought I'd never see you, Edwards, what happened?"

"Afraid I couldn't pass the physical, Captain."

"Your eyes?"

"Yes, Sir. West Point requires just about perfect eyesight when you get in and the same thing when you leave."

"I suppose you want your old job back?"

"Yes, Sir. Sergeant Smith, I think, can tell you that I took this message job back in Louisiana when it was no fun."

"I'll take your word for it. Norris took your place, but he can come back with us."

When Ed Norris and I arrived at the Message Center, the same surprise was uttered by all the messengers. But John Crable said to me, "I just got your letter Don, and I figured you'd be back with us. I knew someone who had been appointed to West Point and he had to be in top physical shape, including his eyes."

"I think I'm in pretty good shape, but I can't do anything about these glasses during my lifetime."

"I'm happy to have you back. Norris was all right but I can tell you he won't volunteer for anything extra like you do."

"I think you know the reason why I sometimes do it."

"Yes, to get notes for your diary. I hope no one ever sees that book you're writing in besides me."

"I know. If something happens to me, just junk it."

"I will if I can."

"How did the attack go?"

"Not too much different from the previous ones. Company E was in the lead for this one. The Germans were back on some ridge and pinned us down. Then, the mortars came down. But our artillery answered them. Company G made a wide flanking movement and got into Gouvy which was our objective. They got part way into the town when they couldn't move because Jerry was holding the railroad station. They had a tank back of the station that we think was a Tiger. Next morning, which was the 23rd, Blue Battalion took over our positions and pushed Jerry back through a town called Ourthe. Seemed like the Germans were doing the same thing they did with you at Berismenil. They hold you up in the day and, at night, pull out. Company E lost two guys."

"Who were they, John?"

"One was Sergeant Sweet. The other was Private Bailey from the first platoon. I think about ten others got hit. A couple were serious."

2. Xhoris, Belgium

Saturday, January 27, 1945

At 0730, Corporal Kern came to our room.

"Breakfast is served. They're going to close at 0800 promptly."

"What do they have today, steak and eggs?" asked Innes sarcastically.

"I don't know, but hurry if you want anything."

373

Only two of the messengers, Crable and Innes, went to eat. They came back shortly after 0800. Innes announced, "Did you guys miss a great breakfast!"

"I'll bet we did," answered Teets. "You guys froze your butts before they dumped those delicious powdered eggs on your pan."

"You're right, George, that's what we had. Crable and I are going to go back to the sack and sleep it off."

After lunch, I had to take one of the normal messages to Company E. Upon my return, I carried the mail for both John and myself. Many of the letters received were written in October and November of 1944. Considering our constant movements, all the messengers were happy that the mail was almost up-to-date. A six weeks delay was considered normal.

In the middle of this afternoon, the messengers had the usual session of what was going to happen next.

"Anybody know what big outfit we're in now?" asked Innes.

"I heard we're attached to the 18th Airborne Corps," answered Crable.

"Airborne?" inquired Simon.

George Teets added, "Fellas, remember back in Claiborne, we had some training on leading a glider. Maybe they're going to have us put it to use."

"But, George," I interrupted. "That's not enough training to know what to do when those gliders land."

"Still they might just put us on one and hope for the best, Don."

"But George, we've got all those replacements. They never had any training. The only thing they know is how to handle a rifle. Even then, the old guys have to calm them down the first time they hear a shell go off."

"I agree with Don," added Crable. "But this Army does some stupid things. This might be one of those stupid things."

Frank Mongus, one of the two quiet Company H runners, summarized it by saying, "You fellas can talk all you want to. We'll do what someone else wants us to do."

374

"I think Frank is one hundred percent right. Whether it's the 18th Airborne or the Seventh Corps, the First or the Ninth Army, we'll have to follow orders," Innes concluded.

Sunday, January 28, 1945

Under many circumstances, Sunday was another day of war. But John Crable and I knew that we should attend Mass as good Catholics if possible. Thus, at 1030, we were present for the High Mass that was said this Sunday in Xhoris. Since the front was a minimum of 20 miles away, we left our rifles and hand grenades in our quarters. But both of us retained the belt containing our extra bullets for our M-1. The sermon and announcements were both in the native tongue which John readily understood. After church, he said, "Nothing was said of any importance except to pray for the soldiers that are fighting. I think that we were included in those prayers."

Church was very crowded since the majority in the Second Battalion still realized that the war was not finished although the Germans had been beaten in the Ardennes.

After church, I was able to secure from Larry Gardiner a small Coleman gas burner that he sometimes possessed. Water was drawn from a nearby well. In a newly found pan, the water was heated. Shaving in hot water was a luxury.

The remainder of the day was spent largely in reading and writing. Periodically messages had to be taken to the various companies. Actually this was a welcomed diversion, since it provided an outlet for some pent up emotions. The situation between my buddy, John Crable, and Hugh Walters was becoming worst. John, of course, was a serious type individual like myself, while Walters was a hell-raiser par excellence.

Monday, January 29, 1945

We had been instructed the previous day that breakfast would be served between 0730 and 0800 each day. No one would awaken us. If you wanted to eat, it was your responsibility to arise on your own. At 0730, I announced, "Guys, time for breakfast for anyone that wants it."

375

"Edwards, shut your fucking mouth."

"Walters, you keep that up and you'll have two guys to contend with."

Three messengers decided to eat breakfast that morning. On our way to the kitchen, Crable, Teets and I discussed the situation about Hugh Walters. I inquired, "George, is there any way you can get him back to your company?"

"Don, they don't want him either. He's just a bad egg. He has been in three or four fights with guys in Company G. He also swung at Captain Ketterer. The Captain doesn't want him. Nobody wants him. We have him."

"My guess is that if he doesn't leave, John or I are going to have a fight with him. And each of us will probably assist the other. Nobody is going to help him. There's going to be big trouble if he reaches for his weapon, for I won't hesitate to shoot him, if required. I'm serious!"

"I'll ask for both of us when I go this morning. But don't hold your breath. Nobody but nobody wants him."

Although our battalion was in a rest area, the formation for any meal was the same as that which existed closer to the front. Every man had to stay five paces apart from the others. Food was to be eaten under cover or alone. We had been warned that in North Africa, many men had been killed or wounded because the Luftwaffe planes had caught them in large concentrations when they were eating. Although none of us were worried for this reason, the German break-out the previous month was still in everyone's mind. No one violated this order.

Each day most of the messengers read the 'Stars and Stripes' with avid interest. Upon its arrival, someone would usually ask, "How far are the Russians from Berlin today?"

Walters would invariably retort with, "What does that concern us?"

Someone would explain that if the Russians captured Berlin, it might mean the end of the war for us. No one wanted any more fighting if it could be avoided. However, all of us knew the Germans would not surrender unless it was hopeless. We had heard too many rumors about Hitler.

376

Tuesday, January 30, 1945

It was a miserable day. Rain showers were prevalent throughout the entire day. The only consolation was that the rain was melting the snow that had started over a month ago. We were thankful that our battalion was not on the line.

Rumors continued to circulate as to the next move. In the afternoon I conducted a poll as to our fate. I asked, "How many think we're going to go back to the line in Germany?"

Four including myself raised their hands.

"How many think we're going to remain in Belgium?" was my next question.

Three raised their hands. One was missing. I questioned Charlie Simon, "Charlie, where do you think we're going?"

"Don, I think they'll put us in the line in France."

"Well, you know they're still fighting in France down by Switzerland. The 84th seems to be the Division they put anywhere in the line, so we'll probably go to the line in France. Simple isn't it?"

None of us agreed with Charlie.

All the messengers did agree that the 84th had had a much tougher time in Germany than in Belgium. Company E had suffered the majority of its casualties in Germany although they had seen more action time in Belgium.

About 1600, John and I went to Company E to secure our pay. Although a few still complained about being paid, some of the wages that we received could be spent in the nearby cities and towns. One Hugh Walters would take advantage of this opportunity.

Wednesday, January 31, 1945

At breakfast that morning, I asked Sergeant Rochester, "Sarge, do you want to go with me to Aywaille to buy anything?

"What could I get there, Ed?"

"I can't say but it looked like a nice place to me when I was just there for my physical exam."

"If we can get away, I'll go with you."

377

Our journey started at 0830. Since the main road was two miles away, it was necessary to walk there to thumb a ride to Aywaille. Just before we reached the main highway, we observed some companies practicing some close-order drills. We stopped to look at them. A GI came walking by us. I inquired of him, "Private, what outfit is that?"

"Part of the First Battalion, 333rd."

"What are they doing?"

"Close order drills."

"What's the reason? That doesn't do any good up front."

"All the guys know that. You ought to hear the bitching. But it's part of the training we do every day."

"How long has First Battalion been doing this?"

"When we got off the line, we had exactly one day of rest. Then training started the next day. Only good thing is that the guys are tired each night."

Rochester and I departed. I said to him, "Sarge, hope the word doesn't get back to our new CO."

"Ed, you and me both."

Upon reaching the main road, we stuck out our thumbs. Within five minutes, we were picked up by an Army truck. In fifteen minutes, we were in Aywaille.

Sergeant Rochester and I walked about the town looking in the various shop windows. Then, we entered one which contained all types of souvenir articles. Rochester decided to purchase some small wooden shoes for his two children. My purchases consisted of colored handkerchiefs for my mother and sister. After our buying spree, we walked into three or four bakeries to purchase some bread and pastries. Our efforts were in vain. Since rationing was in full effect, nothing could be secured without coupons. Money we had, coupons we didn't. Aywaille was the headquarters for the 84th Infantry Division. This meant that there were numerous U.S. Army vehicles and personnel of all varieties. The local population seemed to be next to nil.

Just after 1100, a slight drizzle began. The Sergeant and I decided to return to Xhoris. A quickly secured truck ride brought us back to our junction. A half hour walk then

378

brought us back to the messenger quarters. We displayed our purchases to the other seven present. The new person to join our group, for resting purposes only, was Larry Gardiner. He and Walters seemed to enjoy each other's company. As John remarked to me in the afternoon, "If Gardiner is here, Walters doesn't seem to bother me. What about you, Don?"

"Same thing. I'm actually glad to see Walters has someone whom he likes and who likes him. They're two of a kind."

During the remainder of the day, rain came intermittently. The snow continued to melt.

Thursday, February 1, 1945

The trip that Sergeant Rochester and I had taken the previous day proved to be a stimulus to others in the messenger's room.

At 0830, Crable and Teets left to acquire some souvenirs in Aywaille. A half hour later, Walters and Gardiner decided to go all the way to Liege, which was the nearest large city. All of us knew they were going to satisfy their human passion for female companionship. As Gardiner left, he mentioned, "Right now, I'm loaded. Loaded with money and weeds. Loaded with pussy juice. When I come back, I won't have either. Here I come, you Belgian broads!"

Since both Company G messengers had departed, their work was divided among the five remaining messengers. This posed no problem for those of us remaining in Xhoris.

A movie was scheduled for the entire Second Battalion at 1000. But it was postponed due to the lack of a suitable projector. At 1400, it was shown. The movie was entitled, "Music in Manhattan." It would prove to be my favorite flick while on the European continent since it was viewed four times in less than a year.

The remainder of the day was devoted to resting. But all of us began to wonder what was wrong. Our previous rests had lasted less than four days. A week had passed. We knew the front was being tightened but our rest period seemed unreasonable.

379

That night, there were only seven men sleeping in the messenger's quarters. Walters and Gardiner had not returned from their excursion. As we retired, Teets noted, "I'll bet anything those guys are lying between some broad's legs right now. And will all night long."

"What's the matter, George, are you jealous?" retorted Rochester.

"Rochie, you're damn right I am. But I'm not going AWOL for no ass."

"George, I think I'm going to take a look around for some myself."

Friday, February 2, 1945

Another movie was scheduled for 1000. It was canceled without any explanation. No rescheduling was made.

Throughout the morning, a large number of trips were made to Company E. I said to John, "Something's up John. I think we're getting ready to go back up front."

"I think you're right, Don, but the question is where?"

At 1300, Sergeant Butler came to the messenger's room.

"Has anyone seen Gardiner?"

"Sarge, he went to Liege with Walters yesterday," Crable volunteered.

"So I heard. He'd better be back here soon or he's AWOL. I think you know we're going to leave today."

"We figured that out Sarge," answered Crable. "Wasn't one of those messages giving the time the trucks would arrive?"

"I believe it was. I'll be up with more orders later."

Two hours later, Corporal Kern came to our room.

"Men, here are some new orders. All shoulder patches are to be removed. All bumpers on all vehicles are to be painted over. All the maps are to be returned to regiment. We're to be ready for anything."

"Corporal, what does anything mean?" I asked.

"Edwards, I really don't know. I've heard we're going to some airport to fly out of here into Germany. Someone else said we're going to Holland to be part of the British Army. It's really mixed up."

At 1830 the trucks arrived. One messenger from each company took a designated number of vehicles to his company. The seven messengers proceeded to wait. Although Gardiner had finally returned at 1700, Hugh Walters was still absent. If all the messengers were sent back to their companies, his absence would be noted. As we waited, Innes noted something unusual.

"Guys, have you noticed that we haven't been issued any K-rations?"

His partner, James Rochester, added, "The only outfits we've seen that have their kitchens at the front are the English."

None of us ruled out joining the British Army since the 84th Division had originally been at the northern end of the American line while in Germany, next to the First British Army.

At 2300, our wait ended. Sergeant Butler ordered the messengers to report to their respective companies. As we left, Simon inquired of George Teets, "George what are you going to tell your First Sergeant about Walters?"

"I've got to tell them the truth. What else can I do?"

"You could tell them that Walters is coming."

"Yea, I could but if he doesn't show tomorrow, what then? I think First Sergeant Bratton will understand for he knows Walters."

Upon our arrival at Company E, the order to load the trucks was issued. We proceeded, per the usual Army style, to wait. One thing was different. Our trucks had their full headlights on. Our destination was still a mystery.

3. Schaesberg, Holland

Saturday, February 3, 1945

At 0005, the truck wheels turned. I had taken my usual position which was at the end of row. As soon as we started, almost everyone drifted off to sleep. During most of the long ride, my companions would drift in and out of sleeping, and I was no exception.

At first the convoy traveled through open country. Two hours after we left Xhoris, the trucks passed through the streets of a deserted Liege. It meant that our destination was north. Some time later, we rolled through the streets of Aachen. I could identify the latter city, for at its outer edge were some discarded trolley cars that had been seen on our journey southward to Marche over a month ago. We were back in the Fatherland.

At 0530, Sergeant Smith shouted, "Headquarters out of the truck. Unload the equipment. Then, stay here until you hear from me."

With my pack at my side, I sat down on the pavement. Another member of Company E and I decided to sit back to back to give each other support. We drifted off to sleep.

At 0700, Crable shook me and said, "Don, get up, the company's moving into their quarters."

"John, where are we?"

"I don't know yet. But you can see we're in a village square of some type."

There were a few civilians on the streets. Their faces showed a mild shock to see American soldiers here. Sergeant Smith was issuing orders to the Headquarters platoon. I questioned him.

"Sarge, where are we?"

"Holland."

"Holland. You're sure?"

"I'm positive. We are in Holland."

The first house selected for the location of the Headquarters platoon was that of a well known Nazi sympathizer. It was quickly vacated. A house was selected on the north side of the village square. After the headquarters of Company E were established, John and I were ordered to report to our post of duty. No difficulty was experienced in discovering that the message center was in a house located in the southeast area of the square. John and I were the last messengers to arrive. Sergeant Butler gave us instructions.

"Men, I'm sorry that all the rooms in headquarters are taken. There's a barn out back where you can stay."

"But Sergeant, there's plenty of houses in this town. Can't we get in one of them?" protested Crable.

"Crable, that seems reasonable. I'll try to get Wiles to ask around and see what we can do for you."

Less than an hour later, Wiles returned. He announced, "Fellas, I've been successful. There's a house just down the street from here off this southeast corner. The three ladies said you could sleep in their bedrooms upstairs. You can have the use of the rooms downstairs on the first floor."

"How old are the ladies?" inquired Rochester.

"I'd say each of them is over 60! You are not getting any young chicks."

The seven messengers marched down to our designated dwelling with our equipment. A rap was made on the front door. An elderly Dutch woman with gray hair about five feet tall answered. She motioned for us to follow her. She led us through an entrance hall, up the stairs to the second floor. She then pointed out a large bedroom. Connected to it was another small bedroom. I asked in my best German.

"Ihr schlaffen hier?" (You sleep here?)

"Nein, in dem kellar. Soldaten schlaffen hier." (No, in the cellar. Soldier sleep here.)

"Danke." (Thank you.)

There were three double sized beds. We pondered what to do when Rochester announced, "Guys, don't count me in. I think I'm going to seek a little entertainment at night. If you know what I mean."

"We all know what you mean, Rochie," replied Innes.

None of the beds had any bedding on them but since we had our own sleeping bags, this was not a problem. After inspection, George suggested, "Don, do you think they'll let us look at the downstairs?"

"I think so, George, since Wiles said we could use that part of the house too."

The first floor consisted of three rooms. One was a large living room which was not used inasmuch as our hostesses could not afford to heat it. Next came a dining room which held six chairs and a small dining table. At the end of this room was the kitchen where the three elderly Dutch ladies cooked and ate. On one side of the living room and dining room ran a small hallway which, also, was not heated. Back of the kitchen was an entrance to a cellar which we never entered during our stay. We presumed it contained their sleeping quarters. In the dining room, we noticed a small radio. I secured permission, in my bad German, from our hostesses to listen to it whenever we were in their home and they did not use it.

After we had unpacked upstairs, I made a suggestion to the other six messengers.

"Men, let's ask Sergeant Butler or Gooding to install a phone in this house."

"What do we need one for?" asked Innes.

"Well, in that way, whenever there's a message to be run, Kern or Butler do not have to come to get us. Also because of the close locations of the companies, only two of us have to be here at one time."

"Go ahead and see what you can do." encouraged Vernon Dawes.

I walked to the battalion message center which was about 100 yards away. I confronted Sergeant Butler.

"Sarge, I know there are extra phones. Let me install one in the board and run it to our house. Then, you or Corporal Kern won't have to walk each time to get us. Just phone us whenever we're needed."

"Sounds great to me, Edwards."

Upon further inquiry to Sergeant Gooding, he, too, approved of the idea.

"Edwards, I'll get one of the linemen to assist you."

"Thanks, Sarge, but I can do it. I was in the wire station when I was with Regimental Headquarters Company. I still know what to do."

After securing the necessary equipment, I had our own private messenger phone line installed in half an hour. I procured enough telephone line so that our phone could be next to my bed at night and during the daylight hours it extended down the stairs to the dining room.

My first message run to Company E came at 1030. At the main message center, I inquired, "Where are we in Holland?"

"Edwards, we're in a town called Schaesberg." replied Corporal Kern.

"Where is that?"

"I think from your house, which is almost at the end of the block, you can see Heerlen, which is about four kilometers away."

"And where is Heerlen?"

"Heerlen is about eight or nine kilometers from Palenberg. You know that place?"

"Palenberg, I know, Corporal. In other words we are back at the front we left in December."

"That's what it looks like right now."

After our usual hot supper meal, the six messengers listened avidly to the AEF division of the BBC. We were following the progress of the 78th Infantry Division in their drive toward the Roer River dams. Until these dams were taken, there could be no crossing of the Roer inasmuch as the Germans could easily let the water out and strand any American troops that might cross. No one told anyone that the 84th was going to cross the Roer. Everybody just assumed this as a fact.

Before retiring that night, our three ladies made us a snack. They seemed delighted to do this for some of us had brought back raw materials from our kitchens for their use. We realized that only a portion of what we brought would be served to us and the remainder would be used to supplement their own meager diets.

A PRIVATE'S DIARY

At 0730, John Crable and I arose to attend mass at the local Catholic Church. It was located just three blocks south of the village square so there was no trouble finding it. Since combat was still a distinct possibility, the attendance from the members of the Second Battalion was excellent. In the morning I had learned that the area in which we were located was the Catholic area of the Netherlands. Both John and I were under an illusion that the Dutch people were solidly Protestant from its northern areas to the south. The sermon and announcements were, of course, given in the native tongue. We had become accustomed to this arrangement.

Just after 1300, George Teets came back from a message run to company G with news for us.

"Fellas, Walters is back!"

Crable immediately spoke, "George, is he coming back here?"

"No, he's been AWOL since we left Belgium."

"Is anybody coming to assist you?"

"Yea, the First Sarge said they'd send someone over tomorrow. But they didn't tell me who."

"What's going to happen to Walters?"

"He's going to be court-martialed."

"Any idea what for?"

"Some of the fellas at the company think it's going to be for desertion. That's worse than AWOL."

After George had finished and we were alone later, John spoke, "Don, Walters not coming back was one of the greatest things that ever happened to me."

"I know, John."

"I think that if he would have been here about two more weeks, we would have been fighting. And knowing him, he might have shot me."

"I don't think he would have gone that far."

"Maybe yes, maybe no. But I was ready for him."

386

Bernard J. Cohn — Baltimore, Maryland

Monday, February 5, 1945

The strength of the messengers returned to its normal eight. At 1000, George brought over Bernard Cohn who would replace Hugh Walters. I asked him,

"Bernie, what have you been doing up to now?"

"You may remember that in England, regiment formed a special platoon to remove mines and mine fields."

387

"Did you ever remove any fields?"

"We removed a few down in Belgium. Most of the time they just kept us in reserve in case the line broke."

"Don't they have any further use for you at the present time?"

"No, I guess they figure that Jerry won't have much time to lay many fields any more. Our platoon leaders said they thought the Germans would do the same thing they did in North Africa where they used millions of them. But they've used very few lately."

Private Bernard Cohn was very silent the remainder of the day. In a week he would be chatting as if he had been a part of the messenger's group since the start of our combat effort. I would learn that he was married. His wife and one small son were living in Baltimore, Maryland.

About 1400, Hugh Walters came back to visit his old group. John Crable wisely went to visit someone in Company E.

Since Rochester had begun to lay with various Dutch girls every night since our arrival in Schaesberg, he inquired, "Walter, how was the pussy in Liege?"

"Just fabulous, just fabulous. Those Belgian kunts were all over the place. Not too many of our guys were on the streets either."

"What did you finally get?"

"I finally shacked up with a blond whose boobs must have been a 40. They were terrific. She let me suck on them day or night. She just opened up her blouse and let me go to it. Her ass was out of this world. She could keep me out or let me in. I don't know how she did it."

"What else did she do?"

"Rochie, you name it, she did it. Anything and everything. We didn't leave the room except to get some meals."

"How much did she charge?"

"Didn't pay her a cent!"

"Walters, you're a damn liar. She didn't do all this because you're such a great fucker."

388

"Certainly. I'm a great stud. All you guys know it. She knew it."

"I don't believe it. Those Dutch dames I'm laying with get something from me."

"What are you giving them, Rochie?"

"Cigarettes, chocolate. Bring them food from the mess."

"Oh, I gave this whore my cigarettes."

"How many cartons?"

"Think I left her with four or five. Or maybe more. I forgot."

"How much are our cigarettes worth in Liege?"

"I think I heard about two dollars a pack."

"And she got five cartons from you, Walters?"

"Rochie, I didn't pay for those cigarettes. I traded for them with all of you here. So it didn't cost me anything. I'm not worried what she got for those weeds. She was worth every last cigarette I had."

"How long did Gardiner stay with you in Liege?"

"He and I were with these two blonds just the one night. Next morning, he got cold feet about being away from this lousy outfit. He took off with his tart a little after noon on the Second. I told him I was staying until I ran out. Got here yesterday after going back to Xhoris. Someone said battalion was up in Germany."

"What's going to happen to you?"

"I don't know Rochie. Damn guys won't let me come back here as messenger."

"Anybody tell you anything yet?"

"No, not yet. If I ever get out of this damn Army alive, I expect them to help me the rest of my life."

After a few more minutes of the same type of conversation, Hugh Walters left. Everybody breathed a sigh of relief upon his departure. The grapevine told us later that he was convicted of AWOL and was sent to prison for a year.

Crable did not return until supper time. Upon his return, John asked me, "What did Walters have to say?"

389

"John V. Crable of Elwood City, that's one of the most stupid questions, you ever asked me. What does Walters talk and think about all the time?"

"Women."

"I'll give you a 100% grade for that, John. I know your delicate ears aren't used to this sort of thing in this Army, but he just ranted on about how great he was with some tart he picked up in Liege."

"Do you think he'll come back?"

"I doubt it. They'll throw the book at him. Whatever Army lawyer they pick to help him defend himself, I'll bet Walters won't be very cooperative. When you've had three wives who divorce you because you beat them up, you know he's a real trouble maker."

"Don, double that in spades."

Tuesday, February 6, 1945

Just after 0930, the messenger's telephone rang. I picked up the receiver.

"Messengers, White Battalion."

"This is Sergeant Butler. All messengers are to report immediately. No exceptions!"

"One isn't here, Sergeant Butler."

"Who's that?"

"Sergeant Rochester."

"Leave a note to tell him to report to me when he comes in."

At that moment, Sergeant Rochester walked in the door. I instructed him to come with the others.

After we were all assembled, Sergeant Butler addressed us.

"Men, at 1300, we are going on a field exercise. You are not to tell anyone in this town where we are going or where you have been. When we get there this afternoon, most of you will recognize the place. We're going to practice crossing a river. That's all I can tell you now. You'll get instructions this afternoon."

At 1300, all eight messengers boarded their designated truck in the village square. Within five minutes, the entire Second Battalion was on board and ready to roll. At 1310, the convoy left Schaesberg.

Several small towns in Holland were proceeded through. Then, the German border was passed. A strange transition took place. In the Netherlands, all the houses were intact. In Germany we saw blown-in walls, shell holes and other grim marks of war. We guessed that the Germans had retreated right to the border of their homeland before they decided to fight again. The first German town we entered was Palenberg, our former rest area. At the western edge of Palenberg was the Wurm River. All the trucks stopped. The battalion scrambled out.

A group of Army engineers split the Second Battalion into various groups. Lectures and demonstrations were given on how to cross a river in an assault boat. After the oral instructions, the five companies practiced rowing across the Wurm River. The Major, in charge of the Engineers, warned us, "Men, remember that the Roer is a much wider stream. It's going to take a lot more effort on your part to get across."

I thought the Wurm was actually a small stream that could be easily waded. I did not know what the Roer was like. After the rowing exercise was completed, the Major again addressed the entire Second Battalion.

"Your battalion, men, will be the fifth to cross the Roer. By that time, we hope to have a foot bridge for you. Up this river, we have one now. We're going to practice going across that bridge. There will only be two men on that bridge at one time. No more, no less. When you get on that bridge, get off as soon as you can. You might have artillery firing at you or the enemy might be strafing the bridge with his planes. Get on and get off. Let's everyone try it!"

Since about 800 men had to run across the foot bridge, a considerable amount of time was consumed. But the practice had gone well. By 1600, the exercises were completed. The return journey to Schaesberg was without incident.

Upon our return to our quarters, our three hostesses were there to greet us. The oldest one asked me, "Wie is Deutschland?" (How is Germany)

"Deutschland?"

"Ya, du in Deutschland, heute." (Yes, you in Germany today.)

"Wo ist Deutschland?" (Where is Germany?)

"Zehn Kilometers." (Ten kilometers)

"Ya, wir in Deutschland, aber nicht heute." (Yes, we in Germany, but not today.)

I was lying. The three ladies knew I was lying. Although no Dutch civilians were to be informed as to our whereabouts, every single person in Schaesberg knew the Second Battalion had been in Germany that day.

Wednesday, February 7, 1945

In the morning, the rumor mill was in full operation. We could make a reasonable calculation that when the Roer River dams were captured by the 78th Infantry Division, the whole 84th Division would soon be on the march. No one wanted to go back to the front. The entire Second Battalion appeared to be having excellent relationships with the Dutch people in this area. Very few of the townspeople had refused to take any American soldiers into their homes. All the eight messengers were surprised that our three elderly ladies had consented to do so. In my conversations with them in my poor German, they stated that on the night of May 10, 1940, two Wehrmacht privates had stayed with them. Very few soldiers had ever been stationed in Schaesberg prior to the arrival of our battalion. During the long occupation, the Germans simply sent patrols through the town.

The messengers had fallen into some routine with our hostesses. Each evening, the seven of us listened to the 2300 news over the BBC. This was followed by hot rolls and coffee that they had prepared for us. The ladies always served us like we were in a restaurant. After that we retired upstairs. By 0700 the next morning all were up for breakfast. The one exception was Sergeant James Rochester.

Thursday, February 8, 1945

Just after lunch, Company E was visited by a reporter from the 'Stars and Stripes.' The story was ice cream. Soon after our arrival in the Netherlands, Sergeant Harland Smith had found some discarded equipment for the making of ice cream. With some experimentation on his part and some cooperation on the part of the Company E kitchen, he began to supply ice cream for the members of this company. John Crable and I ate this day at Company E. As part of the story, pictures were taken. These appeared a few days later in the Army newspaper. Company E's menu was the envy of the other four kitchens in the Second Battalion.

Since John and I were attacked to Battalion Headquarters Company, we were technically ordered to eat with the latter outfit. But each day, we compared menus. We selected the better of the two offerings. As John stated, "Don, this job has got to have some benefits. Let's take advantage of any that we have."

"John, does that mean we should have two meals all the time?"

"Don, let's not get hoggish. Just select the best, that's all."

Since we were known to both kitchen crews, we never encountered any difficulty in constantly switching our dining place.

The kitchen of Company E was located in the town's flour mill. The mill, as I learned, was owned by our three hostesses and their nephew who lived two doors away. Mr. Herman von Oermann, the nephew, was married and had two daughters— Maria who was 13 and Anna, seven years of age. After our second day of residence, they came daily to see their aunts and the new American soldiers. They were extremely curious about our weapons. We usually left our rifle and other weapons in the bedrooms. Only once did I bring my rifle, unloaded, for them to look at and examine. To bring the hand grenades that we

393

carried for their observations was impossible since the accidental pulling of the pin could bring death and serious injury to them. Each afternoon, after school and after supper, they would appear. I discovered that Maria could play the piano. Each day during our stay, I urged her to play for us. She would say to me, "Ich nicht sehr gut." (I'm not very good.) My charm never worked since she simply would not play.

We knew that the two girls and their parents had no American soldiers living with them. On this particular day, Innes wondered aloud, "Guys, I wonder why this nephew never took any of us into their house?"

"Skinney," I replied, "their excuse was that the Frau was sick."

"Don, I've seen her. If she's sick, I'm sick."

"Skinney wake up. Don't you know why they didn't have any of us?"

"No, I haven't been able to figure it out. The two girls seem so nice."

"Skinney, what would happen if your buddy, Rochester, was in that house now?"

"He'd probably proposition that Frau. And he'd do it day and night."

"Innes, you finally got the right answer. Sure, I can't blame that nephew. If he had trouble with any of our soldiers, he might complain, but would his complaint be heard? He's just not taking any chances. Our three ladies here have no worry."

"Ed, I never thought of it that way."

Friday, February 9, 1945

At 0900, the messengers received a telephone call on their private line. Sergeant Butler asked, "Can someone come to the message center?"

Teets volunteered to get the required information. Upon his return, he announced, "Guys and gals, get ready to move. Butler wants us to review all the plans for a river crossing. If anyone doesn't understand what's to be done, see him in the next sixty minutes."

394

After lunch, we reviewed the plans that were to be carried out by the messengers. As usual, four were to be with the attacking force while four were to remain behind with the base headquarters. With nary a word, John and I knew it was my turn to be with the forward party.

At 1600, all eight messengers had a hot meal. We sat in our quarters and waited. We listened to the AEF of the BBC. Our three ladies did not bother us since they knew we were about to depart. At exactly 1900, the telephone rang.

"White messengers. Edwards speaking."

"Edwards, Corporal Kern. Tell the messengers the move has been canceled."

I repeated the message to loud cheers. Rochester immediately departed for his nightly entertainment. We had been previously informed that the Dutch inhabitants of Scheasberg were going to put on a show for their American guests. The entertainment was scheduled for 2000. A telephone call to the switchboard confirmed the fact that the show would go on as planned.

Six of the messengers departed for the village square and the show. One had to remain in the event of an emergency. At exactly 2000, the show began. It consisted of a small orchestra of Dutch Army personnel, a few tumbling acts, bicycle riding and jokes about Holland and the U.S. Army. We enjoyed it tremendously. This was conveyed to the show people. The best tribute I ever witnessed while overseas.

Saturday, February 10, 1945

A repeat performance of the previous day. At 1000, the messengers were informed of the imminent move. Again, after supper at 1600, we sat, listened to the radio and waited. At 2000, the telephone rang. This time, the move was postponed indefinitely. Again there were loud cheers from all of us.

We were not surprised. The AEF newscast at 1800 had stated that the Germans had, in the morning, blown the Roer River dams. They had been captured by the 78th Infantry Division that afternoon. Water was flowing downstream. This

395

meant that a river crossing was not feasible. Cohn expressed the sentiments of the runners in stating, "I hope that the flood lasts a long, long, long time."

I added, "But we all know it can't last forever."

Teets noted, "Maybe Jerry will surrender and it will all be over. They did in World War I. Why not in World War II?"

"George," I stated, "this time their leaders don't know when to surrender. I'll bet you Hitler won't surrender as long as he has one Division left."

Sunday, February 11, 1945

John and I slept until the late hour of 0900. We did not go to the Catholic Church until mass was held at 1015. There were fewer men present than the previous Sunday. I muttered aloud, "John, I'll bet the announcement that we're going to stay a little longer made some of the fellas a little more relaxed."

"Right Don. They think they can go to church when danger presents itself. In that way they can go to heaven if they are hit."

Our walk that morning to church had to be made solely on the streets. During the previous week, artillery ammunition began to be stored right on the sidewalks of Schaesberg. The town looked like a small arsenal. Every type of shell seemed to be on the walkways. On one of the message runs, Simon questioned me, "Ed, why are they using Schaesberg to store this ammo?"

"Simple Charlie. The Germans wouldn't think to bomb this town. It's not on any rail line. It's small. There isn't any industry in this town. It's the logical place. I'll bet you dollars to doughnuts that no ammunition like this is stored over in Heerlen."

"Seems like a good idea to me when you explained it that way."

THE LONG REST

Monday, February 12, 1945

We had been informed through the grapevine that the Second Battalion would spend this entire week in Schaesberg. The waters of the Roer River would take that long to subside to their normal banks.

I suggested to the group, "Fellow messengers, I think it's been a month since our last bath. I move we all take one today. Anybody second that idea?"

"Edwards, quit showing us you know some law, would you? But I agree with your idea. Where can we get one?" answered Teets.

"I've made inquiries George. There's a mine about a mile north of town where we can get a shower. Supposedly, it's just like we had when we rested in Palenberg last December."

By consensus, Innes, Cohn and I went on the first shift to the mine. When we arrived at the mine house, there was not a single person to converse with. The three of us went in, hung our clothes on the pulley chains and took our shower. We redressed in the same clothes and walked back to our quarters. This shower was only the second of the year for Innes. It was my third while Cohn was taking his fifth. On our return, Innes and I jousted Bernie on his clean body.

Upon our return, the other four messengers departed for their showers. Rochester, in the meantime, had departed for other pleasures of his own. The other seven runners agreed that he needed the shower most of all, but that was not his feelings about this matter.

One of the messages delivered this day was one which permitted the enlisted men to order Easter flowers. Although Easter was six weeks away, the message stated that delivery was guaranteed if the money was transmitted within the next few days. The price for either flowers or a plant was $5.00. All eight messengers selected something to be sent to their loved ones back in the States. I selected flowers. From a letter that was received later, my mother thanked me for the lovely plant that had been delivered to her on Good Friday. Where the mix-up occurred was unknown but something had been delivered. Just normal Army procedure.

As we chatted in the evening, Vernon Dawes, normally the quietest of the messengers, noted, "Did you ever notice how the BBC reports things?"

"Like what?" answered Innes.

"The air raids for example. If the English have a bombing raid, the raid was conducted by the RAF. But if it's done by our Air Force, the raid was conducted by the Allied Air Force."

"What do they say about the fighting on the ground?"

"About the same thing. But they will mention that a certain American Division conducted the operation, which is better."

Overall, all the messengers were happy that we could listen to a radio each and every day. We had electric lights and reasonably good food. Our three hostesses had a single request regarding the use of the radio. Each evening, they listened to a Dutch radio broadcast which came over the BBC. It appeared as if they had done this during the German occupation.

Tuesday, February 13, 1945

Just prior to breakfast, I proposed to George Teets, "George, let's walk over to Heerlen and see if we can buy something to go back home."

"Don, I've got nothing to buy. My wife and kid have all they need right now."

"George, your wife might like something from Holland, besides how do you know?"

"I don't, but what do I get if I go with you?"

"I think we've got fried eggs this morning. I think you know I eat eggs only one way, scrambled." I'll get those fried eggs for you. Then we'll go to Heerlen."

"That sounds like a good deal."

Although George and I could have walked along the established highways, we decided to take the shortest route. This meant walking across a large open field at the end of our dwelling block, then, continuing along the rail line which ran into Heerlen.

Heerlen, the capital of the province of Limburg was crowded with people including many American soldiers. Two permanent American hospitals were located in the city. We counted, at least, six different infantry patches being worn. Two or three movie houses were reserved for our Army personnel. George and I went to several shops looking for bracelets. The prices were definitely inflationary, thus, no purchases were made. Next an attempt was made to purchase Dutch cookies or bread. Without coupons, no purchases could be made. The only place in Heerlen where food could be purchased by us was the American Red Cross. The regular coffee and doughnuts were available in unlimited quantities. After we had consumed a half dozen each, we purchased a whole bagful to take back to Schaesberg for our hostesses. As we toured the city, George noted, "Don, see the outdoor johns."

"I sure do, George, just like in France."

"Wonder how they ever got them?"

"My guess is that years ago, it was more convenient to have them out in the open where they could flush them down with water. Guess it also prevented less stink in their own backyards which aren't very big."

"Sounds good to me. Wonder why they have only urinals. You don't see anything for the women."

"Women usually stay at home, George. Men in the past were the only ones who worked and needed to go during the day."

"Don, they sure seem strange to me. Outdoor johns."

At 1400, we decided to return to our quarters in Schaesberg. Our trip back was via the same railway tracks and the wide open field on which nothing was growing nor had any seed been sown.

Upon our return, we detailed our trip to the big city. We teased Rochester by saying to him, "Rochie, if you run out of women here, they're roaming the streets of Heerlen."

"I haven't run out yet, but I'll keep it in mind."

399

A PRIVATE'S DIARY

Wednesday, February 14, 1945

After breakfast, four of the messengers decided to visit Heerlen. All tried to encourage Bernie Cohn to go but he absolutely refused. Thus, Crable and Teets decided to travel together while Innes and Simon made up the other twosome. As long as we had two messengers on duty, there would be no trouble in taking care of the required messages inasmuch as the four lettered companies were located on or near the village square.

The visiting foursome did not return from Heerlen until late afternoon. All had enjoyed a movie at one of the designated Army theaters. Again more doughnuts were brought back for the enjoyment of all including our three hostesses and the two daily visiting young girls from next door.

After supper, I was given the assignment of taking the money collected by Company E for Easter gifts to Captain Nablo. He now had two functions. He was the S-1 of the Second Battalion staff as well as Company Commander of the Second Battalion Headquarters Company. The staff officers lived in a dwelling at the northeastern corner of the square. The stairway to their second floor quarters was exceedingly dark. Upon my admittance, I saw a beautiful living room with upholstered chairs and sofas. Several officers were playing cards. Captain Nablo led me to the dining room where he proceeded to count the money. Seated at a nearby table was Lieutenant Colonel Learman who was studying some German maps. On the nearby telephone was Major Lamb. When he put down the receiver, one of the card playing officers inquired, "Who was it?"

"Some God damn enlisted man."

"What did he want?"

"He didn't seem to know and I could care less."

After receiving a receipt from Captain Nablo, I departed.

Thursday, February 15, 1945

Each day the messengers had work to do. But this was not true of the majority of the GIs in the Second Battalion. To keep everyone in good physical condition, a training program was instituted. Complaints were rampant on the need for exercise.

Since it was required that four messengers be on duty, four would have to participate in this training. No one volunteered. John lost the toss of a coin on who would initially represent Company E for training purposes.

At 1000, the village square echoed to the sounds of "Hup, two, three, four." Close order drill was in progress. This was followed by calisthenics. Then came some short and long foot races.

Upon their return, the four messengers—Crable, Rochester, Cohn and Simon—moaned about their sore arms and legs.

The afternoons were still free. Since none of us had any ideas on the length of our stay, four of us decided to take another shower at the mine. This time, we were able to persuade Rochester that his night time activities would be better if he was clean.

About 1700, Sergeant Butler appeared in our quarters with an important message.

"Men, I've got some equipment to issue to you."

"What new equipment is available, Sarge?" inquired Innes.

"It's not new. It's new gas masks."

"Gas Masks!" came the choir of eight voices.

"You heard me. Gas masks. My orders are that each man is to have a gas mask on him when we go back to the line."

A number of us protested saying, "Sarge, you know what's going to happen to these masks?"

"I think I do."

I became the spokesman for the group.

"Sergeant Butler, everyone in this whole Army knows what happens. Those masks become excess baggage. Excess baggage is discarded. We've had those things issued twice before. Each time everyone loses them."

"Edwards, I agree with you, but those are my orders. Everybody must take one. At least, keep it a few days."

After the Second Battalion had passed over the Roer River, not a single officer or enlisted man could be found carrying a gas mask. The threat of a gas attack was just too remote. The Germans were never that stupid.

401

That evening, an order came that all messengers were restricted to quarters. The order affected the entire battalion. Since Sergeant Rochester had not spent a single night in the messenger's assigned quarters, Innes asked him, "Rochie, are you going to stay here tonight?"

"I can't. My girl is expecting me tonight."

"None of us is going to cover for you tonight. Remember that. We did it for Walters for a day but none of us will ever do it again."

"Skinney, this dame has the sweetest ass. How do I know what she'll do if I don't show up."

"Rochie, she'll take care of herself. How old is she?"

"Nineteen. And packed."

"And what number is she?"

"Number three. The first two were dames whose husbands are working in Germany. They just needed me for a night or two. This one is like a furnace who needs constant poking. And besides I got a cherry last night with her!"

"Who was this last one?"

"Sister of my hot tomato."

"How did you happen to get a virgin?"

"Well, my Gretta, that's her name, sleeps in a bedroom with her 15 year old sister. I've been going there the last three nights. We fuck all over the room, on the bed, on the floor, in the chair. Guess the young one wanted to find out what her sister was enjoying. She got me out of bed about midnight. I gave it to her. She was real tight and I hardly made her. She started to bleed a little after I finished. But I took care of her with a towel I found in the room. Then, I got in her again this morning. I think I can take on both of them again tonight. So I'm leaving."

"What are you giving these women?"

"Just cigarettes and chocolate. And I bring some food from our kitchen."

"Rochie, I've got to warn you that you've got to be here when I go to training tomorrow. If you're not, no messages will be taken to our company."

"Skinney, I'll be here. You know I come every day. I ain't goin let me get in the same trouble as Walters. That's for sure."

After Rochester departed, Innes turned to the other six messengers.

"I hope all of you remember when he was going to church and praying all the time last December. Now we're seeing the real Rochester."

Cohn questioned, "Isn't Rochester married and has some kids?"

"That don't stop him. He tries to lay any girl he can get. And his wife knows it. Back in Claiborne, the rumor was that she was getting her fun on the side after she found out what he was doing."

Friday, February 16, 1945

This was my day for training. My body was a little stiff from the lack of real physical exercise but in comparison to most of the men in the Battalion Headquarters Company, I did not suffer too much. Credit had to be given to the fact that the messengers still had work to do in the rest area. The usual training routine was followed. First came close order drill. Some calisthenics followed. Last came the foot races. I won every race in which I participated due to the fact that I was in a little better condition.

The afternoon was left free for everybody.

In the evening, Bernie Cohn and I attended the local cinema to see my favorite movie, "Music in Manhattan."

After the news, the usual snack was served by the three ladies.

Saturday, February 17, 1945

In the morning, the other four messengers had to engage in the Battalion's training program.

Early in the afternoon, I learned by inquiry at our battalion headquarters, that my friend, Harry Ackerman, was located only a short distance of three miles from our dwelling. About 1500, I walked to the Headquarters of Company A. The First

403

Sergeant there informed me that Harry was on a hike through the countryside. However, he consented to take a message that I would return after supper.

At 1900, I returned and chatted with Harry. I noted, "Harry, you're now a Staff Sergeant. You're moving up in this world. I'm still a private."

"Thanks, Don, but if I had my choice, I wouldn't have it. I'd rather be a good private in some Quartermaster outfit. It's safe in the rear."

"I know that Harry, but both you and I know ASTP was a big, big mistake. If I hadn't gone to that specialized college program, I'd be a good clerk in the Air Force. You'd be distributing supplies in some rear depot, and we'd both think how tough it was doing that."

"You're right. I read the story about you and West Point. What happened?"

"Just failed the eye exam, that's it."

"That's tough for you. You know, Don, what I'm hoping for now?"

"No, what, Harry?"

"I want to get wounded."

"Wounded, are you sure?"

"I don't mean lose an arm or leg. Something serious but not too serious. Like a bullet in the buttocks."

"But Harry you can't predict those things."

"I know, but I figure that either I get wounded or I'll get killed."

"How do you figure that out?"

"First, how many men do you think started out last November in this first platoon of this company?"

"Should be about forty."

"Know how many are left without being killed or wounded?"

"I'd say eight or ten."

"Exactly three. Only three of the original 38 are left. I know my number has got to come up some day. I just hope it's soon and not too serious."

404

"Don't you think you have a chance to get through this thing?"

"Not unless the Krauts surrender or give up. I don't look for that. What happened to your group since November?"

"One was killed, another seriously wounded. I got hit twice lightly but I don't think it was too bad."

"That's three out of eight then. And you're not in the rifle pits. I heard that four of the messengers in our First Battalion have gone."

Our conversation lasted nearly four hours. My job obviously was to attempt to improve Harry's morale. He wanted to get out of the war with a small injury. Later his desire would be granted. And only one of the original 38 would survive less than six months of combat.

Sunday, February 18, 1945

As usual, John Crable and I attended the local Catholic Church for mass at 1015.

Just after lunch, we were informed that our regimental chaplain would say mass for the Second Battalion at 1630. I asked John, "Should we go to mass a second time today?"

"It won't hurt us. A little extra prayer might save us from some harm."

At the designated time, we attended our second mass. The sermon was, of course, in English which we had not heard since last November. Attendance was fair. Our prayers were to keep all from harm in the future.

Monday, February 19, 1945

Today was my turn for the training program. In the morning the usual drills and exercises were held. There were, also, two lectures. One was a refresher on first aid. The emphasis was on the stoppage of blood flowing from a battle wound. Close attention was paid by almost everyone since this was practical knowledge that might be put to use in the near future. The second was the proper loading of assault boats in a river crossing. Here the emphasis was on teamwork and speed. Time and again the engineer in charge said, "If you work fast together, you'll be across the river without delay. Delay may prove fatal.

No one slept at this lecture.

At 1300, a ten mile hike was taken. Near its end, many of the GIs in the Second Battalion were complaining about sore legs and thighs. But no one said it wasn't necessary.

Upon our return to Schaesberg, the village square was loaded with tanks from the 771st Tank Battalion. The tankers proceeded to conduct a clinic on the methods of operating a tank, its firepower and limitations. The Lieutenant in charge stated repeatedly, "Never hesitate to ask for help from us when you need it."

In return, the tankers stressed the fact that, at times, the Infantry would be needed to protect them against anti-tank devices and weapons. Although the lectures were for the benefit of the men in the Second Battalion, the most interested and curious spectators were the children of Schaesberg. They were extremely hesitant to get near the 'iron monsters.' The loudest murmur came when one of the tank turrets was turned and pointed at a group of them. Yet, none of them came near those tanks!

Tuesday, February 20, 1945

At 0830, the entire Second Battalion was loaded on trucks in the village square. Our journey took us back into Germany. The border was crossed near Palenberg. The convoy did not stop but continued onto Geilenkirchen. This was the first city captured by the 84th Division in its initial attack last November. As expected, the city was in shambles. All of us noted that the U.S. Army railroad engineers were busily engaged in repairing the railway tracks that led to Linnich and the Roer River. Less than two miles outside Geilenkirchen, the trucks made a turn onto a small dirt road. The men detrucked. We saw the Wurm River.

The remainder of the morning was spent in the practice crossing of the Wurm both in boats and on foot bridges. In this practice run, each man was assigned to a specific group. The four designated messengers were assigned to go with the S-3 and the S-6 of the battalion's staff. They were Captain Frank Price and Lieutenant Colonel Birdsey Learman, our commander. Because of my past experience with radios, I was given the task of carrying a Model 284 radio similar to one carried by Corporal Bergett. This was to be an extra wireless in the event of some emergency. In our assault boat was Corporal John Kern. His task on the river crossing was to carry pigeons. They were to be released on the far bank of the Roer at periodic times. He did not bring them along for the dry run. But the birds were in his possession back in Holland. As we waited for our practice runs, the American artillery batteries could be heard firing at the enemy across the river. The sounds of these guns were familiar. Their firing brought no pleasant thoughts. The practices were without incident. The entire battalion was back in safe Holland for lunch. It was very safe as far as every GI was concerned.

Although all of us considered Schaesberg to be very safe, this was not true of the civilian population. Almost every evening, the Germans would launch some V-1 rockets which flew overhead in the direction of Antwerp or Liege. Whenever the rockets would appear, the messengers would be outside to observe them. The three Dutch ladies would flee to their cellar.

During our stay in Schaesberg, the German Luftwaffe paid a few visits to Heerlen. Whenever their planes would appear, the American anti-aircraft batteries in Heerlen would pour their fire into the sky. The flak did not seem to bother the enemy pilots. They would pass over Heerlen and drop a few bombs, then leave. We wondered if they knew the situation in our little town. A few well-placed bombs in Schaesberg would have set off a tremendous fireworks and raised considerable havoc among both the civilians and the visiting American battalion.

A PRIVATE'S DIARY

Wednesday, February 21, 1945

Just after breakfast, Sergeant Butler called for me.

"Edwards, you're to report to the Battalion Aid Station."

"Any reason Sarge?"

"I think you're going to the hospital today."

At the Aid Station, a jeep driver was assigned to take me to the 11th Evacuation Hospital in Heerlen. General Bolling had ordered that a new blood pressure test be given to me plus a more thorough eye examination.

Upon arrival, the Major, a physician, who was to conduct both tests took me into a consulting room.

"Private Edwards, you know the General wants you to pass both these tests."

"I realize that Sir. But if I truthfully can't see those letters on the Snellen eye chart, I'm not going to say that I can."

"Most men in your job would do anything to pass, you know that?"

"I do, Major, but I'll just have to take my chances."

Since I had been in a rest area for a long time, I passed the blood pressure portion with flying colors. But this new attempt at the eye test was the same. The Major conducted refractions test which largely involved putting drops in my eyes, examining them, and conducting another examination. I simply could not pass.

During my absence, four of the messengers went on the regular training program. George Teets had consented to take all the messages to Company E.

While listening to 'Duffel Bag' on the radio that afternoon, Maria, the 13 year old neighbor girl, came into the kitchen with her school books. I asked her, "Maria, bringen mir das school buches." (Bring me your school books)

"Ya, ich will." (Yes I will)

She went back to converse with her great aunts while I looked at her school books. The geography book proved to be fascinating to me. The map of the continent of Europe was completely distorted. It surpassed any railroad timetable I had ever seen in the United States. The Netherlands was a huge

408

country in comparison to its natural size. It appeared as large as any other nation or country in Europe except for Russia. Each of its provinces was shown in very great detail, like some military maps I had seen. I called for Maria to come back and asked her, "Ist das Nederland ein gross nation?" (Is the Netherlands a large nation)

"Ya, mein soldat. Meine Nederland ist eine grosse nation." (Yes, the Netherlands is a large nation)

"Ist das Nederland grosser das meine nation?" (Is the Netherlands larger than my country?)

"Das Nederland ist grosser das America." (The Netherlands is larger than America.)

"Danke, Maria."

The fifteen minutes with Maria and her books had taught me how nationalism was instilled in European youngsters. Although I could not exactly remember my geography, I doubted the entire Netherlands was as large as my home state of Michigan with its two peninsulas. Yet, Maria believed her Netherlands was larger than the entire United States.

Each evening at 1800, another lesson was given to the messengers on the nationalistic spirit of the Dutch. At that appointed hour, the three Dutch ladies would enter the dining room and turn the radio dial to the Dutch station. We believed it was located in Heerlen inasmuch as most of Holland was still controlled by the Germans. Initially, I could not understand the Dutch language spoken in the normal manner. After a week, I could comprehend that the announcer spoke of the Dutch Army. It was supposedly on the offensive in the northern part of their nation in the areas still held by the enemy. I related these facts to my fellow messengers who treated it as a big joke.

One evening the announcer mentioned that the Dutch Army had advanced three kilometers. After the five minute newscast ended, I inquired of our hostesses, "Die Nederland Armie gehen drei kilometers heute." (The Netherland Army went three kilometers today.)

"Ya, mein soldat, sie gehen drei kilometers heute." (Yes, they went three kilometers today.)

At 1900, the messengers listened to the AEF-BBC news. In a normal announcement of the days' news, the newscaster stated that the Canadian First Army had advanced three kilometers that day in heavy fighting. We knew that the Dutch had a battalion or a regiment attached to the Canadians. But any Army would be several thousand men. My memory said that the Dutch Army had largely surrendered in the German invasion of 1940. Yet, our three ladies were firmly convinced that their small nation had an entire army fighting.

Thursday, February 23, 1945

This would prove to be our last full day in the Netherlands.

At breakfast each morning, the enlisted men always had spectators. The eating part was not difficult. But the GIs had to contend with the children of Schaesburg. Since the Dutch children, as well as their parents, were on rations, the youngsters attempted to secure extra food from the good-natured American soldiers. The arrangements for the kitchen of the Battalion Headquarters Company were such that all the enlisted men had to eat out in the village square or take their food to their billets. Most chose to eat in the square. The tots carried small pails in which the GIs could put any left-overs. Most men did not mind giving them anything they had left. But shortly after our arrival, it was not unusual to be bothered six to eight times during the meal itself. When the battalion had initially arrived, this distraction was not minded. After a week, the enlisted personnel became annoyed. Word must have gotten to the Dutch officials because begging ceased two days later. The average GI could still give the children anything left after he finished eating in peace. However, the amount of garbage was practically nil. The youngster took anything and everything that was not eaten. The champion of the Dutch kids was a little blond girl, not more than five years old. She was always dressed in the shabbiest clothes but looked extremely cute in her small blond curls. The men seemed to take pity on her and gave her more left-overs than any other child.

410

Upon one of my morning message runs to Company E, Ed Norris mentioned, "Don, I've taken your place as the favorite."

"Favorite what Ed?"

"You remember that you used to draw KP more than any other private in Company E. Now I'm it."

"Ed, what are you saying? KP where?"

"Right here. In Schaesberg, Holland."

"Ed, you mean that the privates in the Company are on KP again?"

"That's what I mean. The day after we got here, the mess sergeant and the cooks complained that they had too much work to do. They must have convinced Captain Thompson of this. Sergeant Goodpasteur started assigning KP the very next day. Every guy is teed off about it. Some guy told the cooks in great language he would trade places with them any day of the week."

"Norris, I agree with them. For days, while we ate the K's, the cooks in the kitchen didn't have to prepare a single meal. Now they've got to work a little extra and they complain. They ought to be ashamed of themselves. Isn't the company still using their mess kits?"

"Sure, so they have no dishes to wash. The guys know that lazy kitchen crew of ours just hates to wash pots and pans. When they brought food to us near the front, they could do it, why not now?"

"Any other reasons, you've heard?"

"You know the usual, Don. The rumor is that the first day all the cooks including the mess sergeant started laying with some of the locals. If they had to wash pots and pans after supper and clean up, they might miss their Dutch asses."

"Norris, sounds logical, knowing their reputations."

Early in the afternoon, the attack plan for the crossing of the Roer was confirmed. The Second Battalion would be the fifth unit crossing the river. If the first wave was successful in its initial crossing, the engineers promised that the foot bridges would be in by late afternoon or early evening. The first bridge that would be built would be for the tanks to cross. All knew that tank support was needed as soon as possible.

411

Every messenger was present the entire day including Rochester who, as usual, had spent the night hours away from the group.

At 1700 each day, we always tuned to 370 meters on the radio dial to listen to the German radio station designed for American soldiers. At this particular hour, the Nazis had a program entitled, "Home Sweet Home." Anna, the female who broadcasted the program, usually read messages from American Prisoners of War inside Germany. There were always short talks urging the American GI to surrender and be placed in the safety of a POW camp until the war was over. We always listened with interest to these German newscasts. We were surprised that their news communiques were truthful. However, they were given in a different slant. If the Germans had retreated, they had a disengaging movement in which the enemy always suffered heavy losses. The Allied air raids were just harassing and a nuisance. Our air strikes were always driven off with heavy plane losses. Besides Anna, there was Hans. He directed his talks to the British and Canadian troops. His line of reasoning was a little different for them. In a few days, we could imagine Anna talking about the casualties suffered by the Americans in their crossings of the Roer. Yet, these German programs actually boosted our morale instead of lowering it. All of us remembered Malmedy in the Ardennes where American POW's had been gunned down by the German SS after they had surrendered.

At 2030, our three hostesses prepared us the largest snack we had ever had. They realized it would be the last one they would serve us.

At 2130, all eight messengers laid down to catch a few winks. The telephone would tell us when to assemble.

XX

ROER TO THE RHINE

1. The River Crossing

Friday, February 23, 1945

At 0100, the telephone at the side of my bed rang. I answered, "White Battalion messengers."

"Who is this?" asked Corporal Kern.

"Edwards."

"Edwards, tell everyone to drag themselves out to the square. We're ready to leave. Don't forget the phone."

"Will do, Corporal."

Crable, who had been awakened by the telephone ring, proceeded to shake the other six messengers.

The telephone was disconnected and the line put out into the street. Upon hearing our shuffling feet, the three Dutch ladies must have arisen. They met us downstairs. Each of us shook their hands and thanked them for their gracious hospitality. Their eyes appeared as if they had been crying since each held a hankie.

We proceeded to the Message Center and waited outside for further orders. Our teeth chattered since the night air was chilly. We had become accustomed to a good soft life.

After a half hour, we were ordered to the village square. The entire Second Battalion was assembled here. Around the square were numerous 2½ ton trucks.

At 0200, the order to board the trucks was given. Since the

413

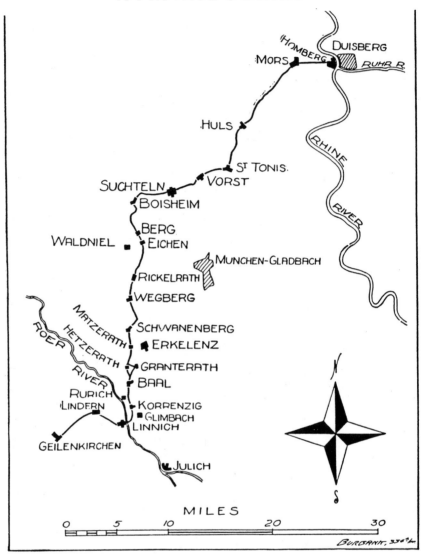

Map—Roer River to be Rhine River

entire battalion would remain together for some time, all the messengers were permitted to stay with the Battalion Headquarters Company. In ten minutes, the trip toward the Roer River had commenced. The route did not seem familiar to anyone but

414

we knew that the trucks were headed in the direction of Linnich where our crossing would take place.

Everybody in the truck was awakened at 0430. The pounding of artillery guns was plainly heard. The vehicles were motionless. No one knew what to expect.

In another half hour, the trucks moved slowly ahead for a short distance. Another long wait ensued. All around us were the heavier artillery batteries. Every ten minutes the guns would fire another salvo. This situation reminded me of a like one some four months ago upon our entrance into the combat zone. Yet none of us had quite the same fear as we possessed last November.

At 0530, the trucks again moved ahead a short distance. We were in a deserted German village. We waited. Shortly after 0600, the order to detruck was issued. The Message Center was placed in a nearby house, which like all the others, had no windows plus having numerous holes in the walls. I inquired, "What town are we in?"

"Beeck," answered Sergeant Butler. "I'm sure you've heard of it."

"I remember, Sarge."

Beeck had been one of the first objectives in the initial attack of the entire 335th Regiment. Although I had never been in the town, I knew it well. We proceeded to sit on the floor and await further developments.

At 0730, the entire Second Battalion was served with a hot breakfast. All ate heartily. The next hot meal was unknown. I mentioned to John,

"Wonder if the kitchen at Company E can use a KP?"

"Don, tis not funny. Your jokes leave much to be desired."

Although the messengers were quiet and sleeping on and off, the artillery surrounding Beech was providing plenty of fireworks that morning. We knew that this was another D-day in the march of the United States Army toward victory. The guns outside were the big 155 mm. It seemed like every half hour another truck would appear with more shells for the artillery guns. What we noticed most was the lack of any return fire from the enemy's artillery. Only two German shells were heard in over two hours.

At 0900, an order was given to assemble. I secured the radio that I was designated to carry over the river. We waited. A half hour later, the command came that the march was canceled. As we went back to the message center, someone wondered aloud, "Men, you know what that means?"

"How many guesses do I get?" asked Cohn.

"I'll give you just one," I stated.

"My guess is that the 334th is having a hard time. If they can't get across the Roer, the engineers can't set up the bridges. It means that we all are in trouble, real trouble."

All the messengers took off their packs and waited. We tried to catch some sleep which was difficult because of the noise from the barking artillery guns. For lunch, we were back to K rations. They seemed strange after the length of time since we last devoured them. We took our time eating our cheese.

At 1245, another readiness signal to assemble was given. Two minutes later, Lieutenant Colonel Learman said to the Battalion Command Party, "Follow me."

With the Command Party in the lead, the route of the Second Battalion went across some open fields. They were the same ones used to reach Leiffarth and Lindern in the past. The ground appeared to be much firmer. Another great change had occurred. All the pillboxes that had formed part of the Siegfried Line were just masses of concrete. The Army Engineers had dynamited each and every one of them. The concrete heaps looked wonderful.

About two miles west of Linnich, the Command Party reached the tail end of the First Battalion of the 335th. The march stopped. The Battalion Commander decided that his party should fall back behind the two lead rifle companies. We were next to the heavy machine gun section of Company H. Behind us was the third rifle or reserve company. About 25 to 35 yards off the road was a group of shallow trenches. On the left side of the highway were five tanks dug in the ground and acting as additional artillery. Every ten or fifteen minutes, their guns would fire another salvo. No one paid any marked attention for about thirty minutes. Then, the Germans must have apparently discovered where the tanks were. They started an artillery duel with them. After one enemy shell landed, every single GI in the entire battalion discovered the shallow trenches. The yardage to them was covered in a new record. After the German artillery fired a few more rounds, the tanks moved to a new location. Very few men of the battalion ventured about but remained in or near the trenches. We were back at war.

As the battalion lay in the trenches, we could observe some P-47's on the other side of the Roer raising havoc with the enemy. The usual game of flying around until some target was seen, was being played. Whenever an American plane would dive, machine guns would start chattering but this seemed to have little effect upon the tactics of the American pilots. Just after 1600, a large number of B-26s were observed coming back from their bombing missions in the German Reich. Most of the formations appeared complete although a few planes lagged behind. One of the trailing bombers began to lose altitude after passing over the American side of the line. It was last seen coming down far behind our front but it did not seem to crash.

While watching the bombers go over our battalion, a number of remarks were made which seemed typical of the infantryman's reaction to the Air Force.

"Well, if it ain't the fly-boys. The big brave aviators are out again winning the war. Only thing you forgot to tell the Bosch is that they were supposed to give up after you plastered them. Jerry was supposed to just let the god damn infantryman just walk in."

"Come on down here you son-of-a-bitches. We only lost half a company per attack, that's all. Just a few poor boys who didn't have a chance to leave this war after thirty missions. Ah, just 30 missions and you leave the war and live in glory from the home folks."

"If I ever get back home people will look at me as if I didn't do a thing to help win this war. But you fly-boys will get all the credit."

"Just life I guess. And speaking of life, don't forget to give her one for me back in gay Paree when you bums drink another round on your magnificent victory in the air, not on the ground."

"Yea, give her another one for me as for I'll be in a lovely fox hole thinking of you fly-boys. That's the life for me. Glory, drink, and women, all combined into one. Nothing could be sweeter."

After another long wait, the Second Battalion returned to the highway. The pace was extremely slow. The twin row column would move a hundred yards. Then another break would be taken. The vehicular traffic on this road was very heavy. Vehicles from both the 84th and 102d Infantry Divisions were trying to get across the single pontoon bridge that we heard was in operation. Some vehicles of the engineering units had priority signs on them. Anytime they went into the west bound lane to pass, another vehicle coming back from Linnich would be met. Since no shoulders existed on the road, a traffic jam would result since the jeeps, trucks and armored vehicles were lined up bumper to bumper and could not move in any direction. It was the biggest traffic tie-up that I ever witnessed in my Army career.

Darkness was descending rapidly. The Second Battalion had just entered Linnich proper. It had taken over three hours to go less than two miles.

The progress of the battalion was still exceedingly slow. The only consolation the foot soldier had was that the vehicles were not moving any faster. At times, the marching column moved faster than the long line of jeeps and trucks. Instead of following the road, we entered a house by the front door and came out at its rear. When entering the house, the two rowed column joined into one. This was one of the bottlenecks in the marching route. But it was a necessity since only a single row column could be used to cross the river. The regulation that five paces had to be kept between each man was still in force. It turned out to be a wise rule. Behind the house was a large field. This had to be crossed before another dwelling was reached. A few stops were made in the open field. By 2100, the next dwelling was reached.

The long single column was completely stopped. For the messengers it was fortunate that it did at this point. I dropped the radio which I was carrying. I took a short walk to the rear of the dwelling. There the Roer River could be seen. By usual American river standards, it seemed like a good size stream. Its width did not appear to exceed 125 yards. A foot bridge was seen but did not appear to be in use. I then returned to the main single column. Bernie Cohn, who was on his first attack mission, asked quietly, "Don, what did you see?"

"Just the river and a bridge. I think the foot bridge we're going to use is up ahead."

It was now 2130. It was quiet. Then, 'Skinney' Innes questioned, "Do any of you hear an airplane?"

None of us answered. The noise of some aircraft did not require an answer. The air seemed to be filled with planes. We hoped they would be ours. We knew they would be from the Luftwaffe. It was obvious that their objective would be to knock out or damage the American bridges over the river. From their sounds, the messengers guessed that they were four or five of the new jet aircraft that had been developed by the German Air Force.

Inasmuch as Linnich was in total darkness, the Luftwaffe pilots decided to have some light. Two or three of the planes were slightly north of the town and dropped some flares. They drifted slowly toward us. They brightened the whole Linnich area. The planes waited until the flares were right over the town and the Roer River.

Then the real action or phase one began. Since the Americans were not going to let the German pilots have an open field day, 50 and 30 caliber machine guns started to fire over the entire area. The sky was aglow with tracer bullets attempting to discover the planes. Nevertheless, the Luftwaffe pilots dove along the river and dropped some heavy bombs. A pontoon bridge seemed to go up. After the first attack the planes sailed back into the sky. Inasmuch as the flares gave off a tremendous amount of light, there was little doubt in our minds that the long infantry column had been sighted. When the first attack

419

started, everyone threw themselves next to mother earth. All the communications' personnel including the messengers were literally hugging the building.

The second phase began a few minutes later. The planes opened up their machine guns on the infantry column. One plane could not be seen by us but the sounds of his chattering guns could be heard. The bullets whizzed off to the left of the dwelling. We realized they were only a few feet away. My position against the building had given me protection but yards away some men were moaning, indicating that they had been hit. The medics, who were behind us, came up to give them aid. A large group of GIs, largely from Company H, who had been in the open field ahead, fled back to the safety of the battered house. Just to the rear of this dwelling was a U.S. Army trailer. At least a half dozen soldiers were under that trailer. One was Corporal John Kern with his pigeons. All through the air attacks, they just kept cooing. During all these attacks, the American machine guns kept firing away. One searchlight in back of Linnich tried to pick out the air raiders. The searchlight crew would try a small beam, then a large beam. All were without success.

The third and final phase of the air attack commenced. The planes swept over the center of Linnich and dropped some 'eggs'. When the bombs landed, the earth shook. The impact was greater than normal since one of the bombs apparently landed on an ammunition depot. Fireworks exploded everywhere. Confusion seemed rampant. Some fires were started in the town buildings, but little attention was paid to them. The German planes flew away.

We shook ourselves from the ground and looked around. The comments that came forth were very bitter.

"Where was our Air Force?"

"Those brass hats should have known Jerry would try to knock out these bridges after dark."

"You guys know our Air Force works only daylight hours. They're back in Paris celebrating tonight. We're supposed to take care of ourselves."

The battalion column reformed. The march had to continue. We went forward toward the footbridge. Less than twenty yards from the dwelling, the real results of the air attack could be witnessed. Medics were fixing the wounded. A few of the GIs lay motionless. They needed no service from the Medics. One of these proved to be a former messenger, Frank G. Mongus of Azusa, California, who had returned to Company H prior to our departure from Schaesberg. We guessed there were twenty or more casualties. But there could be no waiting. Getting across that river was the prime objective.

The battalion column kept inching forward. Finally, I reached the footbridge. At the bridge was an engineer who was keeping the proper intervals between the men as they crossed the Roer. Bergett with his radio was ahead of me. When he was half way across, I followed. My eyes did not see the water. My only interest was to get across that river before the Luftwaffe returned.

A hundred yards beyond the right bank, a hard surfaced road was met. The battalion turned to the left. Marching by single file continued for only a short distance. Then a break was taken. The battalion reformed into two normal rows, one on each side of the road. The foot journey continued. Some American jeeps now came up the highway. Just before the next town was reached, everything came to a halt. I approached the standing jeep.

"What outfit are you from, men?"

"Chemical Mortar Battalion, 84th," answered a Sergeant. "Where are you from?"

"Second Battalion, 335th. When did you get across the Roer?"

"Just a few minutes ago. We were outside Linnich when the airplanes came. Where were your men?"

"Just getting ready to cross the footbridge."

"Anybody get hit?"

"I'd say about a dozen."

"Too bad. Where were you last night?"

"In a little town in Holland, called Schaesberg. Where were you?"

421

"We've been in Brachelen over a week. Been firing our mortars daily at Jerry in a place called Rurich. It's the second village up this road. We're supposed to be over here to give some support to the 334th which crossed this morning."

Their vehicles began to inch forward while the marching column remained stationary. In a few minutes, we started to march. About 2345, the battalion entered the town of Korrenzig.

Saturday, February 24, 1945

There were only three messengers. Charlie Simon, the Company H runner, had become separated from the other three. The Command Party entered a house where the Battalion's Command Post was to be located. Corporal Kern and the three messengers were placed on the first floor. I was directed to find the location of Company E. This was done in less than a quarter of an hour. At 0200, we laid down for some sleep. At 0330, I was instructed to take a message to Captain Thompson. Upon my arrival, I spoke to the Captain,

"Captain, I am to inform you that there is a German counter-attack underway in front of Baal."

"I received it Edwards. We'll sleep unless somebody hears them coming."

At 0500, I made another message run. My report was that the German counter-attack had been unsuccessful.

At 0730, the entire Second Battalion was ready to move forward. An hour later, we had not moved a single step. Then a single German Jet aircraft appeared in the sky. Immediately all bodies were prone. The plane flew over our bodies and began to strafe the highway behind us. We found out that there was a convoy of tanks in that area. The three of us got off the ground and returned inside to the message center.

Just after 0900, some American tanks appeared in front of the command post. At this time, Bernie Cohn and I were looking at some training manuals giving instructions for German infantrymen. The enemy began to shell the tanks. There was nothing to do except lay down until the barrage ceased. None of the tanks were hit. But a few houses in the area were re-damaged. One had a fire within its walls. The flames soon engulfed the whole structure.

Just after 1200, Charlie Simon appeared. We had not seen him since the air raid in Linnich. He would not speak to any of us. We never understood his reason. He held a conference with Corporal Kern, then left.

Shortly after 1230, the three remaining messengers were herded into a jeep. We sped up the highway until a small village was seen. The jeep made a left turn toward the town. Just to the right of the road were foxholes full of riflemen from some other battalion. They were part of the front line.

The jeep came to a halt in Rurich. The entire Second Battalion was lodged in dwellings in the village awaiting the next order. I asked Gardiner, the Company E Jeep driver, "Larry, where is battalion?"

"The last house in town."

Just as Skinney, Bernie and I arrived at the dwelling, Captain Thompson and Lieutenant Colonel Learman came out.

The first platoon of Company E was ordered to cross a railway track which ran northward along the east side of the Roer. The Battalion Command was behind the lead elements. A woods was entered. An attempt was made to cross another rail line, running eastward from the Roer. The Germans opened up with machine gun fire. In the woods all were safe until the mortars or artillery fire would come. A flanking movement to the left was ordered. The lead elements ran into a swamp. The Battalion Command went back out of the woods. A conference was held with the three commanders of the rifle companies. The whole battalion was pulled back. Company F was ordered to follow the eastbound rail line. The track ran between two small hills. In the side of these hills, we could see some vacated German bunkers. Five minutes after starting up the rail line, the well-known 88s were heard. The shells bursted to the right and left of the track. Some men hit the ground. But the command was "Keep moving, keep moving."

The Lieutenant Colonel was near the head of the advancing column. The three messengers were dispersed among the leading elements. Skinney and Bernie were exactly three men in front of me. A shell burst! Two men in front of me fell. The GI in back of me fell. All including myself dropped. Still the command was, "Keep moving, keep moving."

Everyone arose and continued forward. The shells continued to fall for another five minutes. There were more casualties. After marching another twenty minutes, we entered the town of Baal. It had been captured the previous evening. The shelling had come from the left of Baal in territory still held by the enemy. The British on our left had not been as successful as the Americans. The Battalion Commander stopped in a dwelling for a few minutes. Around us was a battalion of 4.2 chemical mortars. They were firing at the Germans. A few minutes later, the German artillery hit the area. But there were no casualties.

The entire Second Battalion continued its march northward and eastward. Our objective, we learned, was the next town. Another railway embankment was crossed and a flat field entered. The messengers continued with the lead elements. Shouts began to come from the rear to slacken the pace. After going onto a highway, a break of twenty minutes was taken. We were no longer being shelled by the Germans.

Ahead we could see another village. Two or three houses were on fire. As we rested, I noticed a jeep. I said, "I know that driver, it's Novak from Company E."

I hailed him. "Novak, where are you going?"

"To find the Company."

"They're back in the column out in the field. How long have you been trying to get them?"

"About two hours, Edwards. I've been in the village ahead. It's being partially held by Red Battalion. I'm going back to get some things I left in the last town. But tell Sarge I'll be back with the other jeep."

"OK. I'll relay the message to Goodpasteur."

The signal was given to march up to the next town but not enter it. In an half hour of slow marching, the village of Dovern was noticed.

Lieutenant Colonel Learman went into the very first house to conduct a conference with the Commander of Company F.

He ordered me, "When Captain Thompson comes by, tell him to see me in the cellar."

"I'll do that Colonel."

Company moved on in a few minutes. When Company E appeared, I hailed Captain Thompson. "Captain you're to report to the Colonel in the cellar immediately."

After ten minutes, Captain Thompson reappeared. Company E moved on. Bernie Cohn repeated the same procedure to his Company Commander.

Colonel Learman reappeared. He ordered the messengers.

"Men, you three are to wait here until the company jeeps appear. Then take the jeeps to your respective companies."

I asked the Battalion Commander, "Colonel, we haven't been informed as to where our companies are located."

"Each company after they've taken their positions is to send someone to inform us. Make sure that it's reported to me also."

At 2230, the two jeeps assigned to Company E appeared. I instructed Novak and the other driver.

"Lou, you'll have to wait here until Norris and some others come to tell me their new location."

They came in and sat down on the floor with the messengers.

Sunday, February 25, 1945

Shortly after midnight, Ed Norris and two others from Company E appeared. I asked, "Ed, what took you so long?"

"Don, you'll see. The Germans have erected all sorts of wooden road blocks. We had to make all sorts of detours to get here."

A trip by foot was taken to Company E. It took ten minutes. However, the two vehicles, because of the blockades, took over a half hour to reach the new headquarters of Company E. Upon my arrival at the dwelling of the Company, I noted a number of German prisoners standing around. As I started to leave, Sergeant Smith said, "Edwards, take these PWs back to battalion."

425

"How many are there Sarge?"

"Twenty."

"Sarge, I can't handle twenty by myself."

"You've got a carbine, a pistol and two grenades. But I guess that's a little too much for one man. I'll get you help."

Another GI, a replacement that arrived in Holland, was detailed to assist me. We put the prisoners in two columns with their hands firmly clasped behind their heads. Each of us took a position slightly to the rear and side of the two columns. We proceeded without incident. Our guns were kept securely in our hands in the event of trouble. Battalion headquarters was easily located since the adjoining house was still raging on fire.

The PWs were delivered to a large room where they joined some others. A battalion guard or two watched them as they sat on the floor. I went to a nearby room and laid down on some old German blankets. My watch showed 0300.

At 0430, Captain Price shook me.

"Edwards, go down to your company. They have some more prisoners they want to get rid of."

"I'll try to find it, Captain, but I'm not sure of the exact route."

I went outside. I wandered around. Several times while wandering, stops had to be made. Since there were still large gaps separating the companies in Dovern, I did not want to become a PW myself.

After more than an hour, I reported back to the Battalion's S-3.

"Captain Price, I can't find the way to Company E."

"OK Edwards, for now it will wait. I think you might be a little tired. Go back and get some sleep."

"I'll try, Captain."

As I put my body on the blankets again, my watch showed 0600.

At 0800, Captain Price shook me.

"Edwards, I have a message which must be delivered to Company E. Can you find the way?"

"If it's daylight, I should have no trouble, Captain."

In this second try, no difficulty was experienced in reaching the headquarters of Company E. The message was delivered. On my return journey, I was delegated to escort a single prisoner back to the Battalion. He was a very short man, about five feet four, and appeared to be over 40 years of age. His gray Wehrmacht uniform was very ragged. He appeared to be very dejected.

We proceeded to plod along the road. My carbine, loaded but no bullet in the chamber, was loosely held in my hand. Suddenly I heard shouts of "Kamrad, Kamrad!"

I turned with my carbine ready to fire. Three Wehrmacht soldatens were running toward me with their hands high in the air. They wanted to surrender to me. They had come from the side of a hill where there appeared to be a cave or hideout. I tried to calm my nerves since I realized that the three of them could have easily captured or killed me at that moment. I made the four prisoners with their hands behind their necks walk in front of me. As we passed a group of houses, a terrific German mortar barrage started. I yelled, "In dem haus."

Without any hesitation, all were inside. One of the prisoners said to me, "Der kellar, der kellar."

"Neine, nein," I replied. "Bleiben sie hier." (Stay here.)

They sat down as ordered. Five minutes later, the shelling ceased. We went outside and resumed our march. I delivered the four PWs minutes later.

Upon my return to the other two messengers, I related my story of how I captured three Germans.

Before leaving Holland, all the messengers had agreed that a month would pass before the 84th Division would be on the Rhine River. Those calculations were based upon past performance when very few of the Wehrmacht surrendered. I mentioned this to Bernie Cohn who replied, "Don, if this keeps up, we'll be at the Rhine in less than two weeks. I wonder what's up with the German Army?"

"Bernie, I think it's quite simple. When the Germans lost that Battle of the Bulge, their soldiers knew it was the beginning of the end. I think their generals have known it all along but I don't think the common Wehrmacht soldier knew it until now."

"Sounds good to me, Don. Let's hope we can save some of those poor Jewish souls."

I had just sat down to have a fuller discussion with Bernie, when Corporal Kern called, "Edwards, they need a stretcher down at Company E for some wounded. Can you take the Medics down there?"

"I sure can. But tell them it's much easier to walk than ride. There's two wooden road blocks between here and Company E."

The Medics decided to walk. As we arrived near the headquarters of my company, the Germans rained down some mortars on us. We were inside a vacated building without any sweat. During the shelling, the three medical men and I sat in some comfortable living room chairs waiting for the firing to cease. While waiting, I looked out the window to see some German infantrymen advancing toward us. They quickly jumped into some foxholes but did not advance. I wondered why.

I questioned Ed Norris. "Ed, was I seeing things when the Germans jumped into some vacated fox holes?"

"No, Don, your vision is poor but not that bad."

"Are we retreating?"

"No, the platoons just pulled back into the houses. If Jerry comes any further, we'll ask for assistance. But I don't think they will."

"Why not, Ed?"

"Because in back of them is another battalion from the 333rd. They'll soon find out they're surrounded and give up. We figured to let them think they are having a successful attack. No one is worried here. We'll probably pull out this afternoon anyway."

His prediction turned out to be accurate. A return was easily made to battalion without any new PWs.

About 1230, shortly after we had devoured our K ration lunch, the enemy started another one of their frequent shellings, mainly from the area where the British were supposed to be. It upset none of us initially. When the first few shells landed, they seemed close to us. Innes noted, "Bernie, Don, let's go into the next room. I think it's a little safer in there."

"Skinney, seems ok in here to me but I have no objections to moving," was my reply. I started to move.

Innes had already gotten off the floor and had taken three steps. A loud crack was heard. A shell had hit the roof. Skinney turned and said, "Fellas, I'm hit."

Bernie and I rushed to his assistance. A small piece of shrapnel had gone through his jacket and hit his shoulder. Luckily the wound was not too serious. Nevertheless Innes quickly went to the aid station where the wound was dressed.

Just after 1300, Crable, Rochester, Teets and the new messenger from Company H, Vernon Dawes, arrived. For the next hour, the three of us described our experiences since leaving the other four on the other side of the Roer. We were unable to explain the loss of Charlie Simon.

At 1400, the messengers were notified that the attack would continue this afternoon. Crable went forward to represent Company E.

Since Martin Innes obviously did not like our present dwelling, we moved to a beer garden located a few doors away. There was no beer available. Some straw was secured to be placed on the floor. Other members of the Second Battalion's Company also spent their night on the bar room floor. At 2100, Bernie suggested we all try to get a good night's sleep.

Monday, February 26, 1945

At 0730, the three of us were ready to proceed. We believed our battalion was in the next town. The 335th Regimental Headquarters were in Dovern. Since Regiment usually had their kitchen available, we took advantage of their hospitality. We had a hot breakfast of cereal and toast. In return we were asked to devote some of our free time to guarding the German PWs who seemed to be surrendering in ever increasing numbers.

During the morning, Blue Battalion passed through Dovern. We knew they probably were to continue the attack against the enemy.

A PRIVATE'S DIARY

For lunch, we secured another hot meal. Pork chops were the main course. They were definitely superior to K-ration cheese.

At 1500, Gardiner came for us in the jeep. The entire communication platoon including the message center, was moved to a large farm house which was situated by itself. The other four messengers were already present. All of us remarked on the unusual facilities. In our trips, limited as they were, throughout France, Holland, Belgium and Germany, the farmers lived in small villages and farmed the surrounding area. This was like the American way. The entire Second Battalion Company and the Battalion Staff were quartered in the 'Chateau,' as it was titled.

Soon after my arrival, Crable and I were ordered to deliver a message to our Company. Company E was located in the town of Houverath which had been taken by them the previous day. The route taken went through an open field in which there were all types of tank tracks. John and I could only summarize what had occurred just a few days ago.

The headquarters of Company E in Houverath were located in the deepest cellar we had seen in Europe. While we waited for some reports to be made out, Captain Thompson and Lieutenant James W. Sandifer, the Executive Officer of Company E, proceeded to razz us.

"Lieutenant, did you ever see any easier job than these men have?"

"No, Captain, it's the softest job there must be in the whole United States Army."

"All they do is come to visit us and get reports, reports, and reports. They're wasting our time all the time."

"Battalion really ought to give them something useful to do, Captain."

This razzing continued for about five minutes until we could depart with the required reports. During the harrangue, we said nothing. It was better to suffer some verbal abuse than to get into a meaningless argument with the two officers.

When we departed, I mentioned to John, "You may remember back in November that Captain Thompson wanted

430

me to leave this job to be his jeep driver. I didn't want to remind him of that."

"I'm glad you didn't, Don."

Since the 'Chateau' was so large, it was necessary to post guards at various points. The messengers were designated to take one of these posts. By a draw, I was assigned the shift from 1900 to 2030 so no sleep was lost.

Upon my return from guard duty, the weekly PX ration had been distributed. The Army was very faithful about the issuance of these added items while we were at or near the front. There was no charge made for any of these supplies. Only once or twice had the rations been cut. This occurred at the beginning of the Belgian campaign when the cigarette ration was cut from the usual five to two packs per week. Candy and gum were among the regular items issued. Usually there was an odd assortment of juices, soap and pipe cleaners. These were difficult to divide into equal shares. After the distribution process, the usual swaps of various items were made. Since neither John or I smoked, the real 'pack-a-day' smokers always came to us for bargaining purposes.

2. The Breakout

Tuesday, February 27, 1945

By 0700, everyone in the "Chateau" was ready to move. Since no K rations had been issued, breakfast was omitted. The entire Headquarters Company moved on foot and in their vehicles to Houverath. Here all the companies of the Second Battalion were assembled. They were standing around in the open. This was strange. Usually all tried to stay under cover as much as possible. Rumors were rampant. Then, each company commander addressed his men. Captain Nablo spoke to his company, "Men, there as been a break out through the German lines. A task force is on its way back through the German rear.

431

Our regiment is to try to catch them. Our aim is to keep the enemy on the run. We think he's having a difficult time forming a defensive line. If he doesn't form one, he can be driven into the Rhine. Listen to these orders. Company F is to be the lead company. Company G will follow. H will be next. Headquarters will follow them. Company E will be last in the order of march. Remember to keep alert. This is an operation that we've never conducted before."

The Second Battalion was formed into two rows as instructed by Captain Nablo. At 0745, the march started. We learned that actually the entire 335th Regiment was in a long column with our White Battalion in the middle. At the beginning, the marching pace was slow. Sometimes a move of less than one minute would be made. At other times, we would march five straight minutes before another break would come. The first town that we entered, Golkrath, was occupied by Blue Battalion. They were also standing outside waiting for us to pass through. Just after 1100, the march began to pick up speed. There seemed to be no specific line of direction. The column would go along a road, across an empty field or through a patch of woods. The number of prisoners being taken was astonishing. The PWs were told to keep their hands behind their head and keep moving toward the rear.

For the first time in Germany, a large number of civilians were encountered. Previously, the towns we had been to, were devoid of civilians except for a few that had stayed behind. In the first small village after leaving Golkrath, all the civilians — men, women and children — came out with their hands high in the air. An order quickly came that we were to tell these civilians to remain in their homes until an order to come outside was issued. In one section of a woods, the column passed all types of German ammunition that was neatly stacked in tiers.

The line of march was carefully picked to avoid all mines. We knew that the Germans in the past had used them to excellent advantage. During one of our frequent halts, the messengers were seated on some stones looking over a large field. A jeep from Company H attempted to go from the open field onto the nearby road. Before most of the Second Battalion,

432

that jeep shot high into the air. Second Lieutenant Jean Chovet lost his life. The jeep driver was seriously wounded.

About 1500, the battalion emerged from a small pathway through some woods onto a wide concrete highway. Just as we came onto the highway, some German youths, numbering about a dozen, went screaming into the woods. They were probably terrified of American soldiers. Their wild hysterical shouting caused a few GIs to become trigger happy. The next thing I knew, bullets were whizzing over my head. From instinct many of us immediately dropped to the dirt at the right hand side of the highway. I looked up to see where the firing was coming from. It was possible that the Germans would try a flanking movement against this long column. What I saw was unbelieveable. Two American soldiers were standing upright, pointing their rifles into the woods. They were ready to fire again. Anger overwhelmed me. I cursed at them.

"You God damn fools, put down those rifles!!"

"But there are Germans in those woods!"

"You ass, yes Germans, but no soldiers. We're not out to kill the civilians. Where have you been, you stupid dummy?"

"Sorry, I just got in the 335th in Holland."

"That explains it. I'm telling you that before you fire that thing make sure who you're firing at. Do you realize that you almost killed six or ten of your own men! Do you want their blood on your hands the rest of your life?"

"No, I'm sorry."

"Sorry isn't the word for it. Keep the rifle under control. I'll bet you've fired that piece almost as many times as I have in four months. Learn that you don't fire unless you need to."

The swearing and epithets hurled at those two men by the others who had nearly lost their lives was more than horrendous.

Ahead on the concrete highway we could see a good size city. Just before entering this city, the 88s began dropping. But the shells were going over our heads. No one hit the dirt. That included the two trigger happy GIs. Some tank movements were heard. The shelling ceased after a few minutes. We entered Wegberg. I will never, never, forget Wegberg.

We learned that the 334th Regiment had been through the city but still left many German soldiers behind them. A great amount of confusion ensued. German soldiers were being picked up all over the area. For the first time, we noted that other branches of the Wehrmacht were being captured besides the usual Infantry men. After several moves, the message center was placed in the cellar of an old building. Two hours after our arrival, the real enemy shelling of the city commenced. But there was no attack on the part of the enemy to dislodge the battalion. That night we learned that we had covered almost ten miles. This meant the Germans no longer had any solid front.

Wednesday, February 28, 1945

Today was to be a break for the Second Battalion in the drive against the enemy.

After breakfast, a number of the not-so-tired GIs looked about for something to do. No civilians appeared on the streets during the entire day. Some men found a near-by horse barn. They took the animals from their stalls and rode them throughout the city. Several like myself found bicycles on the streets. We proceeded to go up and down the streets of Wegberg. The city was not heavily damaged except in isolated spots. Once in a while the Germans threw in a few shells but no one seemed to be worried about their effects for some reason.

As was expected, some of the battalion found some stores of liquor. The alcohol seemed to flow like water. During the day, John Crable and I had been to Company E jointly and separately. We knew that both the officers and enlisted men of our company were enjoying themselves. Thus, when Sergeant Butler told me to take a message to Captain Thompson, it appeared to be a routine message run. This was just after supper, about 1830.

The headquarters of Company E were located in the cellar of a house about two blocks away from the message center. Since the message had to be delivered personally to Captain Thompson, I went directly to his section of the basement. As I entered, I could easily ascertain that both Captain Thompson and First Sergeant Goodpasteur were drunk. Lieutenant Sandifer had been drinking but was not in a stupor. As I entered, Captain Thompson yelled, "Why Edwards, you old son-of-a-bitch, what are you doing here?"

"Captain, I've brought a message for you. You're to look it over, sign, and I'll return it to battalion."

"Come over here and let me see it."

I went to his table and handed him the sealed message.

The Captain tried to open the envelope. As he was fumbling around, Sergeant Goodpasteur drunkenly uttered, "What good is Edwards, anyway?"

In his hand, Captain Thompson had placed a loaded revolver. He kept waving it around. He spoke, "Why, he's no good. Always bringing orders, orders and orders from damned battalion. He shouldn't even be living."

With that statement, he swung around with the 45 still in his hand and brought the gun to within six inches of my midsection. I could see that the safety catch was off. The Captain had his finger on the trigger.

I was petrified. My stomach wanted to bring up the food it had recently taken. Although I had a carbine on my shoulder, I realized one false move and I would be a deceased casualty. Although I had never seen a man or woman suffer the results of a 45 slug, I knew from experience the results of a 30 caliber from many distances. Around my midsection were my usual extra bullets. I had left my two grenades back at our quarters.

Captain Thompson shouted, "Tell me Edwards, just what good are you?"

"I try to do what I'm told to do, Sir."

"Did you hear that Sergeant, he tries to do what he's told to do."

Up to this point, Lieutenant Sandifer had said nothing. He must have realized the gravity of the situation. He wanted no murder. He spoke, "I think Edwards does his job, Captain. Why don't you let him go back to battalion?"

I realized the First Lieutenant was trying to defuse the situation. However, Captain Thompson screamed, "Edwards, you're a God-damn good-for-nothing, I don't know whether you're good enough to live!"

Lieutenant Sandifer replied, "Let him go back, Captain, you can see him some other time."

Apparently this gave a clue to Sergeant Goodpasteur, who, although drunk saw what might happen. One shot would have blown me to bits. He mumbled, "Hey, Tommy, let's go over and fuck that woman. See Edwards later."

This apparently appealed to Captain Thompson. He put down the 45 and shouted, "You're right Goody, we've got to fuck her tonight. You're absolutely right. Get out of here you lout."

I turned and slowly walked out of the room. I did not have the message with me.

Outside the sweat poured out of my body. I believed it could have filled a rain barrel. I slowly walked in a daze back to the message center. It took me ten minutes to cover the two city blocks that I could normally do in less than two. Since I had been instructed to deliver the signed message to Sergeant Butler, I report to him.

"Sergeant, I'm sorry but I can't bring back that message from Captain Thompson."

"Any reason, Edwards."

"Yes, Sergeant. I know you won't believe this but Captain Thompson almost shot me."

"Captain Thompson! What kind of story is this?"

I then proceeded to relate what had occurred. He listened in stunned silence. Captain Thompson had, for a long time, been his Company Commander. I finished my tale. I added, "I am not going back to get that message, Sarge, even if General Eisenhower personally ordered me to do it. I don't think any court-martial could convict me."

"Considering the circumstances, Edwards, I don't think it's necessary for you to go anywhere. You are excused from any further duty tonight. I am going to check with someone about this."

I then returned to the bedroom where John and I had secured a good-sized bed. I laid down on the bed and started to cry. Crable, who was in the next room, heard my sobbing and came to see me.

"Don, what's your trouble? Get a Dear John letter today?"

"No, you know I have no steady girl."

"What are you crying for?"

"I nearly got killed."

"Don, I told you you can't tell jokes too well. If they had a course called Comedy 102 at your University of Michigan, you'd flunk. You didn't run into a sniper?"

"No, Captain Thompson almost killed me."

"Captain Thompson! Why would he want to kill you? Explain that to me."

Although constantly sobbing, I managed to get the whole story out to John. He just sat and listened. I don't know whether or not he believed me. As I finished, Major Lamb appeared at the bedroom door.

"Private Crable, would you accompany me to Company E?"

"Yes, Major."

The appearance of Major Lamb was a surprise to both Crable and me. Unless we were in an attack or dangerous situation, the messengers normally did not deal with the officers of the battalion staff.

I drifted off to sleep. I felt exhausted. No day in combat had ever shaken my nerves in this manner.

About a half hour later, John shook me.

"Don, wake up. I think you'll be interested in what I have to say."

"OK John, I'm interested. Proceed."

"I accompanied the Major to the headquarters of Company E. Just as we got there, Captain Thompson and Sergeant Goodpasteur arrived. The Major then went up to Captain Thompson and drew him aside. He talked to him about his recent conduct. He reminded him that he was an officer of the United States Army. He stated that his conduct simply was not proper. Then the Major ordered the Captain to go back inside and get some sleep. Your name was never mentioned but everybody seemed to know what conduct they were talking about.

The Major turned to me and said, 'Crable, let's go back to battalion.' He never said another word to me."

"What do you think, John?"

"Don, I don't think we'll ever be harassed or razzed again." John turned out to be correct.

This incident would cost Captain Thompson his command after V-E day.

Thursday, March 1, 1945

At 0500, Sergeant Butler shook both Crable and me. He said, "Someone get Captain Thompson. There's a conference to be held."

I turned to John and uttered, "I think you should go, considering last night's episode."

"I don't think so, Don. It's like riding a horse. You've got to get back on as soon as possible or the terror gets worse. Just make sure your piece is in your hand this time, not on your shoulder. Put a clip in this time."

"Guess you're right, John, but I sure hate to do it."

After putting on my boots, I was at Company E in about three minutes. I asked Sergeant Goodpasteur to have Captain Thompson come with me to the Battalion CP for a meeting. In one minute Captain Thompson appeared and said, "Let's go, Edwards."

No other words were spoken between the two of us on the short trip back to battalion. I don't think either one of us wished to discuss the incident.

Shortly after 0600, the Second Battalion was on the streets of Wegberg. On the roads in and about the city were the tanks and vehicles of the 8th Armored Division. They were lined up bumper to bumper. Since the morning air was quite chilly, men from both the infantry and the armored were running around and waving their arms to keep warm.

At 0700, the battalion started marching. We went past the 8th Armored vehicles. The men from the 8th just peered as if to wonder where we were going. Off to the left of Wegberg, artillery firing could be heard but no shells fell in the city itself.

At the edge of the city was a row of 2½ ton trucks. These were to be our troop carriers for the day. After boarding, the usual wait ensued. Then, the trucks started their forward motion. The direction of the truck's route seemed to be north and east, largely to the north. As we traveled we noticed a great deal of discarded military equipment, largely German.

At 0830, the trucks halted. The sounds of battle seemed to be to the left of the highway. According to rumor, the towns in the distance had already been captured by American forces. We waited fifteen minutes. The sounds stopped. The trip became slower. After the initial hour of travel, we rode for no more than ten minutes without a break.

At 1100, after traveling about 5 to 8 miles, the convoy came to a halt. We were in the open countryside in front of a group of houses. The order came, "Fall out and take cover."

The houses were deserted. In the back of these farm houses were barns and sheds containing both farm equipment and live stock. Someone shouted, "Hey guys, we've got our lunch right here."

"What's for lunch?"

"Chicken and eggs."

Within the next half hour, every chicken and all the eggs had disappeared into the stomachs of the Second Battalion. Wood was found lying around which furnished the necessary heat. Some of the jeep drivers had pans in which to do the cooking.

The messengers were placed on the second floor of one of the farm houses. While we waited, the heavens opened up. A rain shower soaked everything on the outside. Downstairs on the first floor was the constant chatting on the radios to the regimental headquarters and the other two battalions. A meeting of all company commanders was held at 1330.

At 1430, the entire Second Battalion climbed back on the trucks which had not moved during the farmyard break. The journey resumed. The trucks were speeding in an almost northerly direction. A main highway was met. The convoy turned right. We passed some stationary vehicles.

439

"Guys, look at those trucks, I can't believe it," yelled someone in the center of the open truck.

"What are they pulling?" asked another.

"It's our Division artillery. First time I ever saw them ahead of the Infantry. This is sure a screwy war."

The convoy slowly entered the city of Dulken. Up ahead, we could hear the sounds of bursting shells. Soon the trucks stopped. No oral orders were given. Fifteen seconds, none needed to be given. A German 88 hit one of the nearby buildings. In record time, the trucks were vacated. A slow foot advance was started. After several blocks of advancing, the order was given to halt. We had run into the rear of a battalion from the 333rd Regiment trying to clear Dulken of the enemy. The Second Battalion set itself up in the surrounding shops and houses. Everyone knew it was only temporary.

Shortly after 2000, silence fell over Dulken. It meant the Germans had left the city. Across from the house where we were located was the first evidence of German propaganda we had seen. On the large side of a stone wall was the German slogan, "Silent. The enemy may be listening."

Since the messengers had heard all types of rumors of what was happening, I asked Sergeant Butler, "Sarge, can we lay down and try to get some sleep?"

"Edwards, I'm afraid not. Everyone is to stay ready to go in two minutes."

At 2200, we were granted permission to take off our boots. We laid down on the wood floor to sleep.

At 2300, Corporal Kern appeared.

"Men, there's going to be a night attack. Four messengers must be ready to go with the Colonel."

"When do we have to go, Corporal?" asked John.

"Put your things on and report to the Colonel immediately."

Crable and I had previously agreed that he would go on the attack. After he and the other three left, the remaining messengers went back to sleep.

440

Friday, March 2, 1945

At 0130, Corporal Kern again appeared and announced, "Men, the next town has been taken. Be ready to go in two minutes."

A short time later, we were traveling in a jeep through the countryside. A few German roadblocks were met. But the Engineers had already taken down enough of the wood to permit a jeep to pass.

At 0215, we arrived at the new Battalion's CP in Süchteln. We went upstairs to see if we could sleep in one or more of the bedrooms. I opened the first door.

"Ach, Amerikaner soldatens!" a woman screamed.

"Ya, meine Frau aber bleiben sie hier," I replied (Yes, Mrs. but you stay here.)

After a hurried consultation, the messengers decided to sleep on the living room floor. We let the German civilians alone who must have been surprised to be awakened in their own house.

At 0400, Sergeant Butler shook me.

"Edwards, go to the CP next door. Your company has brought in some prisoners and there's no one here to guard them."

"I'll do it, Sarge, but get the battalion guard there as soon as he arrives."

Next door, I found Ed Norris and nine German prisoners. Ed noted, "The company rounded up these nine PWs. I've got to be back so you can take care of them, Don."

"See you later, Norris."

For the next hour, the nine prisoners and I stood outside in the chilly night air. Lieutenant Lusby, who was walking into the dwelling, noticed me.

"Edwards, are you cold out here?"

"Yes, Sir, I am."

"Well, after your interesting evening last night, let's go upstairs to some room where you can watch them."

The Lieutenant led the nine prisoners and myself to a vacant room on the second floor. The room contained one

441

chair, one table, and one candle. I lit the candle and placed it on the table. I sat in the chair next to the open door. I had my carbine in my hand, fully loaded. My finger was next to the trigger. The nine Germans went to the other side of the room and laid down on the floor. They all went to sleep. I was jealous of them.

Just before 0600, a battalion guard came and escorted the prisoners away.

I proceeded to the message center and went back to sleep. John and the other three messengers had returned and were sleeping.

At 0700, all messengers were up. I asked John how the night attack had done.

"Don, it's the easiest one I ever been on. We just kept marching. There might have been a few Germans in this town but I think they left before we got there. A few surrendered here and there. After one company got through this town, they went across some canal or river. I think the engineers are up there building a new bridge already."

From our maps, everyone in the battalion knew that the main objective was the large city of Krefeld. I questioned John, "What are they going to do today?"

"My understanding is that the Germans have few defenses in this area. Red Battalion, you know, was already going through about 0500 when we came back. I think the idea is to get into Krefeld as soon as possible. That's only a few miles from the Rhine."

By 0730, everybody was ready to march again. But we waited. During the interval, a liquor store, completely furnished, was discovered. A giant raid took place. Several men got drunk but it involved only one of the messengers, namely, Sergeant Rochester. He could hardly walk. His fellow messenger, the wounded Martin Innes, was his crutch the entire day.

The battalion formed into two columns, one on each side of the road. Krefeld was only 15 kilometers from Süchteln. As usual, the march was slow. It was rare to sustain ten minutes of walking. Ahead we could hear gunfire which was probably holding up the advance of the First Battalion.

The second factor holding up the advance was the weather. It was the strangest encountered in Europe. Just before 1000, dark clouds appeared. Next came a blinding snowstorm. All the dogfaces tried to hide behind a tree or standing vehicle or lay in the ditch beside the road. The wind was whipping the heavy wet snow into our faces. In a half hour, the snowstorm ceased.

A bright sunshine sprang out. Then some more clouds appeared. A heavy rain fell. Combined with a strong wind, all in the battalion were soaked to the skin. At 1130, the sunshine was back. Alternating periods of rain and sunshine followed. By mid-afternoon, the sun finally triumphed.

As we battled the elements, we could hear machine gun fire off to our left flank. Zooming artillery shells were falling in our rear. We knew the war was a wide open affair since we seemed to be in the enemy's rear a good part of the time.

About 1245, most of the messengers were lying in the usual ditch for we were always apprehensive of a shelling, when a jeep with two silver stars passed.

"Holy Shit!" a voice shouted. "It's General Bolling."

At the time I was dozing in the ditch with my face under my helmet. I asked John, "Crable, is Bolling really here?"

"Sure is, Don, and you ought to see what the jeep behind him is carrying!"

"What's in the second jeep, the Corp Commander?"

"No, it's a whole load of MP's. Looks like they're guarding the General."

Along with many other eyes, we followed the slow ride of the two jeeps. They had gone a little more than a quarter of a mile when three 88s hit the highway ahead of them. The General's forward progress ceased. The jeeps turned around. They headed toward the rear. As they passed the spot where I lay, some GI remarked, "Kind of tough up here, isn't it old man."

Yet, the majority of us discussed the fact that he had no business up in this vicinity. Major General Bolling was not a Patton or Rommel type. We knew that someone had to do the staff work in the Division. We believed the General should have remained in the rear. We thought the MP's could have been put to a much better use.

About 1400, the battalion finally entered the town of Vorst. Vorst was five kilometers from Süchteln. Our progress was about one kilometer per hour. Near the eastern edge of Vorst, the Second Battalion made a wide detour across a field to avoid being on the highway. We guessed that the highway at this point was mined. In about a half a mile we proceeded back onto the highway. As we did this, ten tanks from the 771st Tank Battalion came lumbering through the open fields. They proceeded past us right into St. Tonis where Red Battalion was trying to oust the enemy.

Just a little after 1800, we entered the city of St. Tonis. The five member companies were spread throughout the town until the next move could be made. All eight messengers were placed on the second floor of a large brick house. Crable and I held a conference.

"Which one of us should try to find the company?" I asked.

"Don, I'll take it this time. I think I know just about where they went. See you shortly."

John departed.

He had not departed three minutes when a heavy German shell exploded and shook the whole house. Everyone knew it was larger than a reliable 88. Every man, within three seconds, was in the cellar. The enemy proceeded to give us a pounding by both mortars and heavy artillery. The house seemed to shake with the landing of the heavier German shells.

While waiting, I took note of the basement of this house. It was outfitted with three beds. Yet only the husband and wife were still there. They huddled close together as the shelling continued for the next quarter of an hour. The American soldiers just sat and waited. When the shelling ceased, the messengers returned to their second floor room.

A half hour after his departure, Crable returned.

"Don, I've been walking around. I can't find the company."

"Forget it, John, let's have our supper. Then, I'll try to find it."

444

After finishing our K rations, I left. While walking around, I repeatedly inquired, "Does anyone know where Company E is located?"

No one had heard where they were located. Yet two men from F and G companies knew they were in St. Tonis. In an hour, I returned.

"John, I can't find the company. I've looked for an hour."

"Don, let's both go out. Maybe two heads are better than one."

At 2130, we left the message center. Upon inquiry, we learned that both Red and Blue Battalions were in St. Tonis. This meant there were 15 companies in the city. As we tramped around, we turned the corner of one of the darkened streets. We bumped squarely into a member of the Wehrmacht. He threw up his hands and yelled, "Kamrad, kamrad."

"Sehr gut, sehr gut," was my answer (Very good, very good)

We had the German PW place his hands behind his head and march in front of us. About ten minutes later, we found an MP and turned the prisoner over to him. But the search for Company E was unsuccessful.

Upon our return to Battalion CP, we reported directly to Captain Price.

"Captain," I stated. "We can't find our company. We're very sorry but we tried for over two hours to find the headquarters of Company E."

"I believe both of you. Don't worry. We've just contacted Captain Thompson by radio. He'll be over here for a conference shortly. Edwards, you go back with him to his CP. You won't have any trouble with him. I'm sure of that."

I sat down on the floor in the hallway of the Battalion CP and waited for Captain Thompson to finish the conference.

Saturday, March 3, 1945

About 0015, Captain Thompson emerged from the conference. I accompanied him back to Company E. To get to the company involved many turns in the streets of St. Tonis. Upon

445

our arrival, I had been instructed to receive a report from the First Sergeant. When it was completed, I returned to the battalion. I was ready for a good night's sleep at 0130.

At 0300, Sergeant Butler shook me and said, "Edwards, you've got to deliver a message to Company E. They must be ready to move in one hour."

"Anything else, Sarge?"

"Yes, you are to remain with your company until the next objective is reached. Then report back to battalion. You should be able to find it without too much trouble as I understand."

I complied with the order.

At 0400, the entire Second Battalion marched out of St. Tonis. The march was a fast one in comparison to yesterday's slow pace. My place in the battalion's column was the last man at the end of Company E. In one hour, we entered the city of Krefeld by passing under a railway viaduct. All the five companies were quartered on the main street of this large city. After Company E was settled in its new quarters, I reported back to the Message Center which was located only one city block away. I tried to get back to sleep at 0630.

At 0800, John shook me and stated, "Don, we've been placed on the alert. We must be ready to go at any time."

"OK, John, but just let me sleep a few more minutes."

"Roger, Don, but be ready."

Everyone realized that the real objective of this drive was the Rhine River. From Krefeld, it was only three or four kilometers to the giant river. Until that was reached, there could be no rest for any member of the 84th.

At 1000, I was up and ready. My breakfast K ration was eaten. I looked outside to note that the battalion was situated in an area where almost all the houses and buildings were intact. We were on the second floor of a vacant house.

At 1100, all were ordered to be on the streets for the trucks. But at 1130, no trucks had arrived. The order was canceled.

At 1400, another order to entruck was issued. At 1500, the 2½ ton vehicles arrived. We stood around and waited. At 1600, we boarded. The trucks left immediately. Our direction was toward the center of the city and eastward. Here we witnessed the first large scale effects of the Allied air attacks. The downtown area of this metropolis was completely in shambles. Destruction of a greater magnitude had been seen in the small villages in the Siegfried Line. But that was expected with the bitter fighting that had taken place there. This destruction was awe inspiring. If a block had as many as three buildings standing, it had been fortunate. Everything else was just heaps of rubble. Every soldier of the battalion was standing and gazing at the ruins.

"Is this what Anna called a nuisance raid?" asked Innes.

"That's what she called them Skinney," replied Teets.

"I wonder what a non-nuisance raid is like then?"

"I think what we're seeing is just slightly more than a nuisance."

The trucks moved through the center of Krefeld. During our short stay, we had not seen a single German civilian. The streets were deserted.

At what seemed the main junction of the city, the trucks turned left.

"Hey, Don," asked the usual silent Vernon Dawes. "What direction is the Rhine River?"

"Vern, according to the German map I have, it's due east. A city called Uerdingen is there."

"Let's everybody look for Uerdingen everyone that's what Edwards says we should be going to."

As we left the city of Krefeld, we saw one of the more gruesome effects of war. A German horse-drawn artillery carriage had, it appeared, been hit from the air. The bodies of both the two horses and the men in the carriage had been splattered around the area. There was no single piece of flesh that could be identified in any way, shape or form.

At 1800, the convoy stopped. We sat for ten minutes before the order to detruck was issued. A march on foot started. The usual progress of starting and stopping was made. The pattern seemed to be to walk slowly for five minutes then rest and wait. While we were resting in the usual ditch, Rochester noted something in the adjacent field.

447

"Hey, Edwards, what's that going on in that field?"

"Rochie, I believe Cannon Company is setting itself up for work."

"Have you any idea why they're here or where we are?"

"None, Rochie. None."

Darkness had descended. When daylight ceased, Cannon Company with their small 105 howitzers began to fire at the enemy. Soon after their batteries started, the German artillery returned the fire. But the incoming 88s were far over our heads. The enemy did not have the right range yet.

The night was very still. The atmosphere became cold. Because of the darkness the situation was confusing. The question on everyone's tongue was, "How far is the Rhine?"

Dawes questioned me again with "Edwards, what did that last sign say?"

"Vern, it said that Kapellen was two kilometers and that Mors was five kilometers."

"Where does your map say Mors is?"

"I can't find Mors on my map."

We could do nothing but wait. As we lay in the ditch, some American light tanks were going back in the direction of Krefeld. Had the enemy launched a counter offensive? Ten minutes later, a tank destroyer battalion went forward on the same highway. We wondered if heavy German tanks were ahead?

Shortly after 2030, the air became electrified with the sounds of screaming air raid sirens. We needed no second guess to know who was warning whom. Our maps had shown us that our battalion was approaching the industrial center of Germany, the Ruhr. We realized we were near the giant industrial city of Duisberg.

Fifteen minutes later, the atmosphere was filled with the humming of British bombers. Although we could not do anything about when and where their night air attack would be directed, we wondered if Duisberg would be the target that night.

Five minutes later, the air bombardment was directed at Duisberg. The German anti-aircraft batteries began to shoot skyward. It was the largest display of fire power I had ever witnessed. We could listen to the bombs as they hurled through the sky. Although we were some miles away, the ground shook under us. Periodically a British bomber would be hit and burst into flames. The war in our area seemed to stop to watch the RAF at work. Within the hour, silence again prevailed. We had not moved an inch in over two hours.

Sunday, March 4, 1945

The new day started with the messengers still in the ditches. Then, the enemy began to shell our area with mortars. Rochester exclaimed, "Fellas, let's find a house where it might be safer!"

"I'm with you, Rochie," said someone.

We quickly found a vacant house where we gathered. After ten minutes, I mentioned to Teets, "George I think we should find out where the battalion CP is. I think something important is going on."

"We'll wait here. Anybody want to go with Don?"

"Yes, I'll go with him," answered Rochester.

Locating the CP of our battalion proved to be a difficult task. We bumped into numerous American soldiers. Almost all were from the 334th Regiment. No one seemed to know where any other unit was besides his own. Rochester mentioned, "Wonder what the 334th is doing here? I thought only the 335th was to be in this area."

"Rochie, I don't know but they're here and no one knows where our battalion is now. Maybe we're lost."

We wandered down the road a good distance in the direction of Mors. But as we failed to meet any more Americans, I turned to Rochester, "Rochie, I think we've gone far enough. Let's go back the other direction."

"I'm with you, Don."

It proved to be one of the most important moves I ever made.

After walking back about a mile, Sergeant Rochester and I bumped into Captain Thompson and another Company E offi-

449

cer. They along with First Sergeant Goodpasteur had just attended a battalion conference. Goodpasteur was elated to see me.

"Edwards, I'm happy to see you!"

"What can I do for you, Sarge?"

"We just brought these six PWs with us. No one at battalion has any room for them. I'm going to turn them over to you right now."

"I'll take them Sarge. I've been trying to find either the company CP or the battalion CP. Sergeant Rochester and I went walking down that road that forks to the left about a hundred yards."

"Edwards, how far did you go down that road?"

"I'd guess about a half mile to a mile. Why?"

"Did you know you were inside the German lines?"

"No! No one stopped us."

"You're lucky you aren't a PW yourself instead of taking care of these six prisoners."

The six German PWs were led back toward the rear. As we started down the road with them, we met Lieutenant Lusby.

"Edwards, where are you going with those prisoners?"

"Lieutenant, we're going to take them back to the rear and turn them over to someone at regiment."

"You can't do that now."

"Why not, Sir?"

"Because the situation is too fluid. You and the Sergeant take them over to that barn you can see from here. Watch them until you can turn them over to some MP from regiment."

The prisoners were marched to a large barn about 500 yards and slightly off the road. Rochester lit a candle so that we could see them at all times. One of the prisoners, a lance corporal, was badly hit in the upper left thigh. After the prisoners were on the straw, Rochester took out his bandage and stopped the flow of blood from his leg. So I could observe the other five at all times, I lent my flashlight to Rochester while he worked. When he was fully bandaged, the prisoner said, "Danke, mein American soldatens."

With the prisoners comfortably settled in the straw, Rochester and I decided to alternate periods of guarding them. But events proved that we both were to watch the six Wehrmacht soldiers.

Just shortly after 0100, it seemed as if every type of German weapon seemed to erupt. The sound was almost deafening. I said to Rochester, "Rochie, watch the prisoners. I'm going to see what's happening outside."

I went to the barn door. Based upon past experience, I slowly stuck my head outside. A stream of machine gun bullets went whizzing by. Down the road about a quarter of a mile was a German tank. It periodically spit out some bullets from its machine guns. Mortar and artillery shells of all descriptions came down around the area but none hit the barn. Outside, I could hear the words, "Counter-attack, Counter-attack!"

Then the sounds of firing came from back of the barn. It was obvious that American mortars and artillery were shelling the area just beyond the crossroads. I saw two of our tank destroyers firing away at the German tank. A small battle had developed for the crossroads less than three hundred yards from the barn. The firing lasted for less than an hour. The noise slowly diminished until silence prevailed.

During all the shooting, the German prisoners did not attempt to move. Rochester covered them at all times while I had my head just outside the door in the event any German infantrymen appeared. None came. During this excitement, the one German officer attempted to try some of his English on us. Whether he was going to urge Rochester and myself to surrender was unclear. But we both forbid him to talk until the firing stopped. He remained silent.

About 0400, I noticed two MPs on the highway. I hailed them. They took the prisoners from our care.

Rochester spoke, "Don, I think we should try again to find the battalion."

"Rochie, let's give it another try. But let's be a little more careful than we were last time."

As we got to the road, we bumped into Crable.

451

"John, we didn't make it back to that house, because Rochester and I were detailed to take care of some prisoners."

"I know about that. But none of us has been able to locate battalion yet. Let's try to do that."

For the next hour, the three of us wandered about the area. In desperation, we went into a house occupied as a headquarters by the 909 Field Artillery Battalion. I found a hard straight chair and went to sleep.

At 0630, John awoke me.

"Don, it's daylight. I think we can find battalion."

"OK, let's go, John."

The headquarters of the Second Battalion were discovered just three houses away from those of the 909th. We reported to Sergeant Butler.

"Glad to see you three. The other messengers are already here. Stand by to move at any moment."

"Sarge," I asked. "Can you tell us what's happening. We just heard firing through a good part of the night."

"The best I can gather is that Company E started to go on an attack from those crossroads and met a German counterattack head on. There was a lot of firing on both sides. Our tank destroyers made the Germans withdraw their armor. A lot of Jerries surrendered after their tank left."

"Any idea what's happening today?"

"About 0700, the battalion's going to attack Mors. If they get through the town, they are going to try to get to the bridge crossing the Rhine."

"Haven't the Germans blown it yet?"

"Apparently it's still there."

At 1000, the entire communications platoon marched toward Mors. The community was completely deserted. Our guess was that the civilians had retreated with the Wehrmacht over the Rhine.

At the eastern edge of the town, we stopped. Sergeant Carlson issued an order. "We're stopping here for now. Everybody go into that tavern on the other side of the street. Wait for further orders."

452

"Sarge, can we drink anything we find?" inquired a voice in the back.

"No one is to drink anything except what's in their canteen. That's an order from headquarters."

The tavern was a two story brick building. The bar was located on the first floor with an apartment on the second. It was 1200. A discussion of what the situation was ensued.

"Anybody know what's happening?" inquired a voice.

"Rumor has it that the rifle companies are near the river. And the bridge is still there."

We sat on the bar floor and waited and waited. About 1700, I asked Sergeant Butler, "Sarge, have I your permission to go upstairs and look out?"

"Edwards, you can, but be careful. No one knows where the enemy is and what he will do."

I went upstairs into one of the bedrooms and looked eastward. The area toward the east seemed to be in semi-darkness. There seemed to be a bridge over a river with shells falling over the bridge as well as the area immediately in front of it. But little seemed to be moving anywhere. An hour later the entire area was completely dark.

Upon my return downstairs at 1845, Vernon Dawes asked, "Ed, what could you see?"

"Not much. I thought there's a bridge toward the east but nothing was moving anywhere. My guess is that we'll just have to wait."

"But that's what we do most of the time anyway."

"Vern, I believe that's what most of the war is about. Hurry and wait."

At 2100, Sergeant Butler issued an order to the eight messengers. "Since we don't know exactly the situation, we will have to post a guard. Each messenger will be on guard two hours during the night. First shift will be at 2200. Arrange among yourselves the hours."

The eight of us decided on the various shifts. I was to be on guard with Bernie Cohn. Our shift was to start at midnight.

453

3. At the Rhine

Monday, March 5, 1945

With the new day guard duty started. Bernie and I chatted the entire two hours in a low voice. But we heard or observed nothing. At 0200, we turned the task to Simon and Innes.

At 0700, every messenger was up and ready for further orders. Sergeant Butler gave us the news on the battalion's advance.

"Last night the Germans blew the bridge over the Rhine. All three rifle companies are on the river. The Second Battalion will go into a defensive position. During this phase, the messengers will divide into the two usual groups. Four will be at the forward CP, four will be at the rear CP. I will be at the forward CP and Corporal Kern will be at the rear CP. I think all of you know your duties. We will depart for our new locations at 0900."

Each of the four twosome held a conference. Crable and I decided that he would be at the forward CP while I would stay at the rear CP. Usually this meant that John would be closer to the front line, but ironically this would not be true in this instance.

At the appointed hour, Innes, Cohn, Simon and I marched to a house in the city of Homberg. We were located on the west bank of the Rhine River. The other side of the bank was held by the enemy. The famous river appeared to be about a mile wide and flowed peacefully northward.

During the afternoon, the four messengers went to nearby houses and secured bedding for our resting that night. Each of us had our own mattress. During the entire day, not a single shell fell in our area. We welcomed this type of silence.

That night all in the communications platoon stationed at the rear headquarters expected a full night's sleep. At 2300, a terrific concussion was felt in the dwelling. But there was no need for an alert. Early that evening, a battery from the 327th Field Artillery of our Division had started to move into a field just behind the battalion's headquarters. We had hoped that no

454

firing would be made until the next morning. However, the artillery crews were extremely quick at setting up their new positions. Their periodic firings suited no one. Every time their guns fired, the house shook. After being awakened the third time, Bernie Cohn quipped, "This is almost worse than being shelled by the Heines. You can get away from the noise by going into a cellar. We can't get away from our own noise if we want to. But it sure is safer."

Tuesday, March 6, 1945

The five kitchens of the companies forming the Second Battalion brought hot food to their men commencing today. Three hot meals were to be served until further notice. No one drew KP since the kitchens where the food was prepared was still far to the rear and out of the range of the enemy's artillery.

After a breakfast of hot cakes, the four messengers decided that cleaning was the order of the day. All of us took off our clothing down to the skin. We shook everything to clear them of some of the dust that had accumulated in the last ten days. Everyone changed his socks. A cleaning was made of either our rifle or carbine. Each of us took about an hour to shave our beards. The last previous shave had been on February 22. No hot water was available in our location. But it felt good.

In the afternoon, I made the necessary arrangements with Bernie to take any messages that would come for Company E. I had decided to visit a squad of the Field Artillery unit stationed nearby.

Upon approaching the 155 mm piece, it looked deserted. The howitzer was firmly placed on the ground with supports blocking its wheels. Over the gun was a large camouflage net which completely covered the large gun as well as a huge area around it. Just back of the artillery piece were two small openings which led back into the side of the hill where the crew apparently stayed when they were not working.

When one of the artillerymen saw me examining the gun, he exclaimed, "Hey soldier, come on back here with us."

455

Their well constructed shelter had a blanket for a door and fitted well back into the side of the hill. Inside were five or six artillerymen which formed the basic crew. One asked me, "What outfit are you from?"

"Second Battalion, 335th."

"Oh, you're from the Infantry!"

"Yes, I am. Is that strange?"

"Yes, it is. We don't see too many of you since we left Claiborne. What job do you have?"

"I'm with the battalion's communications platoon. Basically I'm a messenger but I have helped with the radio and wire at times."

"Have you been up front at all?"

"Yes."

"Can you explain what happens up there?"

During the next half hour, I tried to explain my role and what it entailed. The small audience listened to every word that I said. My guess was that they had had no one explain the situation to them. At the end of my explanation which was interrupted by numerous questions, three or four of them asked, "What do you think of the artillery support that's been given to you? Tell us the truth since our officers always tell us it's not too good."

"For myself, fellas, I've been satisfied. Although I could not tell you for sure, I think your shelling has made the Germans withdraw in lots of situations. I know in Leiffarth it made a big difference."

"You seem honest, Private Edwards. What's the true picture about the casualties that the line companies have suffered? We've heard so many different stories."

"That depends. In November, the fighting was tremendous. The Germans seem to get weaker as time goes on. My guess is that my own battalion has turned over once in the rifle companies since we started. I think some outfits in the 334th have turned over twice. How have your casualties been?"

"We haven't had any since our first experience in Germany. One crew got hit during the first offensive. But that's all so far."

456

Since we had had a discussion for over an hour, I thought it was time to leave.

But the crew chief who was a Sergeant had other ideas and insisted, "Stay around until we fire the next round. You can help us with it."

We continued to talk and talk for the next hour. Just before 1600, the telephone rang. The order to fire was given. The gun crew ran from the dugout to their assigned positions.

"Load," was the command. The huge shell and powder were placed in the chamber.

"Fire," was the next command. As the honored visitor, I was given the signaled honor of pulling the cord. I pulled. The whole barrel shot back and the chamber door opened. It happened in two or three seconds. The sound was deafening. All the regular artillerymen had cotton in their ears. I never thought of that necessity.

My experience as an artilleryman ended as soon as it started. I relinquished my position as the detonator. Five more rounds were fired by this artillery crew before the cease fire came. As each shot was fired, orders would come wherein the crew had to adjust the firing for the next round. Watching them was a treat in that each man had an assigned position. It was his job to carry it through in clock-like precision. As soon as the firing ceased, my hearing cleared and I said, "Gentlemen of the artillery, it's been a real pleasure for me to visit you. Keep up the good work. We need you."

The crew chief replied, "Private Edwards, it was our honor to have you come. We may not have another opportunity to talk with another person from the Infantry. We know what the average Joe has to contend with up front. We appreciate your efforts. Do come back again."

The night guard duty was again instituted. There was no fear of a direct enemy attack but there was always the possibility that a German patrol would come across the Rhine and wander through the area. We wanted to make sure there was a welcome committee for them.

A PRIVATE'S DIARY

Wednesday, March 7, 1945

Although our group had the normal amount of messages during the day, there was very little other activity. Letter writing and reading took up most of the time. An afternoon nap was always available to anyone who wanted it. The only noise was that of our own artillery.

Just after lunch, I persuaded Sam Cohen, a radio operator from Forest Hills, New York to take a walk and investigate what we could see.

Our battalion's rear CP was on the northern edge of Homberg. This small city was located across the Rhine from the giant industrial city of Duisberg. As we walked, Sam and I noted that the bomb damage was spotty. It appeared as if some stray bombs might have fallen from some of the Allied aircraft. The streets were naturally deserted. White flags and sheets fluttered from the houses. We saw a few civilians in their small back yards but none came to look at us. Shortly after our walking tour commenced, an elderly man hesitantly came out of his house. He approached us and trying some type of English asked, "Mai, ich gehe zu Haus ober there?"

"Ya, du gehe," was my reply.

He quickly walked across an empty lot and a street before disappearing into a dwelling. He appeared very nervous.

In our walk, we could see the bridge that had been the objective of the latest attack. Although we could not get close for an inspection, the steel girders laying in the Rhine could be observed.

Sam and I walked for over two hours. Except for the single German male civilian, we did not encounter any person, either military or civilian. We knew, of course, that many of the houses were occupied by our own soldiers but unless there was some type of action, few soldiers were going to leave them.

Each evening, while our watch on the Rhine continued, one or two German planes would fly over the area. Most of them were of the 'Bed-Check Charlie' type on reconnaissance missions. Tonight about 1900, the whole area shook. Two German bombers were attempting to knock out some of the Ameri-

458

can artillery in the rear. After the first bomb was dropped, the American anti-aircraft battalions started firing at the German aircraft. Prior to this bomb dropping, our Army had been content to let the Germans look over our defenses. After the third bomb was dropped, Charles Simon asked me, "Don, do you think Jerry is going after those artillery pieces. You know, the ones you saw?"

"I don't think so Charlie but one never knows. If those German bombs get any closer, we'll just have to go to the cellar and hope, that's all."

Thursday, March 8, 1945

Since our guard duty was on from 2100 one evening until 0600 the next morning, that task interrupted one's sleep at some time during the night. My shift on this day came from 0300 to 0400. Our purpose, of course, was two-fold. First, as usual, was to stop any German military personnel from prowling. Second, that no German civilians were to be on the streets after and during darkness. We had little problem in either area since the Rhine effectively limited any German patrols and the civilian population was still in fear of the Americans.

About 1000, someone yelled in to all of us, "Hey, there's a German plane in the sky. He looks like he's going to drop something."

Everyone in the communications building was outside looking at the Luftwaffe aircraft as it circled around. Then, as if out of nowhere, appeared three American P-51s. They were on the tail of the German aircraft inside of a few minutes. Soon smoke began to pout out of the battered Luftwaffe plane. As it descended rapidly, the German pilot ejected himself out over the American lines. He was captured about two miles north of our dwelling.

After lunch, Sam Cohen was again persuaded to walk around Homberg. Our objective this afternoon was the huge eight inch howitzers, one of which was stationed two miles from our quarters.

459

After a walk of 30 minutes, we reached the site of this gun. It was of a monstrous size. The gun belonged to the 256th Field Artillery Battalion. An extremely large pit had been dug for its placement. The piece had a platform built on which the crew could load the gun. I asked one of the crew, "How often do you fire this eight inch gun?"

"Whenever we get the order to do so."

"How often does that happen?"

"Usually twice a day, once in the morning and once in the afternoon."

"At what do you fire?"

"Only at very selective targets. Apparently the Army doesn't want to waste this huge shell on just a single tank or something like that. It takes us a whole day to set up the place for this gun. Why don't you fellas stick around for a while?"

"What time is the next firing?"

"I'd say about 1700."

Sam wanted to stay but my arrangements with the other messengers prevented me from waiting until that time. We agreed to return the next day to watch a firing.

Saturday, March 10, 1945

My tour of guard duty came from 0100 to 0200. As usual nothing happened. To stay awake during the dead silence was the most difficult thing one had to do.

Just after breakfast, Corporal Kern appeared.

"Good news men. We're going to be relieved this afternoon. You're to take the orders to your companies. The companies in the battalion will move out piece meal."

"Where are we going, Corporal?" inquired Cohn.

"I think we're going to stay in Krefeld until we go across the Rhine. Nobody knows when that will be."

Just after the noon meal was completed at 1230, some trucks appeared ready to take us on our next journey. We were ordered outside but waited a considerable amount of time before boarding.

At 1400, the small convoy left Homberg. The trucks were carrying only the Second Battalion Headquarters Company. The apparent plan was to take the five companies back one by one. In Mors, we saw two or three companies from the 75th Infantry Division. They were to be the replacements for the 84th for the watch on the Rhine.

After an hour's slow travel, the trucks stopped in front of a group of apartments on the Urdinger Strasse in Krefeld. The Message Center was placed on the second floor of one of the apartments. The messengers were assigned a bedroom with two beds. I was able to secure one for Crable and myself.

Company E arrived back from Homberg two hours later. They were placed in a group of duplexes just two blocks from Battalion Headquarters.

Luxury was the name for these apartments. First there was electricity available for our use. The city had been taken so fast by our Division that the retreating enemy had not had time to destroy the power station. Second, and probably more important, we had running water. In every previous rest area, except Holland, the only water available either came from wells or from the water cans that were brought by the kitchen personnel. In our bedroom, there was a radio which we connected to a loudspeaker that had been left in this apartment. We could have loud music if desired.

The kitchen from the Battalion Headquarter Company set up their equipment in a beer garden. Although there were no free suds, the facilities for eating and serving the food were the best we had enjoyed since leaving Camp Claiborne.

All eight messengers were back together that evening. The favorite topic which was hashed and rehashed many times was "When will this war end?" That evening, a poll was taken of the eight messengers on the date the war would end and why each believed in that specific date.

Crable led off. "I think the war will end about May 1. By that time, we should have met the Russians somewhere between here and Berlin. All of us will see the end of the war."

Sergeant Rochester came next. "I believe the war will end in about a month. The enemy has no strength left. If we could

Front Row — Martin Innes, Bernard Cohn
Back Row — John Crable, George Teets, Donald Edwards

go from the Roer to the Rhine in ten days, who will stop us now?"

Martin Innes followed. "When Hitler surrenders, the war is over. I think he might commit suicide because the Russians will torture him to death if they capture him. His death will be the end of the war. My guess is about April 15."

George Teets was next. "I can't see the war going much beyond the end of April. It depends on when they get over the Rhine. If the Americans have to wait a long time for the British to catch up at the river in Holland, the Germans could get their defenses organized but I doubt it. Jerry has lost his strength."

The other Company G messenger, Bernie Cohn spoke. "I hate to make a guess because there are so many things that could go wrong. The Germans may hold the front against the Russians in the east and let us come into Berlin. When Berlin falls, that's the end of the Third Reich. I think Hitler will flee to some spot like Ireland. He could murder Jews but he doesn't want to lose his own life. All of us will be living when the end comes on April 30."

The senior of the two Company H messengers followed. Charlie Simon said, "I don't talk much fellas so I'll say the war will end sometime in early May. The Germans are foolish to continue but some of them will fight to the end. They should hold off the Russians and let the Americans occupy their country."

Vernon Dawes talked. "I'm not good at guessing games. But since everybody but Edwards has guessed, I'll try. I like May 1. But if we get across the Rhine without any trouble, it could be ten days sooner."

Since I was taking the poll, I was the last to speak. "My observation is that the Germans know the war is coming to an end. I think they might try to make a stand in Bavaria. My guess for the end will be May 10. It's still going to be tough unless the Allies get some type of break. A lot of lives could be saved if Hitler could only realize the end is in sight."

On one item, every messenger agreed. The Rhine was the last barrier the Germans possessed. Once the Allies got across that river, they had no hope. The optimism we possessed was in stark contrast to what we felt was going to be a long war in November.

Sunday, March 11, 1945

This was to be a complete day of rest for the entire Second Battalion. It was expected that some would still perform duties which always included the messengers since Army reports never ceased. John and I actually welcomed the opportunity to walk two blocks to our company and chat with some of the members of our outfit.

During the morning hours, some baseball equipment was discovered or brought to Krefeld for our use. Soon a number of GIs were playing the American national pastime in the streets. There were no German spectators since civilians had yet to appear on the streets of Krefeld. The only traffic were vehicles from our own Army.

Shortly after our usual hot lunch, Crable and I decided to look into and at a German Tiger tank that was situated about

463

five blocks away on the Urdinger Strasse. Before leaving, we secured the usual permission to be absent for a short period of time.

As we approached the tank, I noted to John, "John, I don't think this tank has ever been hit by any shell. Wonder what happened?"

"I'll bet the crew just got out and surrendered. You may remember that up in Mors, there were two Jerry tanks just standing in the streets. Let's look inside first."

The condition of this tank was excellent. Although it must have traveled some distance, it did not have a single mark that would show the effects of shelling. Inside the hull, the tank was expertly constructed. It carried a crew of five men. They were naturally crowded but all had an assigned spot. There were still twelve 88 shells inside the hull. As I sat in the tank commander's seat, I noticed that he had a periscope that he could use in the event the tank had to button up because of shell fire. The plating on the outside was much heavier than on the Sherman tanks used in our Army. Crable and I were impressed by the outline and construction of the tank. As we inspected it, I wondered aloud, "John, what do they do when they fire and the recoil mechanism comes back. There's hardly any room here."

"Don, good thought. Maybe the 88 doesn't have too much of a recoil. That's why the Germans can use it in any type of defense or offense when they want to. But we'll never know that first hand."

Monday, March 12, 1945

The staff of the Second Battalion was not going to make the same error of letting the enlisted men grow lazy. At 0830, every company was out doing drills and calisthenics. This day, the exercises lasted only 90 minutes but no one was going to get soft as many did back in Holland.

At 1030, those men that desired were given the opportunity to take a hot shower. Less than 50% took the opportunity to get clean. The trucks took the potential bathers back to Süchteln. The truck drivers got lost trying to find the showers and wandered for half an hour before discovering them. No one minded since it was not cold outside. The black Quartermaster outfit was found alongside the Niers River. Most of us thought of it as a good small creek. For some unexplained reason, there was no hot water. Cold showers appealed to only a handful of men from the battalion. I believed that another opportunity would come soon.

That evening, I gathered some pots and pans that were in the apartment. Since there was an electric stove, I heated four large pans of water. Two smaller ones were warmed. The pans were hauled up the stairs to the second floor. The water was put in the bath tub in our apartment. It wasn't as good as a shower but it was adequate. As I emerged from the tub, Teets exclaimed, "Don, you would think you were going on some fancy journey and needed to bathe in order to go."

George turned out to be correct.

XXI

A PASS TO PARIS

Tuesday, March 13, 1945

This was to be another day for keeping in shape. There were to be exercises in both the afternoon and morning. The messengers had just returned to their quarters at 1100, when Sergeant Butler called me and said, "Edwards, you're wanted on the telephone."

"Who's calling?"

"Someone from Company E."

Upon picking up the receiver, a voice said, "Is that you, Ed?"

"Yes, this is Edwards."

"This is Sergeant Fitzgerald down at the company."

"What can I help you with, Sergeant?"

"I just called up to let you know that you're going to Paris tomorrow."

"Are you sure?"

"Yes, I'm sure. Your name was one of the three drawn from a hat, you lucky dog."

"Are you positive, Sarge?"

"I certainly am. When you come down this afternoon, we'll give you all the stuff you need about it. Roger."

After gently putting down the receiver, I went back to the bedroom of the messengers. Teets immediately asked, "Don, what did they do, fire you?"

"No, George, I don't think that will happen too soon. Company E just notified me that I'm going to Paris."

"How did you rate that?"

"My name was drawn to go from a hat."

"You lucky stiff. How do you like that for luck?"

The other six messengers congratulated me on my success. After lunch, I talked with John about the proposed trip to Paris. I stated to him, "Maybe you should go, John. Your French is good and you'd enjoy the French capital. You've taken care of me when I've been sick. It's my way of saying thanks."

"Thanks, Don, but I can't do it. You were chosen by a draw. I think it's best that you go. You never know yet, but it might be your only opportunity. But I don't think it will be. I expect both of us to see the end."

On my next trip to Company E, I asked how the drawing had been conducted. Ed Norris explained to me.

"Any man that has been with the company since February 1 had his name put into Sergeant Goodpasteur's hat. Then, the First Sergeant drew three names. You may remember you brought down the order for the passes. Your name was the third one to be drawn. Some guys didn't think you and Crable should be eligible to go. After your name was drawn, there were a few murmurs. But Captain Thompson just said that you have been doing the job that was assigned to you. Sergeant Smith also remarked that no one wanted the job back in Claiborne and you were willing to do it then. The complaints stopped."

About 1400, I secured a jeep ride to the 335th Regimental Headquarters where I was able to exchange my money into French francs. The pass to Paris was to last for 72 hours.

Since I was going to Paree, I went to Sergeant Warren Jeune, the supply sergeant for the Battalion Headquarters Company, to inquire about the possibilities of securing a new uniform.

"Sarge, do you have a new uniform I can wear on my Paris pass?"

"I have a couple, Edwards, but you're to get your new duds at regiment."

468

"That's not my understanding, Sarge. When we get to regiment, we're supposed to be ready to go."

"Well, I heard that's the way it operates. So I can't give you anything."

"If possible, give me a new uniform. If, when I get to regiment, I don't need it, I'll get it shipped back to you. I know some fellows in Headquarters Company who will bring it back to you."

"Wish I could do that, Edwards, but I can't take the chance. I know they will give you new clothes at regiment. Have a good time in Paris for me."

I was fuming but nothing could be done. I did not deem it important enough to consult with Captain Price. I thought the Sergeant should have realized that having the same shirt and pants on for two weeks, night and day, might not make them too presentable.

Just before supper time, Lieutenant Bernice Morgan gave a short talk to the entire communications platoon. He summarized a speech General Bolling had given in the morning to the officers of the 335th Infantry Regiment. The Railsplitter Division was the first unit to reach the Rhine of those outfits that had initially crossed the Roer. Not a single GI commented on the remarks. Everyone was happy he was still living and breathing.

During the evening hours, John and I packed the articles that would be necessary for my forthcoming trip to the French capital. He empathized with me over the omission of a new uniform.

Wednesday, March 14, 1945

Since I was going to Paree, I was excused from all morning exercises.

At 1030, the lucky enlisted men and officers from the five companies of the Second Battalion assembled in front of headquarters to be driven to downtown Krefeld. In that area, all the pass personnel from the entire 335th Regiment would gather. A small truck took the 17 enlisted men and the three officers to the Service Company of the Regiment. The division of the pass personnel was not in proportion to the normal enlisted men to officers ratio. The usual ratio was about 25 GIs to one officer. The passes had been issued on a less than four to one basis. But I still considered myself lucky to go.

Before boarding the 2¹/₂ ton trucks for our journey to the railhead in Belgium, all the enlisted men were inspected by Major Hunter, the former Commander of the Second Battalion. When he came to me, he asked, "Soldier, couldn't you get a better looking uniform?"

"I tried yesterday, Sir, but our supply sergeant stated they would be available at regiment today."

"Who is your supply sergeant?"

"Sergeant Jeune, Second Battalion Headquarters Company."

"Oh yes, I remember him. I understand your circumstances. After inspection, go over to Service Company and see what they can do for you. Weren't you with me some place, Private?"

"Yes, Sir. I was."

"Where was it?"

"In the taking of Berismenil, Sir. I was a messenger with your party."

"I remember. You had the radio for awhile, didn't you?"

"Yes, Major, I did."

"Good to see you again."

Next came a short talk by Lieutenant Colonel William Stone, Commander of the First or Red Battalion of the 335th.

"Men, you've been selected to represent the 84th Division in Paris. I want all of you to have a good time. But I think a word of caution is in order. First, stay out of any trouble. If any man is picked up by the Military Police while we are in France, that man will be severely punished. Second, be careful of your valuables and money. Paris is a large city. There are all sorts of people who will want to take your money, legally and illegally. Third and most important. For every man that returns to Germany 'sick', there will be one less man to go on pass the next time to Paris. I want all of you to remember your buddies who would like to go the next time. Don't become 'sick' and stop them from going."

No explanation was needed to anyone that the word 'sick' meant only one thing, i.e., venereal diseases.

After the inspection and short talk, I managed to get to the supply sergeant of Supply Company. He was willing to exchange my old uniform for a new one. For my trip I had only one old item, my shoes. But they had been polished the previous night.

At 1145, the order to board the trucks was issued. Fifteen minutes later, the wheels turned. The journey to Paris had commenced.

The route taken was familiar to every man in the convoy. Very little traffic was encountered as the trucks raced through Süchteln, Dulken, Wegberg and Baal. However, more German civilians were noticeable about ten miles westward from Krefeld. After leaving Baal, a break was taken for lunch. Every person on this pass trip had previously been instructed to take his food along since none could possibly be served on the truck or on the train.

After the lunch and necessity break, the journey resumed. The Roer River was crossed on a sturdily built Army pontoon bridge. The waters of the river appeared extremely peaceful. Linnich was seen as we passed by on its outskirts. Next came the well-remembered town of Geronsweiler. No tanks or other signs of conflict were present. But the battering the small village had received was plainly evident. The entire area looked strangely serene as the convoy continued on Route 57 through Alsdorf into Aachen. Although the latter city was still in ruins, we noted that the rail line was functional into the city proper. On the rail siding were hospital trains. Next came the Germany-Belgium frontier with its concrete barriers. Shortly the city of Verviers was entered. Just a few miles beyond, we came into the village of Pepinster. This was the end of the truck ride. The trip had taken about three hours. But to push the Germans back out of this same area had been a six month's task.

471

A PRIVATE'S DIARY

The personnel from the 335th hauled their baggage onto the railway station platform. We stood nearby our belongings while Lieutenant Colonel spoke.

"Men, we are very early. The 335th is apparently the first unit to arrive. There are others from the various divisions and corps who will ride the train with us to Paris. You are free until 1900. But everyone must be back at that time. We are scheduled to board the train at 1930. To watch our baggage, I need one volunteer to stay here until 1800. Will anyone stay here until that time?"

I raised my hand.

"Thank you, Private. I'll talk with you in a few minutes. Everyone is dismissed until 1900. Don't get in any trouble. Stay in this town. Dismissed."

The 335th pass party slowly departed. Lieutenant Colonel Stone came to speak to me.

"What is your name, Private?"

"Edwards, Sir."

"I want to thank you again for watching these belongings, Private Edwards. Can I get anything for you to read or write with?"

"No. Colonel, I have some writing that I can take care of for a few hours."

"That's good. I don't anticipate any trouble. When enough of the party has returned, you are free."

For a little over two hours, I was the sole guardian of the baggage. During that time, I attempted to bring my diary up-to-date as far as recent events were concerned. I did not know if Lieutenant Colonel Stone would approve of my notes concerning his speech back in Krefeld.

During the next four hours, groups from other outfits on the Western Front came into the station area. All followed the same procedure as the 335th. One or two men were left to guard the luggage of the others.

Just before 1800, a train load of reinforcements passed through Pepinster. We believed they would end their journey in Aachen. As the new enlisted men rode through the station area, they cheered. Those on the platform shouted various remarks.

472

A PASS TO PARIS

"You'll be sorry."

"Go back while you can."

"There's nothing up there that you want. No dames, no lights, no beds."

"Get out while the gettin is good."

At exactly 1900, a roll call was taken. Every man from the 335th had returned from their visit to Pepinster. My break had been limited to the securing of a cheese sandwich and a cup of coffee in a small cafe.

At 1930, all the groups boarded the rail coaches. The coaches were of the second class European type with hard wooden seats. Eight men were placed in each compartment. With luggage on top and on the floors, no freedom of movement was possible.

For over the next three and one-half hours, the coaches remained stationery on the siding at Pepinster. The first hour passed without too much grumbling. Then everyone started to get restless. Out the windows came a variety of shouts.

"When's this coal train going to start?"

"Let's get out and shove this thing."

"That pussy in Paris is waiting for my prick."

"Those French mademoiselles can't wait until they see my organ."

"72 hours will pass before I get my first French ass."

Strict orders had been issued that no one was to leave the coaches. This made the waiting more difficult. More than one GI wanted to return to the quiet front rather than sit and wait in a Belgian railway station.

Suddenly at 2307, a terrific jerk, awakening any who had been fortunate enough to fall asleep, rocked the coaches. All now attempted to get some sleep. Most were unsuccessful in their attempt to do this. To sleep sitting on the hard wood was almost impossible. A few of us including myself went into the aisle which ran alongside the compartments. Each of us placed a blanket on the floor. This gave us room to stretch out our arms and legs. Those remaining in the compartments then had some room in which to lean against each other. Sweaters, jackets, overcoats and any other soft material available were used as

473

pillows and blankets. The coaches were unheated but we had good air-conditioning in the form of broken windows throughout the entire train. But air-conditioning at this time of the year was not welcomed. As we tried to drift off to sleep, one GI murmured, "Why in the hell did they want us to get clean clothes? Sleeping like this is going to make us look like a pack of rats."

During the night time ride, the locomotive kept constantly stopping and starting. The next morning, another GI stated, "I swear this fucking train stopped 232 times during the night."

Thursday, March 15, 1945

By 0900, the entire coach train was up. Breakfast of the day consisted of the usual K rations.

With everyone up and out of the aisles, the guessing game of how far we were from gay Paree started. Estimates ranged from one to ten or more hours of train travel.

Just after 1000, the troop train pulled into the city of Laon. Maps were consulted. Paris was only 75 miles away. If the train went 40 miles an hour, we should arrive by noon. But the locomotive moved forward ever so slowly. A slow, slow freight back in the States would have passed us.

In the compartment with myself and six other privates was the First Sergeant from Company I of the Third Battalion. He was a veteran of campaigns in North Africa and Europe. First Sergeant Leslie Gratten was with the 34th Infantry Division in both North Africa and Italy. After 18 months of duty, he had been returned to the States and given a similar job with the 84th. His experiences were almost unbelieveable. How he escaped being killed or wounded was a source of wonderment. While discussing his adventures, someone asked Sergeant Gratten, "Are the Germans as good now as they were in North Africa?"

"No, I don't think so. An exception might be some of those we met in Belgium. The Krauts in Africa were the cream of their army. They weren't afraid of anything. They didn't surrender like they do now."

Another question was put to the First Sergeant.

"Sarge, which do you think was worst, Falaise in North Africa or the Bulge in Belgium?"

"Falaise was far worse. Jerry broke completely our lines at that time. All of us were brand new. We thought we were goners. The Luftwaffe had some control of the air. The Germans had good troops and better equipment than in the Bulge. We didn't know if the Boche would ever stop going forward. But I think they just didn't have enough good troops. The Italians weren't much help to them at any time."

"What was your worst experience, Sarge?"

"Twas two days before Christmas last year in Rochfort. That night, the Germans and their tanks came right up to Company I headquarters and fired right inside the building. I decided to get all the men from Company I that I could muster. We were going to high tail it out of there for we were just about surrounded. On the way to round up my men, I met Lieutenant Carpenter, who was commanding Company K. He said his men would join us. About two in the next morning, I and the others just ran out of Rochefort as fast as we could. I didn't stop for a breath of air until a woods was reached which was about two miles away. How we got back to the American lines, I'll never know. But we did."

One GI commented, "I hear that Lieutenant Carpenter got the Silver Star for that while you only were awarded the Bronze Star. How do you feel about that difference?"

"I can't complain. Remember it all depends who you are as to what you receive."

The tales of First Sergeant Gratten took up the entire morning as the train stopped and stopped. His hair-raising stories provided some of us with thought. Most of us believed that the 84th had had all sorts of experiences in combat. We had had many but other outfits had many more. At the end of the morning, the First Sergeant from Company I said, "I can't see the war lasting much longer. The Germans are down to their last man, especially, when we begin to get lots of prisoners in their early 40's."

A PRIVATE'S DIARY

Just after 1200 and our K ration lunch, the train passed through Soisons. All began to look impatiently for Paris. We looked for almost four hours. Just before 1600, the French capital was entered. From a distance, the only distinguishing feature was the famous Eiffel Tower. The train still continued to poke along. At 1645, we came to a stop in the Gare du Nord.

All the Army personnel aboard were ordered out. I noted that this railway station had over 25 sidings on which trains entered the station. Many of the lines had electric wiring above them. As we walked toward the station proper, one GI remarked, "If some nut had used the trolley line, we'd have been here five hours sooner."

Although we could see the main lobby ahead, the GIs were ordered to remain outside under the shed. All our passes were collected. Our arrival time had to be stamped upon them. As usual we waited. Every other group that had been on the train started to depart periodically. At 1800, the only outfit under the shed was the 335th Regiment. Tempers began to flare. Words started to erupt.

"Leave it to the 84th to fuck up. They can really do that."

"I came to Paree to live it up, up, up. What can you do in a railroad station?"

"We'll be here all night guys. Get your blankets ready."

"Bolling, you may be great in Germany. Get your act together when we're in Paree."

At 1830, Lieutenant Stone returned with our passes. He issued orders.

"Men, there has been a mix-up as to where you were to stay. Someone goofed. But it's been straightened out. Follow the noncoms to the buses. They will take you to your hotels to register. We will see every man back here at 1900 on Sunday. Don't get 'sick.' Have a good time."

Our officers had already departed since they were staying at different hotels.

The enlisted men entered the buses that were parked outside the Gare du Nord. Each bus had about 40 seats in it. In a few minutes, the ride through Paris began. Darkness was starting to fall over the city. Yet, the streets were full of all types of

476

people. A few of the famous sidewalk cafes were seen with occupants that were eating and drinking. After what seemed like numerous twists and turns, the buses came to a stop in front of the Hotel Escosse. Since we had no officer, the senior non-commissioned officer, First Sergeant Gratten, was in charge. He told the group, "Everyone is to get off the bus. Just stay in front of the hotel. A couple of us will go in and make the arrangements for your sleeping here in Paris."

Another wait ensued. While we waited, several GIs from the 28th Infantry Division emerged. They were going back to their units since their 72 hour passes were about to expire. Conversation between our group and theirs immediately sprang up. We did all the questioning.

"What did you think of Paris?"

"It was swell. Nothing could beat it."

"Did you have any trouble getting rid of cigarettes?"

"Not in the slightest. Why this morning, I sold my last two cartons to the barber where I got a haircut and a shave."

"How about the women?"

"There are so many available. You can have your pick. Some of the prices are high, but you can make them settle for less. Pigallie is the place for them."

"How did you ever find your way around?"

"Get a Red Cross map of Paris when you sign up for your room. This city is sort of twisted until you know a few key spots. The biggest place to remember here is the Gare St. Lazare. You're on the Rue d'Ekimbourg now. But don't worry, you'll know where you are within 24 hours unless you shack up tonight. Don't get too far away from here. This town is really open."

Several other bits of advice were given out until the men from the 28th Division had to leave for their train back to the front.

Two non-commissioned officers appeared at 2000.

"All of you are to go inside and register. They have hotel rooms for two, three and four persons. You've got to pay for all three nights in advance, whether you use the room or not. Every guy has to sign in."

477

A PRIVATE'S DIARY

Since I had been attached to Battalion Headquarters Company for a long period, I secured a room with Sergeant Paul Kottage, a radio operator, and Private Jay E. "Chuck" Roe, a jeep driver for the Second Battalion's S-2 section. They were the two representatives from that company. After our registration was completed, we had a meal at the Hotel Ecosse. The cost for a complete meal was an amazing ten francs, which was about 20 cents.

We decided to go to our assigned hotel which was located about four or five blocks away. Specific directions had been given to us by the registering clerk so that no difficulty was encountered in finding our way there. We found the Hotel Russie which was located at the corner of Rue de Batignolles and Boulevard des Batignolles. As the clerk explained to us, "Both of these streets have the same last name. If you can find either, you'll find your hotel."

Paul, Chuck and I were shown to our room with three single beds, which faced the Boulevard. Sergeant Kottage then made a wise suggestion.

"Let's all wash up. Then let's go to the Grand Central Club and see what we can see."

After completing our washing, we proceed to the Grand Central Club of the Red Cross which was located in front of the Gare St. Lazare. Although only five blocks from our room, two Frenchmen had to be consulted before we found the club.

We looked around and noted what events were scheduled for the next two or three days. Since it was near midnight, I suggested that we return and get some sleep. My two companions agreed. However, Roe said, "I've got to go to the jon, fellas, but I'll be back."

Kottage and I waited over a half an hour before deciding to leave without our companion. We experienced no difficulty in getting back to the Hotel Russie.

For the first time since London, I slept in a real bed with real clean white sheets and a good pillow. It was like floating on a cloud.

A PASS TO PARIS

Friday, March 16, 1945

Since each of us had been given a hotel key to our room, Paul Kottage and I did not worry about Chuck Roe.

Shortly after 0130, we heard the door open. Kottage spoke, "Is that you Chuck?"

"Yes, it is."

"We were wondering what happened to you?"

"When I came out of the jon, I couldn't see you. So I decided to go to a bar about a block away. I sat down and was having a whiskey when this dame just came up and sat next to me. Her English wasn't too good but we made a deal. She wanted two packs of cigarettes but settled for one. We went upstairs just next to the bar. She wouldn't do anything except a straight lay that that's all I wanted just now. I went back to the bar and had another round. Then I came back here."

"Boy, Chuck, you really wanted something fast, didn't you?"

"Not too much. She was kinda old but still good. I'd like something younger the rest of the time I'm here."

By 0730, I was completely showered, shaved and dressed. But neither of my room mates wanted to get up. I left them a note stating I probably would be at the Red Cross Club if they wanted to catch me. I wasted my time in doing this.

Breakfast, this morning and the following days, consisted of real eggs, orange juice, rolls and coffee. There was no limit on the amount one could eat. All our meals had to be taken at the Hotel Ecosse since this was stamped on your pass.

After finishing my breakfast, I proceeded to the Grand Central Club. A ticket was purchased for the guided tour around the city of Paris. The charge was only 70 francs.

The tour began promptly at 0845. It was designed to last almost three hours. The first stop was the Madeline, an old church of significance to the French. The second was the Place de la Concorde, the site of the famous guillotine. A turn was made onto the Avenue des Champs Elysees, the best known street in Paris. At its end was the massive Arc de Triomphe. The bus halted while the group inspected the tomb of the

479

unknown warrior. The Arc was inside a traffic circle from which no less than a dozen streets radiated. The guide explained that in a normal time, there would be a tremendous traffic problem in this area. At present, there were few vehicles on the streets. Then followed a visit to a statue honoring Victor Hugo. Next a stop was made at the Palais de Chailott. We were directly across the Seine River from the Eiffel Tower. Since there was an Allied radio station at its top, all visitors were barred from ascending it. The bus went across the Seine to the Ecole Militaire, the equivalent of our West Point. The guide pointed out the rifle scars that were present as a result of the fighting last August. Next on the itinerary was the Hotel des Invalides.

Inside the Hotel was a large circular base. As one looked down, the Tomb of Napoleon could be seen. It was made of a dark brilliant marble. As we looked at it, the guide said, "Hitler was here himself about five years ago and looked at this tomb."

The tombs of the other relatives of Napoleon were noted. Our guide pointed out one new one in particular.

"After France's fall in 1940, Hitler had the remains of Napoleon's son brought here. He hoped to gain the good will of the French people. It didn't succeed."

The famed Sorbonne was next on the tour. The Seine River was recrossed to visit the Notre Dame cathedral. A visit and tour were made of the church. Another section of the Seine was crossed to see the Paris City Hall and the Palace de Louvre. As the bus traveled on the Rue de la Paix, with the guide chattering about the exquisite perfume shops, some one in the rear exclaimed, "Why, I've heard of this place. It's in a song about a gal in a perfume shop."

The last point of interest was the Opera. But we could not enter. We returned to the Red Cross Club. Just before our departure, the guide said, "If you wish to leave anything for the driver or myself, give us cigarettes since they are better than any amount of money."

His wish was granted for the two men collected over seven full packs of cigarettes for their trip. Later I learned from a GI stationed in Paris that those packs were better than a weeks' wages.

After a tasty lunch, a visit was made to the Paris Post Exchange store. While on pass, each American GI was permitted to purchase a weeks' rations and, more important, to buy perfume that could be sent back home. After one's purchase was completed, the pass was stamped. The stamp for the perfume was separate and distinct. This perfume department was available only to personnel that were in Paris on leave.

Upon exiting from the PX, your cigarettes and any other tobacco items could be sold immediately. At the street were several Frenchmen dealing in the black market that would purchase your goods. You could secure cash, sex or some other French products like perfume and hankies.

The remainder of this afternoon was spent at the Olympiad Theater which featured a vaudeville show that was available only for American troops.

After supper, that was served with French wine and still cost only ten francs, I went for a stroll with a GI from the 30th Infantry Division. His name was Sam Howman. He worked in the Division headquarters as a clerk. We walked to the Champs Elysees and attended the famous Follies there. Sam and I enjoyed the show which featured huge costumes over basically nude female bodies. On this famed avenue, we saw very few of the Mademoiselles plying their trade. A return was made to the Red Cross club to attend the nightly dance that was held for the Americans. The French girls that attended were anxious to dance every number played in the jitterbug style.

That evening, I had the hotel room to myself. I had a good idea where my room mates were staying.

Saturday, March 17, 1945

During the previous afternoon, I had made arrangements to go shopping this morning. The Red Cross provided a free shopping service wherein French girls would accompany you in your shopping for French articles.

I was paired with one Bill Gibson, a private from the 29th Infantry Division who worked in a regimental headquarters office. Our guide was Marie who had jet black hair, very dark eyes, a tan skin and stood about five feet, five inches. She was a very able shopper and knew the good from the bad. We walked through, at least, eight different stores. Since I had had about a dozen requests to purchase perfume for wives and sweethearts, I had to do a lot of sniffing. To me, most of the perfumes seemed satisfactory. I would say to Marie, "I think I like that one."

In return, she would say, "Let's see what the price is."

She would inquire from the clerk waiting on us the cost. Then she would say, "That's a good price, you can buy that one."

But she might say, "That's too high. I tell them you don't want it."

Marie was a university graduate. Her aim was to teach the English language in some French school. In August or September of this year, she hoped to get to England to either practice her learning of the English language or teach French to some English students. I told her in our wanderings, "Marie, your English grammar is better than mine."

"But, Don, I don't know the, as you call it, the slang. When you know that, you really know the language."

"Marie that might be true. Some of the men I'm with know all the slang and could use a few lessons in grammar. I think you know there's both good and bad slang."

"I know the bad slang in French. I'll just learn the good slang in English."

Whenever Bill or I tried to ask Marie about the German occupation of Paris, she always tried to direct the conversation to other topics. Only once did she tell us a little about how the Germans really ruled France. She closed the subject by saying, "That black period is gone. Now I can look forward to something better."

Since Bill Gibson had previously shopped in France, his purchasing ended about 1130. I asked Marie to go to lunch. She

482

inquired from me, "Is it possible for me to eat at your place where you eat?"

"No," I stated. "Only American soldiers can eat there. Why did you ask?"

"Some of the girls I know said that if you go with an officer, you can eat at their eating place."

"I don't know about the officers' requirements about guests, but the enlisted men are not permitted to bring them. I'm sorry."

Marie picked out a small cafe near the Opera. I just had a cheese sandwich and a glass of wine. I told Marie she could have as much as she could eat but she replied, "No, Don, I don't want you to spend all your money on, I think you call it, a French chick."

She followed my example in having the same sandwich and wine plus a French pastry for dessert.

My shopping spree lasted until the middle of the afternoon. Arrangements were made to take Marie to see the Glenn Miller band that evening. Upon her departure, she said, "I need to talk English the American way."

"I don't think you'll have any trouble, Marie."

Since a wrapping service was available at the Central Registration Bureau, all my purchases were taken there for shipments to the proper places in the United States.

Upon my arrival at the Grand Central Club that evening, there was a note from Marie for me that read as follows:

"Don, I'm sorry, but I cannot get there tonight."

I decided to attend the dance at the local Red Cross Club that evening. I learned that the attendees at these dances consisted mainly of Americans stationed in Paris. The Red Cross clubs were their recreational centers. After the dance, I persuaded a soldier stationed in a map making unit in Paris to accompany me to the area around Pigaille. John Harrington, before we left, remarked, "Don, it's nothing but trash. And really trashy. Don't say I didn't warn you."

The walk to Rue Pigallie was only three or four blocks. It was London's Picaddilly Circus all over again, only French style. However, the French ladies-of-the-night were much more

483

forward. They would often hail the GI to solicit his business. Along the entire area were cheap nightclubs and bars. These were filled with American or British soldiers. John and I stopped in two of them to have a glass of wine. When we gave our order to the barely-covered waitress, she exclaimed, "Wine, I think no American drink our wine. You don't want whiskey?"

As we watched some singers and dancers, a young French miss or two of them would come over to your table to 'get a drink from you.' At many of the tables, the women would be seated in the lap of some GI. In some situations, they would be fondling each other. Periodically, some couples would depart for some other place to continue their enchantment with each other.

After we finished our wine in the second establishment, John and I departed. He asked me, "What do you think of Pigallie?"

"Same as Picaddily. But the women see a little more anxious for business than in London. Is the method of payment the same as it seems in all of Paris, cigarettes?"

"Yes, the bargains are made on the basis of how many packs will exchange hands. I understand the girls really don't want money for their services."

Both of us returned to the Red Cross club and went our respective ways.

Upon my arrival at the hotel well after midnight, my room mates were still away.

Sunday, March 18, 1945

After a good breakfast, I went to mass at the St. Augustine church. The attendance was very poor. There were only two other American soldiers present.

Sergeant Kottage arose just after 1100. He inquired as to what I had been doing during my visit to Paris. After explaining what had occurred, he sadly noted, "Don, I've been in this place for over two whole days. I've had a great time with these French dames but I could have done the same thing in Boomtown back in Claiborne. I wonder if I can ever look anyone in the face later on and tell them what I really did in Paris in March of 1945."

"Paul, why don't you go with me on the Versailles tour this afternoon?"

"Don, I wish I could. But I've got to recover from my two big nights and they were really big. Last thing I remember was some cabbie bringing me to the door at the hotel. I don't even know where I came from."

Sergeant Kottage and I went to lunch. When entering to pay for our meal, Paul could not find a single penny or franc on his person. I lent him 10 francs to buy his meal. As I paid for his meal, he remarked, "I didn't think they would take everything from me. At least, they left me my clothes."

Most of my afternoon was spent on the trip to Versailles. How our bus managed the ten mile trip out and back seemed unbelieveable since it coughed and spat during the whole outing. The huge palace was a slight disappointment since there were only large empty rooms to be seen. The guide stated that, because of costs, keeping the palace in good condition was impossible. This was not true of the huge gardens. They were in splendid condition with large beds of flowers and pure white fountains throughout the area. The smaller palaces where the mistresses of the Bourbon kings lived seemed in better shape than the main palace. After seeing the dazzling coaches of Louis XIV, one GI exclaimed, "No wonder France is so poor if they had to pay for all this stuff."

On the return journey to Paris, the bus passed the Headquarters of SHAEF (Supreme Headquarters Allied Expeditionary Force) which were housed in a large hotel. Just as we re-entered Paris, the guide proclaimed, "You are back in the United States."

All of the bus laughed. He continued, "You don't believe me! Well there is the Statue of Liberty!"

True to his word, there appeared a small replica of the famous statue which had been built on one of the bridges crossing the Seine River.

A PRIVATE'S DIARY

Upon my arrival about 1745 at the Hotel Russe, my two room mates were ready to leave. I asked Chuck Roe how he had enjoyed Paris.

"Well, Don, on Friday morning, I went to the PX and got some things to send back home. I sold some cigarettes and bumped into this cute brunette chick. She spoke pretty good English. She invited me to her place about six blocks from here. I spent the rest of Friday and all day Saturday with her. Gave her all the cigarettes I had. When I left her early this morning, I see I had exactly 10 francs left. She must have got all my money too. Paul tells me you did the right thing. I think I should have taken that morning tour with you on Thursday, then, gone out and had a good time. I don't know what Paris is famous for except women."

"At least, Chuck, she left you with 10 francs more than Paul has."

"You're right. Can you lend us both something to get to the station?"

Since taxicabs were scarce on Sunday, the three of us used the Paris Metro or Subway to get back to the Gare du Nord. In most aspects, the Paris system reminded me of the Philadelphia system. The Parisians rushed to get into the subway cars. The car doors shut quickly. But on the Metro, you could purchase either a first-class or second-class ticket. We purchased the latter although I offered to buy the best class for my two companions. The trip to the Gar du Nord began on the Nation-Porte Douphine line. Then a change was made to a different level to catch the Clegnoncournt-Porte d'Orleans line.

At 1900 in the lobby of the Gard du Nord, a roll call was had. Every enlisted man and officer of the 335th was present. Lieutenant Colonel Stone seemed to breathe a sigh of relief. In back of me, one GI noted, "If this roll call had come at 0700, I think a few guys might have been missing."

We proceeded to wait one and a half hours before we were allowed to board the train. We sat on the lobby floor. A few including myself had purchased some French bread which all the GIs enjoyed in large hunks. When the gates opened, there was a scramble to get to the coach and claim a place in the aisle

486

where one could sleep in some fashion. We knew the coaches would be well air-conditioned. On this return trip, there were more empty windows than ones with glass. At 2130, the locomotive gave a good jerk. We were on our way back to Germany and the war.

Monday, March 19, 1945

When all had arisen in the morning, the troop train had just cleared the city of Avesnes in northeastern France. Belgium was entered. Namur, Huy and Liege were soon memories. The journey came to an end at Pennister. Another roll call was made to insure no one had left the train along the line. The 2½ ton trucks from our regiment were there to pick us up immediately. At 1430, the truck convoy started. The return route was the same as the one taken four days earlier. We arrived in Krefeld at 1730.

After a quick hot meal, I spent the remaining waking hours answering and fielding questions on the what and why of gay Paree. My last remark before retiring to the six other messengers was, "Paris has something for everybody. It has wine, women and song. High fashions, high prices. It's something to see."

XXII

CHASE OVER THE RHINE

Thursday, March 20, 1945

Upon arising this morning, I asked John Crable, "John, where is Charlie Simon?"

"He took sick on the 16th when you were gone. None of us know what's wrong with him. He went to the aid station. Corporal Kern got a phone call to bring his things over there. The Corporal picked them up day before yesterday."

"Who are they sending for a replacement?"

"There is none yet. We've heard that there will be none at this date. My guess is that Company H feels the war is coming to an end and that two messengers are no longer needed. I believe the same thing would happen if one of us got sick. I don't think Captain Thompson would send any replacement."

After breakfast, the entire Second Battalion of 800 men went on a six mile hike. It took nearly two hours since the hike was more like a stroll than a march. For the first time, in the city of Krefeld, I noticed a large number of German civilians on the streets. They were very polite as we marched by and gave us a wide berth in our walking. None of the sections on this hike were severely damaged although an isolated house or two might have been hit.

After the hike, I went to Company E and secured my duffel bag which had been brought up from the rear. I again thanked both First Sergeant Goodpasteur and Captain Thompson for allowing me to be selected to go to Paris. Captain Thompson told me, "Edwards, I'm glad you enjoyed Paris.

489

Lieutenant Tucker said he enjoyed himself. Did many men get 'sick' as far as you know?"

"I don't know of any, Captain. But from what I saw in Pigallie, I wouldn't be surprised if some are 'sick' in the near future."

During most of the afternoon, I wrote letters and brought my notes up-to-date. The latter were placed back in the duffel bag for safe keeping. As I was writing, John remarked, "Don, I think some people would sure like to know what you write about them."

"I agree, John, but they'll never know unless you tell them what I'm doing."

"What did you say about that episode with Captain Thompson?"

"I wrote everything including the part that I cried."

Wednesday, March 21, 1945

After breakfast, the entire Second Battalion took another hike. The length was increased to ten miles. It took a little over two hours to complete. I did not mind the walking but some men did, particularly a private in Company F.

After lunch, a lecture was given by the Interrogation Officer, one Lieutenant Owens, on the interrogating of German prisoners. In his talk, the Lieutenant told us how valuable prisoners sometimes are. He noted, "Men, in one instance, a prisoner was carrying a piece of paper giving every German Division in a large sector of the front. This information, I am sure, saves some lives. I particularly want to stress that no prisoners should be killed. Killing them does no good since that PW could save your life."

His talk was well received for it gave us an insight on how the prisoners were interrogated after they were captured. His last remark showed how valuable a private might be for intelligence.

"Usually the higher the rank a German has, the more difficult it is for us to secure information. The private or corporal in the Wehrmacht is very important to us."

Thursday, March 22, 1945

The usual hike, lengthened to 12 miles, was taken in the morning with the White Battalion.

Upon our return, I decided that another bath might be in order. Water was heated in the two giant kettles that we had. They were brought up the two flights of stairs and poured into the bathtub. I was beginning to get a reputation for being a 'clean GI Joe." Most of the men in the communications platoon would not be bothered with this chore of heating the water for his own bath.

During most of the afternoon, the GIs played a variety of sports. A volleyball court had been set up behind one of the apartments. The games were quickly played. In comparison to baseball, which took a long time to complete, volleyball was the preferred sport.

Every other day at the supper meal, we were being served ice cream. The recipe that Sergeant Smith of Company E had developed had spread to all the kitchens of the Second Battalion.

Friday, March 23, 1945

In place of a hike in the morning, close order drills and exercises were the order of the day.

In the afternoon, the entire battalion marched to a nearby open field. A demonstration of how mortars supported an attack was demonstrated by that section of Company H. The men showed how directions were telephoned back to the mortar crew. The crew then zeroed in on a haystack which was blown sky high by their shelling. Although this same demonstration had been given at Camp Claiborne, it was done to show the many replacements the functions of the mortars.

Upon returning to our quarters, I washed my field jacket in cold water and hung it to dry. Because of the spring like weather, all the messengers shed their wool sweaters which we had been wearing since our arrival in Europe.

491

A PRIVATE'S DIARY

Saturday, March 24, 1945

After the usual morning workout, Lieutenant Morgan announced, "This afternoon, an inspection of your pieces will be held."

Upon our return to our quarters, comments on this inspection were rendered by different messengers. Cohn said, "I thought we were through with inspections. By now we should know about our rifles."

Teets echoed his sentiments by adding, "If we don't know how those rifles should be kept, those Krauts gave us a darn good reason."

Crable, however, put some sense into the reasons for the inspections.

"Let's face facts. If we aren't kept busy, some men will do nothing. Back in Holland, I paid a visit to my old platoon. Some of those men weren't getting up until noon every day. The enlisted men have to do something to get ready and the officers have to make reports on their inspections."

At 1500, the inspection was held. Lieutenant Morgan looked at the weapons of every soldier in the communications platoon. While we were training at Camp Claiborne, random selections were made during the inspections. After he finished, the Battalion Communications Officer announced, "Men, every piece I examined is in first class shape. Keep up the good job you're doing. Dismissed."

As Teets had correctly noted, no soldier near the front had to be told to keep his rifle in shape.

That night at 2000, the Second Battalion Headquarters Company had a beer party. The suds, which were better than the normal 3.2 beer, were apparently shipped to the company from the rear area. A number of both officers and enlisted men proceeded to drown all their woes and sorrows in the glasses of brew. The lack of female company was particularly noted.

Sunday, March 25, 1945

White Battalion of the 335th was given a whole day of rest. This never applied to the messengers since we still kept busy by delivering, at least, ten messages a day. Vernon Dawes was the only one to complain since he was the sole messenger from Company H. The message runs for Company E were split between Crable and myself. No comments were ever made by either of us on the work or jobs we had to perform on these resting days.

Religious services were held for those desiring to attend. A nearby school which had been cleared of all its furniture was the site for the services. Protestant's services were held at 1000 followed an hour later by the Catholic mass. Attendance at both services was poor. A number of us chided Sergeant Rochester for not attending. He became very angry with us stating, "I'll go when I need to go. None of you have to tell me."

When he later went on a message run, Innes stated, "I'm a good fortune teller, guys. He's back to his normal routine. If he gets afraid, he'll be back to church, not before."

The afternoon was spent largely in playing different athletic contests.

Since the beer party on Saturday evening had been a success in the eyes of a number of GIs, a repeat was held this Sunday evening. Some men really got 'bombed' the second time around. The party lasted well past midnight. Four or five men from the communications platoon awoke the entire platoon when they arrived back at the apartment. They were singing, "Show me the way to go home." Several voices shouted, "Shut up and get to bed."

"Don't you boys want to go home. Get out of this fuckin Germany. Let's go home everybody."

A mini riot ensued. Those who were drunk wanted to make lots of noise. Others wanted peace and quiet. A few rifle butts hit a few heads. Fists started swinging. Luckily no shots were fired. In a few minutes, Lieutenant Morgan appeared. He ordered, "Every man is to get into bed immediately. I don't care what clothes you have on, get in bed. That's an order."

493

A PRIVATE'S DIARY

Silence prevailed.

Monday, March 26, 1945

At 0900, the entire communications platoon assembled on the Urdinger Strasse in front of the three apartments that we occupied. Lieutenant Morgan spoke, "I do not want a repetition of what happened last night to occur again. I mean never again. You may go to any authorized party. But you cannot disturb others by your actions. Any individual who is caught creating unnecessary noise will be given extra details. This includes KP. No matter whether you're a sergeant, corporal or private, you will be assigned KP if you cannot behave yourself. Last night when I arrived, one man had his rifle pointed at another. Company E, as all of you know, had a situation where some of their own men were shot by someone in their own outfit. This will not happen here!"

The usual drills and exercises followed.

In the afternoon, every enlisted man in the whole battalion was given a new and different task. The Division insignia was to be painted on everyone's helmet. Not on the back but on the front. Since we were known as the Railsplitter or Lincoln Division, the axe splitting a rail, would be visible to any who saw us. Previous to this time, all had been warned that the insignia was not to appear on anything, men or equipment. All vehicles of any type were to display the insignia on their bumpers. No reason was given for the change. None needed to be given. Whether or not the enemy could identify the units of the United States Army was no longer of any importance.

Tuesday, March 27, 1945

After our usual drills and calisthenics in the morning, the communications platoon was assembled for a lecture by Lieutenant Morgan. The topic was censorship.

"I think all of you know the reasons for censorship. If the enemy is able to get any letters sent by you, they might be able to know the whereabouts of a whole Division. The officers do not take out anything of a personal nature. The only thing we

494

delete is of military importance. I think all of you know about the 'blue' letter. If you have something of a personal nature that you do not want an officer to read, you may use this. But the 'blue' letter is not to be used for criticizing the officers. It will be censored but that will be done by a Division officer. Any questions?"

A hand shot up in the rear.

"Lieutenant, you say we still have to have censorship. Then why did we put the insignia on everything the Division has?"

"That's a good question. I don't know. I was given an order to discuss censorship this morning. I have done that. Dismissed."

Upon our return to our quarters, I decided to take a poll. Since any 'blue' letter would have to come through our hands, I wanted to know how many had been sent by the members of this battalion. I questioned John who replied, "I've never delivered any. One man asked me to get one for him and he got hit the next day."

For Company F, Innes and Rochester replied together, "I've never seen one."

Bernie Cohn deferred to George Teets for the answer from Company G. "Don, as far as I know, there has never been any from my company."

For Company H, Dawes stated, I've never had one in my hand. And I doubt Simon ever had one."

It was the conclusion of the messengers that not a single 'blue' letter had ever been sent by a member of the entire Second Battalion.

During the afternoon, some of the messengers went to the local athletic club to do a little exercising on their large athletic field. During our walk to the field, we watched a battalion from the 102d Infantry Division marching down the Urdinger Strasse. They halted just in front of us. I asked, "Where are you going men? On a hike or to replace someone?"

"We're going up to Uerdingen on the Rhine."

"Is the 102d on the line there?"

"Yea, we've got two regiments on the river and one back resting."

495

"How long have you been back here?"

"Four or five days. How long as the 84th been back here?"

"I think about two weeks."

"Two weeks! You guys are sure lucky."

"But remember the Ozark Division spent all that time up here in Germany when we were in Belgium."

"Gee, I forgot about that. Guess your outfit does deserve a break."

The battalion from the 102d commenced marching forward.

That evening, after seeing the movie, 'Three in a Family,' we heard the sound of artillery fire. From the sounds, we knew that a crossing of the Rhine was imminent or going on.

Wednesday, March 28, 1945

Today was the giant rumor day. The Allies had crossed the Rhine at Wesel about 25 miles north of Krefeld. The idea spread that the 84th Division was through with fighting and would remain in Krefeld occupying the territory adjacent to it.

Another idea that spread was that our Division would retire back across the Roer and occupy that area. Every day the GIs listened to the radio hoping that Hitler would surrender his forces.

The consensus of the seven messengers was expressed by Teets who said, "They aren't going to let the old 84th rest too much."

Thursday, March 29, 1945

The usual morning and afternoon routines were again followed.

But the big news of the day was brought by Innes when he returned from a message run around 1400. He had run all the way back from Company F with his news. This in itself was unusual since each messenger tended to take a great deal of time in transporting the messages in the rest area. He exclaimed, "Fellas, did you hear the news about General Bolling?"

496

"No," answered Cohn. "Did he get shot or something like that?"

"No, he's OK. But he called a guy from my company to see him."

"The General calling a private! What gives?"

"This is the story I got from the guys in Company F. One Private Sheldon Lowenkopf was sort of pissed off about taking hikes in this rest area. He wrote a letter to the B-bag column of the Stars and Stripes. You know the column that the guys gripe in. It's coming out in today's issue. Well, apparently, General Bolling got notified of the letter by someone in the rear. He telephoned Lieutenant Hodges in our company to have Lowenkopf brought to the headquarters of the 84th this morning. Lowenkopf said he was very polite but firm. He wanted any complaint sent direct to him, not to any newspaper. This was to be true for any enlisted man or officer in the Railsplitter Division."

At 1500, the messengers were called to deliver the 'Stars and Stripes' to their respective companies. Teets noted, "For once, let's read the paper before we deliver it. It's hot today."

In two seconds or less, George had located the letter. He said, "Lowenkopf says that his company hiked 35 out of 42 miles from the Roer to the Rhine on foot. He wondered why hikes had to be taken in the rest area. He goes on to say that hikes shouldn't be required of any foot soldier. Pretty strong stuff I'd say."

After the delivery of the papers, the messengers inquired from Corporal Kern what he had heard from the grapevine. He answered, "The vine has it that General Bolling doesn't want anybody or nobody to write to the Stars and Stripes. If a letter is published from anybody, the officer in charge is supposed to take the appropriate action."

"Like what?" inquired Dawes.

"My guess in the case of the messengers is that if any one of you wrote, you'd be the point man in the next attack by this battalion."

"We get the point, Corporal," answered Innes.

When we got back to our quarters, Dawes noted, "I thought this was the American Army not the German or Russian one. We know they can't do it in theirs, why not ours? Aren't we supposed to be fighting for freedom and that other stuff?"

Crable answered, "You are right, Vernon, but I think we should all take heed to what Corporal Kern said."

Friday, March 30, 1945

After breakfast, I decided to clean up our little apartment where the messengers lived. Four messengers left for a run and the remaining two were asked to leave. As he departed, Bernie Cohn razzed me, "Don, you sure try to keep every place we stay in neat and clean. I appreciate it but I don't think some of the others do."

"Thanks, Bernie, but I figure it's better to try to stay clean if one can. I realize we can't do it all the time but it's nice to be clean when one can."

"How are you able to do it with Rochester around?"

"Rochie isn't too bad if you tell him the place has got to be clean. The only trouble with him is that chewing tobacco that he always has. Remember in Schaesberg, he didn't even live with us. When he gets the opportunity again, he won't stay with us."

"Don, I know you're right there."

Before noon, Crable and I had been notified that a Catholic service would be held in the afternoon in a large church in downtown Krefeld. We made the necessary arrangements to attend.

At 1600, the Catholic Chaplain was ready to begin. Before commencing, he turned around and saw several German civilians present in the church. He asked a few of us, "Men, would you remove the Germans from the church?"

Inasmuch as we were armed, there was no trouble in persuading the civilians to leave. Many of them seemed surprised that we asked them to leave their own church. A guard was then posted at the front door.

Before the mass started, the Chaplain explained.

"Probably men, nothing would have happened during our services here today. But if just one unhappy Nazi shot any of you, I could never forgive myself for letting it happen. I know it's not the Christian thing to do, but this is still war."

At 1900, the entire Second Battalion was paid. The currency given out was the new invasion marks. We knew they had to be accepted by the German population. Most, if not all of my pay, went to pay off my debts incurred for the Paris trip. Since I received very little in cash on any pay day, it had been necessary for me to borrow from Crable, Innes and Teets. John was the only one that was not repaid in full on this date.

Saturday, March 31, 1945

Just after breakfast, Sergeant Butler called the messengers together.

"I think we all have been expecting this but I just received an order that the Second Battalion will leave Krefeld tomorrow. The trucks are scheduled to arrive sometime after lunch."

The messengers received the news with mixed emotions. George Teets spoke first. "I was hoping that we could stay here until the war ended. It's so peaceful here compared to where we might be going."

John Crable noted, "We're not in the quartermasters or ordnance or some outfit like that. Being in the infantry you're expected to chase the enemy. The Germans are retreating but there'll still be a few battles yet."

A number of GIs in the Headquarters Company had already had a taste of occupation and found it enjoyable. It was evident to all members of the White Battalion that the "non-fraternization" policy ordered by the brass at SHAEF was not going to work. When the battalion came back to rest in Krefeld, a movie was shown to every man in the battalion on the manner in which the German people had supported Hitler. Thus, we were not to associate with his supporters which meant the entire German population.

499

However, the biological urge in some of the GIs could not be suppressed by anyone unless every man was kept under a 24 hour guard. This was impossible.

A few days after our arrival in Krefeld, we were eating or about to eat our supper one evening on the tables that had been placed outside the tavern itself. We were lined up in the chow line waiting to be served, when, across the street, someone noticed a German female peering out of her apartment. Some of the men waved at her. She returned their greetings with a broad smile. That evening, a call was paid by three sergeants of the Company who were, of course, searching for weapons in German homes. The practice started to snowball. No one was fraternizing. The enlisted men were just doing their duty to make sure that Krefeld was a safe place to be. As Dawes sarcastically noted, "The only place any guy seems to search for weapons is where there is a German frau or fraulein. And there's no order to state how long you can stay in your search for weapons."

It was quite easy for a GI to roam the streets at night since all the military personnel had the correct password for the night.

All seven messengers listened to the radio carefully that night. We realized that in a day or two, we might be very familiar with the names in the news.

Sunday, April 1, 1945

Easter Sunday.

Catholic services were held at 0900 followed by those for the Protestants an hour later. Attendance was greatly improved over the previous Sunday. No explanation was needed for anybody.

The trucks arrived before 1100. All the equipment needed by the battalion was loaded by 1200.

Easter dinner consisted of chicken with all the extra trimmings possible. For dessert we were given ice cream. When the next hot meal would come was unknown. Every enlisted man, during the morning hours, was issued his three or four K-rations which he carried in his pack.

At 1345, the trucks were boarded. Fifteen minutes later another journey had started. The route took the battalion north and west from Krefeld. We were told that we could not ride near the Rhine since the German artillery still might be able to shell the convoy.

The small villages of Huls, Ionesberg, Schasphuysen, Rheurdt and Sevelen were quickly passed by the roaring trucks. At Issum, Highway 58 was reached. The convoy turned in a northeasterly direction toward the Rhine. From the radio and the newspapers, we knew this area between Issum and the Rhine had been one of the last German footholds on this west bank of the Rhine. The scars of battle were shown by broken tree branches, shattered houses, burned out vehicles, foxholes and trenches of all kinds. This gave evidence to the known fact that the Germans had made a stout defense before retreating.

Just before 1530, Cohn shouted, "Fellas, the trucks are slowing down. I'll bet the Rhine is close."

Fifteen minutes later, our truck rolled onto a pontoon bridge. We slowly crossed the famous European waterway. At the area crossing, there was an immense amount of activity taking place. There were two pontoon bridges in place. Each carried vehicular traffic in one direction. A Bailey bridge was almost completed. Edging back and forth across the river were numerous U.S. Navy vessels. Pile drivers were at work setting up the foundation for a rail bridge for which the approaches were already completed.

As we slowly crossed the Rhine, Teets noted, "This is the first river I've seen in Europe that can be called a river. All those other rivers would be like streams or creeks back in the States."

Once across the Rhine, the city of Wesel was entered. As our trucks entered the city, I exclaimed, "Why this place is just like the villages in the Seigfried Line."

Crable added to this idea. "Don, there's nothing left. Remember on the radio, we heard that the RAF had hit this place with a 1,000 plane raid. It sure shows it."

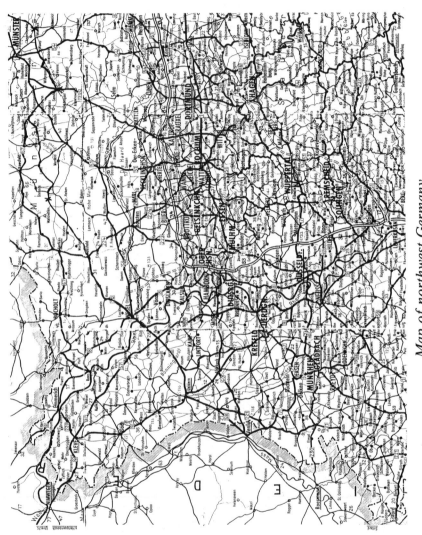

Map of northwest Germany

The entire city of Wesel was totally obliterated by bombs and shells. We knew that Field Marshall Montgomery, who directed the crossing, was an advocate of plenty of fire power before an offensive was launched. Fires were still burning in Wesel. All the men in our truck just stood up and appeared semi-bewildered by the complete destruction of the area.

Just east of Wesel, we observed a new sight, Cohn saw it first and shouted, "Hey, look at those gliders and parachutes."

We realized that this must have been the jump and landing area of the 17th Airborne Division in this Rhine crossing. The gliders, which seemed to number about 100, varied as to their condition. Some had made perfect landings. Others had collided with trees and other obstacles. The gliders were in the fields on both sides of Highway 70 on which the battalion was traveling.

After passing through the towns of Brunen and Raesfield, the truck convoy left the main highway. We entered the German countryside. The next town that we entered was Heiden. No further towns were seen that day. Back dirt roads were traveled. About 1800, the trucks pulled into a large farm establishment. The place seemed like a country estate. The Message Center was placed on the second floor of the main house. Sergeant Butler gave each messenger unit an assignment.

"I have the location of each company. After I give it to you, get to your First Sergeant and bring back the morning report."

"What if he doesn't have it done?" asked Innes.

"Wait for it. Since there has been no action, it should be simple for him to make it out."

Crable and I found Company about a mile away. They were also lodged in a farm establishment of four buildings which housed the 200 men of the company. When we arrived, Sergeant Goodpasteur spoke, "I'm ready for you two. There's the report for battalion. Are either of you going to ride with the company tomorrow?"

"No, Sarge," I answered. "We've been instructed to stay with battalion until we reach some type of front."

Upon our arrival back at battalion, John and I were informed that guards would be posted that night. Corporal

Kern gave us our assignments. "Edwards, you're on guard with Cohn from 2000 to 2200. I don't think you'll have but one shift tonight. We're scheduled to leave tomorrow."

Bernie and I patrolled the grounds during the appointed hours. As we walked about, he said, "Don, look out in those fields. What do you see out there?"

"Bernie, they look like ack ack guns."

"They're not ours, are they?"

"No, we wouldn't be up this far. I think they are German ones which were abandoned when the Americans advanced through here. I'll bet the Germans lived in those houses where we are staying tonight."

"Seems logical to me."

After our guard duty was finished at 2200, Cohn and I went to the adjoining barn which housed the kitchen of the Headquarters Company. We ate a hot meal. It was dinner by candlelight since we had heard aircraft in the sky during our guard shift. Whether they were friendly or unfriendly could not be determined. But no light could show outside the barn. As we ate, Bernie noted, "The front must be miles away. Our kitchens wouldn't be this close to any fighting."

Because of the guard shift changes, all the messengers were able to sleep in beds.

Monday, April 2, 1945

At 0630, we were awakened by Sergeant Butler, who reminded us, "Don't forget to set your watches one hour ahead this morning. We're now on Double British Summer Time."

"What's the purpose of this Double Summer Time, Sarge?" inquired Dawes.

"I really don't know except we could chase the Krauts longer in the daylight."

At 0830, the new time, we had a hot breakfast. John and I made several runs to our company. On one of them we brought Captain Thompson back for a conference.

After dropping us off last evening, the vehicles had departed. Without them we would not be able to cover many

504

miles. We waited. At 1145, a hot lunch was served. We sat and waited. After eating, Corporal Kern had informed us, "Everybody should be ready to go in a moment's notice."

"When do you think we'll leave, Corporal?" asked Rochester.

"I heard in about thirty minutes we'll go."

Although the trucks arrived at 1230, we did not board them until 1530. The journey did not start until 1600.

The convoy's speed was slow. There were long breaks of sitting. We inched through the town of Lette. One of our numerous stops was adjacent to a German military training camp. It was deserted. It did not seem to measure up to the outward standards of our military caps in the United States.

The next towns noted were Rorup and Darup. In the latter town, the trucks went onto Highway 67. In Darup, we noticed that members of some unknown infantry outfit were already in their German quarters for the night. They stood outside their dwellings and watched us pass by. Many German civilians were also outside. A few had white hankies in their hands indicating surrender.

As we passed through the city of Nottuln, some pretty German frauleins waved at us. This brought forth comments as follows:

"Let's stay here for the night. The women want me."

"They know we're good. Let's show them something tonight."

"I've tasted it in Krefeld. I'm ready for Nottuln women."

When our convoy entered Appelhusen, a real traffic jam developed. Our trucks had to pass Highway 51 which led directly into Munster. We understood the city was surrounded by the 17th Airborne Division. With the MPs permitting only a few trucks across the main highway at one time, the convoy of our battalion took nearly 90 minutes before it reassembled on the south side of Highway 51.

The trucks proceeded in a southeasterly direction. Darkness had descended. Overhead we could hear the sounds of aircraft. A guard was posted on each truck to watch the sky. In the town of Senden, the entire battalion was ordered off the

505

trucks. We seemed to walk in circles as all of us attempted to find a place where all could sleep. A barn was located by Sergeant Carlson who ordered the entire communications platoon to sleep there. The seven messengers were placed on the second floor where just plain wood was to be our bedding for this night.

At 2300, as I had just fallen asleep, Corporal Kern awoke me.

"Edwards, a message must be run to Company E."

"Any idea what for?"

"Yes, they need some spare batteries for their radios."

Upon my arrival at Company E, about a mile away in another barn, I met Ed Norris.

"Don, what are you bringing at this hour?"

"Battalion said you needed the spare batteries now."

"No, we don't. We told them to deliver them as soon as they could, but that didn't mean immediately. Too bad they got you up."

"Well, Ed, it's just part of the job."

Tuesday, April 3, 1945

At 0600, every man in the entire Second Battalion was ready to leave. The trucks were expected at any moment. We sat and waited. The whole morning passed.

All the messengers had their K-ration lunch just after 1230. We realized that the trucks had to return for gasoline each time they departed, but no one could give the reason for the long delay. Shortly after 1300, I approached Sergeant Carlson and asked, "Sarge, do you have any objections if some of the messengers go into the farmhouse and shave?"

"Edwards, sounds like a good idea. I heard the trucks wouldn't be here for two hours, at least. Can you finish in that time?"

"I think we'll manage, Sarge."

Crable and I secured some wood from a log pile; pulled out a large iron pan and lit a fire in the wood stove in the

506

kitchen. We shaved and washed. As John noted, "It's better to do this than sit around all the time."

Supper time came. The usual K rations were eaten. At 1830, someone yelled, "The trucks are here."

At 1930, the order to board was issued. Foreseeing a long hard cold ride through the darkness, Crable and I brought some rugs from the farm house to act as blankets. All the other messengers followed our example.

The convoy started to move at 2100. The trip was slow and cold. Because of the hard wooden seats, little good sleep could be obtained.

Wednesday, April 4, 1945

The usual journey of forward a little, wait a lot continued. About 0200, the convoy went across the body of water, the Dortmund-Ems Canal, on a pontoon bridge. Just after 0500, the convoy stopped in Wolbeck. We sought out homes that were vacant. By 0515, everyone was fast asleep on his rug or blanket on a good hard wood floor. The last words I heard were, "Why didn't I take a nap yesterday?"

At 0730, everyone was up for another day of travel. My map that I carried showed that during the night, the convoy had passed through the towns of Amelsburen and Hiltrup. As I pondered over my map, Innes inquired, "Don, can you figure out what we're doing?"

"Skinney, I think so. The Airborne people have Munster surrounded. We are going around it on the south side. We wasted a lot of time, but it might be worth while in the next few days."

At 0815, the order to board the trucks was given. A half hour later, the wheels turned. We were on our way again. A half hour later, the convoy entered the town of Telgte. We were due east of Munster. A right turn was made onto Highway 64. The trucks picked up speed.

As we sped eastward, the opposite side of the highway was filled with civilians. Most appeared to be French, Dutch and Belgian workers who had been shipped to Germany to work for

507

the Third Reich. Others looked like Germans who seemed to be returning to their home which they had vacated when the Allies advanced. In Warendorf, the next town, our convoy was cheered wildly by the imported laborers who stood on both sides of the streets. We cheered back and threw them our cigarettes.

In Warendorf, the convoy left the main highway. The drivers proceeded to open the throttles. We could not believe the speed of the convoy. The trucks started to become widely separated from each other. One GI expressed concern saying, "This is just great. But let's hope Jerry doesn't hit us when we're spread out like this."

The town of Sassenberg was just a passing glance. At Versmold, the convoy slowed. In the village square was a German light tank and a similar one from the American 5th Armored Division. Both had been knocked out and the insides gutted by fire. We wondered if the front was near but no firing could be heard.

The convoy resumed its journey but at a somewhat slower speed. By 1200, we were in Halle where Highway 68 was crossed. After moving through Hager and Enger, the trucks stopped in the tiny town of Hiddenhausen. It was 1430.

Orders were given to detruck. The entire battalion began to wonder about Hiddenhausen. Several houses were entered. The German occupants were terrified initially. Then, they began to serve the 800 plus men with free lunches in their homes. The messengers were invited by two elderly German ladies to have a lunch of some dark sausage and cheese. We hardly spoke during the whole meal. At its end, I thanked them for their hospitality on behalf of the messengers.

After leaving this dwelling, we began to discuss what had occurred during the day. Teets addressed everyone by asking, "How far does anyone think we've gone today?"

"Twenty-five miles," answered Innes.

"I think it's more like seventy-five," replied Cohn.

"Let's ask our driver how much travel we've put in today," noted Dawes.

I was delegated to secure the answer. Upon my questioning, our driver replied, "I didn't note the exact distance, but I believe it's about 52 miles so far."

I figured out that the convoy was going better than 10 miles an hour. This was a phenomenal pace.

During our long break, some GIs of the battalion found some liquor. Where it came from was unknown. But there were bottles and bottles of what was called 'yellow lightning.' It was distributed throughout every truck in the whole convoy.

At 1700, we were ordered back on board the trucks. Shortly we went by Red Battalion who were on the streets to watch us. During this next portion of the ride, the liquor began to flow like wine. George Teets and James Rochester each had an entire bottle to himself. There were at least seven other bottles in our truck which carried 20 men. In a few minutes, rain came down but some were too far gone to feel anything.

The city of Lohne was entered. It appeared as if the entire population of this town including the slave laborers were on the streets. Looting was taking place. The rifling was especially notable at the railway yards where coal was being placed in baskets of all types. But the convoy did not stop. The trucks went across the Nerre River. They pulled into a school yard where everyone got out.

Fully half of the communications platoon was inoperative. The five messengers who still had their senses took Teets and Rochester from the truck to a nearby tree. We placed each on one side of the tree and laid their weapon a short distance away from them, Crable remarked, "I sure hope the Germans don't stage one of their famous counter-attacks. They'd drive this battalion right back to the Rhine and capture 400 men."

From appearances, half of the Second Battalion would not have been able to raise their rifles to defend themselves in that early evening.

As we milled around the school yard, Corporal Kern said, "I understand that we're to stay in the school tonight."

Ten minutes later, one of the Battalion's CP guards appeared and stated, "Everyone listen. The six houses across the street have been cleared of all civilians. Battalion Headquarters is to occupy them."

The communications platoon took one full house for its use. In a few minutes, I was ordered to take a message to my company. Since liquor had almost been my downfall a few weeks ago, I placed a full clip in my rifle chamber. I had the gun in my hand, not upon my shoulder. I was prepared this time. However, upon my arrival at Company E, both Captain Thompson and First Sergeant Goodpasteur were completely sober and greeted me in a most friendly manner. I asked the First Sergeant the condition of most of the enlisted men. His reply was, "Edwards, we couldn't repel any German attack in this condition. But I've learned my lesson."

I did not think any reply on my part would be appropriate.

At 2000, Sergeant Butler issued an order that each messenger would perform one hour plus of guard duty. Again, no one mentioned anything about the Sergeant or Corporal Kern's failure to perform this task. My shift with Innes was from 2100 to 2215. We chatted the whole time. Teets and Rochester, now somewhat sober, jointly relieved us.

XXIII

THE WESER CROSSING

Thursday, April 5, 1945

The morning brought a lull in the chase against the enemy. The messengers did not arise until the late hour of 0830. As we sat in the morning, the war seemed in another part of the world. But the rumors were rampant. Innes inquired of me, "Ed, you've always got those German maps with you. Where do you think we're headed?"

I secured my Esso and Bevaulin maps from my pack. All the messengers were interested in what might be coming. After looking at them a few minutes, I replied, "Skinney, up ahead is the Weser River. Unless the 5th Armored got a bridge intact, that's where we are headed."

"Don, what's the biggest city on that river?" asked Cohn.

"Bernie, it's a city called Minden."

About 1000, Corporal Kern reported the latest news from the grapevine. "Men, the word is that the 5th Armored has seized a bridge intact over the Weser."

"What does that mean for us?" inquired Dawes.

"If they got a bridge like we did at Remagen on the Rhine, it means that there probably won't be a river crossing by the Division."

"I don't think that will happen again," I answered. "Back in Krefeld and in Paris, I heard the Germans got drunk like some fellas did last night and they just failed to blow that bridge in front of the 9th Armored. I don't think they'll make the same mistake twice."

511

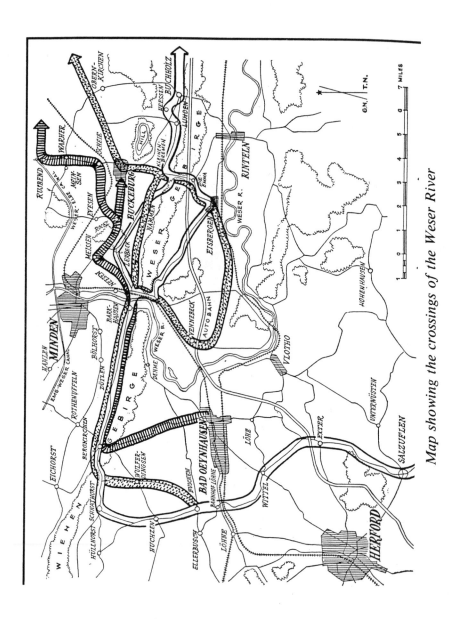

Map showing the crossings of the Weser River

"You're probably right about Jerry," replied Kern. "But let's hope he hasn't learned to blow all the bridges yet."

Just after 1100, the order came that the battalion would make a move in the afternoon.

At exactly 1400, the trucks arrived and loading commenced. The next sixty minutes were spent waiting. This wait was fortunate for Sergeant James Rochester. He had left the Message Center just before 1200. He failed to tell anyone of his future whereabouts. Just before 1500, he returned grinning from ear to ear. Teets exclaimed, "Rochie, we know where you've been. How was it?"

"Just great, just great!"

"Couldn't you find some tail faster than this? You know we almost left without you?"

"You wouldn't have left without me, would you?"

"Sure we would have. And you'd be another Walters. In real trouble."

"George, I just had to have some German pussy. I couldn't find any fraulein available until I took out a pack of cigarettes and started to wave it around. Some madchen came down from her apartment above a store and asked me to come in. She wanted two packs of weeds, but she only got one from me."

Only three minutes after Rochester arrived, the trucks pulled out of Lohne. The forward motion was slow. The first town entered was Wulferdingsen. There were no civilians present. It meant the front was near. The next town, Bergkirchen, was the same story. Just outside of Bergkirchen, the convoy began a descent from the highlands onto a low flat plain. As we started down, John noted, "Look around everybody, there's the 5th Armored. It means just one thing."

"What does it mean, John?" asked Skinney.

"The Germans have blown the bridges over the Weser. Until the Infantry gets a bridgehead, the Armored can't move any place."

The convoy pulled into Haverstadt which was located on the west bank of the Weser. A vacated school was the original site for the Message Center for this night. But before we could enter, another site was selected. It was a large farm house which

513

had just been liberated by the Russian and Polish DPs who were the 'slave laborers' there. John and I secured a straw bunk in their former quarters. The former laborers occupied the main farm house since the owner had vanished.

About 1900, Sergeant Butler gathered the messengers.

"Tomorrow, there's going to be a crossing of the Weser. Red and Blue Battalions are going first and White will follow them."

"What time is Red crossing?" I asked.

"They are to start at 0500."

"When do we cross?"

"No definite time. Colonel Learman wants three messengers from the rifle companies to accompany him. Who is going this time?"

"Edwards for Company E," was my answer.

Innes would go for Company F while Cohn would represent Company G.

While packing that evening, I told John, "I'm going to travel light tomorrow. I feel confident there won't be much trouble. I'm taking only one K ration with me."

"Suit yourself, Don, but I'd take another in case the Engineers don't get the bridges up by dark."

That evening, a party was put on by the liberated Polish and Russian Displaced Persons. They knew where their former master kept his liquor and beer supplies. They had liberated these items and invited all the members of the communications platoon to join them. Since there were four women in the former slave labor group, many of the GIs took advantage of the offer. Those going on the crossing could ill afford to have big heads in the morning. As I drifted off to sleep, the playing of music and loud singing could be heard.

Friday, April 6, 1945

At 0445, Sergeant Butler shook me and announced, "Edwards, get with Innes and Cohn over to headquarters. The battalion's starting to move toward the river."

THE WESER CROSSING

When the three of us arrived at the Battalion CP, Captain Price informed us, "Edwards, Colonel Learman just left. Get a jeep and you'll find him just down the road."

We quickly secured a jeep which took us to the side of the Battalion Commander. We were in the small town of Porta. The three rifle companies and the heavy machine gun section of Company H were lined up on both sides of the street.

At 0600, daylight came. No shells had been heard. The First and Third Battalions were almost across the river intact. There had been no shelling at the crossing site. The Germans must have woken up for at 0630, the mortar shells began to come in what seemed like droves. The first one sent all scampering into the houses lining the road. Naturally there were no civilians present. To the rear we could hear the American artillery firing.

Several German mortar shells demolished a tavern. There were no injuries since the GIs were in the cellar at the time. But very few 88s were coming in.

Between the lulls in the German firing, the whole battalion would slowly move forward. The Battalion Commander spoke to the three messengers.

"Men, we're going to the river crossing. Let's run down there before another round starts."

"Lead the way, Sir," shouted Cohn.

We trotted about a half a mile to a small house which stood about 200 yards from the Weser. This was the last stop made before the run to the boats was made. We were to wait until all three rifle companies were across the river.

From this observation point, the Weser River was not a large one by American standards. It appeared to be about 150 yards wide. About a half mile northward was the demolished bridge laying in the river. Near the crossing site was a two-thirds complete foot bridge. We heard that insufficient equipment had been brought up for the crossing. But White Battalion had to get across that river as soon as possible.

The crossings were being made in about a half dozen flat bottom boats. These craft kept shuttling back and forth across the Weser. A large group of soldiers, usually a platoon of 35 to

515

40 men, would trot up to the house. They would wait a few minutes. If no shells were dropping, there would be a run for the boats and the subsequent crossing. Considering all the difficulties, the procedure was quite rapid. No one wasted any time. The flat land, just before the boats were reached, was full of shell holes. Yet the crossings continued. Periodically, there would be mortar shellings of this flat land.

Since we had some time before our crossing would be made, we proceeded to look through the rooms and closets. Four beautiful sabers were found in one of the closets.

Innes inquired of everyone. "How can I take one of these with me?"

I answered, "Skinney that's great if you don't care for your life. You'll never be able to fall with one of those attached to your side."

He wisely decided to leave the saber.

At 0815, Lieutenant Colonel Learman announced, "It's time to go men. Follow me to the boat."

We ran toward the crossing site. Just before reaching the boats, some mortars fell behind us. A few men stopped. The Battalion Commander yelled, "Get in those boats, now!"

In quick fashion, I was in the boat with a paddle in my hands. We seemed half way across the river before I wondered about those mortars. Within five minutes, we were at the right bank of the Weser. The engineer who grabbed the boat said, "Leave the paddles. Watch yourself when you get out."

His words had just passed his lips when everyone was lying flat in the mud on the river bank. Overhead flew bullets from some German machine gun nest. A few rifle bullets also seemed to be whizzing around. A crawl was made to the right. I kept going forward since there was a group of houses ahead which meant safety. After crawling for about 20 minutes, I decided to make a dash for the dwellings. The machine gun stopped as I reached the street facing the river.

Lieutenant Colonel Learman arrived a few minutes later. He too had been in a prone position. A meeting took place between the Battalion Commander and the three rifle Company Commanders.

THE WESER CROSSING

The Second Battalion was, on the east bank, in the town of Hausberge. The three rifle companies formed themselves and marched out northward along the river. Just as the battalion started out, about ten German prisoners were brought into the building. They were placed in the large courtyard behind the house where a guard stood over them.

All realized that the general objective of the whole 335th Regiment was to widen the bridgehead so that the 5th Armored Division could get across and plunge deeper with their tanks into the Third Reich.

At a road junction 500 yards from the starting point, the Second Battalion split into two columns. F and G Companies took the left fork while Company E went right. Just after leaving the junction, resistance was met. Every house had to be searched thoroughly. But the advance went forward. Actually little firing from the enemy was heard. We noted that their artillery seemed to be non-existent.

As we traveled with the Battalion Command Party, the messengers could hear the radio reports coming from the three rifle companies. Company G was having the greatest difficulty. Two of their platoons were pinned down by enemy fire. A call for artillery fire was made. The enemy then retreated.

The Battalion Commander decided to be with Company E. Their radio was only one block ahead of us as the advance continued. The most surprising thing was the huge number of Wehrmacht soldatens that were giving up. Initially they were accompanied by a guard to the rear. By 1500, a guard was no longer necessary. We just kept waving them to the rear.

Just before 1600, the Battalion Commander asked the three messengers to accompany him to the front. We slowly walked through Company E. It was strangely quiet. As we got nearer to the moving front, a private from Company E shouted at us, "Colonel, don't go any closer, I think the enemy is just ahead."

Lieutenant Colonel Learman heeded the advice and turned around. He suggested that all of us look for a suitable Command Post. All four of us peeked into a few vacated houses.

A PRIVATE'S DIARY

Suddenly the Battalion Commander suggested, "Are any of you thirsty?"

"Colonel, none of us have any water left in our canteens so we could use some water," was my reply for the three of us.

"Let's all go in here for a glass of water."

Innes proceeded to open the door to a beer garden for the Battalion Commander. All the chairs and tables were in perfect order. There seemed to be no one in the place. Then, from behind a small curtain, a frightened small partially-bald German civilian appeared. He came smartly to attention and saluted. The Commander did not return the greetings. The German spoke, "Ja, mein Herr."

"A glass of water."

"Ja, ein glass wasser."

The bartender proceeded to secure a glass and filled it with water. He offered it to our Battalion Commander.

"You drink it first," came the command.

"Ja, mein Herr."

The German did as commanded and then refilled the glass.

"Gut, sehr gut, mein Herr."

Lieutenant Colonel Learman drank the second glass. A glass of water was then procured for each of the three messengers. Each time, the proprietor refilled the glass, his hands trembled and shook. His brow was sweating profusely. I had never seen a man in such a nervous condition. As we drank, I wondered if the bartender thought we were going to harm him in some way. Although the Battalion Commander carried only a pistol, the three of us each possessed four hand grenades plus our M-1 rifles.

After looking the place over in great detail, the four of us left. I was sure there was one greatly relieved bartender. We proceeded to look at more houses. In one house, a private from Company E was guarding some prisoners. When we entered, every German prisoner, numbering about twelve, snapped to attention and stood in a ramrod position. The Commander instructed the guard to send the prisoners down the road by themselves.

Just after 1730, Colonel Learman motioned to me.

"Edwards, go back to the crossing site. The lead vehicle should be ready to cross the bridge right now. I'll send one of the others to give you the exact location of the CP."

"Anything else, Colonel?"

"Yes, if you see any prisoners, herd them back to the crossing site."

The long walk of thirty minutes back to the crossing site was uneventful. On my walk, I dragged the body of a young Wehrmacht soldaten, of about 16, from the middle of the road since I did not think it proper that he should be mutilated further by our military vehicles which would soon be traveling this road. Upon my arrival back in Hausberg, the vehicle bridge was almost completed. This bridge had been built a little south of the boat crossing. A little to the north of the crossing site, a pontoon bridge for heavier trucks and tanks was nearing completion.

While I waited for the convoys to cross, I noticed just in back of the road along the rise toward a hill a huge camouflage net. It had actual branches and twigs interwoven into the framework. This net was at the foot of a steep hill. A railway spur ran directly into the hill. I knew it to be an underground factory for which the Germans were well known. But there was no time to explore the factory. Fifteen minutes after my arrival, Innes appeared. "Don, I've got the exact place of the battalion's CP."

"OK, Skinney. Just sit down here. There's nothing to do until that bridge is completed."

For the next fifty minutes, we watched the engineers put the last sections of the bridge into place. On the other side of the river, we could see long lines of vehicles waiting to cross the Weser. The tanks of the 5th Armored were at the river's edge.

At 1930, the first jeep crossed. The first group of vehicles were from the Red Battalion which had been the first unit across. Next came the lead vehicle of our White Battalion in which Captain Price was riding. I motioned for the vehicle to stop. "Captain, we've been instructed to lead you to the CP."

"Get in, Edwards and Innes. Take us there."

519

In a few minutes, the lead jeep was at the CP. Captain Price turned to me and requested, "Edwards, go back to the bridge. Lead the wire team up here. The Colonel will want to talk to Regiment on the phone as soon as possible."

Another walk was made to the bridge. On the highway were all types of Army vehicles. At the bridge, I found Sergeant Brazil, the wire chief.

"Sarge, are you ready with the wire team?"

"Lead the way, Edwards. Seifert and Merritt will follow you."

Since Privates Hoyt Merritt and George Seifert had to lug a huge carrier of wire, it took nearly an hour before reaching the CP. The telephone was quickly installed. Inasmuch as it was dark, it was imperative that the password be given to the rifle companies. A walk was taken to Company E. After I had given the password, Sergeant Goodpasteur remarked, "Edwards, I thought for a minute that you and the Colonel were going to lead the attack. You stopped just in time."

"Anything happen, Sarge?"

"Just as you turned the corner, Jerry let go with a machine gun blast. We think he was retreating and didn't want us to catch him too fast."

I returned to the Battalion CP at 2255. The messengers had a room on the second floor complete with electricity and a radio. Since all the messengers knew a newscast came on promptly at 2300, we decided to tune the radio to the AEF-BBC. The newscaster stated that the Allies had two bridgeheads over the Wester River. One was the American one at Porta while the other was a British one north of Minden. It was the only time I ever heard of the battalions' activities on the same day on which they occurred. The sensation of hearing about your own unit was most unusual. Because of the fluid situation, the messengers were not permitted to retire. About 2345, I heard the rumble of an American tank on the street outside. I searched out Captain Price and requested, "Captain, can we go to sleep now? I believe I heard the tanks outside."

"Edwards, go to sleep. Everything is under control."

I returned upstairs with the message. Before we turned off the lights Cohn asked me, "Don, do you walk this much every time there's an attack? My feet are killing me!"

"No, Bernie. I've walked more today than I've ever walked. And that includes those 25 mile hikes back in Claiborne. Skinney, how many miles do you think we've done today?"

"My feet feel like it's about 50. I don't know, but it's a lot. Any ideas from you Don?"

"I estimate somewhere between 30 and 35 miles. All I know is that my feet are tired and I need some sleep. It's been a long, long day."

We clicked off the lights just as the new day was about to start.

Saturday, April 7, 1945

By 0730, Skinney, Bernie and I were ready for any new event. During the nighttime, we could hear more vehicles of all types passing our dwelling. During the morning runs to our companies, more and more prisoners kept streaming toward the rear. I noted that none of them were from the Wehrmacht infantry.

Just before 1200, elements of the 334th Regiment passed by on their way forward. The artillery from our Division was on the east side of the Weser firing at the fleeing enemy.

At 1330, the remainder of the message center personnel arrived. The three of us related the previous day's events to the other four messengers.

In the middle of the afternoon, Crable and I decided to walk about a mile to the railway tracks to look at the abandoned rail guns. On the tracks were two large 128 mm artillery guns. They were on railway platforms and pointed in the direction of the crossing site.

"John, I wonder what happened? I don't think they fired at us during the crossing. I know artillery shells when I hear them."

"You were lucky. Someone spotted them as they got ready to fire. Some tanks on our side of the river fired at them and knocked out the crews. We heard that they never fired a shot at the battalion."

The accuracy of the American tank crews was soon evident by bits of flesh that were scattered around the platform. We also noted a series of elaborate trenches that had been used for these anti-aircraft guns. All the ack ack guns had been rendered useless by some American outfit since their barrels at the ends were split. As John and I strolled back to the CP, he said, "Don, I think you'd be interested in what happened at the farm house after you left for the crossing."

"Anyone get hurt?"

"No. But you remember that when you went to sleep Thursday night, some of the fellas and the DPs were having a great party. During the party, they persuaded one of the Russian women to lay for all the guys in the morning. She started taking them on a little after 0800. Someone kept going up to lay with her about every 15 or 20 minutes. Most of them said she was a big as a house. Rochie took his turn. A little after 1100, George Teets decided he would go up. He got up to the bedroom but she refused to open her legs for him. He came down in about ten minutes. He couldn't understand the reason for her refusal. In the afternoon, we heard she just got tired and didn't want any more guys on top of her. But George's ego was sure crushed."

"John, if I know George, his ego has just been aroused."

The evening was spent in listening to the radio. From the conversations around the CP, we knew the next big objective of our Division would be the large city of Hannover.

XXIV

HANNOVER

Sunday, April 8, 1945

Since the Second Battalion was not scheduled to move in the morning, the messengers were permitted to sleep until the very late hour of 0930. During the remainder of the morning, various units of the 84th Division passed through Meissen where we were located. Among the outfits was the Division's artillery. When Innes saw them, he remarked, "White Battalion better get ready to move. We never stay behind the caissons."

Prisoners continued to pour in. However, there was an unusual one today. Just after 1030, Corporal Kern announced, "Company G has captured a 'field wife.' "

Dawes asked, "What a field wife?"

"You know. She accompanies some Wehrmacht officer and lives with him while his outfit is on the line."

"Fellas, let's go see this field wife."

All seven messengers went to observe her at the PW compound. She was an attractive tall blond, about 5 feet 6 inches in height. Over her body she wore a long German field coat. Naturally all eyes were on her while she was at the compound. We knew from rumors that the European armies like the French, German and Russian that this arrangement was the practiced custom. As we watched her, Teets remarked, "I wonder if that custom will ever be seen in our Army?"

The alert to move was given at 1300. We sat and waited. By 1600, no trucks had arrived. A hot meal was served at 1630. At 1800, we finally boarded the trucks. The ride took less than

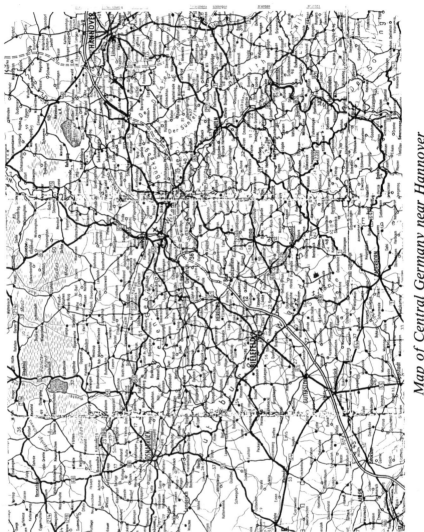

Map of Central Germany near Hannover

an hour. We arrived in the town of Kleinenbremen. This was to be our location for that night.

An hour after our arrival, two planes from the Luftwaffe appeared in the sky over Kleinenbremen. The 55th anti-aircraft battery which was in the town with us started pouring their shells and machine gun fire skyward. This failed to deter the German pilots who continued onto the Weser where their bombs were dropped. Every man in the communications platoon was outside observing the action. This was clearly against regulations but some were no longer being enforced because of the changing situation.

John and I made three message runs to Company E before retiring at 2130.

Monday, April 9, 1945

At 0510, the messengers were awakened to partake of a hot breakfast. At 0700, the whole battalion was ready to board the trucks. After waiting one hour and a half, the order to board was issued. The convoy proceeded due north to Buckeberg. Here a long wait was had while the other two battalions of the 335th assembled. When the other units had fully arrived, the long convoy started out on Highway 65. If this road was followed, we would go directly into Hannover.

After passing thru Venlen, the convoy turned off the highway and went due north. When the village of Summern was reached, a right turn was made. This brought us back to Highway 65 at Stadthagen.

Bernie Cohn turned and made an inquiry of me. "According to your map, Don, why didn't we just go straight ahead on 65?"

"Bernie," I replied. "I think the answer is mines. The enemy can't mine every road so the best idea is to mine the main roads."

At the next town, Bad Nenrdorf, the same maneuver was repeated. A right turn was made at Haste. A few miles beyond, the trucks moved onto one of the German Autobahns. It was a

525

four lane highway. The two concrete lanes going in opposite directions were separated by a moat.

But the directions puzzled us. We were going south, away from Hannover, on the Autobahn. Teets looked at my maps and noted, "I'll bet we're going back to 65."

His prediction turned out to be true. Our long detour had caused us to miss only two or three miles of Highway 65. We guessed that the road was mined. Just as we turned onto Highway 65, a stop was made. The order came, "Hit the ditches."

Ahead we could hear the rumble of artillery fire. But it soon ceased. The journey continued on foot.

At 1600, The Second Battalion entered Lathwehren. We were ordered to move into some vacated houses. After occupying a vacant bedroom, John and I went to see Company E which was lodged about a mile ahead in the town of Kirchwehren.

Just after 1800, the Luftwaffe made their nightly appearance. Since there was no anti-aircraft outfit nearby, the heavy machine gun section of Company H fired at the two planes. As usual, all the men in the whole battalion were outside to watch the fireworks. But a half dozen were injured by flying shrapnel. One hour later, Sergeant Butler called a meeting of the messengers.

"I've been informed by Captain Nablo that no one is to be outside when there is an air attack or an air raid. Some men in the battalion have suffered some needless wounds. I am going to enforce this from now on. Any questions?"

Rochester asked, "If we go out and fire our pieces, can we be outside?"

"No way. Our rifles can't bring down any aircraft. Colonel Learman doesn't want anyone injured because of our own actions."

Fifteen minutes after his lecture, Sergeant Butler returned.

"The attack on Hannover is on for tomorrow. Colonel Learman wants three messengers from the rifle companies to accompany him. Who is going?"

Crable, Rochester and Teets raised their hands. All the messengers knew the correct arrangements.

Since John was going on the attack, I made all the necessary runs to Company E that evening. My last run was completed at 2245. I went to sleep.

Tuesday, April 10, 1945

At 0045, Corporal Kern shook me.

"Edwards, you're to take a Lieutenant from the 771st Tank Battalion to your company."

"I'll be there as soon as I put on my boots."

Outside the CP was a jeep with the Lieutenant and his driver. In two minutes we were at Company E. I stayed some time while the tank officer met all the officers of the Company. After picking up a report, I walked back to Lehrwahren.

Upon my arrival at 0200, John, Rochie and George were at the door awaiting the Battalion Commander. I spoke to John saying, "What do you think about this one, John?"

"You never know, Don, but I think the Weser was the last tough one. Jerry will put up some resistance, but I don't think they have many tanks left to defend Hannover very long."

"I hope you're right. Expect to see you tomorrow evening."

"I hope so too, Don."

By 0600, the entire Message Center was up. Ninety minutes later, we went by jeep to Harenberg to await reports on the attack on Hannover. The day was bright and sunny. This meant that the Air Force could be called upon if the situation became sticky.

During our waiting, the messengers were detailed to search the German PWs as they arrived. This was necessary because they might try to keep weapons on their person back in camp. The procedure was routine until Bernie called the three of us to note a prisoner before him.

This Wehrmacht soldaten was a man over 40 years of age. He was small, only about 5 feet 5 inches in height. He looked as if he was carrying everything he owned on his person. He had on a full pack plus another small bag and loaded pockets. Bernie instructed him to pull out everything and display it on the ground before him. The prisoner complied. Bernie noted,

"This guy is carrying everything. There's his money, his family pictures showing his wife and three kids, his keys, four pencils, two pens and notes of all types. Don, would you and Skinney pad him down?"

Innes and I proceeded to do this. We made sure he wasn't concealing anything on his person. After we finished, Cohn told him to repack and proceed to join the other prisoners.

In the afternoon, we continued with our searching detail. Just after 1330, Dawes returned with some unusual news.

"Fellas, the 84th just liberated a Jewish concentration camp. Some of the Jews are sitting on the road about two blocks away. Who wants to go with me to see them?"

"Vern, I'll go if Bernie and Innes don't mind."

When Dawes and I arrived, there were ten small Jewish boys eating some food that had been provided by some American soldiers. One of the Jewish men, who looked to be about 12 years of age and was from Poland, spoke good English. I started to talk with him.

"Son, how old are you?"

"I'm 18."

"How long have you been held by the Germans?"

"A little over two years. They picked me up in the ghetto in Warsaw."

"How many camps have you been in?"

"This is my third camp."

"What's been the worst thing that happened to you?"

"The beatings by the SS guards. Whenever they wanted to, they just hit you. It might be with a butt, a whip or their hands. They seemed to like to hit us."

"What have they been feeding you?"

"Usually we got a bowl of soup a day. We might get something more often but lately it's been just one bowl a day."

"Did you know we were coming near Hannover?"

"Yes, for the last two weeks, the SS guards have told us that they would kill all of us before the Americans arrived. Most of them left just two days ago."

All ten of the Jews had little or no flesh on their bodies. Welts were present everywhere from their toes to the top of their heads. We later wondered what the SS had done to their private parts. As we watched and talked to them, a lieutenant from another outfit warned us that they were not to be given any food, regardless of our inclination to feed them.

After an hour, Vern Dawes and I left. As we walked back to our detail, I remarked to Vern, "Vern, what I've just seen, I don't think I'll ever forget. The war will probably fade from memory, but those were the most pathetic human beings I have ever seen or hope to see in my whole life."

"Don, you really said the right thing then."

Upon our return I related to Cohn and Innes what we had seen. They departed and came back a half hour later. Bernie sat down and cried for fifteen straight minutes.

At 1530, a jeep came to take us into Hannover. The Germans had left the city.

Upon our arrival, the streets were crowded with people of all types. We could see that many were looting the shops along the streets. Most of the throng appeared to be persons who were not German. We guessed that they were DPs who had been liberated by the 84th Division.

Just after entering Hannover on Wunsroger Strasse, a right turn was made. The jeep stopped before a group of apartments where we were to reside. John, Rochie and Teets were already in an apartment on the third floor. They had taken over an apartment consisting of a living room, a small kitchen and two bedrooms. Crable had secured one of the bedrooms for us. Later Cohn and Dawes would be the occupants of the other. I asked John how everything had gone in the attack.

"I think it was the easiest one the battalion ever had. Near the railroad that you passed under, Company G ran into some machine gun fire. But the tanks came up and lobbed some shells and sprayed the area with their machine guns and that was the end. Our company lost two men when they went after a German tank withdrawing over the river in the city. But then the real trouble started. As the Germans kept retreating, the civilians came out into the streets. There was more excitement in the rear than in the front. Fights started breaking out all over the city. F and G had to stop their advance and clear the streets. If they hadn't done that, that mob would have gotten out of control. I think some of the other units from our Division are trying to clear the streets now."

"Anything else to report, John?"

"Yes, I got interviewed today."

"By whom?"

"We had just entered the city and this guy asks me what's going on. I told him the only thing I knew was that some rifle fire was going on. But he insisted he should be told more. Then, I found out he was a correspondent from some New York newspaper. He had never been to the front before and couldn't understand that all of us didn't know what was happening. I tried to explain to him that the further back you are, the clearer the picture is. I was a little peeved at his attitude. I also told him that the next time he came forward to bring a gun."

At 2000, we were fed a hot meal from the Company's kitchen. There was no danger of any counter-attack. Everyone knew the Germans had run out of gas.

After finishing our meal, all the messengers were ordered to the nearby grain elevator where the civilians were still gathering food. It took 25 GIs almost an hour to clear the area. A dozen or so of the civilians absolutely refused to leave. It then became necessary to have a few rifle shots fired over their heads before they knew we were serious about the orders we were giving.

Wednesday, April 11, 1945

Breakfast was served at 0730.

Back in our apartment, I noted that we were in a complex of apartments that formed a triangle. Battalion Headquarters Company occupied just one complete side of this triangle. The messengers' apartment had a view from two sides. In front of our apartment was a large open space. It appeared to be a park in peacetime. The space contained many tiny huts which housed many of the bombed-out civilians. At the edge of this park were some gardens apparently used to grow food. The gardens were occupied by tanks of the 771st Tank Battalion. Their tank tracks made one big mess of the soil.

Company E was located over two miles from the battalion headquarters. A round trip by John and me took nearly an hour to complete. Looking out the back window in the afternoon, I remarked, "John, I think the former tenants of this place left their bikes here."

"You're right. Let's grab one and tell the others about them. Their companies are farther away than ours."

Within ten minutes, every messenger possessed a German bike.

Twice during the day, we were called upon to assist in chasing the civilians away from the coal and lumber yards that were about two blocks from our apartment. In each instance shots had to be fired before some people would move from their task of looting.

After our supper meal at 1830, Skinney Innes and George Teets approached John and me. George spoke for the two of them and asked, "John, Don. We'd like to ask a favor of you."

"George, what is the favor?" I replied.

"Well, Skinney and I are going to do a little scouting. Rochie has already left. So if there are any messages for Company F, will one of you do them?"

"We'll take care of them, George. How long will your scouting last? The whole night?"

"Skinney and I are going to look for the SS."

"What SS? The Germans don't allow any women in their army. What SS are you talking about?"

"Sexually-starved German women. We thought we'd help them get over their hunger."

"George, I think you'll succeed in your venture and satisfy a few appetites."

Each night until we left Hannover, there would be only four messengers to occupy the apartment the entire night.

A PRIVATE'S DIARY

Thursday, April 12, 1945

Because of the constant looting that was taking place at the nearby coal and lumber yards, the Battalion Headquarters Company was assigned permanent guard duty. The general tour of duty was to be for a two hour period. We were instructed that we should fire above the heads of the looters if they refused to move. The authorities believed that, in most cases, a few whizzing bullets would be force enough. Since all seven messengers were required to stand guard duty, I warned Rochester, Innes and Teets.

"We'll take your messages if need be at night, but none of us are going to take your tours of duty on guard."

All three agreed to this stipulation.

During the day, messages were taken to the four companies instructing them to disburse their companies over a wide area and to set up road blocks at various points throughout Hannover. A curfew was imposed on all except the military.

After supper that evening, Sergeant Butler came to the four remaining messengers.

"Men, some of the company jeeps are going to look over the Jewish concentration camp at Ahlem. Who wants to go?"

All four raised their hands. Sergeant Butler continued with, "I'll hold any messages until all of you return."

Larry Gardiner drove us to Ahlem, about three miles away, in less than five minutes.

The Ahlem camp was surrounded by two barb wire fences. The outer one had been electrically charged to prevent escape. At each of the four corners of the compound was an elevated guard post mounted with two search lights to illuminate the area between the two fences. Just inside the huge gates was a well built barracks. This was for the SS guards. There were two offices plus two bedrooms, each of which contained two beds. Just at the end of this barracks and attached to it but with a different entrance was a huge bare room. This was the gas chamber. There were only two doors to this concrete built structure. Not a single window. At this camp no other torture chambers existed.

532

HANNOVER

In the middle of this camp was a large open space where the inmates must have assembled for roll call. To the left was a large barracks which housed the kitchen. There was, of course, no dining hall for the prisoners. Since we were told that each man had only a small soup bowl and a spoon with which to eat, he took his food back to his cot.

On the other side of the open grounds were two large barracks. The windows in each of them, of which there were about three, were about 25 by 30 inches. They were covered with paper. The barracks themselves were constructed of some flimsy wood. Upon stepping into one of the barracks, a terrible sight and smell were encountered. The stench drove us out for a few seconds. Crable remarked, "I've been used to slit trenches and out door latrines but this odor is beyond description."

All four of the messengers then reentered the barracks. Inside was a very narrow aisle down the center. On each side of the aisle were two rows of bunks. Each bunk was three tiers high. The distance between these bunks was so narrow that none of us could get through without difficulty. On each bunk was a thin straw tick. Over that was one old tattered blanket. There was a stove in the center but inspection revealed that it had not been used for a long period of time. On the floor were piles of human excretion. Vomited food was also present on the floor. Dirt had been allowed to accumulate on the wood floor until it was no longer possible to clean it. Every tick stenched with urine. Inside the hut, we noted several huge bull whips as well as some cat-o-nine tails. We knew their use.

When we emerged from our inspection of the horrible barracks, we noticed an old bus in the middle of the open area. About 20 former Jewish inmates were waiting to be taken away. One of them spoke excellent English so I asked him some questions.

"How do you feel now?"

"Not too bad, considering everything that has happened."

"How long have you been in this camp at Hannover?"

"I'm not too sure, but I think it's over a year."

"Were you in any other camps before coming here?"

"Yes, two others. This is the best of the three."

"Where did the Germans pick you up?"

"In Poland. At the beginning of 1943."

"How do you feel about your bad treatment?"

"I don't know, because I thank my God I'm alive."

"What work did you perform at this camp?"

"Seven days a week, we went out to do work on the roads or clean up the rubble."

"Did the German civilians ever see or talk with any of you?"

"We saw them every day, but they just ignored us. I think they were afraid of the guards."

"What happened if you couldn't work?"

"After a few days, you are taken away and put in that building over there. You know what that is, don't you?"

"Yes, the guide showed the chamber to us."

"And whenever new people would come, the guards would take the weaker ones away."

"Did anyone ever try to escape from the camp?"

"No, because we were weak and the first fence would stop you if you tried to get away."

"Did you ever think the Americans would come to release you and the others?"

"We knew that you would come because the air raids kept getting worse and worse. My friends and I thank you Americans for coming in time to save us. We all thanked God that you came."

After a few more questions, we departed for our jeep which was parked outside the camp gates. Upon exiting the grounds, Bernie Cohn again began to sob quietly. The rest of us tried to cheer him up telling him the worst for these Jews was over.

When we arrived back at our apartment, John said, "Don, I may forget parts of this war, but I don't ever think I'll forget that visit to that concentration camp."

"I think that will be true of me, John. When they show on Movietone news how the concentrations camps looked, they'll never be able to convey the stench."

534

HANNOVER

Friday, April 13, 1945

While standing in the chow line for breakfast, Sergeant
Hal Brazil mentioned, "Did all of you hear the big news?"

"What happened?" I replied.

"President Roosevelt died."

"You're kidding. I almost forgot we had a president since
the Yalta Conference."

"We've got a new President."

"Who is it?"

"Name is Harry Truman. And I heard that a relative of his
is on the Division staff. So we've got pull in Washington."

"I hope it does some of the men who want to get out early
some good."

At 1000, I started my guard shift with Skinney at the grain
elevator which was adjacent to the coal and lumber yards. We
patrolled all three places.

During our two and one half hours of duty, many German
civilians would come and peer at us. When they did this, Skinney and I would take our rifles from our shoulders and place
our weapon in both our hands. No one ventured to challenge
our authority.

After supper, Crable and I decided to start a bike tour of
Hannover. Our aim was to see various parts of Germany's
twelfth largest city each night until our unit was ordered to
move forward. For this evening's tour, we pedaled into the center of the city. It was in complete ruin. The only place we could
recognize was the site of the Hauptbahnhof or main railway
station. As we toured, John noted, "I guess it's appropriate that
all the buildings around Adolf Hitler Place are gone."

"I agree, John, but I don't think anyone back home could
realize what destruction has been caused by the Allied bombers
unless they can see this."

Our tour took over three hours.

535

A PRIVATE'S DIARY

Saturday, April 14, 1945

Guard duty on this day was undertaken in the morning from 0800 to 1000 and in the afternoon from 1400 to 1600. Fewer civilians were peering at us today.

After my morning guard session, Corporal Kern informed the messengers, "About eight blocks from here is a German factory that made Army Jackets for the Wehrmacht. Somebody says that there are jackets for all."

Inside the clothing mill, we found hundreds and hundreds of short German Army jackets. They were very short in the style of the Eisenhower jacket. Since we had no short jackets with us, souvenirs were taken to our quarters. Since they were a light brown, many of the GIs began to wear them inasmuch as they blended in with our brown pants. Two days later an order was issued banning their use.

For our evening bike tour, Crable and I visited the eastern section of Hannover. Since our quarters were located in the far western section, it was necessary to bike across the center part of Hannover.

Near the eastern limits of the city was a huge DP camp. It housed, at least, 5,000 people of all nationalities, although Polish and Russians persons were in the majority. We stopped at the gate to converse with the guards from our Division. I inquired, "Can we go inside the camp?"

"You sure can, but I don't advise it."

"Anything wrong in there?"

"Nothing, but chances are you'll be approached by the women to have some fun. You know what that is?"

"We do."

"Two nights ago, some GIs from the 333rd were in there and while they were having their fun, everything they had was taken from them. They came out to the gate here and were naked. We laughed but it wasn't funny to them. We got them some new clothes but we're trying to warn guys about the risk they're taking."

536

HANNOVER

Sunday, April 15, 1944

Since the units in Hannover were spread over a wide area, no Catholic service was held this day.

After supper, I made a visit to Ed Nelson, who was now a medical aide man attached to the Anti-Tank Company of the 335th Regiment. My last visit with him had been in November in Prummern.

"Ed, how has the world been treating you?"

"Fine, Don. I can't complain yet although I enjoyed being at the Aid Station rather than this job."

"What do you do with Anti-Tank?"

"The other Medics and I sort of stay behind the Company when they set up a defensive screen with their guns. Then, if anyone is hit, we try to come to assist them."

"Have you had much work?"

"Not lately. I think the Company only lost one man killed in action in 1945, but there were several last year. I don't look for any more but you never know in this war. How have things been with you?"

"Pretty good, Ed. My worst experience came with my Company Commander."

"How did that happen, Don?"

My encounter in Wegberg was explained to Ed Nelson. After I finished, he asked me, "Did you really think he was going to pull the trigger?"

"Ed, I thought so!"

Monday, April 16, 1945

Just after breakfast, Corporal Kern came to see all the messengers.

"I've got bad news and good news for you."

"Give us the bad news first, Corporal," stated Teets.

"The 335th Regiment is going to take up the attack today from the 333rd and 334th which passed through us the day after we took this city."

"When do we leave then?" asked George.

537

"That's the good news. The Second Battalion is going to stay in Hannover. Only Red and Blue are going to try to reach the Elbe."

"Oh, you lucky women of Hannover, you're still going to have me to take care of you for a while longer," answered Teets.

"I'll continue to help you, George," echoed Rochester.

Since both John and I had taken our assigned guard duty in the morning, we decided on an afternoon tour to the far east side. Our destination was the Hannover zoo.

Since the zoo was located next to the main rail line, large craters and shattered cages were seen in all parts of the area. However, all the living animals were very quiet. No visitors had been permitted in over a year because of its hazardous location. The heavy bombing had made visiting impossible. We seemed to be a curiosity to many of the animals.

As we traveled around Hannover, we noticed that the rail tracks were the apparent objective of our Air Forces. The main railway in the city ran in a general southeast to northwest direction. Damages to houses along the right of way was always heavy regardless of the district. The surprising thing was that the tracks themselves were in excellent condition. It was apparent to us that the third Reich's top priority was to keep their rail system in first class condition regardless of the destruction to the surrounding areas.

Tuesday, April 17, 1945

Inasmuch as the guard duty during daylight hours at the lumber and coal site had been reduced to one man, Crable and I did not have a tour of duty.

In the morning, John wanted to go to the Hannover Town Hall to ascertain if any former German soldiers had left their Luger pistol around which had been recovered by the police of the city. In fifteen minutes of biking, we were at the municipal building. While John went in to secure a souvenir, I stood watch over the two bikes. If there was no guard, they might easily disappear. I was looking at the park across the street

538

when a British soldier came up and asked me, "Yank, have you got a light for this cigarette?"

"Sure have, Tommy, although I don't smoke."

"Thanks, I like that."

"Are you stationed here or where have you come from?"

"I've been in Hannover here for about three months as a PW. It's been rough, let me tell you."

"When did Jerry capture you?"

"Back in Normandy on June 20. They had a counterattack which cut some of us off. We tried to fight our way out but Jerry was all around me and my mates."

"How was your treatment by the enemy?"

"In France, it wasn't half bad. We got bombed two or three times by our own planes getting into Germany. First, they put us in some camp near Daniz. Then we got moved to Breslau. Finally, we were moved from Breslau to Hannover when the Russians started getting close. Each move kept getting worse. I got on me same shirt and pants as when they took me. Haven't had any soap since October to wash with."

"Sounds bad. What was the food like that the Germans gave you?"

"Same as I told you. It kept getting worse. During the last two months, we had one potato with the jacket on for our Sunday dinner. That was the best meal of the week. The rest of the time, it was soup, soup and soup. It was just water. Guess I lost fifty pounds being a PW."

"How have we been treating you?"

"Oh, you Yanks with the 'white ax' are just great. When you came to the camp, your fellas gave us those great K rations that you have. They are really good."

"I don't think, Tommy, most of my fellow GIs would agree with you on how good those K rations are."

"But you've got to remember that we hadn't eaten for three days. Just before you 'white ax' Yanks got here, those bloody Germans wanted to move us again. Better than three of every four refused. We thought they might shoot us but the guards just left. We thought they might beat us again like they did on the last march. Can you see those welts on my legs? Some bloody bastard kept hitting me with his rifle as we walked."

"I think I should have introduced myself, I'm Don Edwards from Detroit."

"My name is Tom Johnson from Leicester. Have you heard of it?"

"Oh, yes. I'm a soccer fan. It's what you call football in England."

"A football fan. Isn't that a bit unusual in America?"

"Yes, it is. I get kidded about it by some of my fellow soldiers but I still like the game better than the sports that are popular in America."

"Do you think, Don, it will ever become popular in America?"

"I doubt it. Most Americans think of it as a game that only foreigners play."

"Nice chatting with you, Don. I am supposed to get a ride to the back somewhere today. Expect to be home in a couple of days. Thanks for the light."

"Tom, since I don't smoke, you can have a pack of cigarettes from a GI from the 'white ax' outfit."

"Thanks again, you are sure nice guys."

For our evening trip, John and I decided to circle around the fringes of the central part of Hannover. We rode into the center of Hannover. Then a count of blocks without any standing buildings were made. In each of the four major directions, we counted twenty consecutive long city blocks without a single untouched structure. From this circle of twenty blocks there would be another ten to fifteen in which fifty percent or more of the structures would be damaged in some degree. In these ten to fifteen blocks there would be some civilians who were largely living in the cellars of these buildings. As we circled around there was one noteworthy item that John noted, "Don, did you notice that every street is free of rubble. The only place that isn't true is where a railway viaduct has been hit. Those Germans did everything in their power to keep this war going."

I added, "And we know who was cleaning up the rubble."

HANNOVER

My tour of guard duty came from 0500 to 0700. At night two guards were still being used. My companion for this tour was Skinney Innes. He was so tired from his nightly escapade that he asked if he could sleep. His request was granted for I anticipated no trouble.

Just as daylight broke before 0630, I was on the second floor of the grain elevator. I saw an elderly German woman taking coal and placing the chunks into two wooden baskets. I yelled, "Nein, nein meine frau. Gehen sie aus. Nein coal."

She looked up from below and spotted me. She began to run with her two baskets.

"Halt, halt meine frau. Nein coal mit du. Halt!"

She did not stop. I took my carbine and fired three shots far to her left. Upon hearing the bullets, she immediately dropped the baskets and was beating Jesse Owens with her speed.

I ran down to the ground floor where Innes had awakened.

"Don, what's all the shooting about?"

"Skinney, come with me. We have to get some coal back."

I explained what had happened. The next day, I would hear about it.

At breakfast that morning, I sat down next to a soldier who was not a familiar face at the battalion CP.

"Good morning, I'm Don Edwards, I don't think I've met you."

"I don't think you have. I'm John Stinson from the 34th Infantry Division."

"Are they in this area?"

"No, I don't think so. They're probably still in Italy. I've been a Prisoner of War for the last 26 months."

"Why, John, that was over two years ago. Where were you captured?"

"North Africa. I was delivering a message to my company when up popped six Germans on the road. This was near Kassarine Pass."

541

"What did you say your job was?"

"I was a messenger from my company to battalion."

"John, you wouldn't believe it, but that's my job too. Go ahead and tell me again what happened."

"I had a message to deliver to my company commander. I was alone on a road when I was surrounded. I couldn't take on six Germans by myself. I was led by one of their men back to their headquarters where I was questioned. Boy, was I scared. But they knew my unit since there were about 25 other GIs there. I got flown on a plane to Rome and shipped by rail to Stettin."

"What did you do as a PW?"

"A group of us worked in the dock area in Stettin. We loaded and unloaded German ships of all types of cargo. It was easy work until about a year ago. Then, our bombers came. I was lucky and didn't get hit by our Air Force. You may think the Germans know how to bomb and shell. Compared to us, they're way behind. Our bombs come down like a knife cutting paper. Our planes and bombs really terrified the Germans any time they came."

"How were you treated?"

"Good. I think the Americans got the best treatment of any prisoners taken by the Germans. We heard the worst treatment was reserved for the Russian PWs. The food was pretty good until last fall. Even our guards began to complain that they weren't getting enough to eat. When the Battle of the Bulge started, food got better. The guards began to tell us that their armies would be in Paris in a week. But right after Christmas, they wouldn't say anything more about Belgium. We and they knew that they would not win the war."

"How did you get from Stettin to Hannover?"

"When the Russians got within 50 kilometers of Stettin, they started marching us across Germany to here in Hannover. It was tough since we weren't used to walking a long time. During the last month, we had just one whole potato a day to eat. Plus their cheap coffee. Your fellow 'hatchet men' released us a week ago. You've got a nice bunch since they were willing to give us their own food from their packs."

542

"What did you think of your job as messenger?"

"I liked it and I was lucky. If I hadn't been captured, I probably would have been wounded or killed. How has your group fared so far?"

"Frankly John, we've been lucky. Only one has been killed and only one other was seriously wounded. Two including myself had minor hits."

A half hour later, John Stinson of the 34th Infantry Division was on his way back to France and shipment to the United States.

Since it rained and was windy throughout the afternoon and evening, Crable and I postponed any tours through Hannover. However, the weather did not prevent Rochester, Teets and Innes from their nightly activities.

Thursday, April 19, 1945

In the afternoon, Sergeant Butler called me in for a chat.

"Edwards, Colonel Learman got a complaint from some German that you were shooting at old ladies."

"Sarge, let me explain what happened yesterday morning on guard."

The detailed explanation was given. After I finished, the Sergeant added, "You did the right thing. Battalion also heard that everyone is afraid of being shot if they try to loot the coal yard. A little fear may do the people here some good."

In the evening, Crable and I toured the southeastern section of Hannover. There were two more slave labor camps in this area but we decided not to visit them. As we biked, John noted, "More and more civilians seem to be out each night." On Hildenssheimer Strasse, I even noticed some children were playing."

Friday, April 20, 1945

The morning hours brought us the news that parts of the 84th Division had reached the Elbe River. At breakfast, the rumor had been confirmed that the oncoming Russians would be met at this river although they were still fighting in Berlin.

543

After supper, John and I took another tour. This time we went out through the northwestern section of Hannover and reached the autobahn. Our return trip took us through the villages of Garbsen, Seelze and Ahlen. In Seelze, we observed another slave labor camp. We always consulted the guards on duty as to the feasibility of visiting these camps. I inquired of this one.

"Can we go safely into the camp?"

"Yes, you can," answered the GI on duty.

"That's a first," I answered. "We've always been warned not to go in the others. What's different about this one?"

"This is an all Dutch camp. There are a lot more men than women in this one. When we got here, the Krauts had them strictly separated. But I don't think it's that way any more. But you'll be safe in this camp."

As we toured the Dutch camp, we noticed that every hut had flowers growing on the outside. There was no trash to be seen. The men and women of the Netherlands just waved at us but made no attempt to talk with John or me. Compared to the Jewish concentration camp just a few miles away, it was the difference between heaven and hell in appearance.

Saturday, April 21, 1945

At breakfast that morning, Sergeant John Mulligan said, "Red and Blue are attacking this morning at Gorleben near the Elbe. They don't expect much trouble."

"Where is Gorleben?" asked someone at the table.

"The biggest nearby city is Wittenberge. That's on the Elbe. We heard these are the only Germans left on the west bank of the Elbe in the Division's sector."

Upon my return to the apartment, I looked at the maps to ascertain where the 84th was located except for our battalion. I figured that we were over 100 miles from the fighting. The Second Battalion was clearly in the rear at this time.

Outside of the normal message runs which numbered about six to ten daily, the messengers had a great deal of time on their hands. John Crable and I spent much of it reading the books

which were always being sent to the various affiliated companies to be read by the enlisted men. Each afternoon, John, Bernie, Vern and I would play some type of card game, usually,
bridge.

The other three messengers, namely, Rochester, Teets and
Innes spent a good deal of their daylight hours in sleeping.

Each morning, Rochester would boast of the female conquests he had made the previous night. He constantly bragged
that he had a new fraulein each night and that all of them
wanted him to come back since his technique was the best.

Teets and Innes operated as a pair in their nightly prowls.
They experienced little difficulty in their endeavors. They stated
that most of the women with whom they slept had had their
former husbands or boyfriends killed in the war. George's
favorite expression was "they're always wet and ready to go the
whole night long."

For our nightly bike tour, Crable and I went out to the
autobahn or the northeastern side of Hannover. The autobahn
was loaded with trucks that were ferrying supplies to the front
far away. At a bridge near Brink, we were stopped by two GIs
from the 102d who had a roadblock erected to check on the
trucks and other vehicles that were traveling. The usual bull
session was had with them.

"How do you like this duty of checking on vehicles?" was
my inquiry.

"It's not bad. Better than guarding the PWs."

"What do you have to check on the trucks?"

"We see where they are going and that they are not carrying anything unauthorized."

"What is unauthorized?"

"Some of these truckers pick up some women in France or
Belgium and want to take them all over. We've almost had a
fight with one or two guys over that."

"What do you do with these girls that you find?"

"We take them out. Someone comes to pick them up
later."

"Anything else?"

545

"We check to see when they left the place where they picked up supplies to see that they're not wasting too much time stopping in the bars or beer gardens."

"What are you two 'hatchet men' doing in Hannover?"

We explained that our battalion was somewhat of an occupational force in the Hannover area.

Sunday, April 22, 1945

My tour of duty at the grain elevator came from 0300 to 0500. Skinney, who generally slept, and I had nothing happen during that time.

At breakfast, the usual rumors about moving up front were heard. Most of the men affiliated with the Second Battalion dismissed them. The progress of the war was so good that we felt we would never be needed again. The feeling was that our battalion would remain in Hannover until the war would end. Then, we would remain as an army of occupation. No word had been directly received as to what the other two battalions of the 335th were doing near the Elbe. We would learn later that an attack on Blue Battalion was what caused us to leave this area.

John and I attended mass at 1100 in a nearby German Catholic church. Attendance was very poor. Fear was subsiding. The same procedure that was used in Krefeld, was repeated here. No German civilians were allowed at our Army service.

In the afternoon, rain began to come down in sheets in Hannover. John and I decided to remain in our cozy apartment and play cards with Bernie and Vern. As expected, the rain did not deter Rochester, Teets and Innes from their nightly prowls.

XXV

THE ELBE RIVER

Monday, April 23, 1945

Rumors still persisted that our battalion was about to move just after breakfast. The entire morning passed without any movement.

At lunch time, I chatted with Corporal John Kern about this possibility of moving.

"Corporal, do you think we're going to move?"

"The grapevine has it that Colonel Learman went to a meeting at Regimental Headquarters this morning or yesterday. We think he got orders to move."

At 1400, Sergeant Butler appeared in our apartment to announce, "Four messengers report downstairs to take our relief to the companies."

At that particular moment, both George Teets and Bernie Cohn were absent. I conferred with Crable.

"John, you take the relief to Company E. I'll do what's necessary to lead them to Company G."

"That's a good idea, Don."

The four of us — John, Skinney, Vern and I — reported. Instructions were given to us by Sergeant Carlson.

"The Major and Sergeant from the Engineers will take you out to the Autobahn and Highway 3. There you will pick up a jeep a piece and take that to your respective company. After that, return here to battalion."

In front of the Command Post was a large German automobile. In the front seat was a Major and a Sergeant from the

547

171st Engineer Battalion. The former was in the driver's seat. The four messengers squeezed into the back seat. The Major proceeded to drive at breakneck speeds. Rarely did the speedometer go below 80 kilometers (50 miles). Our route was out Highway 3 through northeastern Hannover. While riding on the Alfe Getterheer Strasse, a small dog appeared on the trolley tracks in the path of the speeding auto. The Major attempted to apply the brakes but a 'Yip' was heard. The wheels arose slightly from the roadway. The Major remarked, "Just another damn Jerry dog dead."

After Highway 3 passed under the Autobahn, the vehicle turned around and parked. We were here to await the advance party of the 171st Engineers. We waited nearly three hours. John and I walked around the area but we could do nothing else since we had brought no reading material with us. As we strolled, John noted, "That Major is typically Army. He sped out here like 60, killed that dog, and we've been waiting more than two hours now."

"So true, John, so true." was my reply.

Just moments before 1700, four jeeps appeared. They were flagged down by the Major who conferred with the officer in each jeep. We were called.

The Major spoke, "My understanding is that each of you will lead one jeep to your respective company. Take the officer to your company commander. If you need a ride back to your headquarters, we'll take care of that."

Since each messenger knew where all five companies of the battalion were located, my task of leading my assigned jeep to Company G presented no problem. Upon reach our destination, I proceeded to take my assigned officer to Lieutenant Dean Gattenbein, who was the commander of Company G.

Upon my return to the messenger's apartment, George Teets met me and shouted, "Where in the hell have you and Crable been? Bernie and I have taken three messages to your company this afternoon. Can't you guys stay around here some of the time?"

I lost my temper.

Geeorge W. Teets — Scottdale, PA

"George W. Teets of Scottdale, Pennsylvania. I don't know where Bernie was but I got a good idea that you were out whoring around this afternoon. At two, Butler told us to report to take somebody to each company. I took over for Company G. I've been gone three and a half hours doing your job. I've taken your messages at night when you've been sleeping around with

549

every frau and fraulein in town. Now if you want to make something of it, I'll lay you out flat."

"Ok, Don, ok. I'm sorry. I'm sorry, I didn't realize what had happened."

At that moment, John appeared and told me to control my temper.

After supper, six of the messengers proceeded to pack their equipment. Rochester had to take off for one last fling.

At 1930, Vernon Dawes took a look out our apartment window.

"Fellas, the battalion's on the trucks!"

Everyone picked up their gear and fled down to the trucks. Sergeant Eric G. Carlson, the Battalion's Sergeant Major, met us.

"Where in the hell have you messengers been? We were going to leave you in Hannover."

As spokesman for the group, I replied, "Sergeant, neither Sergeant Butler nor Corporal Kern notified us. This is the first time we have not been in the trucks on time. I think you can check with them."

"I'll do that, Edwards."

After we had squeezed into our assigned truck, Vern Dawes turned to me and said, "Don, you sure have been on the warpath today."

At 1945, Rochester appeared. All six messengers shouted in unison, "Where have you been, dear Rochie? Where have you been?"

"You'd be surprised."

As we waited for the convoy to depart, Rochester began to brag about his amours while in Hannover. Someone asked him, "Rochie, how many did you lay with?"

"Ten in 13 days. Pretty good I'd say. Best night was a week ago when I took on two sisters and satisfied both of them. These Nazi dames just crave my prick. That's all there is to it."

At 2015, the wheels turned. Our departure was watched by a group of about 50 civilians. They just stood in stony silence and looked.

550

The trucks carrying the Battalion Headquarters Company proceeded through the heart of Hannover and northeasterly out Highway 3. The speed was slow since the other four affiliated companies were picked up at various points in the city.

After passing under the autobahn about 2100, rain started to fall on the open trucks. Although it was late April, the night seemed bitterly cold as the water splashed over our faces. Some of the men tried to lay down on the boards of the truck to catch some sleep while the remainder of us tried to do the same sitting on the hard benches. As we kept stopping and starting, someone exclaimed, "You'd think there's a war going on around here."

Tuesday, April 24, 1945

As the new day came, rain continued to pour on us. From my usual station at the end of the row, I could only see that we had passed through Celle and Luchow.

Just after 0300, the rain ceased. All were drenched.

Just after 0600, daylight appeared. At 0630, the convoy stopped for an entire hour before proceeding. But no guns could be heard.

Just after 0800, the convoy entered a small town. Orders were given to disembark. The communications platoon soon found a vacant house. A second floor bedroom was occupied by the messengers. Upon our entry into the room, Dawes exclaimed, "This place looks like it's been hit by a tornado."

This bedroom had two beds but the mattresses were lying next to the window. The contents of two dressers were scattered everywhere. We were in the dark as to the reason behind the disorganized room.

After ascertaining the location of Company E which was about 1,000 yards from the Message Center, the rest of the morning was spent in sleep.

After our lunch, I conferred with First Sergeant Sal Vignato of the Battalion Headquarters Company.

"Sarge, any idea what happened in this town?"

"Yes, our battalion would have stayed in Hannover but Blue Battalion had a German counter-attack here yesterday. They drove Company I, except for one platoon, right out of town. But Blue reorganized and pushed the Krauts into the Elbe which is about two miles from here."

I asked, "But Sarge, don't the Germans know the situation?"

"They do. But about 200 of them got high on some liquor and some SS officer persuaded them that the Americans could be driven back. Too bad because Company I lost about six men and the Germans had, at least, 25 killed.

The reason for the disorganized bedroom now became clear.

For our supper that day, the entire communications platoon had fresh-killed chicken. The reason for this meal was that in the backyards of the occupied houses were some hens that were running loose. A few members of the platoon caught them. They were slaughtered with their bayonets. The chickens were given to the cooks for the preparation of our evening meal.

Wednesday, April 25, 1945

Rumors about the coming meeting with the Russians were in full swing. Our 84th Division had been on the Elbe for nearly ten days and was patiently waiting for the meeting. But in checking our German maps, it showed that Berlin was about 40 to 50 miles from Gartow, where we were residing. And fighting was still going on in the German capital.

Just after 1200, a message was delivered to each company in the Second Battalion that both pleased and alienated the Infantry GIs. Three men from each company were to be granted a furlough to the U.S.A. Since this was the sixth month in which the 84th had been in combat, the general consensus was that the policy should have started after the second or third month in combat. In addition, the policy applied to every single outfit in the whole Division. Some outfits, like the Division's Headquarters Company, had probably not heard an artillery shell burst during their entire stay on the European continent. The discontent was summarized by Private Vernon McDaniel, one of the wire linemen in the platoon, who said, "If this battalion had continued to suffer the same casualty rate we had last November and December, hell, there would only be about three men who would be eligible to go."

The biggest activity for the communications platoon in the afternoon was the antics of two drunk ducks. Three members of the platoon had secured a bottle of liquor, called '45 volts' which was a cheap but powerful German liquor. Two ducks were seized from the backyard of an adjoining house. During the afternoon, the liquor was poured periodically down the throats of the hapless birds. At supper time, which came at 1700, the ducks were dead drunk. One of the two birds attempted to walk. Every time he got to his feet and moved a few steps, he would keel over. The walking of the ducks was watched by the platoon with great mirth until the birds gave up and laid down to sleep.

Although all realized the conclusion of the war was near, guard duty was still required. We were warned that Company I had become careless and had suffered needlessly because they had had no guards posted. Our present bedroom was proof of that. However, this duty lasted only from midnight until 0600 the following morning. No messengers complained after the sight of their bedroom that they had seen on the previous day.

Thursday, April 26, 1945

My tour of duty came from 0000 to 0100. I was alone but saw nothing move except guards at the other houses that were occupied by the battalion.

At 0530, the messengers were awakened. The conversation dealt with what would happen today. Cohn ventured a guess. "My guess is that we're going to cross the Elbe just like we did the Roer."

Only Vernon Dawes agreed with him on his prediction.

The rest of us took Crable's position which was, "We'll be shifted around a lot but we won't cross that river. If we were going across the Elbe, we would never have stayed in Hannover that long."

At 0600, we ate breakfast. We waited for the arrival of the trucks which came at 0800.

Just after 0900, the convoy left Gartow. Since there was no traffic on any roads, the convoy's speed was very fast. The route taken seemed to parallel the Elbe River although the stream itself was never seen. We passed through the large towns of Seehausen and Osterburg. After going through the latter city, where the 335th Regimental Headquarters were situated, the direction veered toward the east. However, the Elbe was not reached. Just after 1100, the convoy stopped in the small town of Hindenburg. The messengers were housed in an apartment above a store and beer garden. Inasmuch as no telephone lines were laid to the affiliated companies, all the messengers were busy the remainder of the day.

In the evening, Crable and I witnessed an incident which illustrated the fear the average German had of the Russians.

After supper, a few men from the communications platoon decided to look around the store beneath our apartment. In the process of snooping around, the wife of the store owner appeared. She screamed at the soldiers, "Ameridaner, Ameridaner, aus, aus."

Little attention was paid to her shouting. Then one of the soldiers said, "What do you want, the Russians? We'll get the Russians here."

Upon hearing the mention of the word 'Russians', the woman fled from the store.

Friday, April 27, 1945

The previous evening we had been informed that on this day our battalion would move into positions along the Elbe. The Second Battalion of the 335th was to relieve the Second Battalion of the 405th, which was one of the three regiments of the 102d Infantry Division.

At 0830, a jeep ride was given to all seven messengers to our new quarters which was about five miles away. The entire

Battalion Headquarters Company was to be lodged in a large villa. It looked to be the home of some well-to-do farmer or wealthy entrepreneur. The dwelling was extremely large — the largest we had seen in Germany. It consisted of a basement and two huge floors. The basement was slightly above ground level. A stairs had to be climbed to reach the first floor. On this floor were several huge rooms which branched off a long hall. At the end of this hall, the corridor split and led to two side entrances. The second floor was reached by a large staircase. There were six bedrooms on the upper floor. Across the huge open yard in front of the main dwelling were a few smaller houses and a shed that housed the machinery of the farm. There was also a stable consisting of 30 stalls for horses. There was a rumor that some Count owned the premises.

The messengers were assigned a large room on the first floor which could be entered from the outside. Upon our arrival, our counterparts from the 405th were still present. We introduced ourselves as from the Railsplitter Division and they did the same from the Ozark Division. We started conversing with them for less than two minutes when it abruptly ended. The eight Ozark messengers started conversing among themselves for our benefit.

We knew from past experience that there was somewhat of a good normal rivalry between the two American Divisions since both had gone into combat about the same time. Their sector usually adjoined ours. We were, also, aware of the fact that the 102d was a little peeved at the publicity that the Railsplitters had received as a result of the Bulge campaign.

Their messengers began to talk about the shelling they had received during the months of December and January. It seemed the enemy was shelling them day and night. And the winters in Germany must have been much more severe than those farther south in Belgium. And the Krauts were always launching counterattacks that their artillery was always breaking up. And that the messages they had to run were always through mortar and machine gun fire. For almost fifteen minutes, their bragging never stopped.

555

After a few minutes of their boasting, I thought Teets and Innes were going to take up their rifles and hit a few of them. As the unacknowledged spokesman for the group, I raised my fingers to my lips and shook my head. With my mouth, I silently said, "No, no, no."

Just before 1100, the messengers of the 405th departed. A wild flurry of words broke forth from the seven of us. Teets started off with, "Did you hear those bastards? Living in those deep protected cellars when we're plowing through that damn deep snow around Dochamps."

Innes added, "I'll bet that Jerry never shelled them once during the time we were down at Marche."

Rochester noted, "Those dumb birds. They don't know how lucky they were staying up north."

Crable tried to calm things down by asking me, "Don, how man attacks or counterattacks did the 102d have while we were gone in Belgium?"

"John, just one. The 102d went after Brachelen and Randerath at the end of January. Both places were deserted when they got there. The reports said they did not suffer a single casualty. Frankly, I think they were just a little jealous of us."

As our messenger group ranted and raved, Private Bill Keenoy, the new message center jeep driver, entered. He motioned to Crable and me.

"Don, John, I want to take you to the new Company E Headquarters. Can you leave this shouting mob?"

"Yes, Bill, we can go," I answered. "They'll calm down in a minute."

Company E was located in a small village called Berge about a mile away from the Elbe. The various platoons were placed in farm houses near the river. But no attempt was made to dig any foxholes or form any type of defensive line.

Upon our return to the villa, the other messengers were shown the locations of their various companies. Since each of the four companies was located, at least, five miles from the Battalion's CP, the messengers secured seven bicycles from the basement of our large dwelling. Pedaling five or more miles was much more desirable to walking that distance.

Just after lunch, a detail was ordered by Major Lamb to return to Hindenburg to clean up the site they had left. The personnel from the message center including the messengers were not included in the order inasmuch as our section usually left our living quarters in good order. However, both the radio and wire sections had to provide personnel to make their former quarters spic and span. The order was most unpopular as was the detail. While waiting to leave, muttered various remarks like, "We beat the Heinies but still have to do the work."

"Why can't those lousy Germans clean their own homes? After all we conquered them."

"So what if they're dirty. Get some PW to clean them."

"They were rotten to start with. We're going to make them better than they were."

Nevertheless the detail did as ordered.

Shortly after 1500, I had to deliver a message to Company E. Since I desired to see the famous Elbe, I secured permission to see the river. I was disappointed. The river seemed less than a quarter of a mile wide. The current moved ever so slowly northward. On the western bank where I stood was a high levee. A similar one could be seen on the eastern bank. In front of the western levee was a large weedy swamp. But the scene was a most peaceful one. On the American-held side, a few men from Company E were lazily strolling around. With my field glasses, I could not see a single soul on the opposite or German-held bank. It seemed like a dream.

Saturday, April 28, 1945

Another day of waiting for the Russians to appear on the river.

One reason for the furor over yesterday's clean-up by members of the communications platoon was the fact that the Battalion Headquarters kitchen as well as the other four kitchens of White Battalion now had German PWs to do the KP duty. Needless to say, this employment of the prisoners met with everybody's approval. Some Wehrmacht soldatens were daily getting across the river by the small ferry that was operated by the S-2 section of the battalion staff.

Midway through the afternoon, I chanced to look in at two German PWs who were processing some of the food to be eaten at our evening meal. One of them said to me, "Hallo there American soldier, how are you?"

"Hello, sprechen sie English?"

"Yes, I do. Sprechen sie Deutsch?"

"Ya, aber mein Deutsch ist nicht sehr gut."

"That's good, I will like to speak English with you. You Americans have really won the war you know. The Russians and English may think they won it, but it really was you Americans."

"Yes, I think we have. What is your name mein soldaten?"

"It is Hans. What is yours mein Herr?"

"My name is Donald Edwards. You may call me Don if you wish, but don't swear at me in Deutsch."

"I will not do that, Donald. You have a pistol and a rifle with you. I have nothing."

"I realize that, Hans, but I never use them unless I must do so."

"Tell me, Donald, is this the type of food you eat all the time?"

"Yes, it is, and most of our soldiers complain about it."

"I have been in the German Army since July of 1939, and I never saw such good food. Even after our Army defeated France, we did not receive food this good. Our Army always ate but our food was rather tasteless. Your coffee, you know, is real coffee. I haven't had that since 1939."

"Hans, I think we are well fed, but you know how some soldiers are."

"I know, Donald. May I ask where you get all those motors?"

"They all came from the United States."

"Does all the American Army have these motors or are you a favorite unit?"

"No, Hans, we are not a favorite unit. I am in the Infantry if you know what that is?"

"Yes, I do. You are a foot soldier."

"That is right. The Infantry or foot soldiers do not have many motors. We are supposed to walk."

"What about the artillery for the foot soldiers. Do they have motors or horses?"

"All our artillery have motors. There are very few horses in the American Army. I do not think we have any here in Germany. I know my Division has none."

"How did all of you Americans get over here?"

"I came over the Atlantic Ocean on a ship belonging to England."

"But we were told that most of the ships were sunk by our navy."

"Hans, you mean by your submarines?"

"Yes, they told us very few Americans got to England."

"That might have been true a long time ago but you can see me here."

"Donald, I am very impressed by what I see in your Army. But you do not act like soldiers."

"I agree with you. Most of the men with me were drafted or taken into the Army. As soon as the war is over, they do not want to be a soldier any more."

"Do you want to be a soldier after the war?"

"No, I intend to become a teacher."

"Ein Lehrer, is that it?"

"Yes, ein Lehrer."

"Where are you from, Hans?"

"My home is Langenzenn. That is near Nurnberg. You have heard of Nurnberg?"

"Yes, that is where Hitler showed up every year to see his Army."

"Donald, you are right. Where are you from?"

"I am from Detroit. That is where automobiles are made in the United States."

"Yes, it is on a big lake. How long have you been away from your country?"

"My Division came to England in September. We came to France in November. Where have you been with the Wehrmacht?"

"I have been in every major campaign. I lay wire for the Army. I am 28 years old and have kein Frau."

"I also have kein Frau."

At that moment, Bill Keenoy poked his head in the kitchen door.

"Hey, Don, can you go with me to regiment?"

"Yes, Bill. I have to say goodby to Hans here."

I turned to the German PW and extended my hand.

"Hans, it has been very good to talk with you."

"I have enjoyed it, Donald. I think I will like the Americans although our radio has said you are monsters. And I still think you are in a favorite unit of the American High Command."

"Hans, I wish I was but I am not. Auf Wiedersehen."

On our jeep journey to Osterberg, Keenoy remarked, "You sure were talking a blue streak to that Nazi soldier."

"I don't think he's a real Nazi. I think Hans didn't believe how much equipment we had in our Army. I think that's true of most of the Wehrmacht soldiers. They can't believe they lost the war. He was a very interesting fellow to talk to."

That evening, I told the remainder of the messengers about my conversation that I had had in the afternoon. Teets' remark seemed to sum up the feelings of the group.

"I guess they are just like us. We think we're fighting for the right cause. They thought they were fighting for the right cause. But we have the better equipment and soldiers to go with it."

Sunday, April 29, 1945

Although the Russian allies had made contact in several sectors, none had been sighted in the 84th Division's area.

John and I biked to a large hall occupied by Company F to hear Catholic mass. In the past months, the sermon had dwelt on the idea of going to heaven if something happened to you. On this day, our chaplain talked on the ending of the war. He stated that we should all be thankful we had remained alive. Further, we should never forget those who had not been so fortunate as well as those who had suffered painful wounds that would always be with them.

A great deal of time was spent by all the men in just resting and sleeping. A few of us who enjoyed books were not bored as many were. The lack of any civilians and fighting made our existence strange.

In the evening, most of us were trucked to regiment to see a poor movie, entitled, "Winged Victory."

Monday, April 30, 1945

The prevalent rumors were that the Russians were some 25 miles from the Elbe River in our sector. At breakfast, one member of the communications platoon remarked, "Hell, we could have taken Berlin in the time we've been waiting for those blasted Russians. Jerry must be really giving them a bad time."

But another said, "Yes, getting across the Elbe would have been easy, but some of us would have gotten hurt. It's not adventure but it sure is a lot safer."

Early in the afternoon, George Teets and I agreed to accompany each other to our respective companies to deliver a message to our company commanders.

After taking the message to Company E in Berge, it was necessary for us to bike on the levee to reach Company G. At only one place along this stretch of the Elbe River did we see any activity to show that war still existed. One of the light machine guns that Company E possessed was emplaced to cover a sector where a landing could have been made on solid ground on the west bank. Two GIs were playing cards, paying little attention to their weapons. As we approached, they just looked up and said, "Hi there, fellows. Nice day, isn't it?"

Just before reaching Company G, we saw the crossing site of the ferry that was being operated by our battalion. On the east bank of the Elbe was a large group of people just waiting. There appeared to be no German military personnel. As the people were discharged from the ferry on the west bank, they simply picked up their belongings and started walking westward. We watched for some 20 or 30 minutes. As we left, George remarked, "I wonder how far some of them have come? I wonder how far they have yet to travel?"

"George, I wish I could answer that question. I can't."

We continued with our assignment. We could not wait or worry about the situation of others.

Tuesday, May 1, 1945

Another visit was made to the Elbe River in the morning. The same serene scene was present as George and I had witnessed the previous day.

The guesswork of the day placed the Russians about 10 to 15 miles away from the river but no one knew exactly where the lead troops of our ally were located.

One of our message runs this day involved the distribution of diagrams and illustrations and other distinguishing characteristics about the Russian Army uniforms. A pamphlet also told of how the Russians had been fighting since 1941 when their country was invaded by the Nazi war machine.

Each day the number of prisoners taken began to rise. This was a good indication to us that the Germans were being pushed back toward the river. But none of the prisoners were from the German infantry.

Wednesday, May 2, 1945

Jascha Heifetz gave a violin concert before an audience of GIs from the 335th Regiment. His concert was given in a small theatre in Osterburg. To the disappointment of many, he was dressed in an army kahaki suit minus the insignias and other paraphernalia worn by the regular soldiers. His accompanist at the piano was also dressed in similar fashion. One person in back of me remarked, "As if I don't see enough guys dressed in that brown color all the time, he has to do the same thing."

I turned around and explained to the GI that the reason he wore the army type uniform was for his own protection. Correspondents for the press did the same thing. He then said, "That makes sense."

After playing a program of nearly an hour, Heifitz answered the request for what he termed the "Horrible Staccato." After he finished, the famous violinist thanked the audience for their work here in Germany. He did not elaborate too much since everyone knew his ethnic background. He wished everyone success in the future.

Upon our return to our quarters, the large yard in front of the villa was filled with German prisoners. Every type of branch of service was present. Their rank ranged from Colonel to private. I asked the guard on duty, "How many are there here?"

"About 800 or 900, no one is sure."

"How many guards do you have?"

"I think we've got about five but I don't think any Jerry is about to escape back across the river."

The German officers stood apart from their enlisted men inasmuch as they went to a separate prison cage.

After supper at 1700, a bike ride was taken with John to Company E in Berge. I asked Ed Norris what had occurred. He answered, "Don, about mid-morning the Germans started lining up on the opposite bank. E and G companies got every boat they could lay their hands on. We've been ferrying them across all day long. From the mob I saw, it's going to take a week to get them all across. We heard the Russian artillery just after noon today."

One of the messages that was delivered to our company gave a warning that no one should go near the river bank. It seemed that the Russians were throwing shells all over the area since they wanted to prevent the Germans from escaping across the Elbe.

Later when Crable and I were outside the headquarters of Company E, I asked John, "Isn't that a familiar sound I hear?"

"That's a German machine gun. But I hear something else."

"John, it sounds like a burp gun. It has a much slower rate of fire. Must be some type of Russian weapon."

A PRIVATE'S DIARY

Just after 2000, flares began to arise from our guns in the rear. The sky was brilliantly lit the entire night. We needed to show the Russians that the Americans were already here.

This night was the last where the sounds of battle were heard.

XXVI

THE RUSSIANS AND VICTORY

Thursday, May 3, 1945

As we ate breakfast about 0800, the air was again peaceful. We were told that the Russians had arrived on the opposite bank of the Elbe. Everyone wanted to go to the river but another move was scheduled for the entire Second Battalion later in the morning.

Just after 0900, word spread that the battalion had taken as a prisoner a Lieutenant-General of the Wehrmacht. At 0930, he was out in front of our dwelling waiting for a vehicle to take him to Division Headquarters. Every member of the Battalion Headquarters Company was outside. Many were taking photos of the captured German General. He seemed to be a perfect specimen of the Prussian aristocracy. In his right eye was a large monocle held rigidly in place by well developed facial muscles. He was about six feet tall and extremely well-built. He stood perfectly erect. His face did not show any emotion as the shutters clicked and murmurs spread among the GIs. He seemed highly pleased at the recognition shown to him. At 1000, the jeep from Division arrived. He was taken away but there was no guard to accompany him. None was needed.

The messengers were duly informed that the entire Second Battalion was to be relieved from its present positions by a single company from the 102d Division. At 1015, Sergeant Butler instructed me, "Edwards, take this Lieutenant to Captain Thompson. He'll instruct him on the duties."

565

As we were riding in the jeep, we noted, in a large field just outside Berge, another host of German prisoners. They must have numbered, at least, 500. when the Lieutenant saw them, he exclaimed, "Why, I'll need my whole platoon to guard them."

My reply was, "Lieutenant, we just had five men guarding a whole battalion. I don't think you'll need that many. The Germans are not in any mood to fight or escape."

The Lieutenant was left with Captain Thompson for further instructions.

At 1130, our convoy left for another location that we knew only to be north of our present site. On our journey, we witnessed more prisoners of the former Wehrmacht being loaded into trucks of the 84th artillery for transportation to the prison cages. Our trip took us through the towns of Osterburg, Seehausen, Arendsee, Luchow and Dannenberg. After leaving the latter city, an area full of dangerous magnetic naval mines was entered. That was something new to the battalion. Bernie Cohn asked a question that was never answered.

"How did Jerry ever plant navel mines on land?"

However, the results of a mine were obvious to us when we saw the remains of a Sherman tank that had its pieces scattered over a wide area of ground. We were warned that the mines were very sensitive and to avoid the area in walking.

Our battalion was scheduled to relieve elements of the famous 29th Infantry Division. We entered the town of Langendorf at 1600. Our counterparts of the Second Battalion of the 116th Infantry Regiment were ready to leave their quarters which the messengers were to occupy.

The seven of us engaged in natural conversation with the eight of them. I asked them, "Have any of you been with the Division since D-day?"

Not a single person answered until one of their messengers said, "I've been a messenger since August. The last original messenger left in December."

"Can you tell me exactly what happened to the original eight messengers?"

The senior member of the group spoke, "Two were killed, one was missing in action and five were wounded. I call this group number two and a half. We've had a total of 21 messengers since June 6. That's not as bad as the rifle companies."

"How many casualties has the 29th had since D-day?"

"We really don't know, but there's a saying in our Division that there has been five 29th Divisions. One was killed. Three were wounded or captured. One is still fighting."

"On what do you base those figures?"

"Well, out of 15,000 in a Division, only half are really up front. Anyone in a battalion is on the front. Regiment may or may not be. Back at the Division level, you're safe. So I'd say about 30,000 casualties, give or take a few hundred."

"What was the worst thing the 29th was in?"

"We don't know directly because none of us were there. But talk to some of the veterans and they say it was D-day. Next was capturing St. Lo in France."

"Anything else we Railsplitters should know before you leave here?"

"Yes, the Russians are not across the Elbe here. The British are on the other side. And we're going to leave you our bikes. I think you can use them."

The 116th messengers departed at 1630.

After supper, Crable and I decided to visit Company E which was located in Brandleben. This small town was directly across the river from the city of Domitz. After visiting our friends at our company, we went to a ferry site on the west bank of the Elbe. As we neared the water, John noted, "Don, look at all those German vehicles. What happened to them?"

"John, it looks as if they got hit from the air by some of our fighters."

Guns and all types of military hardware were scattered everywhere. But there were no bodies. Some of the German anti-aircraft machine guns were being fired by some of the members of Company E.

At the ferry site, everything was peaceful and calm.

On our way back, I noted to John, "Looks like we'll never get to see the Russians."

567

A PRIVATE'S DIARY

Friday, May 4, 1945

At 0730, the messengers were notified that another move had to be made within the hour. Since the distance was only a mile to the town of Gr. Gusborn, all the messengers rode their newly acquired bikes to the new destination.

All the message center and part of the radio section were placed in a small one floor house consisting of two bedrooms, a parlor and a kitchen. Our new residence was in a small but fairly dense forest region. The total number of buildings in Gr. Gusborn numbered only 45. Most civilians had fled the village. The main topic of conversation was, of course, the end of the war. Although the Germans were still fighting in a few isolated areas, every man of the Second Battalion was expecting a radio announcement momentarily.

The big local news was sprung on us about 1000 by Corporal Kern who said, "We have a new officer leading the communications platoon!"

"Who is it?" someone asked.

"First Lieutenant James Masterson."

"Oh, he came from my company," noted Teets.

"That's right, he's from Company G. Lieutenant Morgan has just been transferred out but no one knows to where. After he and Larry Gardiner got into those fisticuffs the day before we left Hannover, it's just been a question of time before Division got him out of here."

"I like old 'Moo, Moo'," added Innes. "But he was always afraid of everything. He always kept yelling that the shells were about to fall when no one needed to be reminded of the dangers, especially, in Belgium."

"What's going to happen to Larry Gardiner?" asked Dawes.

"He's awaiting his court-martial. Most likely he'll get some time for striking an officer although I think both of them were at fault," answered Corporal Kern.

"Larry will soon be joining his friend, Hugh Walters, in some stockade," added Teets.

568

About an hour later, our new commanding officer, Lieutenant Masterson, came by to introduce himself to every man in the whole communications platoon. He seemed anxious to know all the enlisted men that were in his command.

Since leaving Hannover, no romantic adventures had been available to some of those in the communications platoon. About 1330, Thomas J. Bennett, one of the messengers for battalion, came by to make an announcement to the entire communications platoon. Bennie, the nickname everyone used, boasted, "Fellows, I've just lined up a beautiful doll!"

"Who is she, some old hag that's hard up?" retorted Sergeant Marshall Howsden, the radio repairman for our battalion.

"Hell, no. She's blond and really built! You'll see."

"I don't believe that she's going out with you."

"The hell with all you farts. I'll show her to you this afternoon."

Just after 1500, Bennie again came by.

"OK all you twerps. I'm going out with my new girl."

Every single member of the communications platoon, except the one required switchboard operator, was out looking his new girl over. She was a platinum blond with a shallow face and a thin body. As they passed by, someone remarked, "She's it, if I ever saw one."

She turned up the road toward Langedorf and Bennie was following her. As they went strolling down the road, Vernon McDaniel shouted, "Hey Bennie, where are you going?"

Picking up the telephone wire strung along the road, he replied, "I'm going to fix a break in the line."

"Yea, but none of the lines are out."

"One of them is going to be out."

They disappeared over the first small hill out of sight.

An hour later, Bennie was back to tell of his success story with his new German girl.

Later that evening, a few of the other members of the platoon paid a visit to the same German Fraulein with one remaining the entire night.

A PRIVATE'S DIARY

Sunday, May 6, 1945

The religious services for Christians were held at 1000 and 1100. Upon leaving the Catholic mass at 1050, one overheard remark was, "Look at the small number of guys going to the Protestant service."

His companion's reply was, "Yea, but we were considerably understaffed at Mass this morning. And remember the old slogan, 'there are no sinners in foxholes.' "

An illustration of the imminent end of the war took place when Crable and I made a message run to Company E in mid-afternoon. Sergeant Smith called both of us and announced, "Crable, Edwards, you are carrying the wrong assigned weapon."

"Yes, we are, Sergeant, but these carbines we have are much lighter and more suited to our needs as messengers," was my reply.

"But what does the manual call for?"

"I hope carbines."

"You're right and wrong. It does but your code numbers were assigned back in Claiborne to the two company operators. No one else is to have carbines."

"But these carbines are much better for us. We don't fire our pieces very often. A rifle won't do us any more good."

"The manual calls for Garrands and that's what you're going to carry."

"Sarge, experience is the best teacher, right? Let us keep the carbines. Besides, there's going to be no more fighting."

"Experience isn't what the manual says. On your next trip, have those carbines exchanged for a Garrand."

Upon our return to the Message Center, John and I appealed to Lieutenant Masterson. He listened and answered, "Crable, Edwards, I'd like to help you but I have no control over you in regard to weapons. The rules in your company prevail. However, I think you're right but you'll just have to accept the ruling."

John and I were not alone for almost the entire communications platoon had to again shoulder the Garrand. As I remarked to John a day or two later when we had our heavier weapons, "Practical experience doesn't mean a thing in this Army."

"Amen, Don."

At 2200, the messengers from E, G, and H companies had to deliver messages that their outfits would move again in the morning.

Monday, May 7, 1945

Everyone in the communications platoon arose at 0600 sharp. Although the distance to travel was less than 15 miles, the kitchen crew had to have time in which to pack after serving breakfast. All the messengers with the exception of Vernon Dawes secured permission to ride their bikes to our new destination which was the village of Vietze. This town was on the Elbe River itself.

At 0830, John and I set out on our bike ride. Corporal Kern had previously instructed us, "Between the towns of Lasse and Forleben there will be a road leading to Vietze. There will be a sign there."

The Elbe River was seen in many places. It looked serene. There were several roads leading to the river between between Gorleben and Lasse but none pointed to Vietze. We continued on the road to Gartow which was occupied by elements of the 333rd Regiment.

We made inquiry of two fellow messengers in that regiment.

"Can you tell us the way to Vietze?" I asked.

"Sure, just follow the road north about a mile. Fork to the right and you'll run right into Vietze."

His directions were followed through Restorf and Brunekndorf into Vietze.

Vietze was in the shape of a box with one side facing the Elbe River. We were quartered in the best building in town, namely just above the beer garden.

Just before 1600, it was necessary to make a message run to Company E which was located in Revestorf. Upon my

571

A PRIVATE'S DIARY

Vernon Dawes, 12 year old Russian soldier, Martin Innes

arrival, I wondered if I was in the correct site. There were more Russian soldiers wandering about then American ones. Fifty were counted before I stopped numbering them. The average Russian soldier seemed to be much shorter and heavier in stature than his American counterpart. The most noticeable items were their short caps, which seemed to squat on their heads, and their heavy black boots. A few of them had tommy guns which were being examined by members of Company E. The Russians, in turn, were examining our Garrands and carbines. Everything seemed to be peace and harmony. Language was the only barrier. Most Wehrmacht soldiers understood some English words but this was not true of our eastern allies. Spirits of all types seemed to be flowing between all the soldiers. But nary a German civilian was seen on the streets.

Tuesday, May 8, 1945

The official end of the war was announced for the next day. The Army newspaper gave the headlines, "Nazis Quit." All the messengers agreed that the real ending had come when we

572

knew that no more battles were to be fought. That was the day after our arrival in Gartow.

Outside of two message runs apiece, all the messengers spent a very quiet day in Vietze. A few German civilians began to show themselves but most of them had not yet returned to their village.

The seven messengers remained awake until midnight and the start of the new day.

Wednesday, May 9, 1945

V-E Day.

John and I attended Mass at 0900. The message for the sermon was again on thanks that we were here to see the end of the war.

In the afternoon, I visited my favorite officer, Captain Frank Price, to see if he could use his influence so that the messengers could all retain their carbines. He was very sympathetic to the problem but concluded, "Edwards, I think you know what's best for you and the rest of the messengers in regard to weapons. But those Army manuals are made by someone who doesn't know the real situation. I'm afraid I can't help you."

"Do you think anyone can?"

"I doubt General Bolling himself could do anything. Just hope someone back in Washington wakes up some day."

In the middle of the afternoon, I quizzed each messenger who had served all his time with the group what he thought was the most tense situation he had been in during the time from November until this day.

My fellow messenger, John V. Crable, was first.

"Without a doubt, it was the first attack by the battalion at the end of November last year. Although we had been shelled before, I don't think any of us expected the Germans to put up such a fight to stop the companies from taking those few feet of ground."

Martin P. Innes came next.

573

"I have to agree with John. That first attack was murder. If that type of thing had kept up throughout the war, none of us and I mean none of us would be discussing it on this day."

James A. Rochester followed.

"The shelling at Geronsweiler. The Germans threw in more shells at that place than any other we've been in. If we had stayed there, some more of us would have been killed like Mike was."

George W. Teets came last.

"I choose Geronsweiler. When I thought Crable and Edwards had gone with Mike, I thought we had lost three men. If Jerry had kept that up throughout the war, all of us would have been hit seriously some day."

John Crable knew my purpose in questioning the four who had been with me constantly the last five months. The other two never inquired as to why the same question was not asked of them.

A little after 1500, an announcement was made that each man would receive a liquor ration for this most important day. Each GI would share our bottle of brandy per ten men; one bottle of champagne per eight men and one bottle of red wine for four men. The non-commissioned officer in charge of the communications platoon, Sergeant William Miller, was to distribute the liquor at the party that was to be held in the local beer garden.

At 2000, the victory party started. A small band from regiment consisting of six men came for the celebration. A movie, "The Suspect," was viewed. But no liquor was available. When one of the radio operators went to the quarters of Sergeant Mill, he found a sign reading, "These are for the platoon." Along side the sign were three bottles of red wine for use by thirty men. Swearing and cursing in full force broke out when the confiscation of the liquor ration by Sergeant Miller and his friend, Sergeant Howsden, was made known. However, Sergeant Talerek and Sergeant Kottage saved the day and night in bringing forth some schnapps and other liquor they had found when the communications platoon had moved into the beer garden. The party was very merry. We drank to the End and Victory.

As John and I retired that night, I asked factitiously, "John, have you ever considered giving me that hour's notice?"

"Don, I've still got it under consideration!"

We both laughed. We had survived.

Epilogue

Wednesday, February 6, 1945

I had arrived at the Michigan Central Depot in Detroit at 0730. My discharge from active service had occurred two day earlier at Camp Grant, Illinois. At the end of the long runway leading from the trains were my mother and my sister, Blodwyn Irene. When I reached them, my mother started to cry tears of joy for my safe arrival back home. She said, "Don, I was so worried about you when the fighting was going on."

"Let me tell you, mother, I was worried at times, too."

Donald A. Edwards—Detroit, Michigan

APPENDIX I

Enlisted Men

	Headquarters Company	Company E	Company F	Company G	Company H	Total
Grand Total of Number Served	134	319	317	298	206	1,274
Killed in Action or Died of Wounds	2	20	35	23	15	95
Missing in Action	1	5	17			23